Christine Carroll

# Journey

## from
## Mormonism

ISBN: 978-1-4303-0493-7
Copyright © 2005 by Christine Carroll
www.Lulu.com

## Introduction

God has invited us to participate with Him in the accomplishment of His eternal plan. Some time during our journey in life God may reveal to us that we are treading along the wrong path. Such a revelation may come as a whopping, shattering blow to our ego or to our world view. Happily, such a disclosure may serve as a launching pad to the discovery of truth, thereby enabling us to tread along the correct path in life. Liberating joy and peace come to one who recognizes and responds appropriately to truth when revealed.

Jesus said, "I am the way, the truth, and the life: no one cometh unto the Father, but by me" (John 14:6). Yet, in many places in God's Word, we are warned about false prophets who pervert the truth and deceive many. These men ensnare people into a *web* of false Gospel. This book is about my personal journey to that moment in time when I came out of such a *web* and embraced the Truth. My discovery was that *truth* is not a feeling. Truth is a person and His name is Jesus! He graciously invites us to fellowship with Him throughout all of time and eternity. We see God in the face of Jesus Christ. It is the Holy Spirit who comes alongside as helper to reveal that fact.

The truth will set you free, but first it will make you miserable.

*This poster illustrates perfectly what this journey felt like for me. I've had it in my home for many years -and have no idea whom to credit.*

## Mormon Challenges

Wherefore confound your enemies; call upon them to meet you in public and private; and inasmuch as you are faithful their shame shall be manifest.

*Joseph Smith, Doctrine and Covenants, 71:7*

Convince us of our errors of doctrine, if we have any, by logical arguments, or by the Word of God, and we will be ever grateful for the information, and you will have the pleasing reflection that you have been instruments in the hands of God of redeeming your fellow beings from the darkness which you may see enveloping their minds . . . and endeavor with patience and meekness to reclaim from error, and save the immortal soul from an endless death.

*Mormon Apostle Orson Pratt, The Seer p. 15-16*

*And there is no creature hidden from His sight,*
*but all things are open and laid bare*
*to the eyes of Him with whom we have to do.*

*Hebrews 4:13*

## Reader's Guide

This book is full of Mormon references and language. My thinking is that Latter-day Saint (Mormon) sources will provide the most credibility to a Mormon, and that Mormon sources do a fine job of calling into question this false Gospel. Depending on your background and perspective you may want to make a quick review of the *Terminology Differences* and *Glossary* located in the Exhibit Section on pages 193-196 before you begin reading. Capitalization and italics are used to call attention to common Mormon phrases and terminology and to replicate quotes.

With one exception (p. 79) the quotations made throughout this book are from the Mormon *General Authorities* (the LDS Church Hierarchy), and from the Mormon *Standard Works (Book of Mormon, Doctrine and Covenants, Pearl of Great Price, and the Bible)*. The Mormon Church also refers to the General Authorities as modern *Living Oracles*. This designation is used because of the customary recognition that these men speak authoritatively to the church membership about Mormon revelation and doctrine.

**Limiting LDS quotes to the Living Oracles and to the Mormon Standard Works should diminish controversy over the value and authenticity of the references made in this book.**

Each time a reference is made to Joseph Fielding Smith, the tenth Mormon Prophet, I have typed out his full name. This I have done in order to distinguish him from the sixth Mormon Prophet, Joseph F. Smith, or from Joseph Smith who was the originator of Mormonism.

**I labored over which Bible translation(s) would be most useful in this book.** When I was LDS I believed the existence of numerous translations of the Bible was evidence of the general confusion of the mainstream Christian Church. Today I believe this is incorrect. Bible translations generally base themselves on primary documents. In this way, they use the same sources to elucidate various shades of meaning and to adapt themselves to the common vernacular. They do not often differ in meaning, as some would suggest. I mostly rely on the King James version and the New American Standard version. For those readers who fear that I may be 'picking and choosing' translations according to my purpose at the time, I recommend that they read this book alongside whatever translation they are partial to. This practice is common among Bible students, and I feel will show that the Bible message is consistent across most translations.

An **Exhibit Section** is included in the back of the book. Its pages are referred to in the text and it serves only as a preview to a vast reservoir of data available by persons interested in examining Mormonism. The exhibits will help lay out the geography of Mormonism and give you a good foothold for the journey you are about to take.

There are literally hundreds of **books and websites** available on this subject. A few of my favorites are listed on page 125. A full **Works Cited** listing is located at the end of the book.

## Acknowledgments

This book is dedicated to my immediate brothers and sisters and their spouses and children, and all others to whom this book may be an encouragement and enlightenment. God bless you!

Special recognition goes to my son Gilbert, a true humanitarian, advisor and encourager. Hats off to my loving husband Clyde, who for months patiently endured stacks of books in almost every quarter of our home and surrendered our computer entirely over to me for the development of this book. My daughter Valerie, with a broad smile and cheerful disposition, formatted many drafts. I thank each of my other children and their spouses who have encouraged me to 'keep on keeping on' to this book's final form.

Thank you Crystal Zielbauer for your wisdom, foresight, and amazing eye for edits.

A special thanks go to friends Suzanne Rankin, Sherry Clark, and Jeanette Tuxhorn (all former Mormons) for their encouragement or assistance when the task seemed endless.

Lastly, and foremost, God has enabled me to write this book, and it is my desire that it will help others come to see Jesus as He is revealed in Holy Scripture and embrace and receive Him into their hearts as 'Savior' and 'Lord' of their lives. This book goes forth with my deepest appreciation to God, from whom all my contentment is supplied. As King David said, *"Thy word is a lamp to my feet, and a light to my path." Psalm 119:105.*

# Table of Contents

Introduction . . . . . . . . . . . . . . . . . . . . . . . . . . . . . . . . . . . . . . . . . . . . . . . iii
Mormon Challenges. . . . . . . . . . . . . . . . . . . . . . . . . . . . . . . . . . . . . . . . . iii
Reader's Guide . . . . . . . . . . . . . . . . . . . . . . . . . . . . . . . . . . . . . . . . . . . . . v
Acknowledgments . . . . . . . . . . . . . . . . . . . . . . . . . . . . . . . . . . . . . . . . . . . v

## 1. Background. . . . . . . . . . . . . . . . . . . . . . . . . . . . . . . . . . . . . . . . . . . . .1
Honoring God . . . . . . . . . . . . . . . . . . . . . . . . . . . . . . . . . . . . . . . . . . . . . . 1
Salvation Through Joseph Smith. . . . . . . . . . . . . . . . . . . . . . . . . . . . . . . 1
Judging Non-Mormons . . . . . . . . . . . . . . . . . . . . . . . . . . . . . . . . . . . . . . 2
Receiving the Priesthood. . . . . . . . . . . . . . . . . . . . . . . . . . . . . . . . . . . . . 3
Loving the Book of Mormon. . . . . . . . . . . . . . . . . . . . . . . . . . . . . . . . . . 4
Activity in the Church. . . . . . . . . . . . . . . . . . . . . . . . . . . . . . . . . . . . . . . 5
Laboring in Works . . . . . . . . . . . . . . . . . . . . . . . . . . . . . . . . . . . . . . . . . 5
Saving and Communicating with the Dead . . . . . . . . . . . . . . . . . . . . . . 6
Achieving Eternal Exaltation . . . . . . . . . . . . . . . . . . . . . . . . . . . . . . . . . 7

## 2. Jehovah's Witnesses Challenge Me. . . . . . . . . . . . . . . . . . . . . . . .9
Adam God . . . . . . . . . . . . . . . . . . . . . . . . . . . . . . . . . . . . . . . . . . . . . . . 9
Wedding in the Temple . . . . . . . . . . . . . . . . . . . . . . . . . . . . . . . . . . . . 11
My Zeal . . . . . . . . . . . . . . . . . . . . . . . . . . . . . . . . . . . . . . . . . . . . . . . . 14

## 3. Humpty Dumpty . . . . . . . . . . . . . . . . . . . . . . . . . . . . . . . . . . . . . . .17
Building Up My Faith . . . . . . . . . . . . . . . . . . . . . . . . . . . . . . . . . . . . . 17
"Adam" –Again?. . . . . . . . . . . . . . . . . . . . . . . . . . . . . . . . . . . . . . . . . . 17
Palatine, Illinois . . . . . . . . . . . . . . . . . . . . . . . . . . . . . . . . . . . . . . . . . 21
Doctrine and Covenants 71:7 Stirs Me Again . . . . . . . . . . . . . . . . . . . 21
To the Library . . . . . . . . . . . . . . . . . . . . . . . . . . . . . . . . . . . . . . . . . . . 22

## 4. An Inherited Mind-Set . . . . . . . . . . . . . . . . . . . . . . . . . . . . . . . . . .27
Parental Guidance. . . . . . . . . . . . . . . . . . . . . . . . . . . . . . . . . . . . . . . . 29
Superior Claims . . . . . . . . . . . . . . . . . . . . . . . . . . . . . . . . . . . . . . . . . 30

## 5. Changing God and Scripture. . . . . . . . . . . . . . . . . . . . . . . . . . . . .33
The Standard Works Defined. . . . . . . . . . . . . . . . . . . . . . . . . . . . . . . . 33
The Doctrine and Covenants . . . . . . . . . . . . . . . . . . . . . . . . . . . . . . . . 34
The Pearl of Great Price . . . . . . . . . . . . . . . . . . . . . . . . . . . . . . . . . . . 34
Writings of Joseph Smith 1 and 2 . . . . . . . . . . . . . . . . . . . . . . . . . . . . 35
The Mormon Articles of Faith. . . . . . . . . . . . . . . . . . . . . . . . . . . . . . . 35
More Mormon Scripture. . . . . . . . . . . . . . . . . . . . . . . . . . . . . . . . . . . . 36
Watch the Mormon God Evolve. . . . . . . . . . . . . . . . . . . . . . . . . . . . . . 38

## 6. False Prophets and Apostles . . . . . . . . . . . . . . . . . . . . . . . . . . . .47
False Prophecies Make False Prophets . . . . . . . . . . . . . . . . . . . . . . . . 47
Reinventing Zion . . . . . . . . . . . . . . . . . . . . . . . . . . . . . . . . . . . . . . . . 49
Contradictory Teachings of Mormon Prophets. . . . . . . . . . . . . . . . . . 49
Christ Returns to the Garden of Eden – in Missouri? . . . . . . . . . . . . . 51

## 7. Eyes on the Bible . . . . . . . . . . . . . . . . . . . . . . . . . . . . . . . . . . . . . .55
I Replaced My LDS View of the Bible . . . . . . . . . . . . . . . . . . . . . . . . 56
Supposed Contradictions. . . . . . . . . . . . . . . . . . . . . . . . . . . . . . . . . . . 59

## 8. Living Oracles Confess Another Jesus . . . . . . . . . . . . . . . . . . .61
What About a Relationship With Christ? . . . . . . . . . . . . . . . . . . . . . . . 62
The Non-Biblical View of Jesus' Pre-existence . . . . . . . . . . . . . . . . . 64

Was Jesus a Product of a Virgin Birth? . . . . . . . . . . . . . . . . . . . . . . . 64
Jesus Married?  A Polygamist Too? . . . . . . . . . . . . . . . . . . . . . . . . . 65
The Blood of Jesus . . . . . . . . . . . . . . . . . . . . . . . . . . . . . . . . . . . . . 66
Who Forgives Sins? . . . . . . . . . . . . . . . . . . . . . . . . . . . . . . . . . . . . 68
Atonement at Gethsemane? . . . . . . . . . . . . . . . . . . . . . . . . . . . . . . 68
Honor and Exalt the Son, Even as the Father! . . . . . . . . . . . . . . . . 68

**9.  The Gods Concocted a Plan** . . . . . . . . . . . . . . . . . . . . . . **73**
A Mythical Pre-existence . . . . . . . . . . . . . . . . . . . . . . . . . . . . . . . . 73
The Place of the Fall . . . . . . . . . . . . . . . . . . . . . . . . . . . . . . . . . . . 74
Put Your Shoulder to the Wheel . . . . . . . . . . . . . . . . . . . . . . . . . . . 76
Women's Place in Mormon Heaven . . . . . . . . . . . . . . . . . . . . . . . . 77
Men's Place in Mormon Heaven . . . . . . . . . . . . . . . . . . . . . . . . . . . 77
No Worry – All is Well in Zion and Hell? . . . . . . . . . . . . . . . . . . . . . 78
Redefining Creation, God and Humans . . . . . . . . . . . . . . . . . . . . . . 79
The Question of Polytheism . . . . . . . . . . . . . . . . . . . . . . . . . . . . . . 80
Implications of Remaining Polytheists . . . . . . . . . . . . . . . . . . . . . . . 81
Mormon Alleged Proof-texts . . . . . . . . . . . . . . . . . . . . . . . . . . . . . . 82
The Living Prophet and the First Presidency . . . . . . . . . . . . . . . . . . 83

**10.  Where Do You Get Your Authority?** . . . . . . . . . . . . . . . **87**
The First Vision . . . . . . . . . . . . . . . . . . . . . . . . . . . . . . . . . . . . . . . 87
Empty Claims to Priesthood Restoration . . . . . . . . . . . . . . . . . . . . . 88
Proper Lineage and Race? . . . . . . . . . . . . . . . . . . . . . . . . . . . . . . . 89
Aaronic Priesthood . . . . . . . . . . . . . . . . . . . . . . . . . . . . . . . . . . . . 91
Melchizedek Priesthood . . . . . . . . . . . . . . . . . . . . . . . . . . . . . . . . . 92

**11.  The Sixth Mormon Article of Faith** . . . . . . . . . . . . . . . . **95**
What is the Church and Who Belongs to It? . . . . . . . . . . . . . . . . . . . 96
The Church Name:  A Sign of the True Church? . . . . . . . . . . . . . . . . 97
Church Organization . . . . . . . . . . . . . . . . . . . . . . . . . . . . . . . . . . . 97
Messiah Jesus . . . . . . . . . . . . . . . . . . . . . . . . . . . . . . . . . . . . . . . 99
The True Church Forever . . . . . . . . . . . . . . . . . . . . . . . . . . . . . . . . 99

**12.  Temples and Temple Work** . . . . . . . . . . . . . . . . . . . . **101**
Revealed Confusion . . . . . . . . . . . . . . . . . . . . . . . . . . . . . . . . . . 103
Offensive to God . . . . . . . . . . . . . . . . . . . . . . . . . . . . . . . . . . . . . 104
Changes in the Mormon Temple Ceremony . . . . . . . . . . . . . . . . . 106

**13.  The Book of Mormon** . . . . . . . . . . . . . . . . . . . . . . . . . **109**
An Empty Book . . . . . . . . . . . . . . . . . . . . . . . . . . . . . . . . . . . . . . 110
Other Problems . . . . . . . . . . . . . . . . . . . . . . . . . . . . . . . . . . . . . . 111
More Absurdities . . . . . . . . . . . . . . . . . . . . . . . . . . . . . . . . . . . . . 113
Occultic Origins? . . . . . . . . . . . . . . . . . . . . . . . . . . . . . . . . . . . . . 114
Biblical Support for the Book of Mormon? . . . . . . . . . . . . . . . . . . . 115
National Geographic and the Smithsonian . . . . . . . . . . . . . . . . . . . 116
DNA . . . . . . . . . . . . . . . . . . . . . . . . . . . . . . . . . . . . . . . . . . . . . . 116
Two Popular Book of Mormon Verses . . . . . . . . . . . . . . . . . . . . . . 116

**14.  Laughing and Crying** . . . . . . . . . . . . . . . . . . . . . . . . . **119**
Question the Brethren? . . . . . . . . . . . . . . . . . . . . . . . . . . . . . . . . 119
Joseph Smith the Ego Man . . . . . . . . . . . . . . . . . . . . . . . . . . . . . 120
Mormon Potpourri . . . . . . . . . . . . . . . . . . . . . . . . . . . . . . . . . . . . 121

**15.  Mormon Hymns** . . . . . . . . . . . . . . . . . . . . . . . . . . . . . **127**
Dora North Explains . . . . . . . . . . . . . . . . . . . . . . . . . . . . . . . . . . . 127
Jeanette Tuxhorn Adds More . . . . . . . . . . . . . . . . . . . . . . . . . . . . 128

**16. Family Departure** . . . . . . . . . . . . . . . . . . . . . . . . . . . . . . . . .131
    I Wanted Out and Counted the Cost . . . . . . . . . . . . . . . . . . . . . 131
    A Saving Prayer. . . . . . . . . . . . . . . . . . . . . . . . . . . . . . . . . . . . . 132
    A Remedial Twist . . . . . . . . . . . . . . . . . . . . . . . . . . . . . . . . . . . . 133
    My Husband Explains . . . . . . . . . . . . . . . . . . . . . . . . . . . . . . . . 134
    Our Children . . . . . . . . . . . . . . . . . . . . . . . . . . . . . . . . . . . . . . . . 134
    Valerie Tells Her Story . . . . . . . . . . . . . . . . . . . . . . . . . . . . . . . . 135
    Angela's Friend – No Friend . . . . . . . . . . . . . . . . . . . . . . . . . . . 136
    A Curious and Disconcerting Observation. . . . . . . . . . . . . . . . 137
    A Christian Service . . . . . . . . . . . . . . . . . . . . . . . . . . . . . . . . . . 138
    Remove Our Names From the Church Records, Please! . . . . . . . . 139

**17. The Triunity of God: A Heresy?** . . . . . . . . . . . . . . . . . . . . . .141
    Two Great Heresies. . . . . . . . . . . . . . . . . . . . . . . . . . . . . . . . . . 141
    Two Fundamental Themes . . . . . . . . . . . . . . . . . . . . . . . . . . . . 142
    Thayer's Greek Lexicon and Strong's Concordance. . . . . . . . . . 145
    Humanity of Jesus – A Great Mystery . . . . . . . . . . . . . . . . . . . 145
    Fulness of God's Revealed Person . . . . . . . . . . . . . . . . . . . . . . 145
    The Greek word *Protokos* . . . . . . . . . . . . . . . . . . . . . . . . . . . . 145
    Foolish Plan?. . . . . . . . . . . . . . . . . . . . . . . . . . . . . . . . . . . . . . . 146
    Embrace the Name of the Lord . . . . . . . . . . . . . . . . . . . . . . . . . 146

**18. Grace: A Heresy?** . . . . . . . . . . . . . . . . . . . . . . . . . . . . . . . . . .149
    My Nightmare . . . . . . . . . . . . . . . . . . . . . . . . . . . . . . . . . . . . . . 150
    Striving. . . . . . . . . . . . . . . . . . . . . . . . . . . . . . . . . . . . . . . . . . . . 150
    The Greek word *Tetelestai*. . . . . . . . . . . . . . . . . . . . . . . . . . . . 153
    The Greek word *Dikaloo* . . . . . . . . . . . . . . . . . . . . . . . . . . . . . 153

**19. The Book Of Life.** . . . . . . . . . . . . . . . . . . . . . . . . . . . . . . . . . .157
    What is Truth? . . . . . . . . . . . . . . . . . . . . . . . . . . . . . . . . . . . . . . 158
    Heaven or Hell?. . . . . . . . . . . . . . . . . . . . . . . . . . . . . . . . . . . . . 159
    The Never-ending Culmination . . . . . . . . . . . . . . . . . . . . . . . . . 160

**20. The Real Self.** . . . . . . . . . . . . . . . . . . . . . . . . . . . . . . . . . . . . .163
    Nicodemus. . . . . . . . . . . . . . . . . . . . . . . . . . . . . . . . . . . . . . . . . 163
    The Old and New Creation . . . . . . . . . . . . . . . . . . . . . . . . . . . . 164
    Anathema – God's Curses. . . . . . . . . . . . . . . . . . . . . . . . . . . . . 165
    Filters. . . . . . . . . . . . . . . . . . . . . . . . . . . . . . . . . . . . . . . . . . . . . 166

**21. Surrendering.** . . . . . . . . . . . . . . . . . . . . . . . . . . . . . . . . . . . . .171
    Doubts and Fears . . . . . . . . . . . . . . . . . . . . . . . . . . . . . . . . . . . 172
    The Developing Room. . . . . . . . . . . . . . . . . . . . . . . . . . . . . . . . 173
    Counting the Cost . . . . . . . . . . . . . . . . . . . . . . . . . . . . . . . . . . . 174
    The Truth is at Stake Here. . . . . . . . . . . . . . . . . . . . . . . . . . . . . 175
    Mormonism in a Nutshell. . . . . . . . . . . . . . . . . . . . . . . . . . . . . . 176
    Why I Oppose Mormonism . . . . . . . . . . . . . . . . . . . . . . . . . . . . 176
    Taking Offense. . . . . . . . . . . . . . . . . . . . . . . . . . . . . . . . . . . . . . 178
    Be Encouraged!. . . . . . . . . . . . . . . . . . . . . . . . . . . . . . . . . . . . . 179

**22. Reconciliation.** . . . . . . . . . . . . . . . . . . . . . . . . . . . . . . . . . . . .183
    Justice and the Fall . . . . . . . . . . . . . . . . . . . . . . . . . . . . . . . . . . 184
    The Protevangelium. . . . . . . . . . . . . . . . . . . . . . . . . . . . . . . . . . 185
    How to Receive Salvation . . . . . . . . . . . . . . . . . . . . . . . . . . . . . 188

**Exhibits**. . . . . . . . . . . . . . . . . . . . . . . . . . . . . . . . . . . . . . . . . .**191**

    Terminology Differences . . . . . . . . . . . . . . . . . . . . . . . . . . . . . . . . . . . . 193
    Mormon Plan of Eternal Progression. . . . . . . . . . . . . . . . . . . . . . . . . . 194
    Mormon Glossary . . . . . . . . . . . . . . . . . . . . . . . . . . . . . . . . . . . 195-196
    The Biblical Gospel / LDS Gospel. . . . . . . . . . . . . . . . . . . . . . . . . . . . 197
    Adam-God - Journal of Discourses . . . . . . . . . . . . . . . . . . . . . . . . 198-199
    Denouncing Adam-God, Kimball Article . . . . . . . . . . . . . . . . . . . . . . . . 200
    Denouncing Adam-God- England Letter. . . . . . . . . . . . . . . . . . . . . . 201-202
    Brigham Young's Tie Clasp. . . . . . . . . . . . . . . . . . . . . . . . . . . . . . . . . 203
    Blacks and the Priesthood, Journal of Discourses . . . . . . . . . . . . . . . . 204
    How Many in the Godhead? Lectures on Faith. . . . . . . . . . . . . . . . . . . 205
    Polygamy –a Necessity to Godhood, Journal of Discourses . . . . . . . . . . . 206
    Marriage of Jesus, Joseph F. Smith's Letter. . . . . . . . . . . . . . . . . . . . . 207
    Blood Atonement, Journal of Discourses . . . . . . . . . . . . . . . . . . . . . . 208
    First Vision, Joseph Smith's Handwriting . . . . . . . . . . . . . . . . . . . 209-210
    First Vision Comparisons . . . . . . . . . . . . . . . . . . . . . . . . . . . . . . . . . 211
    Condemns Polygamy, Doctrine and Covenants . . . . . . . . . . . . . . . . . . 212
    Salt Lake Temple Decorated with Satanic Symbols . . . . . . . . . . . . . . . 213
    Flaws in the Pearl of Great Price . . . . . . . . . . . . . . . . . . . . . . . . . . . . 214
    Min is not God! . . . . . . . . . . . . . . . . . . . . . . . . . . . . . . . . . . . . . . . . 215
    Doctrine and Covenants Changes -sample . . . . . . . . . . . . . . . . . . 216-217
    Archeology and the Book of Mormon, National Geographic. . . . . . . . . . . 218
    Archeology and the Book of Mormon, Smithsonian Institute . . . . . . . . . 219-220
    Grace and Trinity a Heresy - McConkie Article. . . . . . . . . . . . . . . . . . . 221
    Governor Ford Prophecy . . . . . . . . . . . . . . . . . . . . . . . . . . . . . . . . . 222
    Joseph Smith —the Glass Looker, Justice Albert Neely . . . . . . . . . . . . . 223
    Articles of Faith: Original and Current. . . . . . . . . . . . . . . . . . . . . . . . . 224
    More Accurate Articles of Faith . . . . . . . . . . . . . . . . . . . . . . . . . . . . . 225
    Biblical Defense of Truth . . . . . . . . . . . . . . . . . . . . . . . . . . . . . . . . . 226
    Qualifications to Serve God . . . . . . . . . . . . . . . . . . . . . . . . . . . . . . . 227
    Mormon Priesthood Secrets Chart . . . . . . . . . . . . . . . . . . . . . . . . . . 228
    First Token of the Aaronic Priesthood . . . . . . . . . . . . . . . . . . . . . . . . 229
    Second Token of the Aaronic / First Token of the Melchizedek Priesthood. . . 230
    Second Token of the Melchizedek Priesthood . . . . . . . . . . . . . . . . . . . 231

**Works Cited** . . . . . . . . . . . . . . . . . . . . . . . . . . . . . . . . . . . .**233**

# 1.  Background

*Grace be unto you, and peace, from God our Father, and from the Lord Jesus Christ.*

Philippians 1:2

My name is Christine Carroll.  I come from a strong Mormon heritage.  I was born and raised in Idaho and am the eleventh child in a family of seven sons and four daughters.  We were all born *Under the Covenant*, meaning that our parents *achieved* a *temple marriage,* the marriage necessary for entrance into the highest Mormon afterlife, referred to as the *Celestial Kingdom* of glory.  All eleven of my parents' children *achieved* a temple marriage.

Through the influence of Wilford Woodruff, the fourth Mormon Prophet, some of my ancestors emigrated from England to Nauvoo, Illinois in 1841.  In 1856, they traveled westward with the historic Martin Handcart Company.  Pushing a handcart across what became known as the *Mormon Trail,* they settled in a place they called their own *Zion,* which is today Utah.  The popular call to the nations was *"Come to Zion, Come to Zion"* which Mormons sing about in church gatherings to this day.

My Mormon ancestors were polygamists.  I was raised on pioneer stories about the hardship and suffering our ancestors weathered so that we could enjoy the blessings of the only *restored* church.  The true Gospel, we were taught, had been removed from the earth long ago because wickedness had prevailed over righteousness.  Because the Gospel of Christ was lost from the earth, an event which Mormons term the *apostasy,* a restoration was necessary.  According to the Mormon Church, (also referred to as the Church of Jesus Christ of Latter-day Saints, or Latter-day Saints, or LDS) the restoration and all of its accompanying blessings began at around 1820 through a man named Joseph Smith, God's first prophet of these *latter days*.

## Honoring God

I believe my parents loved truth as they saw it, and responsibly taught it to each of their eleven children.  They maintained high moral standards, and were hard-working ambitious people.  My parents instilled reverence and respect toward God, and God used this to later bring me out of Mormonism.  I am very grateful to my parents for teaching me that a religion worth keeping is worth defending, able to answer to any form of opposition.  I saw it as my duty to defend the church when it was attacked.  Little did I know that what seemed truth to me while growing up and raising a family of my own was, in fact, not the case.

## Salvation Through Joseph Smith

The early 1800's were a time of religious fervor and controversy in the United States. Mormonism teaches that in the year 1820 God and Jesus Christ appeared to a fifteen-year-old boy named Joseph Smith, directing him to restore truth to the earth. In 1830, Joseph Smith founded the Church of Christ.[1] Later, the church name was changed to The Church of the Latter-day Saints,[2] and finally, The Church of Jesus Christ of Latter-day Saints in Fayette, New York, comprised of six members.[3] Shortly thereafter, Mormon settlements operated simultaneously in Kirkland, Ohio and Independence, Missouri. Despite encountered persecution, church influence continued to expand. The church later settled in Nauvoo, Illinois. By 1844 Joseph Smith, empowered by a city charter granted by the Illinois State Legislature, governed some 15,000 people in Nauvoo.

Taking the American ideal of religious freedom to new lengths, Mormon leaders intended to create a new nation where they could pursue their religious and political goals. On May 24, 1844, Joseph Smith said, "I calculate to be one of the instruments of setting up the kingdom of Daniel by the Word of the Lord, and I intend to lay a foundation that will revolutionize the whole world."[4] But after being arrested for destroying an anti-Mormon newspaper, Joseph Smith was killed by an anti-Mormon mob who stormed the jail where he was staying.

The influence of Joseph Smith upon the Mormon Church cannot be overestimated. Of this man, church authorities have proclaimed:

> *There is no salvation without accepting Joseph Smith.*[5]

> *. . . and every spirit that does not confess that God has sent Joseph Smith, and revealed the everlasting Gospel to and through him, is of Antichrist, no matter whether it is found in a pulpit or on a throne.*[6]

> **There is no salvation without accepting Joseph Smith**

> *Joseph Smith . . . will be resurrected and receive the keys of the resurrection, and he will seal resurrection authority upon others, and they will hunt up their friends and resurrect them...*[7]

> *For his [Joseph Smith's] word ye shall receive, as if from mine own mouth, in all patience and faith.*[8]

> *If we get our salvation, we shall have to pass by him [Joseph Smith]; if we enter into our glory, it will be through the authority that he has received. We cannot get around him.*[9]

Mormon hymns proclaim inordinate honor and praise toward Joseph Smith. The hymn *Praise To The Man* declares, "Kings shall extol him, and nations revere. Earth must atone for the blood of that man. Hail to the prophet, ascended to heaven! Traitors and tyrants now fight him in vain. Mingling with Gods, he can plan for his brethren . . . "[10] The hymn *The Seer, Joseph, The Seer* says:

> *He loved the saints . . . unchanged in death, with a Saviour's love, he pleads their cause in the courts above. His home is in the sky; he dwells with the Gods - he reigns; he reigns in the realms above. We'll meet him, we'll meet him our martyred Seer, in heaven.*[11]

We honored Joseph Smith in other hymns, such as *Oh Give Me Back My Prophet Dear*[12] and *We Thank Thee, O God, For A Prophet.*[13] The Mormon Apostle Orson Hyde spoke of grieving the spirit of the deceased Joseph Smith, of whom according to Hyde, has power to forgive sins.[14]

In 1846-47, under the direction of the second Mormon Prophet, Brigham Young, the Mormons left Illinois and made their famous trip to the place that became known as Deseret, later Utah. The Mormon Church established its headquarters in Salt Lake City.

## Judging Non-Mormons

While I was growing up, I remember Mormons being cautioned against contamination with so-called Christian doctrines. We were proud to be living in *our* Zion, among the *pure in heart*. We called nonmembers *Gentiles* and *outsiders*. Church authorities taught us to consider other people, Christians included, unfortunate and much in need of the restored Mormon Gospel.

The early Mormon Apostle Erastus Snow said:

> *. . . it is very difficult to distinguish the Christian from the infidel, unless it be that the Christian is the worst.* "[15]

John Taylor, the third Mormon Prophet said:

> *We talk about Christianity, but it is a perfect pack of nonsense . . . Myself and hundreds of Elders around me have seen its pomp, and glory; and what is it? It is a sounding brass and a tinkling symbol; it is as corrupt as hell; and the Devil could not have invented a better engine to spread his work than the Christianity of the 19th Century.*[16]

> **we talk about Christianity, but it is a perfect pack of nonsense**

We believed we had exclusive knowledge and wisdom. Our thinking went something like this: *We believe like you do. The difference is simply that through the Prophet Joseph Smith and the subsequent restoration of the gospel, we have more important truth. No one else is able to answer all of life's important questions such as 'Why we are here?' and 'Where we are going?.'*

These questions, and Mormonism's answers to them, became primary to the high calling upon our lives to be teachers and saviors to the nations of the world. The Mormon Prophet John Taylor, explained:

> *. . . we are the only people that know how to save our progenitors, how to save ourselves, and how to save our posterity . . . we are the people that God has chosen by whom to establish his kingdom . . . we are in fact the saviours of the world, if they are to be saved . . .*[17]

Spreading the Mormon Gospel was an instinctive part of our lives. The notorious Mormon scholar and Apostle Bruce R. McConkie explained in his book *Mormon Doctrine*, "There is no salvation outside the Church of Jesus Christ of Latter-day Saints."[18] I believed this and was proud to be on the "inside." In agreement with the Mormon Prophet, Joseph Fielding Smith, I was taught: "We are, notwithstanding our weaknesses, the best people in the world . . . and in many ways superior to any other people. The reason is that we have received the truth, the Gospel of the Lord Jesus Christ."[19]

> **we are the best people in all the world**

I grew up believing that Christians know very little about the Bible, and that God uses non-Mormon churches to bring people to a fundamental (if shallow and limited) understanding of truth. Then, through Mormon prophets and church officials as well as Mormon extra-biblical writings, these non-Mormons could grow to a mature and deep understanding of God. I was taught that the reason Mormons do not *proselytize the heathen* is because these people must develop the elementary understanding of God available through Christian Churches before they are ready for the full truth of Mormonism. God uses the marginal truths of Christian Churches as an introduction, further growth and development coming only through the Mormon faith.

## Receiving the Priesthood

Mormons believe they alone have God's priesthood today. Mormonism teaches that the priesthood, once lost, was restored to earth to Joseph Smith. According to Mormonism, before its restoration the priesthood had been absent from the earth for nearly 2000 years. The Mormon *priesthood restoration* reinstituted the necessary Laws and Ordinances (e.g. sacrament, baptisms for the living and the dead, endowments, eternal marriage) necessary in *achieving Godhood* which is their main objective on earth. The process of working through all of the necessary Laws and Ordinances of the Mormon Gospel is termed the *Law of Eternal Progression*. The reward for having worked through that progression is termed *Exaltation*, and those who earn Exaltation achieve their own Godhood. The achievement of Exaltation, fundamental in the Mormon belief system, is acquired only through the power of the Mormon priesthood. As a Mormon, I was taught that we *alone* had the Aaronic and Melchizedek priesthoods, which gave us the exclusive authority to act in God's name:

> *Without the Melchizedek Priesthood salvation in the Kingdom of God would not be available for men on earth, for the ordinances of salvation - the laying on of hands for the gift of the Holy Ghost, for instance - could not be authoritatively performed. Thus as far as all religious organizations now existing are concerned, the presence or the absence of this priesthood establishes the divinity or falsity of a professing church.*[20]

I was taught that during a pre-earth life I had earned the privilege to live in an LDS family which held the priesthood. I learned that my white skin color was a reward for my diligence in that pre-existence.[21] The most noble of the spirits, in the pre-mortal life, were blessed to unite with a body during the greatest of all eras, referred to as *Dispensation of the Fulness of Times*. Differing from its meaning in Christianity, the biblical phrase *Fulness of Times* refers to the *restoration* by Joseph Smith of the Gospel of Christ (Mormonism) in the last days.[22]

## Loving the Book of Mormon

Mormons believe the *Book of Mormon* contains a history of God's dealings with the ancient inhabitants of the American continents from about 2247 BC to 421 AD.[23] Joseph Smith claimed an angel led him to a collection of buried plates made of gold, on which were inscribed ancient hieroglyphic text. Smith, who professed to be a Prophet, Seer and Revelator translated the golden plates by means of a *Urim and Thummim*, such as was familiar to the Israelites of long ago. The church claims that the plates were translated into the present *Book of Mormon*. A written account by Joseph Smith as to how this event transpired is recorded in the *Pearl of Great Price*, Joseph Smith 2.

The Mormon Church claims the *Book of Mormon* contains the *fulness of the everlasting gospel*.[24] Combined with the *Bible*, the *Pearl of Great Price*, the *Doctrine and Covenants*, and the *Book of Mormon* makes up the four *Standard Works* of Mormonism.

When I was a young girl, my mother bought me the *Book of Mormon* in storybook form. I loved the stories in that book just as much as I loved to hear pioneer stories about my ancestors. I felt comfortable and proud of our church whenever I thought about the *Book of Mormon*. As I reached my early teen years, it became more important to me to share Mormonism with non-Mormon friends.

A couple of my childhood friends were not LDS. These girlfriends, Teddy and Daryl, whom I had known from second grade, were sisters who lived on a farm some distance from my home. Sometimes, because they lived so far away, I was able to stay overnight at their house. Each time I stayed overnight, the girls' grandmother read bedtime stories to us from the Bible. This family prayed together, as did my family. I was convinced that if someone would only teach Mormonism to this family, they would make good Mormons.

There came a time around age eleven or twelve that Teddy and Daryl decided to share their conviction that my church was wrong. One day while visiting at my home, they took it upon themselves to tell me that the *Book of Mormon* was false. I loved the *Book of Mormon*. I was terribly upset by my friends' accusation. By this age I believed that one must accept the *Book of Mormon* in order to live in heaven with God. The Mormon Apostle Orson Pratt had said, "The nature of the message of the *Book of Mormon* is such, that if true, no one can possibly be saved and reject it; if false, no one can possibly be saved and receive it."[25]

I grew very protective of the *Book of Mormon*. I was aware that there were verses from the Bible that Mormons believe predict the coming of the *Book of Mormon*. When the girls claimed that it was false, I felt a need to show them how wrong they were. I could remember some of the words Mormons use from the Bible that predict the *Book of Mormon* and I began to share them, though I couldn't recall the specific references. Teddy and Daryl didn't believe those words were in the Bible.

Immediately, I excused myself, went into the bathroom, knelt down, and prayed that God would show me Bible verses to prove to my friends that the *Book of Mormon* was true. I sincerely wanted Teddy and Daryl to believe the book but God never provided me with the verses. Despite my disappointment that God didn't answer my prayer, I believed I could find the verses later for the girls. I felt unprepared and a little guilty for not knowing where the proper LDS proof texts were to show my friends. This personal failure instilled in me the desire to become a better missionary.

During my youth, five of my brothers left home to serve two-year missions for the Mormon Church. This connection increased my feeling of the importance of the church. My mother wrote faithfully to my brothers, and I faithfully read the letters they sent home. I was so proud of my brothers. I believed they were the best missionaries, the most handsome, and strongest young men around. I wished any of my brothers could have been with me to help my girlfriends change their minds about our *Book of Mormon.*

## Activity in the Church

I served in many church capacities. I was taught never to refuse a church job for such a calling was inspired by God. My Patriarchal Bless-ing (a personal blessing –see glossary page 196) made it plain that I must follow my leaders in order to please God. As a teenager I played the piano for Primary (for children under twelve years of age) and later served in the Primary Presidency. In the Young Men's and Women's Mutual Improve-ment Association (MIA) I taught the Beehive and the Laurel teenage classes (youth groups), served as speech director, taught the adult *Book of Mormon* class, and helped with road shows (traveling entertainment). Mormons are very active with social events, sports, drama, teaching, dance, volunteering, studying, etc. The social life of an active Mormon is integral to their religion. I taught the Social Relations class and served in the Presidency of the Relief Soci-ety (an auxiliary for women). I taught the Investigators class (for those investigating the church) in Sunday School and the Gospel Doctrine class. I served as a Stake Missionary in the Chicago area. I was diligent in prayer and fasting. I loved the LDS Church with all my heart.

> *I was taught never to refuse a church assignment*

## Laboring in Works

In an LDS upbringing women are taught to set the tenor in a home. I saw that principle modeled by my mother. She often said, "Where much is given, much is required, and we must endure to the end." Expressions like this one became a part of my vocabulary from an early age. My Patriarchal Blessing emphasized the same, along with the great importance that my example of obedience would influence the lives of my family and close associates, and even assist the dead. Here are some words from the Patriarchal Blessing which guided my lifestyle:

> *God has chosen you to be a leader in Zion, to teach the gospel . . . You will build up faith to those who are inactive . . . if you continue in faithfulness, study the gospel, you will be en-lightened in its principles and be a savior in Zion to the living as well as those who have gone beyond.*

According to LDS belief a blissful eternity awaits all people. The belief that all receive salvation is termed *universal salvation.* Those who keep all the commands of the Mormon Gospel are rewarded with life in the presence of Elohim, the name-title of the self-Exalted Mormon God in charge of planet earth. But to live with the Mormon God in the highest heaven one must through achievement exalt oneself to the station of a God or Goddess. The *Doctrine and Covenants* describes the three heavenly kingdoms to which people are assigned in eternity.[26] The kingdom they receive is awarded according to their works. The Mor-mon Apostle Bruce R. McConkie explained:

> *Contrary to the views found in the uninspired teachings and creeds of modern Christendom, there are in eternity kingdoms of glory to which all resurrected persons (except the sons of perdition) will eventually go. These are named: celestial, terrestrial, and telestial . . .*[27]

Members of the LDS Church who have testimonies of the Jesus of Mormonism and his required works, but who do not exhibit and perform valiantly with devotion to the Mormon Church, are assigned to the Terrestrial kingdom.[28] Mormon revelation proclaims that those who only achieve the reward of this middle prized kingdom are restricted from the presence of the Father God, only to receive the presence of the Son.[29]  Logically it follows then that those of the lowest heaven only have the presence of the Mormon Holy Ghost.  Mormon revelation states that the bodies and spirits which become recipients to the lower kingdoms have less glory than those who earn the Celestial kingdom.[30]

Later in my life, after I was married, my husband shared with me that he felt as though trying to measure up to all that Mormonism requires is like trying to climb a greased pole - impossible!  For me as well it became a struggle to meet the Mormon rules of conduct, with a satisfying level of success.  The *Book of Mormon* states "For we know that it is of grace that we are saved, *after* all we can do."[31]  How was I ever to be sure I'd done all I could do?  Things I did never seemed to be good enough.  The Mormon Church teaches that grace does not refer to the total sufficiency of the gift of Jesus' atoning Sacrifice to reconcile people to God.  The twelfth Mormon Prophet, Spencer W. Kimball, asserts the LDS rejection of the Christian notion of a God of grace:

> *One of the most fallacious doctrines originated by Satan and propounded by man is that man is saved alone by the grace of God; that belief in Jesus Christ alone is all that is needed for salvation.*[32]

So, I labored on for Mormonism.  Works had kicked into overdrive for me at an early age, and were continuing as a major emphasis in my striving for Exaltation.  Some more of my Patriarchal Blessing:

> *. . . the spirit of the Lord will come to your assistance so much that you will be able to do much good to those whom you love and with whom you associate.  Be obedient . . . seek counsel from those who are officiating where you reside, and you will have strength to overcome evil and be able to discern that which is good.*

I certainly had tried my best to be obedient to the counsel of my blessing, and I had sought counsel with the leaders of my church.

## Saving and Communicating with the Dead

Mormons believe that all people who are honest in heart, whether living or dead, are waiting for Mormons to teach them about the restoration of the Mormon Gospel.  According to LDS theology, at the point of death our spirits exit our mortal bodies, and then dwell in one of two places.  The faithful LDS enter Paradise.  The rest of the dead (including those who, during mortality, were not fortunate enough to hear the Mormon Gospel) reside in a place called Spirit prison.  Mormons teach that faithful, deceased Mormons living in Paradise are, at some point in time, sent on missions to the Spirit prison.  There they teach the Mormon Gospel to those who have not yet heard truth.  At the same time, living Mormons seek out the genealogical records of the dead, and then perform proxy temple work on their behalf (baptisms, endowments, sealings, etc).  People in the Spirit prison who accept the LDS Gospel, and have had vicarious temple work performed for them, are then released and move on up to Paradise, alongside other faithful Mormons.

Mormonism teaches that building temples during the millennium and laboring in them will occupy most of the time of the saints.[33]  As the fourth Mormon Prophet Wilford Woodruff said, temple work is also of prime importance now:

> *The spirits of the dead gathered around me wanting to know why I did not redeem them.  Every one of those men that signed the Declaration of Independence with General Washington called upon me as an apostle of the Lord Jesus Christ, in the Temple at St. George two consecutive nights, and demanded at my hands that I should go forth and attend to the ordinances of the house of God for them . . . Brother McAllister baptized me on behalf of John Wesley, Columbus and others.*[34]

In 1944, a church patriarch gave my mother a special blessing to comfort her in a time of added personal responsibility caused by World War II.  In part it said, "I bless you in behalf of your kindred that you may serve in the temples and have joy in temple work, and that you may be rewarded with heavenly manifestations concerning your kindred dead."

God has warned us about contact with familiar spirits who pose as genuine.  The Bible also warns us of false prophets who approve of such manifestations.[35]

## Achieving Eternal Exaltation

While growing up I was all ears when people discussed the subject of *self-Exaltation* to Godhood. The following quotes are from four prophets of the LDS Church: Joseph Smith, Brigham Young, John Taylor, and Spencer W. Kimball. They pertain to Mormon teachers, saviors, tempters, and redeemers, and deal with the Mormon plan of Exaltation:

> . . . *and you have got to learn how to become Gods yourselves . . . the same as all Gods have done before you, - namely, by going from one small degree to another... and are able to dwell in everlasting burnings and to sit in glory, as do those who sit enthroned in everlasting power.*[36]

> *The greatest responsibility in this world that God has laid upon us is to seek after our dead.*[37]

> . . . *and every man who has a friend in the eternal world can save him, unless he has committed the unpardonable sin. And so you can see how far you can be a savior.*[38]

> *They, [the dead], without us cannot be made perfect . . . I say to you, Paul, [N.T. apostle] you cannot be made perfect without us.*[39]

> *It will be a pleasure to know that we have saved all the Father gave unto our power.*[40]

> *Consequently, every earth has its redeemer, and every earth has its tempter.*[41]

> *But I expect . . . that I shall see the time with yourselves that we shall know how to prepare to organize an earth like this- know how to people that earth, how to redeem it, how to sanctify it, and how to glorify it, with those who live upon it who hearken to our counsels.*[42]

Speaking of the Mormon faith Brigham Young boasted "It is the only system of religion known in heaven or on earth that can exalt a man to the Godhead."[43] In a church publication the Mormon Prophet Spencer W. Kimball explained, "And when the ceremony [temple marriage ceremony] is completed you two will go forth from those sacred precincts . . . to conquer and build and love and exalt yourselves and your family."[44] I believed the Mormon Prophets and LDS Scriptures.

In accordance with Mormonism, I believed that church members who overcome all things and earn the highest rank in heaven, will live eternally in a family unit, produce spirit children, and become eternal fathers and eternal mothers.[45]

Later, as a Christian, I learned that it was this goal of self-Exaltation that caused Satan to fall[46] and the same strategy for which he facilitated the fall of Adam and Eve.[47]

1   Book of Commandments, preface, 1833.

2    History of the Church, vol. 2, p. 63.

3   Jesus The Christ, p. 769; Doctrine and Covenants 115:4.

4   History of the Church, vol. 6 p. 365.

5   Doctrines of Salvation, vol. 1, p. 189-190.

6   Discourses of Brigham Young, p. 435.

7   Discourses of Brigham Young, p. 116.

8   Doctrine and Covenants 21:5.

9   Melchizedek Priesthood Study Guide, 1984 p. 129.

10   Mormon Hymnal, p. 147, 1961 printing.

11   Mormon Hymnal, p. 296.

12   Mormon Hymnal, p. 137.

13   Mormon Hymnal, p. 196.

14   Journal of Discourses, vol. 6, pp. 154-156.

15   Journal of Discourses, vol. 25, p. 197.

16   Journal of Discourses, vol. 6, p. 167.

17   Journal of Discourses, vol. 6, p. 163.

18   Mormon Doctrine, p. 670.

19   Doctrines of Salvation, vol. 1, p. 236.

20   Mormon Doctrine, p. 479.

21   Mormon Doctrine, p. 526.

22   Mormon Doctrine, p. 200.

23   Mormon Doctrine, p. 98.

24   Doctrine and Covenants 20:9.

25   Divine Authenticity of The Book of Mormon, p. 1.

26   Doctrine and Covenants 76; 132:16-17.

27   Mormon Doctrine, p. 420.

28   Doctrine and Covenants 76:71-80; Mormon Doctrine, p. 784.

29   Doctrine and Covenants 76:77.

30   Mormon Doctrine, pp. 783, 784.

31   Book of Mormon, 2 Nephi 25:23.

32   The Miracle of Forgiveness, p. 206.

33   Doctrines of Salvation, vol. 2, p. 166.

34   Temples of the Most High, pp. 87-88; Journal of Discourses, vol. 19, p. 229.

35   Deuteronomy chapters 13 and 18.

36   Journal of Discourses, vol. 6, p. 4

37   Teachings of the Prophet Joseph Smith, p. 356.

38   Teachings of the Prophet Joseph Smith, p. 357.

39   Teachings of the Prophet Joseph Smith, p. 356.

40   Journal of Discourses, vol. 9, p. 124.

41   Journal of Discourses, vol. 14, p. 71.

42   Journal of Discourses, vol. 6, pp. 274-75.

43   Journal of Discourses, vol. 10, p. 251.

44   The New Era, June 1975, p. 9.

45   Doctrine and Covenants 132:19-32.

46   Isaiah 14:12-14.

47   Genesis 3:5.

# 2. Jehovah's Witnesses Challenge Me

*. . . wisdom . . . is peace-loving and courteous . . . It allows discussion and is willing to yield to others; it is full of mercy and good deeds. It is wholehearted and straightforward and sincere.*

James 3:17

Imagine the Jehovah's Witnesses and the Mormons together –both claiming to be God's only voice on earth! Both claiming by the very name of their organization God's sanction of approval and their witness to Him.

One day during our years in Vernal, Utah, two Jehovah's Witnesses came knocking at our door. I invited them in. They left me with my first real exposure to what Mormons commonly term *anti-Mormon literature*, and presented a series of quotes by Mormon General Authorities. Included in the materials left for me was this challenging quote from an original Mormon Apostle Orson Pratt:

*Convince us of our errors of doctrine, if we have any, by logical arguments, or by the Word of God, and we will be ever grateful for the information, and you will have the pleasing reflection that you have been instruments in the hands of God of redeeming your fellow beings from the darkness which you may see enveloping their minds . . . endeavor with patience and meekness to reclaim from error, and save the immortal soul from an endless death.*[1]

But of greater impact to me personally was a quote from LDS Scripture I was already familiar with:

*Wherefore confound your enemies; call upon them to meet you both in public and in private; and inasmuch as you are faithful their shame shall be manifest.*[2]

Because of my upbringing I felt responsible not only to defend Mormonism, but also to share its truth with the Jehovah's Witnesses. I wasn't afraid at that time to read the materials they left with me. I had been taught that some people were uninformed, and had been lied to regarding Mormonism. Others, whatever their motives, received some kind of bizarre pleasure from attacking God's restored true church. My desire was to remove the incorrect impressions I believed the Witnesses had regarding us, and at the same time be faithful to church challenges like the ones noted above. Ultimately, these Mormon quotes played a major part in ordering my sense of obligation to study LDS Gospel and being faithful to the church.

## Adam God

The Jehovah's Witnesses showed me some photocopies purportedly of Mormon material about a subject referred to as *Adam-God*. These were photocopies of writings claiming that Adam is God, the father of our spirits, and the very same resurrected God the Mormons worship. Other matters they brought to my attention included the subjects of Blood Atonement and the necessity of plural marriage or polygamy. The photocopies were disturbing to me. I felt certain they were fraudulent or that they could in some way be explained. Regarding polygamy, the Jehovah's Witnesses pointed out to me that according to Mormon Scripture recorded in the *Doctrine and Covenants,* one will be damned if polygamy is not practiced and that plural marriage is necessary for entrance into the highest Mormon afterlife.[3]

I arranged for my Stake (area) missionaries and myself to meet with the Jehovah's Witnesses. The result? We Mormons could not give an explanation! The LDS missionaries simply declared the material to be fabrications, which had been introduced and perpetrated by enemies of the church. I felt the Mormon missionaries disappointed God by not being equipped to respond effectively to the anti-Mormon literature. Their only response, it seemed to me, was one of anger toward the Jehovah's Witnesses for putting them in an embarrassing situation.

If the missionaries from my church had cared for the souls of the Jehovah's Witnesses, I thought, why not apologize for being angry and set up a future time together in order to substantiate that they were utterly wrong in their accusations concerning our church? What better way, it seemed to me, to get a foot in the door to teach them the true Mormon Gospel?

The encounter with the Jehovah's Witnesses left me embarrassed and surprised by my own lack of knowledge. Until then, I'd been proud of all I'd learned from the Mormon seminary which I attended and received credit for as part of my high school curriculum, and the studies I had done independently. I took pride in the fact that I had read much concerning my church, including the entire *Book of Mormon* before I graduated from high school. The Jehovah's Witnesses had taken me down a peg or two. Now I felt a need to be better prepared.

While the LDS missionaries reacted angrily toward the Jehovah's Witnesses, I believed that there were clear answers for the Witnesses' questions. I promised the Witnesses I would supply those answers. I sought out the most informed people I knew to explain what seemed to be a conflict between current LDS teaching and that of the early church records concerning Adam-God. The Mormon leaders with whom I spoke brushed off my inquiry concerning Adam-God and the issues of plural marriage and Blood Atonement. They seemed to feel as though such matters were of no importance, nor were they interested in supplying the Jehovah's Witnesses with answers to their accusations and questions. It was my conviction that a proper explanation was necessary to enable the Witnesses to move beyond their objections, hear the Mormon Gospel, and be converted to the Mormon Church. I was very surprised at my leaders indifference toward the matter! They were prideful, mocking, laughing, under their breath in contrast to the Jehovah's Witnesses, who seemed more genuine and equipped. I felt that as far as sharing and defending our faith was concerned, I alone was left burning the midnight oil.

The Jehovah's Witnesses encouraged me to gain access to the *Journal of Discourses.* They assured me that the Discourses were a good source for checking into Mormon history. I was able to find a set of all twenty-six volumes of the journals. I found this massive compilation of messages from past General Authorities of the church overwhelming and intimidating. Later on I purchased my own set, which I cite in this book. I wondered if there might be an ingredient acquired only in the temple which would enable me to understand more clearly and would take away the risk of being deceived about some of the mysterious things with which I had been challenged. I hadn't been married long, and oh how I yearned to go to the temple, where perhaps God would answer all my questions.

One day I removed from the bookshelf volume one of the *Journal of Discourses* and looked up the reference the Jehovah's Witnesses had left with me to examine. I read the reference aloud to an LDS friend. It was my hope that she would become a soldier of truth with me in defense of the church. I read the following words from Brigham Young, the second Prophet of the Mormon Church.

> *Now hear it, O inhabitants of the earth, Jew and Gentile, Saint and sinner! When our father Adam came into the garden of Eden, he came into it with a celestial body, and brought Eve, one of his wives, with him. He helped to make and organize this world. He is MICHAEL, the Archangel, the Ancient of Days! about whom holy men have written and spoken ---- He is our FATHER and our GOD, and the only God with whom we have to do. Every man upon the earth, professing Christians or non-professing, must hear it, and will know it sooner or later. . . . When the Virgin Mary conceived the child Jesus, the Father had begotten him in his own*

*likeness. He was not begotten by the Holy Ghost. And who is the Father? He is the first of the human family; and when he took a tabernacle, it was begotten by his Father in Heaven, after the same manner as the tabernacles of Cain, Abel, and the rest of the sons and daughters of Adam and Eve. . . . What a learned idea! Jesus our elder brother, was begotten in the flesh by the same character that was in the garden of Eden, and who is our Father in Heaven. Now, let all who may hear these doctrines, pause before they make light of them, or treat them with indifference, for they will prove their salvation or damnation.*[4]

> **Adam is our only God...**
> **believe it**
> **or be damned**

I'll never forget the look on my friend's face as she dropped the subject like a hot potato. She did not become angry, as did the Mormon missionaries during the difficult encounter with the Witnesses, but she certainly demonstrated an indifference just as Brigham Young had warned against in the quote I had just read to her.

I first thought the quote to be a forgery. The missionaries had told us that it was a misquote. When I found the quote was exactly as it read in the *Journal of Discourses,* it was explained that because Brigham Young's speeches were recorded by hand by a secretary, there were misunderstandings and errors. If this were so, I wondered what Brigham Young really meant. Finally, I thought something must be wrong with me, and not the church. Perhaps I was not smart enough, or spiritually worthy to understand the message. I hoped my temple *Endowment* (see glossary, page 195) would clarify it all. For these reasons, at that particular time in my life I made little use of the *Journal of Discourses.* I felt certain that under examination they would substantiate the church.

But - I recalled singing from the Mormon Hymnal, a hymn titled *Sons of Michael, He approaches.*[5] What people sing about can be very telling:

> *Sons of Michael, he approaches! Rise the ancient Father greet; Bow, ye thousands, low before him; Minister before his feet . . . Mother of our generations, Glorious by great Michael's side, Take thy children's adoration; endless with thy Lord preside . . .*

Who, I wondered, was the real Michael in the song, and why bow before him, unless he is really God? Later I leaned, that the song refers to the Adam that was in the Garden of Eden - just as Brigham Young had said.

I remembered a quote the Witnesses challenged me with by the Mormon Apostle George Albert Smith: "If a faith will not bear to be investigated; if its preachers and professors are afraid to have it examined, their foundation must be very weak."[6] I told the Witnesses that I agreed with the quote and was certain that we Mormons could stand steady because our foundation was secure. All objection to Mormonism, I felt certain, could not withstand the acid test of Mormon history explained below:

> *There was no need for eliminating, changing, or adjusting any part to make it fit; but each new revelation on doctrine and priesthood fitted in its place perfectly to complete the whole structure, as had been prepared by the Master Builder.*[7]

I believed that our church records were accurate. Even today leaders of the LDS Church hold to the conviction that the church will be judged from their own church books and histories.[8]

## Wedding in the Temple

I had been taught to endure hardships. I was always taught that living the Mormon Gospel required hard work. In our family we were taught that the Christian religions were the easy way, but since we were blessed with the restored truth, more was expected of us. My strong desire was to follow the example of my parents and siblings –to be faithful, as they were, to the church. With God's help I would do so! There were many rules and regulations, but we must all keep striving! My husband smoked cigarettes, which kept him from being worthy of being married in the Mormon temple. Blessings could come about only through the power of the Mormon priesthood and the required keeping of all the commandments: "But to be exalted one must keep the whole law . . . to receive the exaltation of the righteous, in other words eternal life, the commandments of the Lord must be kept in all things."[9]  In his book *Answers to Gospel Questions*, Joseph Fielding Smith further stated, "In other words if there is one divine law that he does not keep he is barred from participating in the [Celestial] kingdom, and figuratively guilty of all, since he is denied all."[10]

Sometimes my mother reminded me about little sins keeping people from the highest form of salvation.  She spoke of those who would permit a caffeinated cup of tea or coffee to bar themselves from the Celestial kingdom.  Statements affirming these conclusions were made by Joseph Fielding Smith in a book under the heading *Salvation and a Cup of Tea*.[11]  The Standard Works of the church informs church members that when Jesus comes again those who do not tithe to the church will be burned.[12]  A Mormon's reliance on his or her own works to achieve salvation permeates Mormon teaching.

My biggest dream in all the world was to receive my *endowments* and be married to a wonderful Mormon man, in a Mormon temple, for time and all eternity.  Among members of my church community, civil marriages were looked down upon.  In Mormonism, it is believed that without a temple marriage there is no family unit in eternity.  Temple marriage is a prerequisite to Godhood.[13]  Therefore, God and Jesus were both married.  The Mormon Apostle Orson Hyde, is quoted below:

> There was a marriage in Cana of Galilee; and on a careful reading of that transaction, it will be discovered that no less a person than Jesus Christ was married on that occasion.  If he was never married, his intimacy with Mary and Martha, and the other Mary also whom Jesus loved, must have been highly unbecoming and improper to say the best of it.[14]

The Mormon Apostle Orson Pratt said:

> *Each God, through his wives, raises up a family of numerous sons and daughters . . . The inhabitants of each world are required to reverence, adore, and worship their own personal father who dwells in the Heaven which they formerly inhabited.*[15]

| |
|---|
| **each God, through his wives, raises up a family . . . inhabitants of each world . . . worship their own personal father** |

Only Mormon temple marriages, I was taught, are honored by God and acknowledged as the gateway to living eternally with Him.  I desired to have a family which would be a blessing to my husband and myself.  For a Mormon, though, having children also is a necessary step in the Mormon Law of Eternal Progression.  Children serve as the means whereby the necessary tabernacles (physical bodies) are supplied for pre-existent spirits.  If my future husband and I were not faithful to the Mormon call on our lives to supply bodies for spirits, these spirits would end up with wicked families.

> There are multitudes of pure and holy spirits waiting to take tabernacles, now what is our duty?  To prepare tabernacles for them; to take a course that will not tend to drive those spirits into families of the wicked.[16]

Participating in the temple *Endowment* is the most sacred and holy event in a Mormon's life.  And it is extremely important to marry within the church!  Leaders of the church have expressed that it would be better to bury a child than to have him or her marry outside the church.  Joseph Fielding Smith stated:

> I have heard the President Joseph F. Smith say on several occasions that he would rather take his children one by one to the grave in their innocence and purity, knowing that they would come forth and inherit the fulness of celestial glory, than to have them marry outside of the Church, or even outside the temple of the Lord.[17]

I was married in a civil ceremony in 1959 to Clyde Carroll.  Also a Mormon, Clyde was born and raised in Vernal, Utah.  We moved to Los Angeles, California, where Clyde finished his schooling.  Ten months later our oldest daughter, Valerie, was born.  We then moved to Vernal, Utah, where Clyde began his flying career.

Church doctrine made it plain that if I didn't go to the temple, there would be much sorrow on my part at the time of my resurrection.  Failing to do so would result in having to be a servant for all eternity.[18]  I could never become a Goddess, but would be an angel forever.[19]  Throughout all eternity, I would serve those who were more worthy.  This would be a constant reminder of my failure to accomplish my temple duties.

Although not yet married in the Mormon temple, my husband and I were asked to teach the adult MIA *Book of Mormon* class. My husband elected to let me do it by myself and he would stay home with our child. I took this calling seriously and it became a challenge that thrust me, at an early age, deeply into church doctrine.

In 1963, four years after our civil marriage, my husband and I were worthy to answer appropriately to the probing questions asked by church authorities before *Temple Recommends* (certificates of entrance) are issued. At last we were deemed worthy to be married in a Mormon temple. We chose the temple in Idaho Falls, Idaho. There we received our *endowments*, necessary in achieving *Exaltation* in the Mormon highest Celestial kingdom. Inside the temple we were dressed by a temple worker in the clothing of the Holy priesthood, given our *garments* (the temple *regulation underwear* as they are also called), and were instructed to wear them each day for the rest of our lives. They would serve as spiritual and physical protection for our lives. I was disappointed that the actual marriage part of the ceremony only lasted a few minutes while the entire ceremony took hours. Frankly, I felt disappointed with myself and a little guilty for not understanding the particulars behind the temple proceedings. Looking back, they were indeed very strange. But, as I often heard before, "One must return many, many times to understand all of the beauty and significance of the Temple Ceremony." I believed that through my faithfulness the Temple Ceremony would blossom beautifully in my understanding.

In the temple I took symbolic blood oath covenants. The violating of these covenants, I was told, would result in severe penalties, which were symbolically executed in various ways. For example, one such penalty was symbolically executed by placing my right thumb under my left ear, palm down, fingers close together. I then was instructed to move my thumb quickly across my throat to my right ear, dropping my hand to the side, symbolically cutting my throat. Indeed, I swore by the words of my mouth and with the gestures of my hands that I would give my life's blood if necessary for the protection of, and the building up of the kingdom of God (Mormonism). I swore on my life never to reveal what transpired within the temple walls. I swore an oath of obedience to my husband in the temple. Apart from the oaths I took which were very sobering, I also acquired a *new name*. My mate was responsible to remember my *new name*, and by his priesthood authority, he was responsible to call me forth on the morning of resurrection. I now think oaths like this are an abomination to God.

> *I took symbolic blood oaths in the Mormon temple*

The problem was I wasn't sure my husband even remembered my *new name*. According to the church, if my spouse were not faithful but I was, I would be given to some other worthy man for eternity.[20] Whose wife would I become? I recalled the mirrors in the temple, positioned in such a way as to reflect more images of me than I could count. The temple guides had explained that the mirrors were to help me understand that if I remained faithful, there would be no end to my posterity!

And sadly, if I were not faithful to the Laws and Ordinances of the Mormon Gospel I could lose my female gender and end up in a lower kingdom of heaven throughout all eternity. I believed that for a Mormon, (or anyone) this occurrence would be catastrophic! Joseph Fielding Smith said, "I take it that men and women will, in these kingdoms, be just what the so-called Christian world expects us all to be - neither man or woman, merely immortal beings having received the resurrection."[21]

Each part of the Mormon Temple Ceremony is critically essential to Mormon salvation. Each part must be perfectly remembered, performed and heeded. Without strict obedience to all of the Temple Ceremony, it is impossible for a Mormon to pass through the veil into the Celestial kingdom, where by then he has earned eternal life with God. Understanding God's perfect temple endowment and the importance of keeping temple oaths became of great concern to me. Clyde, it seemed, wouldn't have cared if he ever set foot inside a temple again. If I remained faithful I thought I could keep a current Temple Recommend, and go back whenever possible.

Faithful LDS are encouraged to return to their temples as often as possible. Whenever I went back to the temple I wrestled with the information given me by the Jehovah's Witnesses concerning Adam-God, in particular the part Adam plays in the creation segment of the Temple Ceremony.

When I was taking Mormon seminary in high school we had to memorize from the KJV Bible: "And this is life eternal, that they might know thee the only true God, and Jesus Christ whom thou hast sent."[22] This verse, I felt, was of critical interest to Mormons and non-Mormons alike. It made plain that eternal life was based on the knowledge of who God is. We were taught to use this verse to introduce Joseph Smith's first vision of the Father and the Son. This vision denies the Christian understanding of one God and falsely portrays that God and Jesus are two seperate beings with glorified resurrected bodies of flesh and bones. Because the Jehovah's Witnesses had made me aware of the Adam-God issue, a correct knowledge of who God is became the most important question in my mind. Did the answer somehow link with the Adam-God doctrine? I believed that someday I could resolve Brigham Young's words about Adam-God and other topics which my peers seemed careful to avoid discussing. These were issues which the church insisted were misconstrued by the enemies of the church. I wanted to be able to explain the church's position better, both for myself and to others. According to my Patriarchal Blessing, part of what God required of me personally was to study and teach the Gospel. With God's help I would find honest answers to my questions, and be prepared to answer objections from other people as well.

## My Zeal

Although I gave the Mormon measure of setting the tenor in our home great effort, my husband did not respond in the manner I had been taught was his duty as husband and father. Clyde seemed to take my efforts to communicate about spiritual matters as an invasion into unwelcome territory. Repeated attempts for a spiritual connection with him left me hurt and discouraged. Although we always tried to smooth things over, a spiritual barrier came to exist between us. In any religion, the consequences of being spiritually unequally yoked causes marital strife! I felt burdened and confused. I was afraid that if the issue became too big our marriage and family would break up, or that Clyde would grow too spiritually discouraged about being the head of the home in the manner required by the LDS Church. I felt the obligation of not coming down too hard on my husband. This was the cause of greater stress and guilt. At the same time I sensed more responsibility being placed upon myself in the rearing of our children. I felt inadequate and underqualified for the job. I disliked the thought of a woman taking spiritual leadership in a home. I believed this was the man's place! Such a model, I believed, would violate our children's understanding of the importance of God and the LDS faith in their lives. As the years went by I considered my husband's lack of spiritual commitment as proof that he did not consider the church to be important in his life or consequential to the lives of our children. He never came right out and expressed as much to me, but that was the conclusion of my heart. I never felt a sincere encouragement or approval for my zeal. My efforts at good works were encouraged by the church – but I felt uneasy.

1  The Seer, pp. 15-16.

2  Doctrine and Covenants 71:7.

3  Doctrine and Covenants 132:4.

4  Journal of Discourses, vol. 1, pp. 50-51.

5  Hymns, Church of Jesus Christ of Latter-Day Saints, p. 163; 1961 printing.

6  Journal of Discourses, vol. 14, p. 21.

7  Doctrines of Salvation, vol. 1, p. 170.

8  Doctrines of Salvation, vol. 2, p. 200.

9  Doctrines of Salvation, vol. 2, p. 6.

10  Answers to Gospel Questions, vol. 3, p.26.

11  Doctrines of Salvation, vol. 2, p. 16, 17.

12  Doctrine and Covenants 64:23.

13  Doctrine and Covenants 132:4-6.

14  Journal of Discourses, vol. 4, p. 259.

15  The Seer, p. 37.

16  Doctrines of Salvation, vol. 2, p. 88.

17  Doctrines of Salvation, vol. 2, p. 76

18  Doctrines of Salvation, vol. 2 p. 60, 61.

19  Doctrine and Covenants 132:16-17.

20  Doctrines of Salvation, vol. 2, p. 65.

21  Doctrines of Salvation, vol. 2, p. 288.

22  John 17:3.

# 3. Humpty Dumpty

*These were more noble than those in Thessalonica, in that they received the word with all readiness of mind, and they searched the scriptures daily, whether those things were so.*

Acts 17:11

## Building Up My Faith

By 1968 my husband and I had four children and were living in Aurora, Colorado, a suburb of Denver. Clyde was hired as a pilot for a major airline. Although we settled down to the normal routines of working and raising a family, I could not let the issue of Adam-God go. My encounter with the Jehovah's Witnesses generated in me a deeper study of Mormonism, and its defense. I have much to thank the Jehovah's Witnesses for. While I do not agree with their doctrine, I believe God used the Jehovah's Witnesses in my life to expose some of the bitter truths of Mormonism. I felt it my duty – as a member of the only true church – to follow church doctrine. That is, I felt responsible to answer opposition from those outside our church. At the same time, I became increasingly troubled that the leaders of my area seemed either unprepared or uninterested in helping me on this search.

My years in Aurora were a time of study and building up of my faith. I often reflected on my discussions with the Jehovah's Witnesses. They brought to my attention the forceful words of the early Mormon Apostle George Albert Smith, who advised, "If a faith will not bear to be investigated; if its preachers and professors are afraid to have it examined, their foundation must be very weak."[1] Something in my soul called for personal accountability in following the challenge of this early Mormon Apostle.

Besides the Standard Works, a few noteworthy books which I read during these years were: *Doctrine and Covenants Commentary,*[2] *Jesus the Christ, Articles of Faith,* and *A Marvelous Work and a Wonder.* Among the Mormon apologetics I read were each volume of Joseph Fielding Smith's *Answers to Gospel Questions,* each volume of his *Doctrines of Salvation;* Hugh Nibley's, *No Ma'am,That's Not History, Sounding Brass,* and *The Myth Makers;* E. Cecil McGavin's *Cumorah's Gold Bible;* and James E. Talmage's *The Great Apostasy.* Other than in brief passing these books never tried to explain the Adam-God controversy.

## "Adam" –Again?

While living in Aurora an acquaintance gave me a small book entitled *Michael-Adam,* by Ogden Kraut. This book made me think again of Adam-God. Kraut argues that Mormonism is in apostasy and ought still to teach Adam-God as fundamental church doctrine. He maintains that the doctrine was once viewed as critical to one's Exaltation, so much so that it was once included in the Temple Endowment Ceremony. Kraut insists that the doctrine is and always will remain true. While reading his book, I was reminded again of my experience with the Jehovah's Witnesses. Although this small book left a marked impression with me, I felt it probably wasn't presented in a proper perspective. Although I had no way of knowing for certain, I wondered if the Kraut book was authored by a Fundamentalist Mormon. With that in mind, I believed it possible that the author had misrepresented the facts. My church excommunicated Fundamentalists and generally viewed them with contempt. If this book was written by a Fundamentalist, it seemed possible to me the that the author had scrambled the real message of Adam-God. (I later learned that Fundamentalist Mormons hold closer to original Mormon doctrine than do mainstream Mormons of today).

I kept thinking there must be a way to make the contents of the small book square with the current day church. This was my view for some time. It was difficult for me to consider the idea that the church would speak untruthfully concerning the subject of Adam-God. I relied on my church and my Patriarchal Blessing's admonition to follow my leaders; believing the church was unquestionably true. I had complete reliance on my leaders; they had my unyielding devotion. However, the time came when I was cognizant enough about the subject of Adam-God that I could no longer leave this issue on the back burner. I needed answers and frankly, by this time, I wasn't convinced by the church's response to the subject, such as is written in Joseph Fielding Smith's *Doctrines of Salvation*.[3]

Joseph Fielding Smith argues that the sermon by Brigham Young concerning Adam-God was in all probability erroneously transcribed. I found his response inconsistent with the facts that I had seen. I knew enough that I felt uncomfortable arbitrarily or capriciously denying the possibility that Brigham Young taught Adam-God, especially when it so clearly appeared he had in places such as the *Journal of Discourses*.[4]

The church vehemently denied that Brigham Young meant what was written in that reference, or for that matter that Adam-God was ever taught at all. I wanted to believe that response, but I knew it wasn't the answer to the Adam-God issue simply because of the number of references that alluded to this doctrine. It seemed to me that the transcription argument was a convenient way out, rather than the truth about the matter.

Through these years I began to see among my peers a consistent manner of dealing with difficult church issues. The usual route of dealing with controversy, while still maintaining loyalty to the church, was to shoot the messenger. Afterall, from my friends' perspective the church couldn't be at fault –and that left only one conclusion: the problem must lie in me or others who may pursue the church for direct answers to important issues. My questions were not met with ease! Usually, when I brought up doctrinal issues to someone, they were met with reticence. Instead of having the issues addressed, I heard a wide list of other responses including:

> *Don't cultivate a spirit of apostasy.*
> *Have you stopped praying?*
> *If you obeyed the Prophet you wouldn't be confused.*
> *Have you read the Book of Mormon?*
> *Haven't you prayed to receive a testimony?*
> *You leave that anti-Mormon literature alone or you may lose your testimony!*
> *Do you faithfully do your genealogy?*
> *Have you been going to the temple?*
> *You are seeking an excuse to get out of the church because it requires obedience in all things!*
> *Leave the mysteries alone!*
> *You are reading anti–Mormon literature written by enemies of the church, some even apostates!*
> *Do you pay your tithing?*
> *I warn you. You are tossing away your blessings, now and throughout eternity.*
> *...and the most frequently used excuse was: "Can't you feel the truth of the church?"*

The information the Jehovah's Witnesses introduced became my first real experience with what Mormons label *anti-Mormon literature*. This phrase certainly is a misnomer. *Authentic Mormon literature* is more accurate, as the literature usually is straight out of Mormon Standard Works, or from actual messages of Mormon Authorities expounding Mormon doctrine. The phrase is a convenient catch-all for any work critical of Mormonism; it is designed to excuse one from the responsibility of examining Mormonism using available information. This popular phrase defends the inordinate reliance among Mormons on the modern Mormon organization and the men who operate it, rather than any fixed theology.

> the common phrase
> "anti-Mormon
> literature"
> is a misnomer

It seemed beyond my imagination or that of the Mormons with whom I was acquainted to consider that the church could be wrong! I believed that doubting the church was the same as doubting God. The two were one and the same in my mind! While I never considered my quest to study different topics of Mormonism as a sign of apostasy, it seemed that sometimes others thought so. Does examining Mormon doctrine mean one is entertaining the idea of apostasy? No one had reason to reach that conclusion, for I was very dedicated to the church. Somehow, I believed all would harmonize if I continued faithfully to study, pray and seek my leaders' advice. I placed on my shoulders the responsibility to stand up for the church. It was my loyalty to the church that caused me to seek out answers to these difficult questions.

While growing up, I was taught that there is no place in the church for blind adherence. In fact, my Mormon acquaintances often ridiculed the Catholic Church for keeping its members in the dark by advising them as to what they should and shouldn't read. Now I was being told what not to read! I began to find myself among the minority. It seemed to me that many people in the church ignored inconsistencies and contradictions, and some seemed governed by fear. Sometimes I felt fearful also. I was taught that doubts about the church were from Satan, used to endanger our testimony. I observed that most members of the church felt little need to study the Standard Works or Mormon history. Perhaps they were too overwhelmed at the size of the task, or were not interested. They felt good about the church and for them that was sufficient. They relied on the *Doctrine and Covenants* which explains the *burning bosom*:

> *But, behold I say unto you, that you must study it out in your mind; then you must ask me if it be right, and if it is right I will cause that your bosom shall burn within you; therefore, you shall feel that it is right. But if it be not right you shall have no such feelings, but you shall have a stupor of thought that shall cause you to forget the thing which is wrong . . .*[5]

Notice the emphasis on the word *feel*. My testimony feeling was very powerful. I too had experienced a burning in my bosom, but had been unwittingly testing it through many years. During those years of study, I often asked myself, "Why has God allowed all of this conflict to come into my life?" Not until later was I able to understand that God had a glorious purpose in mind as He permitted people into my life to introduce me to literature critical of Mormon doctrine. My personal study had already disclosed that there is much for a Mormon to consider such as these quotes from the *Doctrine and Covenants:*

> *The Glory of God is Intelligence, or in other words, light and truth.*[6]

> *It is impossible for a man to be saved in ignorance.*[7]

> *And if a person gains more knowledge and intelligence in this life through his diligence and obedience than another, he will have so much the advantage in the world to come.*[8]

What knowledge? What intelligence? Obedience to what? While I was studying to defend our church doctrine, I found LDS passages like the ones above either unknown, ignored, or overlooked by all but one Mormon friend, with whom I later lost contact. At that time, some members with whom I tried to share information were cautioning, "You are cultivating a spirit of apostasy! Leave the mysteries alone!" But, I was acquainted with the *Doctrine and Covenants*. This LDS book of purported Scripture is viewed by the church as superior to the Bible. I was fully aware that this sacred Mormon volume teaches that the mysteries of the Mormon Gospel are revealed to worthy Mormons.[9] Truthfully, I was trying with all my heart to be worthy, so I didn't think it was bad to ponder the mysteries. I wondered if Adam-God was one of those mysteries. I concluded that the facts pertaining to Adam-God were understood only by the most worthy Mormons. I entertained the idea that there could be some sort of a hidden code, or secret message of truth understood only by those persistent in the good works of Mormonism. I felt that somehow it tied to the practice of polygamy, as defined in the entire 132nd section of the *Doctrine and Covenants* as the New and Everlasting Covenant.

Brigham Young taught:

> *Why do we believe in and practice polygamy? Because the Lord introduced it to his servants in a revelation given to Joseph Smith, and the Lord's servants have always practiced it. "And is that religion popular in heaven?" It is the only popular religion there, for this is the religion of Abraham, and unless we do the works of Abraham, we are not Abraham's seed and heirs according to the promise.*[11]

> *The only men who become Gods, even the Sons of God, are those who enter into polygamy.*[12]

> *Doctrine and Covenants*:

| |
|---|
| **the only men who become Gods . . . enter into polygamy** |

> *For, behold, I reveal unto you a new and everlasting covenant; and if ye abide not that covenant, then are ye damned; for no one can reject this covenant and be permitted to enter my glory . . . Go ye therefore, and do the works of Abraham; enter ye into my law and ye shall be saved.*[10]

These quotes carry a strong and relevant message about polygamy (plural marriage). Yet, today, those words are disavowed or redefined in Mormonism, and in terms of discussion or study they are now uncomfortable for most Mormons.

At one point I confided in one of my brothers, sending him a booklet containing four lost revelations from the early Mormon Prophet John Taylor. These revelations pertained to the unchangeable necessity of practicing polygamy (as a requirement to Exaltation, or in other words, Godhood). If the account of these revelations as was written in the booklet proved genuine, the present Mormon Church had fallen into apostasy, and the Mormon Manifesto (which officially advises church members to refrain from contracting marriages constitutionally forbidden by the law of the land) violates section 132 of the *Doctrine and Covenants*, as well as the early teachings of Mormon Authorities. The Manifesto, located at the end of the *Doctrine and Covenants*, does not claim to be a revelation. This fact comes as a surprise to many LDS people. For the time being the Mormon Church has suspended the practice of polygamy but retains it as a doctrine.

To this day many people believe *and* practice the Law of Plural Marriage. Known as *Fundamentalists*, these people number in the thousands in Utah alone. Violating the law of our land and negating the advice of the Manifesto, they follow the example of their early Mormon leaders who secretly practiced plural marriage after the Manifesto was issued. This they do to honor the revelation of plural marriage described in the *Doctrine and Covenants 132*, a requirement for achieving the status to Godhood in the Mormon highest kingdom of the afterlife. In these matters I wanted to learn my brother's view and gain his assistance. It never came.

I had been taught from my youth that polygamy will be practiced in the Mormon highest heaven. Truthfully, this seemed an uncomfortable belief, but I just accepted that God would change obedient hearts to embrace this law. In Colorado, I made an effort to learn about other mysterious Mormon buzzwords such as having one's *calling and election made sure*, the *second endowment*, and *receiving the second comforter*.

Joseph Smith taught:

> *I am going on in my progress for eternal life. It is not only necessary that you should be baptized for your dead, but you will have to go through all the ordinances for them, the same as you have gone through to save yourselves . . . Oh! I beseech you to go foreward, go foreward and make your calling and election made sure; and if any man preach any other gospel than that which I [Joseph Smith] have preached, he shall be cursed; and some of you who now hear me shall see it, and know that I testify the truth concerning them.*[13]

In his book *Mormon Doctrine*, the LDS Apostle Bruce R. McConkie explains:

> *Those members of the Church who devote themselves wholly to righteousness, living by every word that proceedeth forth from the mouth of God, make their calling and election sure. That is, they receive the more sure word of prophecy, which means that the Lord seals their exaltation upon them while they are yet in this life.*[14]

I understood this ordination to the station of God was done quietly in the privacy of a select few witnesses, inside a room called Holy of Holies within Mormon temples. This room, as I understood, was reserved for the higher privileges of the Melchizedek priesthood and related to the Exaltation of the living and the dead. I understood that this priesthood ordination was accompanied by a personal visitation from God:

> *Never cease striving until you have seen God face to face. Strengthen your faith; cast off your doubts, your sins, and all your unbelief; and nothing can prevent you from coming to God. Your ordination is not complete till God has laid his hands upon you. We require as much to qualify us as did those who have gone before us; God is the same. If the savior in former days laid his hand upon His disciples, why not in the latter days?*[15]

> *. . . and this is the sum and substance of the whole matter; that when any man obtains the last comforter, he will have the personage of Jesus Christ attend him, or appear unto him from time to time, and even He will manifest the Father unto him, and they will take their abode with him, and the visions of the heavens will be opened unto him, and the Lord will teach him face to face, and he may have a perfect knowledge of the mysteries of the kingdom of God . . .*[16]

What an event for a Mormon to look foreword to! Much concerning the *New and Everlasting Covenant*, the *calling and election made sure*, and the *second comforter* is shrouded in mystery. I discovered that while all of this information was valuable to me, most people with whom I was acquainted had never heard much at all concerning any of these matters. I felt certain that those who received their calling and election made sure, knew the real meaning behind the Prophet Brigham Young's words concerning Adam. I began to seek out those whom I considered the most worthy members of the church. I figured that someday in the temple, if I proved faithful, God would make the Adam-God doctrine and other difficult matters understandable to me.

## Palatine, Illinois

Little did I know at the time of our move to the Chicago suburb of Palatine, that my Mormon faith would be completely shattered and stripped away! That experience resulted in the greatest blessing of my life, a genuine relationship with the true God of the Holy Bible. In the past, the differences in the spiritual needs of my husband and myself had served to drive me deeper into study of the LDS Standard Works and church apologetic writings. Now delving deeper into original Mormonism and its history would serve to educate me right out of that church! God had a wealth of information for me to examine. He sent them through Melaine Layton.

I had just been released from serving a Stake mission for the church. About this time there was talk in our ward of a former LDS woman who had been speaking out against Mormonism on a radio program. Her name was Melaine Layton. Both Melaine and her husband, Roger, professed to be thankful to be out of the Mormon *cult*. Melaine had insisted the LDS Church was not Christian, and that its doctrine had been changed many times to suit the whims of its leaders. I was astonished at such accusations. My assessment of this talk was precisely as I had been taught to conclude: more persecution heaped upon the only true church and its members!

But this woman –a former Mormon? Coming out of Mormonism was, at that time, almost unheard of! I'd never met a former Mormon! A couple in our ward, Toni and Fred Baker, were acquainted with both Melaine and Roger. The husbands had been roommates in college, and Melaine and Toni had been friends. Toni informed me that Melaine had written some material critical of the church, which upset Toni greatly.

## Doctine and Covenants 71:7 Stirs Me Again

Coincidentally, at about this time our teenage daughter, Valerie, brought a school friend over to our house. He wanted to discuss religion with me. This young boy asked me many difficult questions. He was accusing the Mormon Church of inconsistencies much like the Jehovahs' Witnesses had shown me, including the Adam-God doctrine! For a young teen, the boy's knowledge of the Bible was most impressive! I felt the need, as Valerie's mom, to make certain her view of the church was undamaged after the encounter with her high school friend. I still felt responsible to the Mormon Scripture: "Wherefore confound your enemies; call upon them to meet you both in public and in private; and inasmuch as you are faithful their shame shall be manifest."[17] The charges made by Valerie's friend and the critical accusations Melaine expressed on the radio, combined with the challenge of the *Doctrine and Covenants* convinced me to put this matter to rest once and for all. I asked Toni for Melaine's telephone number.

Fearing that Melaine may be a bad influence on me, Toni was at first apprehensive that I should meet with an apostate. I kept persisting, and finally Toni relented and gave me Melaine's telephone number. I didn't want Melaine to meet me in my home. I was concerned that this apostate may be a bad influence on my family. So, I asked her to meet me in a restaurant near where she lived. She cheerfully agreed to do so.

Because Melaine was the first apostate from the Mormon Church I had ever met, I had all kinds of thoughts about what she would be like. None of them were accurate. Melaine was an attractive, soft spoken, and non-threatening mother of five daughters. After awhile, Melaine showed me some of her writings concerning the LDS Church. You can understand how I felt when one subject pertained to the doctrine of Adam-God. Why, this was the very thing the Jehovah's Witnesses had accused us of teaching! I reflected again upon the four lost revelations booklet which I had sent to my brother. Here was more information regarding the very subject I had wondered about for years! Melaine had no way of knowing how much I wanted to inspect what she had written. More than anything else I wanted to probe into what she had written concerning the Adam-God issue. I perceived that Melaine was eager for me to take her materials home. I didn't want to totally satisfy that desire in her, but at the same time I wanted, with God's help, to resolve for myself the Adam-God controversy. Before long I could not hold my eagerness to acquire information from her.

In 1976, around the same time I met Melaine, the following words by Spencer W. Kimball, the twelfth LDS Prophet) appeared in the the November 1976 *Ensign*:

> *We warn you against the dissemination of doctrines which are not according to the scriptures and which are alleged to have been taught by some of the General Authorities –such, for instance is the Adam-God theory.*[18]

The church's position was that Brigham Young's teachings regarding Adam were misconstrued by the enemies of the church. What did Melaine's book have to report? Could I trust her? I certainly could trust God to help me understand the truth. I wanted to study the references she had included in her book *And this is Life Eternal that they might know Thee, the only True God —Adam?*

## To the Library

Melaine also told me about Jerald and Sandra Tanner, the authors of the book *Mormonism: Shadow or Reality?* I had never before heard of the Tanners. Melaine said, "Christine, the Garrett Library in Evanston [a suburb of Chicago] has most of the primary sources you will need to challenge or examine my writing, as well as that of the Tanners. Will you examine the value of our writings? Will you take up the challenge?" Remembering again the command in the *Doctrine and Covenants* 71:7, I said, "Certainly!" I took Melaine's book about Adam-God home with me and quickly ordered a book by Jerald and Sandra Tanner.

Melaine told me that her challenge to me would not be a comfortable or easy one to accept. She also stated that her relationship with the Jesus of Christianity was very different than the relationship I was experiencing with the Jesus of Mormonism. I considered her remark about my relationship with Jesus most judgmental. Was she assuming Christ wasn't with me? I didn't realize at that time that the Bible is about an entirely different Jesus than the Jesus taught in Mormonism. I believed that Mormons, although we were different, certainly knew more about Jesus than the rest of the world. We carried truth in the purest form! How dare she judge us!

I began to research whether there was verification for Melaine's claims. I felt some trepidation, but mostly eagerness to resolve many things which had been troublesome to me for some time. My past experiences of sharing my concerns about various issues had left me with a hesitancy to share with others. Doing so in the past made me feel that, based on church standards, I had become a member of a "doubting testimony club." It seemed that doubting was a sin that should be kept a secret. I believed that most people in the church would question my loyalty and integrity to the church if what I was doing in the library in Evanston became known. So, I arranged to use Melaine's library card, thus protecting my anonymity during my investigations.

The search catapulted me into a period of examination and contrast of early and modern Mormonism. Old issues of the *Millennial Star*, the *Times and Seasons*, the *Elders Journal*, and the *Women of Mormondom*, were only a few of many other fascinating old LDS sanctioned publications in the library. I had at my fingertips a gold mine concerning early Mormonism. From the book *Women of Mormondom* I photo-copied whole sections concerning Adam-God. From the *Times and Seasons*, I copied information contradicting the present Mormon belief of who Jesus is, and for whom temples are are built. These are only a few matters of importance of which I was able to research. This exciting library even contained pictures of the prominent pioneer settlers of Utah and Idaho, including my own ancestors and those of my husband. I sent copies of these pictures, with the accompanying information concerning our ancestors lives, home to our parents in Utah and Idaho. I still have the photo-copies I made at the library, as well as a record of everything I checked out. This record serves as a memento of those days back in Illinois.

Later, Melaine gave me over 300 pages of photocopies of LDS Church documents concerning Adam-God. I have them still. These copies established, without a doubt, that Brigham Young meant exactly what he said concerning Adam-God, and that the information I had received from the Jehovah's Witnesses, and in the Kraut booklet, were not misconstrued as for years I had hoped they were.

I had always believed that somewhere Mormonism had a sure defense against all I had come up against. I felt secure and better equipped before I began to research in Evanston. Ultimately, however, my research at the library established without a doubt that Melaine was correct in all she had said against the church. From that point on, on a daily basis, I saw Mormonism crumble. Then, no matter how it seemed that in the church two-plus-two would always add up to four, it never was able to do so again. The more I looked the more I had to surrender to unreconcilable contradictions and changes in Mormonism. While times were distressing, deep inside I knew God wanted me to face this matter head on! I trusted God to help me do so. I discovered the Tanners' accusations leveled against the Mormon Church were legitimate and genuine, uncovered as they sought to learn and present the truth concerning Mormonism. I now believe that from the viewpoint of the Mormon Hierarchy and many church members, those who challenge Mormonism must be shunned and labeled as enemies of the church, for the enemy approach is the popular church defense.

> *those that question and challenge Mormonism are often shunned and labeled as enemies*

What a sinking feeling! Something of paramount importance was happening here - something that most certainly had to do with eternity and choices. These were choices which would effect my whole family! Often, when I was a youngster, my mother brought my attention to the Mormon Scripture: "But I have commanded you to bring up your children in light and truth."[19] I had always considered it a sacred responsibility to raise our children to love Mormonism, and I had always done so. I was in a state of complete astonishment and bafflement over my discoveries about the Mormon Church. By now, I realized that my responsibility to the children was to cease teaching Mormonism to them. I knew it was false!

I tried to resolve matters with my bishop and other leaders. Because my leaders, family, and friends were not interested in my endeavors to pursue answers to doctrinal problems, I sought out the theological library in Evanston, and people like Melaine, who were willing and able to assist me with information. I went to see a Fundamentalist Mormon (polygamist) in Salt Lake City in hopes to find historical Mormon documents. In Midway, Utah, I examined old issues of the *Deseret News* and other Mormon publications dating back to the latter part of the 19th century, which were discovered by my in-laws in an abandoned attic. I was true to myself and to God, and honest in my efforts to discover truth. Everywhere I turned I found significant historical changes and inconsistencies within Mormonism. I believe this is because God did not bring forth the Church of Jesus Christ of Latter-day Saints.

As it turned out, my discoveries were far larger than just the critical issue of Adam-God. I had to come to terms that in truth the evolved Mormon God was a figment of man's imagination. So are the extra-biblical Mormon Standard Works. The claims to the priesthood, to a pure, unchanged, written account of its own history was shattered before my eyes. I examined loads of facts which could not be classified as insignificant, for they destroyed the case for Mormonism completely! For me it became as clear as the nose on my face: Mormonism is an evil deception! That being the case, I was convinced that Satan was its author, for Satan is *the father of lies*.[20] For days I was in complete shock! The familiar dogma of Mormon doctrine was destroyed.

Mormonism had been a lifeline for me with which I was familiar and comfortable, and life outside its perimeters was foreign. I felt that if our family was embracing a false doctrine, joy and peace would not be among the consequences! In the past, Mormonism had been the most important thing in the world to me. It had been sacred to me, and it was all I knew! Never did I dream I could be living in idolatry. But we all were. It seemed the very basis of my life had been taken away. I wondered how life would be without the church. The thought was very unsettling. I could no longer live happily within Mormonism, for that would be a life under false pretense. I knew I must forge ahead on the trail I believed God was now ordering in my life.

I wondered if the information to which I was now privy was deliberately being suppressed by the church to keep its members in the dark about the actual facts regarding the LDS Church origin. It certainly appeared so. They had at their disposal the entire church archives! Why had I been deceived about something as major as who God is? Knowing God was the most important issue of all to me. Aided by the Holy Spirit's guidance, I was exposed to the facts needed to determine the truth about Adam-God. I could no longer be content to settle for my leaders' statements of denial concerning the Adam-God doctrine. To teach that Brigham Young's words were misconstrued by the enemies of the church, or that the doctrine was only alleged to have been taught, was purely and simply untrue. To call this topic a *theory*, as is often done, when Brigham Young emphatically called it "*doctrine* so important that not believing it would incur loss of salvation"[21] was of major implication and consequence to me.

In 1976, the Mormon Apostle Mark E. Peterson wrote a book titled, *Adam: Who is He?* In the book Peterson offends reason in his effort to avoid acknowledging that the Adam-God doctrine was indeed part of the Mormon Gospel for some 50 years. His explanations simply are contrary to the facts. Interestingly, a few years later, McConkie, who staunchly denied the doctrine in his book *Mormon Doctrine*, admitted the truth concerning this issue. In a private letter to professor Eugene England of Brigham Young University McConkie wrote: "Yes, Brigham Young did teach that Adam was the father of our spirits, and all the related things that the cultists ascribe to him". The letter, which I've included in the Exhibit Section on page 201-202 includes a warning from McConkie to keep this fact a secret.

> **keep this fact a secret**

Who should be believed? The Prophet Brigham Young, the Apostle Bruce R. McConkie, or the Apostle Mark E. Peterson? How about the present prophet? Clearly, false prophets are the issue here! With a hammering blow, I learned that there was far more to grapple with than the Adam-God issue. Mormonism's critical doctrines have been drastically altered and changed in meaning, a fact that is denied and carefully buried by the church itself. I learned that I had been betrayed by the very church I had given myself to and loved so much. Morally, I felt it was my duty to inform my family of that discovery. Should we not protect one another from deceit? How would my family and friends react? I hoped they would want to examine the evidence for themselves.

God made use of the Garrett Library in Evanston, Illinois, and past and present Mormon authorities to help me find truth. In the following chapters we will take a peek at some unavoidable and insurmountable problems within the Mormon Gospel. Consider with me some hard hitting claims made by Mormon General Authorities –claims which do not hold up under scrutiny. Consider the mind-set with which I was reared.

1    Journal of Discourses, vol. 14, p. 216.

2    Historical and exegetical notes by Hyrum M. Smith of the Council of the Twelve Apostles and Janne M. Sjodahl, revised edition.

3    Doctrines of Salvation, vol. 1, pp. 96-106.

4    Journal of Discourses, vol.1, p. 50-51.

5    Doctrine and Covenants 9:8-9.

6    Doctrine and Covenants 93:36.

7    Doctrine and Covenants 131:6.

8    Doctrine and Covenants 130:19.

9    Doctrine and Covenants 76:7.

10   Journal of Discourses, vol. 9, p. 322.

11   Doctrine and Covenants 132: 1, 4, 32.

12   Journal of Discourses, vol. 11, p. 269.

13   Teachings of the Prophet Joseph Smith, pp.366-367.

14   Mormon Doctrine, p. 109.

15   History of the Church, vol. 2, pp. 195-196.

16   Teachings of the Prophet Joseph Smith, pp. 150-151.

17   Doctrine and Covenants 71:7.

18   Ensign, October 9, pp.11, 77.

19   Doctrine and Covenants 93:40.

20   John 8:44.

21   Journal of Discourses, vol. 1, pp. 50-51.

# 4.  An Inherited Mind-Set

*The President of the Church of Jesus Christ of Latter-Day Saints holds the keys of salvation for all men now living because he is the only one by whose authorization the sealing power of the priesthood can be used to seal men up to salvation and exaltation in the Kingdom of God.*

Mormon Doctrine, p. 411

The family I was born into held utmost respect and strong devotion to the church, its leaders and its writings.  Consequently, even as a child I was taught that each man holding the office of prophet, or president of the LDS Church as he is also called, was given his position directly by God.  The Mormon claim to an exclusive priesthood, inspired writings, temple ordinances, and to a living modern-day prophet set our church apart from all others.  We revered Joseph Smith, our first modern-day prophet, through whom we believed God began the restoration of the lost Gospel.

Like other Mormons I held fast to these unique aspects of my religion.  I believed God's truth did not exist outside of Mormonism and that through the Mormon priesthood our leaders alone received direct revelation from God.  Mormons, I believed, were beneficiaries in the only true Gospel plan, and have a special high calling to spread the truth to the four corners of the world.  I was proud of the Mormon Gospel message, revealing to peoples of the whole earth the true nature of God, as well as His saving Laws and Ordinances.  Only our church had a modern-day living prophet, speaking for God on earth.  Our prophets proved to be godly men; they held the solutions to world sorrows and needs!  The Old Testament Prophet, Daniel, prophesied that a kingdom would cover the face of the entire earth.[1]  I was taught that the Mormon Church is this kingdom.[2]

> *Mormonism is the kingdom the prophet Daniel prophesied about*

As church members we boasted of our Standard Works.  In addition to the Bible, which Mormons consider to be genuine notwithstanding its many errors in translation, the Mormon Standard Works include *The Book of Mormon,* The *Pearl of Great Price,* and *The Doctrine and Covenants.*  The current eighth Mormon Article of Faith by Joseph Smith declares, "We believe the Bible to be the word of God as far as it is translated correctly; we also believe the *Book of Mormon* to be the word of God."  No translation problems there!  See the Articles of Faith in the Exhibit Section on page 224.

The LDS Church asserts that, through the power of God, Joseph Smith translated golden plates given to him by the angel Moroni, a resurrected ancient North American who appeared to Smith in order to restore lost ancient records of the American Indians.  Above and beyond the Bible, I was taught that it is the *Book of Mormon* that contains the fulness[3] of the everlasting Gospel.  Mormons view the *Book of Mormon*

> **Book of Mormon
> is the most correct
> book on earth**

as the most correct book on earth.[4]

The coming of the angel Moroni and the translation of the gold plates into the *Book of Mormon* is believed among Mormons to be a direct fulfillment of Revelation 14:6 in the Bible which prophecies an angel proclaiming an eternal Gospel. By sharing in the message of the angel Moroni and the coming forth of the *Book of Mormon*, members of the Mormon Church are taught that they may become saviors on Mount Zion! How thrilled I was to share about the angel Moroni and the coming forth of the fulness of the Gospel which I believed was contained in the *Book of Mormon*.

Mormons claim to be blessed with modern-day revelation. The ninth Mormon Article of Faith states, "We believe all that God has revealed, all that he does now reveal, and we believe that he will yet reveal many great and important things pertaining to the kingdom of God." Much of this latter-day revelation is included in the 136 sections of revelation recorded in the *Doctrine and Covenants*. These revelations purported to be from God to Joseph Smith and his successors came during the early years of the Mormon Church. Mormon Apostle Bruce McConkie explains, "Most of these sections came to Joseph Smith by direct revelation, the recorded words being those of the Lord Jesus Christ himself."[5] The *Doctrine and Covenants* reveal instructions regarding governments and laws in general, church doctrine, accounts of visions, recorded words of angelic beings, and other points of interest concerning the Mormon Kingdom of God.

In addition to the *Doctrine and Covenants* and the *Book of Mormon,* Mormon doctrine is further revealed in the *Pearl of Great Price.* Included within the *Pearl of Great Price* are two small books, titled, the *Book of Moses* and the *Book of Abraham.* The *Book of Moses* purports to be a record of Mosaic doctrine not contained in the original first five books of the Bible. Mormons believe the first five books of the Bible are incomplete, missing much of the doctrine originally contained.[6] The *Book of Moses*, a book of eight chapters, is believed to have been given to Joseph Smith through direct revelation so he could replace this missing information. The *Book of Moses* reveals radically different teachings than the Bible concerning creation, pre-existence, and the purpose of life, the Lord's dealings with Adam and the early patriarchs.[7]

The *Book of Abraham*, on the other hand, is a work claimed to be translated by Joseph Smith from a papyrus record taken from Egyptian catacombs. It contains five chapters. The papyrus allegedly was written by Abraham's own hand. This book describes lost knowledge about a pre-existence of humans, the nature of Deity, creation, and priesthood.

It is important to emphasize once more that the Latter-day Saints accept the following as the Standard Works of the church: the *Bible,* the *Book of Mormon,* the *Doctrine and Covenants,* and the *Pearl of Great Price.* Of equal value are official statements made by the General Authorities. The common belief in the insufficiency of the Bible necessitates the remainder of the Mormon Standard Works. I realized, while still a Mormon, that without our extra-biblical doctrines, we Mormons would not be set apart from Christianity. It never really worried me that our doctrine differed from the biblical account.

In ignorance, I was grateful for our church's added Scripture. My understanding of the creation, the purpose of life, the fall, and the account of human redemption, was based upon the Mormon purported extra-biblical Scriptures. More accurate than the Bible, the rest of our Standard Works were the only authentic, trustworthy, untampered, accurate, complete message in the entire world. Because our writings were perfect, we took pride that there was no need to ever change them.

We boasted a living modern prophet, and of our other important leaders called General Authorities. We were taught that the messages from these men, our *Living Oracles,* were, in fact, God's revealed truth to humankind:

> *Members of the First Presidency, Council of the Twelve, and the Patriarch to the Church - because they are appointed and sustained as prophets, seers, and revelators to the Church - are known as the living oracles.*[8]
>
> *The messages given to us through our General Authorities came through the power of the priesthood and were directly from the Holy Ghost . . .*[9]
>
> *In addition to these four books of scripture, the inspired words of our living prophets become*

*scripture to us. Their words come to us through conferences, Church publications, and instructions to local priesthood leaders.*[10]

> the inspired words of our living prophets become scripture to us

We Mormons shared great respect and trust in our leaders; we believed that through them members of the church could never be led astray. I viewed our leaders as men of utmost character and integrity, worthy of our trust and devotion.

We were taught that the lack of priesthood authority, and other matters of apostasy, such as the Bible's lack of accuracy and comprehensiveness, caused the need for restoration. The necessity of a modern-day prophet was a part of (and evidence of) our restored truth. I learned that the very presence of our prophets and their testimonies, along with Mormon history, would one day testify against all people who had access to our church but chose not to follow it.

The first Sunday of each month brought our *Fast and Testimony* meetings, where our Mormon community bore public testimony to one another of the beautiful Mormon Gospel and our cohesiveness and uniqueness as a people. With pride in our hearts, and often tears in our eyes, members of the church bore testimony of the mission of Joseph Smith and the integrity of our past and present leaders and their messages. We spoke of our dear missionaries serving missions, at their families' expense, so that others may benefit from the *restored* Gospel. We testified to the purity of our extra-biblical writings which we believed to be Holy Scripture. We spoke highly of other components and accomplishments of the Mormon Church. We were deeply proud of our accomplishments and callings. We affirmed to one another that no one could destroy the tested diamond truth of the Mormon Gospel. Our proud heritage was above reproach! As a Mormon I carried a deep commitment toward the church and considered it an honor to share our Standard Works and the Mormon Kingdom of God with non-Mormons. We viewed our church as a place of stability amongst a world of bickering Christians. Each of us were called to shatter the unstable doctrines of the countless denominations that comprised a false Christianity. Our exclusive hold to the truth of God would always spawn misrepresentation, jealousy, persecution and slander among the outsiders. I was also taught that members of the church are made of fiber able to withstand all of the attacks of Christendom's corrupt pastors and teachers and all of their creeds so abominable to God. The strong belief against Christian doctrines, creeds and leaders is taken from the testimony of Joseph Smith as recorded in the *Pearl of Great Price*. This testimony is central to Mormon theology. Smith asked God which church to join. Here is the answer he recorded:

> *I was answered that I must join none of them, for they were all wrong; and the Personage who addressed me said that all their creeds were an abomination in his sight; that those professors were all corrupt . . .*[11]

## Parental Guidance

My father was a quiet man, and when he spoke I listened attentively. He expected us to carry our family name with integrity, never tarnishing our reputation as honorable citizens. He expected his family to stand up for the truth, be true to our word, to be responsible for the way we conducted our lives, always taking into account the long-range effects of our behavior. He expected us to admit to our guilt and to respect the truth.

My Mother strongly emphasized spiritual values. She taught us to place a higher emphasis on the spiritual realm than on the common interests of the world. Both my parents instilled in us a belief that character is discovered through how we deal with the difficulties we battle in life. The standards with which I was raised, coupled with the pride I carried within my heart that Mormonism likewise was true to its name set my course in life. Honoring God and honoring my parents was central in my life. I didn't want to shame my parents nor my church before others nor bear the sorrow that would follow for doing so. My Patriarchal Blessing admonished me to study our church teachings, and I was faithful in doing so.

## Superior Claims

Through the Mormon prophets and writings one can best understand the Mormon God, and what the Mormon world is supposed to be. Mormon writings and statements of their prophets are the very heart of Mormonism, they are unique to Mormonism, as they are not granted authority in any other religion. These aspects of Mormonism; I boasted, set our religion apart as superior to any other. Mormon Apostle James E. Talmage in his book *Articles of Faith*, asserts, "The Word of the Lord through His Prophet Joseph Smith, has never been revoked . . ."[12] In his book *Joseph Smith-Seeker After Truth*, the Mormon Apostle John A. Widtsoe elaborates, "The revelations have remained unchanged. There has been no tampering with God's Word".[13]

This is the mind-set I had as a Mormon, as did my Mormon community, and my Mormon family. The tenth Mormon Prophet, Joseph Fielding Smith, also argued the divine and perfect character of Mormon Scripture:

> *Inspiration is discovered in the fact that each part, as it was revealed, dovetailed perfectly with what had come before. There was no need for eliminating, changing, or adjusting any part to make it fit; but each new revelation on doctrine and priesthood fitted in its place perfectly to complete the whole structure, as it has been prepared by the master builder. The organization of the church in all of its parts and functions has been proclaimed, even by enemies of the Church, as being in its nearness to perfection to any organization on earth.*[14]

In another of his books, Smith stated that you cannot improve on perfection: "Ordinances instituted in the heavens before the foundation of the world, in the priesthood for the salvation of men, are not to be altered or changed. All must be saved on the same principles."[15] In fact, argued Joseph Smith, inconsistency is the mark of Satan. He describes two ways to recognize the presence of Satan in revelation: "By the color of his hair; that is one of the signs that he can be known by, and by his contradicting a former revelation."[16]

Consequently, Mormon history must be extremely valuable to the world. Under the heading "Judgment Out of Church Books and Histories" is written:

> **Mormon history is the most important and most accurate history in the world**

> *The most important history in the world is the history of our church, and it is the most accurate history in all the world . . . Do you know that the time is coming when we are going to be judged out of the books that are written? Therefore we should make these records accurate; we should be sure of the steps we take. We are going to be judged out of the things written in books, out of the revelations of God, out of the temple records, out of those things which the Lord has commanded us to keep and have on file concerning the records of this people . . .*[17]

> *I could take you in the library in the Historian's office in Salt Lake City and show you whole rows of books written by enemies of the Latter-day Saints, with scarcely a true statement in one of them.*[18]

> **books written by enemies . . . with scarcely a true statement**

This is the essence of Mormonism: Since Mormonism teaches that its members will be judged from its history and Standard Works, the importance of keeping truthful and accurate records should not be minimized. Through the Mormon prophets and LDS Scripture, then, one can best understand the Mormon God, and what the Mormon world is supposed to be. The real test of Mormonism is to examine its writings and the statements of its leaders, especially its prophets who claim to be speaking for God. For me as a Mormon, this is where the battle for truth was waged. This is the critical testing ground for the Mormon Church; it is here that Mormonism, as the only true religion, stands or falls. Now we'll look at what I found.

1    Daniel 2:44.

2    A marvelous Work and a Wonder,  p.36.

3    Doctrine and Covenants 20:29.

4    History of the Church, vol. 4, p. 461.

5    Mormon Doctrine, p. 206.

6    Mormon Doctrine, p. 563.

7    Mormon Doctrine, p. 564.

8    Mormon Doctrine, p. 547.

9    Ensign, November 1976, p. 63.

10    Gospel Principles, pp. 38-39.

11    Writings of Jospeh Smith 2:18.

12    Articles of Faith, James E. Talmage, p. 27.

13    Joseph Smith –Seeker After Truth, p.119.

14    Doctrines of Salvation, vol. 1, p. 170.

15    Teachings of the Prophet Joseph Smith, p. 308.

16    Teachings of the Prophet Joseph Smith, pp. 214-215.

17    Doctrines of Salvation, vol. 2, pp.199-200.

18    Doctrines of Salvation, vol. 2, p.199.

# 5. Changing God and Scripture

*God is not a man, that he should lie; neither the son of man, that he should repent: hath he said, and shall he not do it? Or hath he spoken, and shall he not make it good?*

Numbers 23:19

As a teenager I listened to a memorable discussion between my mom and dad. My dad insisted that God is still progressing in knowledge. Mom simply didn't believe that God progresses in knowledge. She strongly insisted that such a belief was never taught by the church, and then shrugged off their apparent disunity as a worthless misunderstanding on the part of my father. My dad asserted that he was so taught, and that the teachings of the church proclaim so. Years later, while doing research, I discovered my father was right; that the church taught this doctrine! Wilford Woodruff, the fourth Prophet and President of the church declared:

> *God himself is increasing and progressing in knowledge, power, and dominion, and will do so, worlds without end.*[1]

While in truth, my mom and dad could not both be correct. The ever-changing Mormon history supported both of their cases. Joseph Fielding Smith was in agreement with my mother. He declared:

> *It seems very strange to me that members of the Church will hold to the doctrine, 'God increases in knowledge as time goes on.' . . . Where has the Lord ever revealed to us that he is lacking in knowledge? . . . I think this kind of doctrine is very dangerous, I don't know where the Lord has ever declared such a thing.*[2]

I have discovered that both views are held among Mormons, and although they are contradictory beliefs, both are supported using various LDS references.

Ultimately, all of Mormonism is crushed under the stress of critical examination. Any serious study reveals an indefensible number of inconsistencies and contradictions. This chapter reveals a few of many.

## The Standard Works Defined

The Standard Works of the Mormon faith could, by themselves, take volumes to write about. LDS apologist Bruce R. McConkie defines the Mormon Standard Works:

> *By the Standard Works of the Church is meant the following four volumes of scripture: the Bible, Book of Mormon, Doctrine and Covenants, and the Pearl of Great Price. The Church uses the King James Version of the Bible, but acceptance of the Bible is coupled with a reservation that it is true only insofar as translated correctly. The other three, having been revealed in Modern times in English, are accepted without qualification.*[3]

---

*The other three [books]
are accepted without
qualification*

The fact that Mormons accept the Bible only with reservation, but accept the other three Standard Works without qualification, is noteworthy.

Some subjects written about in the Mormon Standard Works require more than the limited scope of this chapter. One major problem area in the *Doctrine and Covenants* pertains to the Mormon priesthood. Because Mormonism's claim to authority hinges on priesthood, I have devoted a separate chapter to that subject. Because the Bible and the *Book of Mormon* enjoy more publicity than the other Mormon Standard Works they also are given whole chapters. Here, we shall note a few important aspects of the *Doctrine and Covenants* and the *Pearl of Great Price*. Of their content the Mormon Church boasts both authenticity and unchanged purity of doctrine!

## The Doctrine and Covenants

While reading the *Doctrine and Covenants*, originally called the *Book of Commandments*, one should take care to note that this book is not a translation. Instead, it claims actual revelations directly from God. Since it is not a translation, one ought expect it to be unswervingly correct and require no change. Of the 65 revelations in the original *Book of Commandments*, there have been thousands of changes. I've included examples of various changes in the Exhibit Section on page 216-217.

The 1833 *Book of Commandments,* which was the forerunner to the present-day *Doctrine and Covenants,* contains a revelation in which God grants Joseph Smith only one gift, and that the purposes of God would never include granting him another gift.[4] That gift was to translate the *Book of Mormon*. By 1835, Joseph Smith must have felt hindered by this restricted revelation. Subsequently, in the present *Doctrine and Covenants,* the revelation was changed to appear that this was the first gift God bestowed upon him.[5]

The *Doctrine and Covenants* contains many false prophecies. A few of many are referenced in the following chapter under the subheading *False Prophecies Make False Prophets*. Throughout this book note how the present *Doctrine and Covenants* conflicts with the early versions concerning the Mormon view of God. As aftershocks continue after an earthquake, so the walls of Mormon Zion crumble when the facts surrounding its claims are examined.

## The Pearl of Great Price

The *Book of Moses, Book of Abraham, Writings of Joseph Smith 1 and 2, Articles of Faith*, and Chapter 24 of Matthew's Gospel are included in the *Pearl of Great Price*. The reader may see alterations and a facsimile of the original 1851 edition of the *Pearl of Great Price* in the Exhibit Section on page 214.

A few chapters of Joseph Smith's *Inspired Version* of the Bible (mentioned later) are printed in the *Book of Moses*. Substantive changes have been made from when it was first published in 1885. Excerpts of the *Book of Moses* were lifted directly from the King James version of the Bible, while in other places Joseph Smith made alterations to the King James version to suit his own purposes. Additional words have made differences in doctrine.[6]

Many primary doctrines of Mormonism sail down the tubes with the discovery that the source from which the *Book of Abraham* (which inconveniently surfaced after being lost) was translated is actually an

*pornographic
depictions were
removed and then
replaced in 1981*

Egyptian funeral text, and has nothing to do with Abraham or the time period in which he lived. Joseph Smith's original translation of the *Book of Abraham* was supposedly burned in the Chicago fire. The first printing of the *Pearl of Great Price* included a hypocephalus which, later, because of its pornographic connotation, was removed. It was placed back into the *Pearl of Great Price* in 1981. The replacement occurred after the original (undestroyed) papyri resurfaced in the New York Metropolitan Museum of Art, Nov. 27, 1967. One can see this pornographic phallic change as well as other changes by examining the various editions of the *Pearl of Great Price*. Who had the right to change any of the facsimiles? After all, the church claims that the *Book of Abraham* was written by Abraham's own hand upon the papyrus. When Joseph Smith translated the papyrus, he turned 4 lines from the papyrus into 49 verses in the *Book of Commandments*. Some 15 names of Egyptian pagan gods are mentioned in the funeral text, but not a word about Abraham.[7] The resurfacing of this writing and its content is a tremendous embarrassment to the Mormon Church. See the exhibit titled *Min is not God!* on page 215. Needless to say, the church has attempted to keep the matter quiet.

## Writings of Joseph Smith 1 and 2

Joseph Smith 1 includes Joseph Smith's inspired revision of Matthew 23:39 and chapter 24. Joseph Smith's alterations here neither greatly add to or detract from or explain the biblical account. It is hard to say of what added value Smith saw in adding this part to the *Pearl of Great Price*.

> *Brigham Young never mentions the First Vision in his 363 Journal of Discourses sermons*

Joseph Smith 2 consists of extracts from the *History of Joseph Smith*, volume 1, chapters 1 to 5. This section of the *Pearl of Great Price* includes the account of the first vision of Joseph Smith (his description of his first encounter with God). I never questioned the account of the first vision as it is presently taught by the LDS Church, and I was shocked to learn that the vision (the official version) was first written in 1838, but not published until 1842 in the official church release of the *Times and Seasons*, 22 years later. Brigham Young, in all his 363 sermons recorded in the *Journal of Discourses*, never mentions the first vision. I was very surprised to find there are many versions of the first vision, and critical discrepancies between each account: Joseph's age, why he went to pray, who appeared, when they appeared, all vary between accounts. The exhibit on page 211 compares the versions. The evidence contradicts the Mormon understanding of the Godhead, as based upon the vision.

Also damaging to accepted church history is the fact that the Session Records[8] show that Joseph Smith's brothers, Hyrum and Samuel and his mother, Lucy, were active in the Palmyra Presbyterian Church. This occurred 8 years *after* the supposed first vision of Joseph Smith, a vision which informed him that he must join none of the churches, for they and their professors, were all corrupt. In Joseph Smith 2, Smith states that a revival which broke out in Palmyra prompted him to pray concerning which church he should join. The late Wesley P. Walters, whom I met in the home of Melaine Layton, discovered records conclusively revealing that there was no revival in that area during the years of which Joseph Smith claimed.[9]

In the *Amboy Journal*, of Amboy, Illinois, Walters located church records stating that Joseph Smith attempted to join the Methodist Church eight years after his claimed vision, but was rejected. Why the Smith family remained active for years in churches, which, according to the claimed first vision, were abominable to God and whose creeds and professors were all corrupt, is a mystery. I believe it is because Mormonism was invented, and was never sanctioned by God in the first place.

Of added interest is the fact that Wesley P. Walters uncovered old records which found Joseph Smith convicted of necromancy.[10] A copy of the record is available in the Exhibit Section on page 223. This is one of many artifacts showing Joseph Smith's strong involvement with the occult.

## The Mormon Articles of Faith

The LDS Church distributes a list of its thirteen *Articles of Faith*, also found in the Mormon Standard Works (not be confused with the Mormon book called *Articles of Faith*). The current Articles of Faith are not the same as the originals, which contain fourteen articles. While the versions do not differ greatly, they are deceitful as they carefully conceal the truth about Mormonism. *More Accurate Articles*, written by Robert McKay, provides a contrast and summary of what is hidden between the lines of the Articles of Faith and the present Mormon world view. His points are not intended to offend but only to speak the truth in love. To those who study present-day Mormonism, the Mormon Articles of Faith take on the appearance of a strangely misleading list of beliefs. Pages 224-225 of the Exhibit Section include all three versions of the Articles of Faith.

Of its extra-biblical Standard Works the Mormon Church boasts both authenticity and unchanged purity of doctrine! But we see that Mormon Scripture has been heavily altered and changed. It is difficult to nail down and maintain a solid, unchangeable church message, whether it be from the Standard Works or in messages given by the General Authorities of the church. I have given only a small sum of all the problems within this selection of the LDS Standard Works, but enough to show that Mormonism is not the true church of God. The way I see it, to defend the changes and inconsistencies in the Standard Works makes one as guilty as those who invented the originals in the first place. Unreliable, dishonorable, disreputable and discardable are the extra-biblical Standard Works of the church.

## More Mormon Scripture

As you journey through the remainder of this book it will be helpful to keep in mind the following official statements made by the General Authorities concerning the Mormon Standard Works. Remember that the extra-biblical writings are sacred Scripture to the members of the LDS Church and are included in the Mormon term Standard Works. These claim to divine origin and all of them are credited with more accuracy than the Bible. With this in mind, we can consider the influence they exercise on LDS Church members. A timely question in Mormonism is, "Which deserves more authority, these books God is supposed to have given, or the words of the leaders of Mormonism?" This would not be an issue at all if the two sources of doctrine agreed. But they do not.

How does a Mormon define Scripture? Of the church authorities, the Mormon Scripture titled the *Doctrine and Covenants* helps answer this question:

> And whatsoever they shall speak when moved upon by the Holy Ghost shall be scripture, shall be the will of the Lord, shall be the word of the Lord, shall be the voice of the Lord, and the power of God unto salvation.[11]

And elsewhere Joseph Fielding Smith states:

> What is Scripture? When one of the brethren stands before a congregation of the people today, and the inspiration of the Lord is upon him, he speaks that which the Lord would have him speak. It is just as much scripture as anything you will find written in any of these records, and yet we call these the Standard Works of the church.[12]

To specifically identify Mormon Scripture is more challenging. Consider the following Mormon publications:

### The Inspired Version

Joseph Smith completed his own translation and review of the Old and New Testament. It is published and called the *Inspired Version* of the Bible by the Mormon Church. However, LDS leaders pick and choose from this book according to the need at hand. They both use and excuse Joseph Smith's *Inspired Version* of the Bible. Some authorities of the church say it was never completed, as did the Mormon Apostle Bruce McConkie in his book *Mormon Doctrine*.[13] But, the *History of the Church* states that it was completed in 1833.[14] In fact, the present *Doctrine and Covenants* gives the command to publish the *Inspired Version* unto the nations.[15] If the *Inspired Version* was not completed this commandment to complete and publish it to the world was broken.

### The Journal of Discourses

Various prefaces to the 26 volumes of the *Journal of Discourses* state:

> The Journal of Discourses deservedly ranks as one of the Standard Works of the Church, and

*every right-minded Saint will certainly welcome with joy every Number as it comes forth from the press as an additional reflector of "the light that shines from Zion's hill."*[16]

### Six Volumes of Distorted History

Joseph Fielding Smith stated:

> . . . *the most important history in the world is the history of our church, and it is the most accurate hisory in all the world. It must be so.*[17]

According to the Tanners, *Mormonism: Shadow or Reality?*, "Within the first six volumes of the *History of the Church*, some 62,000 words were added or deleted without any notation. An estimated 17,000 words were added and over 45,000 deleted from the time the history was first printed." More than sixty-percent of the history was written after Joseph Smith's death, yet the church makes it appear that Joseph Smith wrote all of it. "In other words, Mormon historians altered Joseph's words before the first publication of his history appeared. If any legal document had been changed in the same way that the *History of the Church* has, someone would be in serious trouble."[18] In fact, the early church history discredits present Mormon history. Altogether, it staggers one's imagination to see how much Mormon Church history has been altered and reinvented.

### Scripture by Brigham Young

> *I have never preached a sermon and sent it out to the children of men, that they cannot call Scripture.*[19]

A study of early LDS Church history reveals that the Mormon Prophet Brigham Young's sermons and speeches were not to be taken lightly, or downplayed as is often the case today. Therefore, another important question in Mormonism is, "Can a revelation be changed?" One Mormon authority says:

| |
|---|
| *I have never preached a sermon . . . that they cannot call Scripture* |

> *That is modern revelation. May I repeat? Modern revelation is what President Joseph Smith said, unless President Kimball says differently.*[20]

The key phrase in defining Scripture, as far *as it is translated correctly* (eighth Article of Faith) ultimately provides an avenue through which to dismiss the countless discrepancies and errors within Mormonism. At any time the church can counter an inconsistency simply by claiming that the Prophet was speaking as a man, not as the Prophet. After this, one is hard-pressed to discover which utterances are indeed Scripture; only convenience dictates.

### What Happened to the Book of Commandments?

The original revelations to Joseph Smith were compiled into a book known as the *Book of Commandments*. The revelations inside are claimed to be from God:

> *Behold this is mine authority, and the authority of my servants, and my Preface unto the Book of my Commandments, which I have given them to publish unto you, O inhabitants of the earth: - Wherefore fear and tremble, O ye people for what I the Lord have decreed, in them, shall all be fulfilled . . . search these commandments, for they are true and faithful . . . What I the Lord have spoken, I have spoken, and I excuse not myself, and though the heavens and the earth pass away, my word shall not pass away . . .*[21]

If the revelations in the *Book of Commandments* were really of God, who in their right mind would dare change them? Actually, there have been significant and numerous alterations made within the *Book of Commandments*. For example, in order to accommodate the alleged account that the priesthood was restored to the earth, today's version (*Doctrine and Covenants*, section 27) has added 400 words to the original corresponding chapter 28. The *Book of Commandments* ends at verse 7. The prayer of bestowing the Aaronic priesthood (todays section 13) has all been added. The present Section 13 was not a part of the original *Book of Commandments*. Not until 1876, was it included in the present *Doctrine and Covenants*.[22]

In addition, the command in verse two of chapter one to publish the *Book of Commandments* to the inhabitants of the earth did not occur. Therefore, the commandment was broken. If, in the future, the *Book of Commandments* is published to the world, its contents would disagree with current LDS doctrine, for the current *Doctrine and Covenants* differs greatly from the original revelations as they appear in the *Book of Commandments*.

### What about the Lectures on Faith?

> **signified by members raising their right hand to the square**

The *Lectures on Faith*, part of the 1835 edition of the *Doctrine and Covenants*, was approved as doctrine by vote in a general conference of church members, and were considered as such until their removal in 1921, 86 years later. This removal took place by the church leadership without the usual membership vote –signified by members raising their right hand to the square. This action broke another command, given in the *Doctrine and Covenants*, which states that all things must be done by the common consent of the church.[23]

It is very difficult to nail down what is to be classified as the credible works of Mormonism. In Mormonism, truth is what is here today –never mind what was yesterday or what may come tomorrow.

### The Penalty for Having an Unwise View About the Godhead

In a devotional speech given at BYU, March 2, 1982, the Mormon Apostle Bruce R. McConkie warned members of the church that salvation cannot come to those who endorse a false belief about doctrine of the Godhead:

> *There is no salvation in believing any false doctrine, particularly a false or unwise view about the Godhead or any of its members.*[24]

This is a very serious statement, one which commands serious contemplation. In fact throughout my Mormon experience, I heard over and over again the emphasis placed on the *Doctrine and Covenants* which states that, "It is impossible for a man to be saved in ignorance."[25] What then, is an unwise view about God? And what is the correct view of God? The answers to these questions should be found in the authorized LDS statements, records, the Standard Works, and they should harmonize, never changing. However, once again, we are faced with the question of where to place the ultimate authority in the Mormon Church –with the Standard Works given directly from God, or with church authorities speaking for God. They simply do not agree.

## Watch the Mormon God Evolve

Since the essence of Mormonism is in its revealed perfect word, we will now look for the Mormon Father in Heaven as he has revealed himself in the Standard Works of the church, and in the writings and sermons of the Mormon *Living Oracles* who represent the Mormon God.

### Is God a spirit?

The *Book of Mormon* says that God is the Great Spirit. While the Bible speaks of God as a spirit[26] one time, the *Book of Mormon* does so eight times.

Here is one reference from the *Book of Mormon*:

> *. . . Believest thou that this Great Spirit, who is God, created all things which are in the heaven and in the earth?*[27]

The fifth Lecture on Faith, states, ". . . The Father being a personage of Spirit, glory and power: possessing all perfection and fulness . . ."[28] This early Mormon Lecture on Faith agrees with the *Book of Mor-*

*mon* and the biblical quote in John 4:24 (a quote which Mormons view as a mistranslation). But the present *Doctrine and Covenants* shouts in radical discord that the Mormon God has a body:

> *The Father has a body of flesh and bones as tangible as man's; the Son also; but the Holy Ghost has not a body of flesh and bones, but is a personage of Spirit . . .*[29]

The *Lectures on Faith* not only state that God is a personage of Spirit, but that He is everywhere present:

> *We here observe that God is the only supreme governor, and independent being, in whom all fulness dwells; who is omnipotent, omnipresent, and omniscient; without beginning of days or end of life . . .*[30]

This Lecture on Faith contradicts the present church belief that the Mormon God has a body and can therefore occupy only one space at a time. Regarding the Mormon Godhead, McConkie explains:

> *Each occupies space and can only be in one place at one time, but each has power and influence that is everywhere present.*[31]

> *The Holy Ghost can no more be omnipresent in person than can the Father or the Son . . .*[32]

Teaching that God is omniscient, lecture two contradicts the Mormon Law of Eternal Exaltation (that God evolved to godhood). We see that in stern opposition to present Mormonism, which teaches that God has a body and is not omnipresent, and that he earned his godhood. Lecture two and five of the *Lectures on Faith*, states that God is a spirit –omnipotent, omnipresent, and omniscient.[33]

### Many Gods?

While the belief in one God was once part of early Mormon theology, it was later given up by Joseph Smith. Presently there are many Gods in the Mormon view. Within Mormon theology men evolve into Gods. The belief in many Gods is expressed by the term *polytheism*. The words of Joseph Smith:

> *I will preach on the plurality of Gods. I have selected this text for that express purpose. I wish to declare I have always and in all congregations when I have preached on the subject of the Deity, it has been the plurality of Gods. It has been preached by the Elders for fifteen years.*

> *I have always declared God to be a distinct personage, Jesus Christ a separate and distinct personage from God the Father, and that the Holy Ghost was a distinct personage and a Spirit: and these three constitute three distinct personages and three Gods . . . . They are plural; and who can contradict it?*[34]

> **I will preach on the plurality of Gods**

Brigham Young also spoke of countless Gods:

> *How many Gods there are, I do not know. But there never was a time when there were not Gods . . .*[35]

The evolving of the Mormon God from one to many is revealed in *The Book of Abraham* within the *Pearl of Great Price.* The *Book of Abraham* teaches a plurality Gods. For example:

> *. . . they, that is the Gods, organized and formed the heavens and the earth . . . And they (the Gods) said: Let there be light . . . and they (the Gods) comprehended the light . . .*[36]

Joseph Smith taught:

> *In the beginning, the head of the Gods called a council of the Gods; and they came together and concocted a plan to create the world and people it.*[37]

> *We have imagined and supposed that God was God from all eternity. I will refute that idea, and take away the veil, so that you may see.*[38]

As a Stake Missionary I was required to memorize the following words from the first vision of Joseph Smith:

> *When the light rested upon me I saw two personages, whose brightness and glory defy all description, standing above me in the air. One of them spake unto me, calling me by name and*

*said, pointing to the other—This is my beloved Son.  Hear Him.*[39]

This commonly used account of the vision speaks of two persons, each viewed as a God in Mormonism.  I find the vision in question since there are various conflicting versions of the account (see the exhibit on page 211).

I was also required to commit to memory the modern *Doctrine and Covenants* version of God.  It bears repeating:

> *The Father has a body of flesh and bones as tangible as man's; the Son also; but the Holy Ghost has not a body of flesh and bones, but is a personage of Spirit.  Were it not so the Holy Ghost could not dwell in us.*[40]

Each of the above verses describe more than one God having bodies of flesh and bone like a man has.  This is obviously a polytheistic view of God.  In contrast, the current *Doctrine and Covenants* by Joseph Smith, retains references to only one God.  Here is one such reference:

> *And gave unto them commandments that they should love and serve him, the only living and true God, and that he should be the only being whom they should worship.*[41]

**Church members strive for Godhood - How many Gods would this make?**

Faithful members of the LDS Church strive to achieve their own status of Godhood.  This is the basic theme of Mormonism today:  Men can become Gods; there are many Gods; the Gods exist one above the other without number; God was once a man.  Consider this passage from Joseph Smith's most famous sermon, the King Follett Discourse, given April 6, 1844:

> *Here, then, is eternal life —to know the only wise and true God; and you have got to learn how to become Gods yourselves, and to be kings and priests to God, the same as all Gods have done before you,—namely, by going from one small degree to another, and from a small capacity to a great one,—from grace to grace, from exaltation to exaltation, until you attain to the resurrection of the dead, and are able to dwell in everlasting burnings and to sit in glory, as do those who sit enthroned in everlasting power.*[42]

**Two Gods?**

As I looked into early editions of the Standard Works, I discovered more contradictions about God.  Imagine how startled I was to discover that the *Lectures on Faith*, teaches that there are two gods instead of the present belief of the godhead of three.  Consider the following:

> *We shall in this lecture speak of the Godhead: we mean the Father, Son and Holy Spirit . . . There are two personages who constitute the great, matchless, governing and supreme power over all things—by whom all things were created . . . They are the Father and the Son . . . Q. How many personages are there in the Godhead? A. Two: the Father and the Son.*

I have mentioned only a few passages in the *Lectures on Faith* which illustrate the evolving and inconsistent view of the Mormon God.  The earlier editions of the *Doctrine and Covenants* taught that there are two persons in the Godhead, therefore the Holy Spirit is not God at all.  In fact, verse two of lecture five states that the mind of the Father and the Son is called the Holy Spirit.  See the exhibit on page 205.

It bears repeating here that the lectures about God included in the *Doctrine and Covenants*, first written in 1835, were approved by a church vote.  As early and later editions prove, the lectures remained part of the Standard Works of the church until they were removed without the vote of the church membership in 1921, –eighty-six years later.  As mentioned before, the removal of these important lectures without church vote broke the command given in the *Doctrine and Covenants*,[43] which says that all things must be done by the common consent of the church.

### One God?

As noted before, the present *Doctrine and Covenants* contain the following verses as proof that Joseph Smith first taught one God:

> *And gave unto them commandments that they should love and serve him, the only living and true God . . . Which Father, Son, and Holy Ghost are one God, infinite and eternal, without end. Amen.*[44]

In accordance with the verse above, and in an attempt to emphasize that there is only one God, Joseph Smith, in his own *Inspired Version* of the Bible, changed Luke 10:22 to read, ". . . no man knoweth that the Son is the Father, and the Father is the Son, but him to whom the Son will reveal it."[45]

The *Book of Moses*, a small section of the *Pearl of Great Price* is in agreement with the last two quotes; it reads ". . . but there is no God beside me.[46] Furthermore, it repeatedly expresses the early Mormon belief in one God, using the words 'I, God.'" For example:

> *. . . In the beginning I created the heaven, and the earth upon which thou standeth . . . . and my Spirit moved upon the face of the water; for I am God. And I, God, said: Let there be light; and there was light. And I God saw the light; and that light was good. And I, God divided the light from darkness. And I, God called the light day . . .*[47]

The *Book of Mormon* acknowledges only one God:

> *Now Zeezrom said: Is there more than one God? And he answered, No. Now Zeezrom saith again unto him: Is the Son of God the very eternal Father? And Amulek said unto him: Yea, he is the very Eternal Father of heaven and of earth, and all things which are in them are; he is the beginning and the end, the first and the last . . . all . . . shall be brought to the judgment bar of Christ the Son, and God the Father, and the Holy Spirit, which is one Eternal God, to be judged according to their works, whether they be good or whether they be evil.*[48]

> *. . . sing ceaseless praises with the choirs above, unto the Father, and unto the Son, and unto the Holy Ghost, which is one God, in a state of happiness which hath no end.*[49]

> *. . . And now, behold, this is the doctrine of Christ, and the only true doctrine of the Father, and of the Son, and of the Holy Ghost, which is one God, without end. Amen.*[50]

> *. . . I would that ye should understand that God himself shall come down among the children of men, and shall redeem his people. And because he dwelleth in the flesh he shall be called the son of God, and having subjected the will of the flesh to the Father, being the Father and the son—The Father, because he was conceived by the power of God; and the Son, because of the flesh; thus becoming the Father and Son—And they are one God, yea, the very Eternal Father of heaven and of earth. And thus the flesh becoming subject to the spirit, or the Son to the Father, being one God, suffereth temptation . . .*[51]

> **the Book of Mormon maintains only one God**

The preface to the *Book of Mormon* also maintains only one God:

> *—And also convincing of the Jew and Gentile that Jesus is the Christ, the Eternal God, manifesting himself unto all nations—*

### "What" or "Who" is the Third Member of the Mormon Godhead?

Mormon General Authorities have taught the Holy Spirit is like a divine fluid —like electricity, material atoms, a cosmic force, and an impersonal energy.[52] It is interesting that the 1965 reprint changed this information without a notation. Today in Mormonism, the Holy Ghost is the third member of the Godhead. He is a personage of Spirit.[53] I was brought up to believe He would yet receive a body, get married, and work out His salvation, as did Jesus. From a Mormon standpoint, the question arises, "How can the Holy Ghost be a God, if He hasn't already received a body through which to work out his salvation to Godhood?" After all, in Mormonism, receiving a body is a prerequisite to becoming a God! So is baptism. Because He does not yet have a body, how was the Holy Ghost baptized? Marriage is also a prerequisite to Godhood. When was the Holy Ghost married? If the Holy Ghost is one of the Mormon Gods, why is He conspicuously absent in the creation part of the Mormon Temple Ceremony? When I went through the temple there were three main characters in the creation story. We had Elohim (the Father), who gave instructions to Jehovah (Jesus), and Michael (Adam). This account is accurately printed in the creation drama from the book titled *What's Going On In There?*[54]

### Who is Jehovah?

While doing research in the Garrett Library I came upon an old issue of the Mormon publication *Times and Seasons,* which surprisedly conflicted with what I was taught about who Jesus is. Here the church taught that Jehovah is God the Father: "We believe in God the Father who is the great Jehovah and head of all things, and that Christ is the Son of God, co-eternal with the Father."[55] Presently the Mormon Church teaches that Christ is Jehovah: "All revelation since the fall has come through Jesus Christ, who is Jehovah of the Old Testament . . . . Now we know that Jehovah is Jesus Christ."[56]

If the *Times and Seasons* is true, and it was so claimed, Jesus could not as present day Mormonism teaches, be the spirit son of an exalted resurrected glorified God, because the Christ spoken of in the *Times and Seasons* is co-eternal with the Father. Nor could he in a pre-earth life have been our spirit brother, nor a spirit brother to Satan. Actually, the pre-existence, as taught in Mormonism, never did exist!

### Adam-God?

In 1976 while living in Illinois and examining for myself the issue of Adam God, the Mormon Prophet Spencer W. Kimball warned the church membership (see the exhibit on page 200):

> We warn you against the dissemination of doctrines which are not according to the scriptures and which are alleged to have been taught by some of the General Authorities of past generations. Such, for instance is the Adam-God theory. We denounce that theory and hope that everyone will be cautioned against this and other kinds of false doctrine.

Be assured though that true prophets do not contradict each other! Brigham Young never called the subject a theory:

> How much unbelief exists in the minds of the Latter-Day Saints in regard to one particular doctrine which I revealed to them, and which God revealed to me - namely that Adam is our father and God . . . Our Father Adam is the man who stands at the gate and hold the keys of everlasting life and salvation to all his children who have or who ever will come upon the earth.[57]

The Prophet Joseph Fielding Smith:

> President Brigham Young is quoted — in all probability the sermon was erroneously transcribed! — as having said [that Adam is God].[58]

Mormonism did teach that Adam is God, and Brigham Young taught that those who do not believe so will all be damned.[59] To claim that the speech was erroneously transcribed does not take into account the importance Mormons attach to keeping accurate records from which they will be judged, or the numerous other places where Brigham Young taught Adam-God, or that there is no evidence that he ever taught anything but Adam-God. Besides, if this speech was carelessly transcribed, what integrity do any other Mormon historical records have?

To ignore Mormonism's many contradictions and changes about God one must either be consciously apathetic or rebellious toward God, or must have a fuzziness or fog hanging over one's mind, will and emotions. The Mormon Prophets have changed their version from one God –to many Gods. The alleged sacred Mormon writings and history reveals overwhelming inconsistencies and changes in the Mormon view of God. Do you know of any such track record of change? What a contradiction to the *Deseret News* editorial which says of the Mormon God and his Gospel:

> . . . But since He never changes, and since human nature is always the same, identical condi-

*tions are required to bring that human nature into harmony with the unchangeable God . . .*
*For that reason, the gospel must always be the same in all its parts.*[60]

Such strange discoveries! Later I discovered in the *Journal of Discourses* that some of the early Mormon Twelve Apostles did not believe in God, and some believed in the un-biblical teaching of reincarnation.[61] I was not surprised to find among Fundamentalist Mormons the belief that Joseph Smith is the third member of the Mormon Godhead as clearly stated and illustrated in the book *The 3-1/2 Years* by Norman Pierce.[62] In light of the fact that the Adam-God doctrine is taught to this day by groups of LDS Fundamentalists, I can see why some believe Joseph Smith to be the Holy Ghost. The Adam-God doctrine as it was in fact taught in early Mormonism, makes such a conclusion reasonable. It also gives more possibilities to the meaning of the following words of Joseph Smith as recorded by the Mormon Apostle Heber C. Kimball, words which I became familiar with during my teen years:

> *Would to God, brethren, I could tell you who I am! Would to God*
> *I could tell you what I know! But you would call it blasphemy!*
> *— and there are men upon this stand who would want to take my*
> *life.*[63]

I recall a discussion concerning the quote above, at which time it was stated that Joseph Smith may have been identifying himself as the third member of the Godhead. After all, went the discussion, the Holy Ghost still needed to receive a body.

> **must have the**
> **certificate of Joseph**
> **Smith, junior, as a**
> **passport to heaven**

Brigham Young made plain the Mormon reliance on Joseph Smith for salvation:

> *From the day that the priesthood was taken from the earth to the winding-up scene of all*
> *things, every man and woman must have the certificate of Joseph Smith, junior, as a passport*
> *to their entrance into the mansion where God and Christ are — I with you and you with me. I*
> *cannot go there without his consent. He holds the keys of that kingdom for the last dispensa-*
> *tion — the keys to rule in the spirit world; and he rules there triumphantly, for he gained full*
> *power and a glorious victory over Satan while he was yet in the flesh —.*[64]

This statement is an inordinate attempt to lean on the arm of the flesh for one's testimony about God. I find the need to have a passport from Joseph Smith to enter heaven repulsive.

These are only a few of many unmanageable inconsistencies both in the church's written words and its present understanding of God. The truth is, Mormon Scripture has been heavily altered. Consequently, it is difficult to nail down any foundational message whether it be from the Standard Works or in messages given by the General Authorities of the church. What a maze of evolvement the God of Mormonism has undergone! Grappling with historic facts as I discovered them within Mormonism was very disturbing, and I could not casually rationalize the church and its capriciousness. How could what seemed to be of importance today be assured a place of value to the church tomorrow? The changes about God were of such significance and of such magnitude that I was absolutely certain that Mormonism is not the restoration as it claims. By this point in my journey the many things I had once believed would require an impossible leap to embrace. I could not live with false doctrine! How could I or anyone else rest with peace when finally recognizing the evident problems and confusion within the LDS understanding of God?

I believed that, with the track record of Mormonism's doctrinal changes thus far, more changes would likely occur in the future. After my departure from the church I found this assumption correct. Changes concerning the priesthood as it relates to black people, the Temple Ceremony and text within the *Book of Mormon* all have occurred since I requested my name be removed from the LDS Church records. We have touched only the beginning. In the next chapters we shall see a continuation of Mormonism crack, crumble and tumble down. In the face of all the inconsistencies concerning the Mormon God, I find it strange the LDS Church still preaches to the world that they alone have the keys to salvation. The tradition of the Mormon heritage is very strong in the hearts of its members, but Jesus warned: "Full well ye reject the commandment of God, that ye may keep your own tradition making the Word of God of none effect through your tradition."[65] Tradition is well and good so long as it is harmonious with the true and living God of the Bible.

The Bible presents a clear and cohesive Gospel message:

*God is not the author of confusion, but of peace.*[66]

*Jesus Christ the same yesterday, and to day, and for ever.*[67]

*For I am the LORD, I change not . . .*[68]

These Scriptures fly in the face of the slippery Mormon God and his ever changing Gospel.

God has supplied for each of us all that is needed to determine truth from error.  His truth prevails, just as was promised:

*. . . for there is nothing covered, that shall not be revealed; and hid, that shall not be known.*[69]

Jesus alone holds the keys to salvation!  I praise His Holy Name!

1  Journal of Discourses, vol. 6 p. 120.
2  Doctrines of Salvation, vol. 1, pp. 7-8.
3  Mormon Doctrine, p. 764.
4  Book of Commandments, chapter 4:2, p. 10.
5  Doctrine and Covenants 5:4.
6  Flaws in the Pearl of Great Price, pp. 29-62; The Changing World of Mormonism, p. 395.
7  By His Own Hand Upon Papyrus, pp. 41-100
8  Western Presbyterian Church of Palmyra, Session Records, vol. 2.
9  New Light on Mormon Origins from the Palmyra (N.Y.) Revival.
10  Justice Albert Neely's Bill- The Glass Looker, March. 20, 1826, copy of Judge Neely's records.
11  Doctrine and Covenants 68:4.
12  Doctrines of Salvation, vol. 1, p. 186.
13  Mormon Doctrine, p. 383.
14  History of the Church, vol.1, p. 324.
15  Doctrine and Covenants 124:89, 94:10.
16  Journal of Discourses, preface to vol. 8; see also preface to vols. 1, 3, 4 and 20.
17  Doctrines of Salvation, v. 2, p. 199.
18  Mormonism: Shadow or Reality, p. 8, 133.
19  Journal of Discourses, vol. 13, p. 95.
20  BYU Fireside Message, May 5, 1974, S. Dilworth Young, First Council of the Seventy.
21  Book of Commandments, 1:2,7, 1833 edition.
22  The Changing World of Mormonism, pp. 41-66.
23  Doctrine and Covenants 26:2; 28:13.
24  Deseret News, Church News Section, March 20, 1982, p. 5.
25  Doctrine and Covenants 131:6.
26  John 4:24.
27  Book of Mormon, Alma 18:28.
28  Doctrine and Covenants, 1835 edition, vol. 2, Fifth Lecture on Faith, p. 58.
29  Doctrine and Covenants 130:22.
30  Doctrine and Covenants, Lecture 2, 1835 edition.
31  Mormon Doctrine, p. 319.
32  Mormon Doctrine, p. 752.
33  Doctrine and Covenants, 1835 edition, Lectures 2 and 5.
34  Teaching of Prophet, Joseph Smith, p. 370.
35  Journal of Discourses, vol. 7, p. 333.
36  Pearl of Great Price, Abraham, 4:1, 3-4.
37  Teachings of the Prophet Joseph Smith, p. 349.
38  Teachings of the Prophet Joseph Smith, p. 345.
39  Writings of Joseph Smith, 2:17.
40  Doctrine and Covenants 130:22.
41  Doctrine and Covenants 20:19.
42  Journal of Discourses, vol. 6, p. 4.
43  Doctrine and Covenants 26:2, 28:13.
44  Doctrine and Covenants 20:19, 28.
45  Inspired Version of the Bible, Luke 10:22.
46  Pearl of Great Price, Moses 1:6.
47  Pearl of Great Price, Moses 2: 1-5.
48  Book of Mormon, Alma 11:28, 29, 38, 39, 44.
49  Book of Mormon, Mormon 7:7.
50  Book of Mormon, 2 Nephi 31:21.
51  Book of Mormon, Mosiah 15:1-5.
52  Key to the Science of Theology, p. 29, 1855 edition.
53  Doctrine and Covenants 130:22.
54  What's Going On In There?, pp. 20-31.
55  Times & Seasons, vol. 3, p. 579.
56  Doctrines of Salvation, vol. 1, p. 27.
57  Deseret News, June 18, 1873.
58  Doctrines of Salvation, vol. 1 p. 96.
59  Journal of Discourses, vol. 1 pp. 50-51.
60  Deseret News, Church News Section, June 5, 1965.
61  Journal of Discourses, vol. 12 p. 66.
62  The 3-1/2 Years, pp. 56, 102-105.
63  Life of Heber C. Kimball, p. 333, 1st edition.
64  Journal of Discourses, vol. 7, p. 289.
65  Mark 7:9-13.
66  1 Corinthians 14:33.
67  Hebrews 13:8.
68  Malachi 3:6.
69  Matthew 10:26.

# 6. False Prophets and Apostles

*Now taking it for granted that the scriptures say what they mean, and mean what they say, we have sufficient grounds to go on and prove from the Bible that the gospel has always remained the same; the ordinances to fulfill its requirements, the same, and the officers to officiate, the same; and the signs from the promises the same . . .*

Joseph Fielding Smith, Teachings of the Prophet Joseph Smith, p. 264

Joseph Smith's claim (above) is taken for granted to be true for all of Mormon history. We have already seen from previous chapters the falseness of this claim. The Mormon Gospel has not remained the same! This is because Joseph Smith was a false prophet, and the church he began and its prophets are false too.

As a mobile moves entirely when touched in only one place, we find Mormon doctrine affected as the Mormon God moves about. In this chapter and those that follow we will watch as the Mormon God is further exposed as counterfeit. Using conflicting messages from Mormon prophets and apostles we discover that all is not well in Mormon Zion. The term "Zion" is used synomymously with the Church of Jesus Christ of Latter-day Saints.

## False Prophecies Make False Prophets

To prophesy in the Name of the Lord is a very serious action. The Bible warns against false Christs and false prophets[1] and of false apostles[2]. They lure people to false gods and beliefs, thereby enslaving souls. In the Exhibit Section on page 226 I have prepared a list of Scriptures entitled *Biblical Defense of Truth* which will assist in the pursuit, defense, and preservation of truth. Second Timothy says:

*Preach the word; be ready in season and out of season; reprove, rebuke, exhort, with great patience and instruction. For the time will come when they will not endure sound doctrine; but wanting to have their ears tickled, they will accumulate for themselves teachers in accordance to their own desires; and will turn away their ears from the truth, and will turn aside to myths.[3]*

Joseph Smith and his myths have led people directly into the face of a false theology. The God of Mormonism leaves a labyrinth everywhere he ventures. Recognizing his trail should make one shudder and run to the ancient paths[4] of safety preserved within the Bible. God provides us with His standards for testing a prophet. Let's look to a standard now, for God requires that we test those who are proclaimed as prophets.

*If a prophet or a dreamer of dreams arises among you and gives you a sign or wonder, and the sign and the wonder comes true, concerning which he spake to you, saying, 'Let us go after other gods (whom you have not known) and let us serve them,' you shall not listen to the words of that prophet . . . for the Lord your God is testing you to find out if you love the Lord you God with all your heart and with all your soul. You shall follow the Lord your God and fear Him; and you shall keep His commandments, listen to His voice, serve Him, and cling to Him . . . But that prophet or that dreamer of dreams shall be put to death, because he has counseled rebellion against the LORD your God . . . to seduce you from the way in which the Lord your God commanded you to walk. So you shall purge the evil from among you . . . you shall not yield to him or listen to him, and your eye shall not pity him, nor shall you spare or conceal him.*[5]

> **over 50 major false prophecies from Joseph Smith**

*But the prophet who shall speak a word presumptuously in my name which I have not commanded him to speak . . . that prophet shall die. And you may say in your heart,' 'How shall we know the word which the Lord has not spoken?' When a prophet speaks in the name of the Lord, if the thing does not come about or come true, that is the thing which the Lord has not spoken. The prophet has spoken it presumptuously: you shall not be afraid of him. That prophet shall die.*[6]

Note that the Old Covenant (before the coming of God's Messiah) carried a death penalty for being a false prophet. There are over 50 major false prophecies from Joseph Smith alone. He is not the only Mormon prophet who made false prophecies. Remember, as the verse above points out, it only takes one false prophecy to make a false prophet. The following are a few false prophesies:

**The New Jerusalem and its Temple** – The *Doctrine and Covenants* (revelations by Joseph Smith) states that a temple must be erected in the western boundaries of the state of Missouri in the generation beginning in 1832.[7] It never happened.

**United Order** – The *Doctrine and Covenants* says "Verily I say unto you, my friends, I give unto you counsel, and a commandment, concerning all the properties which belong to the order which I commanded to be organized and established, to be a united order, and an everlasting order for the benefit of my church, and for the salvation of men until I come."[8] The United Order failed completely.

**The Civil War** – Mormons believe that the *Doctrine and Covenants* prophesies the Civil War.[9] The revelation states that beginning with the rebellion at South Carolina, war would be poured upon all nations. The civil war did not result in war being poured out upon all nations. The revelation further states that the southern states would call on other nations, even the nation of Great Britain - this never happened. A study of Joseph Smith's *History of the Church* shows this prophecy was actually written after Joseph Smith was deceased. The Mormon Church suppressed from its church members a part of Joseph Smith's own diary, which discredits the revelation.[10]

**Nauvoo House** – This house, according to the *Doctrine and Covenants*[11], is to belong to the Smith family forever. This prophecy was a false one, for the Mormon people departed from Nauvoo and the house no longer belonged to the Smith's.

**Oliver Granger** – Oliver Granger is to be held in sacred remembrance from generation to generation, forever and ever.[12] Most people are not even aware of his name much less what he was to be remembered for doing.

**David Patton** – On April 17, 1838, Joseph Smith prophesied that David W. Patton should sell all that he had, and perform a mission in the spring.[13] David Patten was shot and killed before spring arrived.

**Second coming of Christ** – In 1835 Joseph Smith prophesied that the second coming of the Lord would occur within fifty-six years.[14] This never happened.

**Governor Ford** – Joseph Smith prophesied that governor Ford had dammed himself politically and that his carcase would stink on the face of the earth as food for the carrion and turkey buzzard. This never happened. See the exhibit on page 222.

**Slavery** – Brigham Young said that in spite of the struggle during his day to free the slaves, slavery of the Blacks would never end.[15] Slavery did end.

**Blacks and the Priesthood** – Joseph Fielding Smith denied Blacks the priesthood ". . . so long as time endures."[16] Brigham Young also denied Blacks the priesthood until ". . . after all the seed of

Adam."[17]  See the exhibit on page 204.  Blacks were given the priesthood on June 8, 1978.

**Polygamy and the Union** – Brigham Young said "We shall never give up polygamy to join the union."[18]  In 1890 the Mormon Church postponed polygamy.  This declaration, commonly called the Manifesto, can be found at the end of the Doctrine and Covenants.

## Reinventing Zion

Another false prophecy relates to the Mormon interpretation of *Zion*.  My Jehovah Witness friends and I used to quibble over the meaning of an entire list of Scripture references from my *Combination Reference* or *Missionary Pal* as it is also called.  Published by the church, this list of verses compiled by Eldin Ricks, contain quotes from various biblical prophets and are alleged to promote Mormonism.  One such list of Bible verses attempts to prove that Mormonism is the last days restoration of God's church, headquartered in the Rocky Mountains.[19]

Mormons are taught that the *Book of Mormon* foretells the establishment of Zion on the western continent, in the valleys of the Rocky Mountains.[20]  In 1844, Joseph Smith, through revelation, asserted that all of North and South America comprise the land of Zion.[21]  To a Mormon, the term Zion represents a gathering place.[22]  The church teaches that baptism into the Mormon Church makes one a citizen of Zion.[23]  I used to sing LDS hymns about the Mormon Zion.  A few such songs are: *Oh Ye Mountains High*,[24] *Holy Temples on Mount Zion*,[25] *Zion Stands with Hills Surrounded*,[26] and *High on the Mountain Top*.[27]

*"Zion" in the Rocky Mountains*

Concerning Mormon Zion, an early Mormon Apostle, Heber C. Kimball, said:

> *We are in the mountains; we did not come here of our own accord, but we came by the will of the Father.  We are in the tops of the mountains where the prophet [Isaiah] said the people of God would be in the last days—.*[28]

Fortified, we believed with God's own sanction of approval, the Zion of Mormonism could never be shaken.  Its foundation was the surest of all foundations on earth.  But the idea of Mormonism being God's kingdom, headquartered in the Rocky Mountains, and fulfilling biblical prophecy, is absurd.  As to the geographical location, I have lived to see this belief changed.  Today Mormons are taught differently.  McConkie said, "every nation is the gathering place for its own people."[29]

## Contradictory Teachings of Mormon Prophets

While living in Illinois not only did my LDS perception of God tumble, but it seemed that everywhere I looked there were inconsistencies, changes and absurdities within Mormonism. The following are examples of Mormon Prophets contradicting themselves and changing church doctrine:

**Brigham Young** – "Adam was made from the dust of an earth, but not from the the the dust of this earth."[30]

**Joseph Fielding Smith** – "The Book of Mormon, the Bible, the Doctrine and Covenants, the Pearl of Great Price all declare that Adam's body was created from the dust of the ground, that is, from the dust of this ground, this earth."[31]

——

**Spencer W. Kimball** – "We warn you against the dissemination of doctrines which are not according to the scriptures and which are alleged to have been taught by some of the General Authorities of past generations."  Such, for instance, is the Adam-God theory.  We denounce that theory and hope that everyone will be cautioned against this and other kinds of false doctrine.  See exhibit on page 200.

**Brigham Young** – "How much unbelief exists in the minds of the Latter-day Saints in regard to one particular doctrine which I revealed to them, and which God revealed to me - namely that Adam is our father and God . . . Our Father Adam is the man who stands at the gate and holds the keys of everlasting life and salvation to all his children who have or who ever will come upon the earth."[32]

———

**Joseph Smith** – "For I know that God is not a partial God, neither a changeable being; but he is unchangeable from all eternity to all eternity."[33]

**Joseph Smith** – "We have imagined an supposed that God was God from all eternity. I will refute that idea, and take away the veil, so that you may see."[34]

———

**Brigham Young** – "He (that is, God) created men, as we create our own children; for there is no other process of creation in heaven or on the earth."[35]

**Joseph Smith** – "For behold, by the power of his word man came upon the face of the earth, which earth was created by the power of his word. Wherefore, if God being able to speak and the world was . . ."[36]

———

**Joseph Smith** – "And Zeezrom said unto him: Thou sayest there is a true and living God? And Amulek said: Yea, there is a true and living God. Now Zeezrom said: Is there more than one God? And he answered, No."[37]

**Brigham Young** – "How many Gods there are, I do not know. But there never was a time when there were not Gods . . ."[38]

———

**Joseph Smith** – "And gave unto them commandments that they should love and serve him, the only living and true God, and that he should be the only being whom they should worship."[39]

**Joseph Smith** – "In the beginning, the head of the Gods called a council of the Gods; and they came together and concocted a plan to create the world and people in it."[40]

———

**Joseph Smith** – "Behold, David and Solomon truly had many wives and concubines, which thing was abominable before me, saith the Lord."[41]

**Joseph Smith** – ". . . I, the Lord, justified my servants Abraham, Isaac, and Jacob as also Moses, David and Solomon, my servants, as touching the principle and doctrine of their having many wives and concubines."[42]

———

| *having many wives and concubines* | **Wilford Woodruff** – "God himself is increasing and progressing in knowledge, power and dominion, and will do so worlds without end."[43]<br><br>**Joseph Fielding Smith** – "It seems very strange to me that members of the Church will hold to the doctrine, "God increases in knowledge as time goes on" . . . Where has the Lord ever revealed to us that he is lacking in knowledge? . . . I think this kind of doctrine is very dangerous, I don't know where the Lord has ever declared such a thing."[44] |
|---|---|

———

**Brigham Young** – "Do you think that we shall ever be admitted as a State into the Union without denying the principal of polygamy? If we are not admitted until then, we shall never be admitted."[45]

**Wilford Woodruff** – "Inasmuch as laws have been enacted by congress forbidding plural marriages, which laws have been pronounced constitutional by the court of last resort, I hereby declare my intention to submit to those laws, and to use my influence with the members of the Church over which I preside to have them do likewise."[46]

———

**Joseph Smith** – "I will preach on the plurality of Gods. I have selected this text for that express purpose. I wish to declare I have always and in all congregations when I have preached on the subject of the Deity, it has been the plurality of Gods. It has been preached by the Elders for fifteen years. I have always declared God to be a distinct personage, Jesus Christ a separate and distinct personage from God the Father, and that the Holy Ghost was a distinct personage and a Spirit: and these three constitute three distinct personages and three Gods . . . they are plural; and who can contradict it."[47] This sermon is dated June 16, 1844.

**Joseph Smith** – "Which Father, Son, and Holy Ghost are one God, infinite and eternal, without end. Amen."[48] This revelation is dated April, 1830. Notice that Joseph Smith declares that he has always preached that there is a plurality of Gods, and that it has been preached by the Elders for fifteen years. He claims he has always declared the Father, Jesus Christ, and the Holy Ghost to be three Gods. If you go back 15 years from the date of the July 16, 1829; it's about one year before the revelation above!

———

**Joseph Smith** – "And Enoch walked with God after he begat Methuselah 300 years, and begat sons and daughters, and all the days of Enoch were 365 years, and Enoch walked with God, and he was not, for God took him."[49]

**Joseph Smith** – "Enoch was twenty-five years old when he was ordained under the hand of Adam; and he was sixty-five and Adam blessed him. And he saw the Lord, and he walked with Him, and was before His face continually; and he walked with God three hundred and sixty-five years, making him four hundred and thirty years old when he was translated."[50]

The prophets of the Bible were never plagued by such inconsistency. The biblical prophets presented a consistent account of the eternal God. In contrast, the Mormon Gospel has existed in a state of perpetual renovation. Better to discover for oneself, asking the true God for His assistance to reveal truth, rather than accepting a man's untrue words! How deadly to believe our own way and be wrong.

> *Bible prophets weren't plagued by inconsistency*

## Christ Returns to the Garden of Eden – in Missouri?

In another attempt to rob the Jews of their heritage, the LDS Church teaches that Mount Zion is identified as the New Jerusalem to be built in Jackson County Missouri.[51] This is Mormon eschatology! LDS Scripture teaches that part of the land of Zion (Daviess County, to be exact), is where the actual Garden of Eden was.[52] Regarding *Doctrine and Covenants* 133:18; and Revelation 14:1-5, McConkie stated:

> *Garden of Eden located in Jackson County, Missouri*

> . . . *The Mount Zion spoken of is identified by latter-day revelation as the New Jerusalem to be built in Jackson County, Missouri. . .*[53]

I'm embarrassed for those who participate in such a reinventing of biblical eschatology! The Mormon concept of Zion is ludicrous. I no longer look to the so-called Mormon restoration of the Gospel. There has never been such an apostasy –God has always had a remnant of believers on the earth. How better to render our thoughts captive to God than be persuaded by false prophets and apostles. "Thus sayeth the LORD, Stand by the ways and see and ask for the ancient paths, Where the good way is, and walk in it; And you shall find rest to your souls."[54]

Another favorite Mormon Hymn I loved to sing is titled *Come, Come ye Saints*.[55] The hymn refers to the establishment of the Mormon Zion, now headquartered in Salt Lake City, Utah. The melody is from an old Christian hymn. The words were set to the tune to reflect the Mormon trek across the plains and the settlement of Mormon Zion, headquarted in Salt Lake City. The melody always ends with the words "All is well! All is well!" Now I strongly disagree with those words in the hymn. Truthfully, all is not well in Mormon Zion!

To close this chapter, I select these words by John Jaques, omitted from the 1851 edition of the Mormon *Pearl of Great Price*:

> *Oh ! say, what is truth? "Tis the fairest gem,*

*that the riches of worlds can produce;*
*And priceless the value the truth will be, when*
*The proud monarch's costliest diadem,*
*Is counted but dross and refuse.*

*Then say, what is truth? "Tis the last and the first,*
*For the limits of time it steps o're;*
*Though the heavens depart, and the earth's fountains burst,*
*Truth, the sum of existence, will weather the worst,*
*Eternal, unchanged, evermore.*

I used to sing those words in an LDS hymn, titled *Oh Say, What is Truth?*[56] Had these beautiful words been respected and followed there would never be a Mormon theology in the first place. I find a perpetual labyrinth in Mormon Zion. The fortification walls of the Mormon Zion are not scripturally based and always stand at odds with themselves. I am grateful that God opened my spiritual eyes to see Mormonism crack, crumble and tumble down. What a cracking, crumbling and tumbling down! Joseph Smith and his successors fail the biblical test of a true prophet. I say, all is not well in Mormon Zion!

1   Matthew 24:24.

2   2 Corinthians 11:13.

3   2 Timothy 4:2-3.

4   Jeremiah 18:15.

5   Deuteronomy 13:1, 2, 5, 8.

6   Deuteronomy 18:20-22.

7   Doctrine and Covenants 84:2-4; Journal of Discourses, vol. 10, p. 344; vol. 9, p.71; vol. 17, p.111; vol. 13, p.362; vol. 14, p. 275.

8   Doctrine and Covenants 104:1, August 6, 1836.

9   Doctrine and Covenants 87.

10  Mormonism: Shadow or Reality, pp. 190-192; Changing World of Mormonism, 424-430.

11  Doctrine and Covenants 124:95-60.

12  Doctrine and Covenants 117:12.

13  Doctrine and Covenants 114:1.

14  History of the Church, vol. 2, p. 182.

15  Millennial Star, official Mormon voice in England, vol. 25, p. 787; Journal of Discourses, vol. 10, p. 250

16  The Way to Perfection, p. 101.

17  Journal of Discourses, vol. 7, pp. 290-291.

18  Journal of Discourses, vol. 11, p. 269.

19  Combination Reference, pp. 28-29.

20  Articles of Faith, James E. Talmage, pp. 348-352; A Marvelous Work and A Wonder, LeGrand Richards, p. 235.

21  Teachings of the Prophet Joseph Smith, p. 362.

22  Mormon Doctrine, pp. 854, 855.

23  Mormon Doctrine, p. 854.

24  Hymns, Church of Jesus Christ of Latter-Day Saints, p.145.

25  Hymns, Church of Jesus Christ of Latter-Day Saints, p. 63.

26  Hymns, Church of Jesus Christ of Latter-Day Saints, p. 212.

27  Hymns, Church of Jesus Christ of Latter-Day Saints, p. 62.

28  Journal of Discourses, vol. 10, p. 101.

29  Deseret News, Church News Section, Sept 2, 1972.

30  Journal of Discourses, vol.3 p.319.

31  Doctrines of Salvation, vol.1 p. 90.

32  Deseret News, June 18, 1873.

33  Book of Mormon, Moroni 8:18.

34  Teachings of the Prophet Joseph Smith, compiled by Joseph Fielding Smith, p. 345.

35  Journal of Discourses, vol.11 p. 122.

36  Journal of Discourses, Jacob 4:9.

37  Book of Mormon, Alma 11:26-29.

38  Journal of Discourses, vol.7 p. 333.

39  Doctrine and Covenants 20:19.

40  Teachings of the Prophet Joseph Smith, p.349; also Pearl of Great Price, Abraham 4:26.

41  Book of Mormon, Jacob 2:24.

42  Doctrine and Covenants 132:1.

43  Journal of Discourses, vol.6 p. 120.

44  Doctrines of Salvation, vol.1 p.7-8.

45  Journal of Discourses, vol. 11, p.269.

46  Doctrine and Covenants, section 136, the Manifesto - September 24th, 1890.

47  Teachings of the Prophet Joseph Smith, p.370.

48  Doctrine and Covenants 20:28; Book of Mormon, 2 Nephi 31:21; Alma 11:44, and Mosiah 15:5.

49  Teaching of the Prophet Joseph Smith, p. 169-170.

50  Doctrine and Covenants 107:48-49, also Pearl of Great Price, Moses 8:1.

51  Mormon Doctrine, p. 855.

52  Doctrine and Covenants 116.

53  Doctrine and Covenants 84:1-4.

54  Jeremiah 6:16.

55  Hymns, Church of Jesus Christ of Latter-Day Saints, p. 13.

56  Hymns, Church of Jesus Christ of Latter-Day Saints, p. 143.

# 7. Eyes on the Bible

*And because my words shall hiss forth — many of the Gentiles shall say: A Bible! A Bible! We have got a Bible, and there cannot be any more Bible . . . Thou fool, that shall say: A Bible, we have got a Bible, and we need no more Bible. Have ye obtained a Bible save it were by the Jews?*

Book of Mormon, 2 Nephi 29:3,6

One can see from the quote above that the LDS Church classifies as *fools* those who prize the Bible to contain the total salvation message for mankind. Taking this into consideration makes it easy to see why Mormons generally limit use of the Bible to that of a proof-text for their man-made Gospel. To do this they must twist and wrangle Scripture. Thanks to the discovery of the Dead Sea Scrolls, the Mormons claim that many *plain and precious things* (a Mormon expression) have been removed from the Bible is found to be as ridiculous as it is dishonest. The Dead Sea Scrolls present serious problems with Joseph Smith's Inspired Version of the Bible and with the *Book of Mormon* as they do with Mormonism's mainstream beliefs. The *plain and precious things* essential to receiving true salvation are faithfully recorded in the Bible and have never been removed. This was God's calling upon the Jews, who were God's divine caretakers in order to preserve the purity of Scripture. In this they have been faithful. We would not have the Old Testament if it were not for them. God warns that some will undermine and devalue truth:

*For the time will come when they will not endure sound doctrine; but after their own lusts shall they heap to themselves teachers, having itching ears; And they shall turn away their ears from the truth, and shall be turned unto fables.*[1]

By nature, the human tendency has been to follow our own inclinations rather than heed God's Word. Applicable are the words of the Prophet Jeremiah:

*Thus saith the Lord, "stand by the ways and see and ask for the ancient paths, Where the good way is, and walk in it; and you shall find peace for your souls, But they said, 'we will not walk in it.' "And I set watchmen over you, saying, Listen to the sound of the trumpet! But they said, 'We will not listen'.*[2]

In the first book of the Bible we find Satan casting doubt on God and encouraging the violation of God's Word:

*And the serpent said unto the woman, Ye shall not surely die: For God doth know that in the day ye eat thereof, then your eyes shall be opened, and ye shall be as gods, knowing good and evil. And when the woman saw that the tree was good for food, and that it was pleasant to the eyes, and a tree desired to make one wise, she took of the fruit thereof, and did eat, and gave also to her husband and he did eat.*[3]

Satan never changes his tactics. We read in the Gospel of Luke that during His humanity, Jesus was led by the Holy Spirit into the wilderness, where He fasted for forty days and was tempted by the devil. It

| | |
|---|---|
| *ploys Satan* *uses against us* | is seen that Satan employed against Jesus every possible means through which humans can be tempted.  The ploys Satan uses against us all are described in the Bible: "For all that is in the world, the lust of the flesh, and the lust of the eyes, and the pride of life is not of the Father, but is of the world."[4] |

There is no other way to reach humans.  In the attempt to thwart the plan of God, Satan used the same method to entice Eve.  With Eve, the serpent began his strategy of war against God by persuading her to question the integrity of God's Word.  Satan questioned, "Hath God said . . . ?"[5]  To Jesus Satan questioned "If thou be the Son of God . . .?"[6]  Satan uses the the lust of the flesh, and the lust of the eyes and the pride of life as weapons against us all our lives long!

The strategy of denying the integrity of God and His Word allows for false doctrine and subsequently a false salvation.  Because it differs so much in its teachings, the Bible poses a threat to Mormon theology.

In order to justify its many un-biblical tenants, the Mormon Church must make two claims:  First, a total apostasy from the early church must have occurred.  The early church must have somehow lost the true God-given Gospel, necessitating a restoration at a later period.  If the true Gospel was not lost, there would be no need for a latter-day restoration via Joseph Smith.  Second, the present-day Bible must not contain the complete and essential salvation message.  Mormons believe the salvation message is to be found in extra-biblical sources exclusive to the Mormon Church.  Therefore, complete salvation can only be found within the Mormon Church.  This belief requires a denial of all the biblical claims to the contrary, and therefore a rejection of the authority of the Bible.  Believing these proud assertions and accusations against the Bible places Mormons at odds with the pure biblical message given by the one God of Israel.

| | |
|---|---|
| *"as far as it is translated correctly" an excuse for doctrinal discrepancies* | Except for specific verses removed from their context in order to support  Mormonism, the Mormon Church does not encourage its members to first look to the Bible as a means of determining truth.  The original eighth Mormon Article of Faith states that the Bible is the Word of God; but the modern version inserts the qualification "as far as it is translated correctly."  See the exhibit on page 224.  In practice, the phrase "as far as it is translated correctly" in the eighth Mormon Article of Faith serves as a catch-all excuse for the many areas in which Mormonism differs from biblical Christianity.  The church Hierarchy determines the truth of Scripture. |

Speaking of Bible translation, the Mormon Apostle Orson Pratt, made the following statement:

> *All of the most ancient manuscripts of the New Testament known to the world differ from each other in almost every verse - the learned admit that in the manuscripts of the New Testament there are no less than 130,000 different readings.  No one can tell whether even one verse of either the old or new testament conveys the ideas of the original author.  Just think 130,000 different readings in the New Testament alone.[7]*

The Mormon Apostle Mark E. Peterson said the following concerning the Bible:

> *Many insertions were made, some of them slanted for selfish reasons, while at times deliberate falsifications were perpetrated.[8]*

Joseph Smith made the claim below:

> *Ignorant translators, careless transcribers, or designing and corrupt priests have committed many errors.[9]*

## I Replaced My LDS View of the Bible

During a time of personal frustration, my friend Melaine, wrote a very sweet letter to me, which I still keep.  The letter serves as a a memory of the encouragement and understanding she faithfully gave to me.  In the letter, she continued to motivate me to read the Bible and pray.  I took her advice.

While dealing with countless problems with Mormonism, I began thinking more seriously about the

Bible. I love the following words written in the flyleaf of a Bible by Dwight L. Moody, "Either sin will keep you from this Book, or this Book will keep you from sin."

Instead of an inherited reliance on the LDS Prophets to reveal the meaning of the Bible, a new appreciation for the Bible began to unfold. I had a date in the future with the most wonderful book in the world. I didn't know it, but I was on my way to a personal relationship with the true Jesus, and an absolute trust in the Word of God to determine truth. To this day, although I may be tempted to disobey the Bible, I firmly believe it contains the complete truth of God. God reveals the truth of it in His own times and seasons.

As a Mormon I was taught that the *Book of Mormon* superseded the Bible in accuracy, understanding, and completeness. I later learned that the *Book of Mormon* itself does not claim divine sanction:

> *Nevertheless, I do not write anything upon the plates save it be that I think it be sacred. And now if I do err, even did they error of old; not that I would excuse myself because of other men, but because of the weakness which is in me, according to the flesh, I would excuse myself.*[10]

> *And I know that the record which I make is true; and I make it with mine own hand; and I make it according to my knowledge.*[11]

On the other hand the Bible, claims divine inspiration and purity. The message of salvation was never lost nor removed from the Bible. The Bible claims to be the complete revealed Word of God. Consider the following:

> *All scripture is given by inspiration of God, and is profitable for doctrine, for reproof, for correction, for instruction in righteosness: That the man of God may be perfect, throughly furnished unto all good works.*[12]

> *The words of the Lord are pure words: as silver tried in a furnace of earth, purified seven times. Thou shalt keep them, O Lord, thou shalt preserve them from this generation for ever.*[13]

> *For as the rain and snow come down from heaven, and do not return there without watering the earth, and making it bear and sprout, and furnishing seed to the sower and bread to the eater; so shall My word be which goes forth from My mouth; it shall not return to Me empty, without accomplishing what I desire, and without succeeding in the matter for which I sent it.*[14]

> *. . . The grass withereth, and the flower thereof falleth away: But the word of the Lord endureth for ever. And this is the word which by the gospel is preached unto you.*[15]

> *For verily I say unto you, Till heaven and earth pass, one jot or one tittle shall in no wise pass from the law, till all be fulfilled.*[16]

> **till heaven and earth pass, one jot or one tittle shall in no wise pass**

The promise to *protect the truth delivered once for all time*[17] coupled with the assurance above that not one *jot or tittle* shall pass is as secure and true today as it was when first recorded in the Bible. The Bible teaches that God has always kept a remnant of believers, and that there has never been a total apostasy from truth as Mormonism claims there was. As to the true Gospel, we are exhorted to "contend earnestly for the faith which was once for all delivered to the saints."[18] Note the words "once for all."

At some point in my journey out of Mormonism, I met a young Christian woman who quoted to me the following Scripture verse:

> *For the Word of God is living and active and sharper than any two-edged sword, and piercing as far as the division of soul and spirit, of both joints and marrow, and able to judge the thoughts and intentions of the heart.*[19]

My heart was deeply touched as she shared this passage and the Holy Spirit made plain to me that there was something very significant about the Word of God being alive and full of power - life changing power. I wanted to hurry home and read the Bible - more than ever before! As I read my Bible, truth cut deeply into my inner soul, enlightening my mind. The Bible became so much easier to understand. I came to a deeper understanding that Jesus is the originator of all![20] While reading the Holy Spirit guided me to understand that differing from Mormonism, the biblical Jesus could not have been my spirit brother or a spirit brother to Satan in a pre-earth life. Instead He created all:

*In the beginning was the Word, and the Word was with God, and the Word was God. He was in the beginning with God. All things came into being through Him; and apart from Him nothing came into being that has come into being. In Him was life; and the life was the light of men. And the light shines in the darkness; and the darkness did not comprehend it.*[21]

During this period of time, my friend Melaine, suggested that I read a book by two recognized Christian authorities and educators, Norman Geisler & William E. Nix. The book titled *From God To Us* was just what I needed to read. Here is a conclusive quote from the book:

*Not only is the Bible the most well-preserved book to survive from the ancient world, its variant readings of significance amount to less than one-half of one percent corruption, none of which affect any basic Christian doctrine. In addition, the textual critic has at his disposal a series of canons which for all practical purposes enables him to completely restore the exact text of the Hebrew and Greek autographs of the Scriptures - not only line for line, but even word for word.*[22]

Melaine also gave me an audio tape series by Josh McDowell, a condensed version of Josh McDowell's *Evidence That Demands a Verdict*. I listened carefully to it several times. The tapes blessed my understanding so much that I keep them to this day. Because willing servants of God stepped forth to assist me to a proper understanding, I gained a greater respect and higher regard for Holy Scripture. I learned that the first five books of the Bible (the Torah) consist of 308,000 letters, and when they copied a text, if there was one mark or any one letter out of place they began all over again. When Bible manuscripts were not perfectly copied, even to the *jot* and *tittle*, the entire manuscript was destroyed. How different than the extra-biblical writings of the Mormon faith. Even to this point in our journey (we've just begun) we see that the Mormon Church has multiplied changes, alterations and variations within its extra-biblical writings. While I was struggling with the religion of my family origin which downplays the Bible, I began asking myself, "What would members of the Mormon Church have left to read of their extra-biblical writings, if they applied the same rule as was used by the Jews to secure the original purity and accuracy of the manuscripts of the Bible?" For me, this was a sobering thought.

A study of the reliability of the modern texts or textual transmission in terms of the number of manuscripts is useful in gaining an appreciation of the authenticity of the Bible. For such a study I recommend reading the first volume of Josh McDowell's *Evidence That Demands a Verdict*.

I now see that the Bible is like the Old Testament laver, which was a temple basin made of mirrors. In a mirror we see ourselves. So it is with the Bible; it serves as an aid to accountability in our lives and provides instruction and guidance. As we become obedient doers of the Word of God, and as we meditate therein, our lives become more meaningful and purposeful. I personally took note of how beneficial Bible reading was in the process of discerning truth and in making practical choices in my everyday life. Particular Scriptures captivated my full attention; they were powerful and taught me about the many ways Mormonism and its account of salvation stray far from the realm of biblical Christianity. As I read I became totally amazed at the huge difference between the two! With increasing awareness, my outlook on Mormonism changed from offense to horror. The message of the true Gospel became clear to my understanding and I rejoice to this day for the complete biblical message of salvation contained in the Bible. I rejoice that "Every word of God is pure: He is a shield unto them that put their trust in Him."[23] I tremble with reverence and accountability to the words, "Add thou not unto his words, lest he reprove thee, and thou be found a liar."[24]

The Bible is a book about God and our relationship to Him. It reveals the truth concerning God's redemption for mankind. It explains that Jesus is the Son of God. He died to set us free. The Bible truly is God's Word to humans. The Bible cannot be scientifically proven in a laboratory. To those who acknowledge that there is a perfect, just and Holy Almighty God who cares about us enough to preserve for us His truth, the Bible takes on a dimension beyond that of just another book. The Bible was written by over 40 authors over a span of 1600 years (1500 B.C. to 90 A.D). Internally it carries an amazingly consistent continuity. Its content is unique over any other book. It contains prophecies of future events, many of which have already been fulfilled. The Bible is a perfect picture, a foreshadowing of the first and second appearance of the Messiah. The Bible has in many ways been archaeologically verified. There is more evidence that the Bible has been correctly handed down to us than there is verification for any other classical literature.

I believe that a study of how the Bible came into existence staggers the searching human heart and exemplifies God's faithfulness and His providential covenant making with man. The Dead Sea Scrolls contradict the Mormon explanation that Bible translations throughout history are not reliable. The Bible is consistent, coherent, and dependable. God's Word is sacrosanct and inviolable; holy and venerable. It is true however, that *tranlations* vary in degree of interpretation of words and phrases from the Hebrew and Greek texts. But that is a different matter, and never diminishes the Bible message to the degree Mormons claim.

## Supposed Contradictions

No doubt, the Bible contains difficult passages, but we have the abiding promise that in God's timing and as we become more like Jesus our understanding will be enlarged. I am convinced that there are ways in which we are presently not understanding the full scope of God's ultimate purpose for creation. Even as we may now look back and see prophecy clearly fulfilled, we will continue to do so until all things are fulfilled in God's ultimate plan and purpose for creation. In the meantime the main things are the plain things and the plain things are the main things. Concerning our understanding God spoke through His prophet Moses:

> *The secret things belong to the Lord our God: but those things which are revealed belong unto us and to our children for ever, that we may do all the words of this law.*[25]

Although Mormons are expected to take for granted that there are numerous mistranslations and other problems with the Bible, they are hard-pressed to demonstrate specific instances demonstrating the absence of a consistent salvation message. The following Bible quotes demonstrate how difficult passages are resolved within the text. They are taken from a book by Alban Douglas, titled *God's Answers to Man's Questions*:[26]

> 1. *John 1:8 ---- No man hath seen God at any time: Exodus 24:10 ---- And they saw the God of Israel.*
> *Answer: Actually both statements are true. They did not see God for He is a Spirit; they saw the physical reflection of God. When I look in a mirror I see a reflection of my face but I've never seen my face as others see it.*
>
> 2. *Numbers 25:9 ---- 24,000 died in the plague; 1Corinthians 10:8----23,000 fell in one day.*
> *Answer: 23,000 is the number that fell in one day and 24,000 the total number that died.*
>
> 3. *Acts 9:7 ---- Paul's companions heard the voice; Acts 22:9, 26:14,---- Paul's companions did not hear the voice.*
> *Answer: The companions heard a sound like thunder but did not understand the words.*

In spite of centuries of intense scrutiny, the Bible has survived criticism from philosophers and intellectuals. Even though we cannot prove in a laboratory that the Bible is the Word of God, it is truly set apart from any other book. It still remains the world's best selling and most quoted book. Shall we carelessly interpret, or neglect to cherish and esteem the most wonderful autobiography ever written - sent with the greatest of all possible love? The Bible is credible. It is the Word of God. It proclaims the true Messiah to the nations. It carries within its pages God's own stamp of approval. God's Word will not return to Him void. The fact of the matter is that God has lovingly kept His promise to preserve and protect the Bible throughout all time. The message of salvation is clearly intact here. God has warned us to not add to his Word.[27] From this point, as we contrast Mormonism to Christianity, we shall refer more often to the Bible.

1   2 Timothy 4:3-4.

2   Jeremiah 6:16,17.

3   Genesis 3:4-6.

4   1 John 2:16.

5   Genesis 3:1.

6   Matthew 4:3.

7   Journal of Discourses, vol. 7, pp. 27-28.

8   As Translated Correctly, p. 4.

9   History of the Church, vol. 6, p. 57.

10  Book of Mormon, 1 Nephi 19:6.

11  Book of Mormon, 1 Nephi 19:6.

12  2 Timothy 3:16.

13  Psalms 12:6-7.

14  Isaiah 55:10-11.

15  1 Peter 1:24-25.

16  Matthew 5:18.

17  Jude 1:3.

18  Jude 1:3.

19  Hebrews 4:12.

20  Colossians 1:16.

21  John 1:1-5.

22  From God To Us, p. 186.

23  Proverbs 30:5.

24  Proverbs 30:5-6.

25  Deuteronomy 29:29.

26  God's Answers to Man's Questions, pp. 92-93.

27  Deuteronomy 4:2, 12:32; Revelation 22:18-19; Proverbs 30:6; Matthew 15:6; Isaiah 29:13.

# 8. Living Oracles Confess Another Jesus

*Beware lest any man spoil you through philosophy and vain deceit, after the tradition of men, after the rudiments of the world, and not after Christ. For in Him dwelleth all the fulness of the Godhead bodily.*

Colossians 2:8-9

Toward the last of my research in Chicago, I read in a church magazine an article titled, *The Living Christ*. The article was a written account of a speech that the Mormon Apostle, Bernard P. Brockbank, gave at the annual General Conference of the Mormon Church, held in Salt Lake City, Utah. Addressing the membership of the church worldwide Brockbank confessed, "It is true that many of the Christian churches worship a different Jesus Christ than is worshiped by the Mormons . . ."[1] While still a Mormon, I believed and was proud of our church view about Jesus. I believed what I had been taught and assumed that anything in the Bible which disagreed with Mormonism and it's version of Christ must be a Bible mistranslation. But later, when I viewed the Bible as truly inspired by God and "profitable for teaching, for reproof, for correction, and for training in righteousness"[2] I was stunned to see that the Bible is in opposition to the Jesus of Mormonism.

Brockbank's statement concerning the different Mormon Jesus is succinctly true, and emphasizes the presence of serious differences between the Jesus of Christianity and the one of Mormonism. On June 20, 1998 the *LDS Church News* reported: "In bearing testimony of Jesus Christ, President Hinckley spoke of those outside the church who say Latter-day Saints 'do not believe in the traditional Christ. No, I don't. The traditional Christ of whom they speak is not the Christ of whom I speak. For the Christ of whom I speak has been revealed in this the Dispensation of the Fulness [sic] of Times.'"

Have you ever defined the characteristics you believe comprise the best marriage relationship? Would you define marriage as a sacred ordinance of divine origin - the most sacred and intimate relationship in life? In your marriage what value would you place upon fidelity, integrity, mutual respect, honesty, intimacy, and dependability? It is remarkable that Holy Scripture describes a relationship with God as a marriage relationship. The body of Christ, those having a true relationship with the real Messiah, are termed the bride of Christ,[3] and Christ as the bridegroom.[4] The church, the called out assembly of believers, is to be presented as a chaste virgin to Christ.[5]

Yet, such an intimate relationship with Jesus is viewed improper and perilous by the Mormon Church. This is only one aspect where the Mormon Church does not believe in the same Jesus described within the Bible. The Bible warns people about accepting a beguiling relationship with a counterfeit Jesus. In fact, the Bible warns against being tricked by Satan, the master deceiver, into embracing a different Jesus, a different spirit, false apostles, a different Gospel –and a different way to be saved. We are also warned not to be deceived in the same manner as was Eve. Notice the following verses:

> *. . . I have betrothed you to one husband, that to Christ I might present you as a pure virgin. But I am afraid, lest as the serpent deceived Eve by his craftiness, your minds should be led astray from the simplicity and purity of devotion to Christ. For if one comes and preaches another Jesus whom we have not preached, or you receive a different spirit which you have not received, or a different gospel which you have not accepted, you bear this beautifully. . . For such men are false apostles, deceitful workers, disguising themselves as apostles of Christ. And no wonder, for even Satan disguises himself as an angel of light. Therefore it is not surprising if his servants also disguise themselves as servants of righteousness; whose end shall be according to their deeds.[6]*

The Mormon Church categorically fits each part of the very serious warning made in the verses quoted above. Satan seduced Eve by proposing the thought that God was holding back on her. He cast doubt on God's Word. Satan declared, "hath God said, ye shall not eat of every tree of the garden? . . . God doth know that in the day ye eat thereof ye shall be as gods . . ."[7] I was shocked to understand the obvious connection between the Mormon goal to become a God and Satan's plan of deception; Satan was cast out of heaven for even aspiring to be like the Most High God![8] Yet, he rushed to Eve and lured her into the same disastrous rebellion against God! Adam followed. Immediately, their spiritual connection with God was completely severed and, as a result of their disobedience, they began to experience fear with all its catastrophic effects. These effects are passed on to us. When we buy into Satan's lies he steals from us the very truths God has supplied for our happiness and well being.

> **there are seven things the Lord hates**

An unfaithful bridegroom naturally seeks out persons not recognizing or questioning his disguise or means of relationship. Many Mormons, especially of the later generations, are not aware of unfaithfulness on the part of their bridegroom, who acts as only a false bridegroom can! The Mormon Church professes to the world faithfulness to Jesus, and the God of Israel, assuring its members that they are Christian in the purest form. I am certain that the Mormon Church is led by seducing spirits, and doctrines of devils.[9] Mormonism tickles peoples ears, won't endure sound doctrine,[10] and blows with every wind of doctrine.[11] The church has a form of godliness but denies the power thereof, and is ever learning and never able to come to the knowledge of truth.[12] The Bible explains that there are seven things[13] the Lord hates. These seven things, says the Bible, are abominations to God. Deceit, a false witness, a lying tongue, and wicked imaginations are among them. I expected godly traits of character from the Mormon Church to which I really was married and gave myself to. But instead I discovered the LDS Church guilty of the traits the book of Proverbs describes above. The church deceived and betrayed me as it has countless others. How devastating to the soul! As in a marriage, betrayal is one of the most difficult issues in life.

I wish the Mormon Church, posing as the bride of Christ, would come clean. How *praiseworthy and of good report* (thirteenth Mormon Article of Faith) it would be for the Church of Jesus Christ of Latter-day Saints to admit to its false teachings and preach the true Gospel, thereby releasing its members to adjust their eyes to clarity of vision, and receive a legitimate relationship with the Messiah of the Bible. At a point in my journey out of Mormonism I had to deal with forms of denial that had kept me from looking straight at the facts of the Mormon faith. I confessed my guilt to God. I repented for participating in a false religion. Forgiveness is a necessary part of any healing process. The words of Jesus as recorded in Mark are appropriate here:

> *And when ye stand praying, forgive, if ye have ought against any: that your Father also which is in heaven may forgive your trespasses. But if ye do not forgive, neither will your Father which is in heaven forgive your trespasses.[14]*

I forgive the Mormon Church, and try to speak the truth in love.

## What About a Relationship With Christ?

I am often asked if I believe that some Mormons place their trust in Jesus alone, without the Mormon Church for salvation. There is no way to peer into someone's heart to know if they have done so. In their hearts and in keeping with the Mormon hymn *Choose the Right,* many church members want to please God. I believe that most Mormons have never truly heard the truth of the biblical Gospel and do not believe in the biblical Jesus or that such a Jesus even exists. When I grew up we didn't want to be classified with the Christian *outsiders.* While pretending to the title Christian, Mormon doctrine redefines common words used in Christianity. Differences in terminology separate Mormons from the teachings endorsed throughout the Bible. On page 193 of the Exhibit Section I have included a list of "Terminology Differences" compiled by Sandra Tanner. This list will assist the reader to understand the Mormon language. I find that many people, Mormon and non-Mormon, are unaware that there are terminology differences, nor are they aware of half truths, padded accounts, or the amount of deceit that is hidden or disguised from view.

We have seen that the Bible describes the true relationship with Christ as that of bride and Bridegroom. This is the most sacred and intimate personal relationship life can offer, one not to be avoided but sought after and safeguarded. Warned against having a relationship with the true and faithful Bridegroom of the Bible, members of the LDS Church do not recognize nor understand that the life they are living could be more rich. Always, as a member of the LDS Church, I was taught to address only the Father in prayer and that it was most disrespectful to God to think too highly of Jesus. I was taught to be only reverentially grateful to Jesus. Before I left Mormonism, I began noticing how seldom Jesus was emphasized in church meetings. Also, I began to realize that my knowledge of, or relationship with God seemed unimportant in temple interviews and tithing settlements, even though I was always asked if I supported the general and local authorities of the church. This, I have realized, was because Mormons do not separate the institution of Mormonism from God. It is as though they see Mormonism as God, and consider breaking allegiance with their church the equivalent of abandoning God. In this respect Mormonism is an idol, something one gives his time, energy and passionate devotion to in place of God. It is a God substitute. After I departed from the church the Mormon Apostle Bruce McConkie gave a speech to the BYU students which expresses the way I was raised to believe. He argued that one should not have a personal relationship with Christ:

> *It is no secret that many false and foolish things are being taught in the sectarian world about our need to gain a special relationship with the Lord Jesus . . . in an effort to be truer than true they devote themselves to gaining a special, personal relationship with Christ which is both improper and perilous . . . There is no salvation in believing any false doctrine, particularly a false or unwise view about the Godhead, or any of its members.*[15]

> *. . . You have never heard one of the first Presidency or the Twelve, who hold the keys of the kingdom . . . you have never heard one of them advocate this excessive zeal that calls for gaining a so-called personal relationship with Christ. We worship the Father only and no one else. We do not worship the Son and we do not worship the Holy Ghost. Our relationship with the Father is supreme, paramount, and pre-eminent over all others. He is the God we worship. It is His gospel that saves and exalts . . . He is the one who was once as we are now . . . Our relationship with the Son is one of a brother or sister in the pre-mortal life . . . gaining a personal relationship with Christ is both improper and perilous. Our prayers are addressed to the Father, and Him only. They do not go through Christ, or the blessed Virgin, or St. Genevieve or along the beads of a rosary.*[16]

> *a personal relationship with Christ is both improper and perilous.*

Gaining a relationship with Christ is both improper and perilous? From McConkie's speech, can you see why, as a Mormon, I had undervalued Jesus? And of the Father, Mormon Apostle Milton R. Hunter said:

> *Yet, if we accept the great law of eternal progression, we must accept the fact that there was a time when Deity was much less powerful than He is today . . . how did He become glorified and exalted and attain His present status of Godhood? . . . From day to day He exerted His will vigorously, and as a result became thoroughly acquainted with the forces lying about Him. As He gained more knowledge through persistent effort and continuous industry, as well as absolute obedience, His understanding of the universal laws continued to become more complete. Thus He grew in experience and continued to grow until He attained the status of Godhood.*[17]

None of these beliefs are hinted at anywhere in the Bible. The God of the Bible never became acquainted with the forces lying about Him –He was the originator of them!

As to not worshipping the Son, the *Book of Mormon* disagrees: ". . . Christ is the Holy One of Israel; wherefore ye must bow down before him, and worship him with all your might, mind, and strength, and your whole soul; and if ye do this ye shall in nowise be cast out."[18] "And when Jesus had spoken these words he came again unto his disciples; and behold they did pray steadfastly, without ceasing, unto him; and he did smile upon them again; and behold they were white, even as Jesus."[19] Members of the LDS Church should read their *Book of Mormon* and realize that this community did pray to Jesus. (Also, note that the reward for steadfastness was to be white, even as Jesus.)

The following words concerning the Mormon Jesus, and others of the Mormon Godhead are shocking and grievous to Christians who uphold the biblical purity of the nature of God:

> *Jesus is greater than the Holy Spirit, which is subject unto him, but his Father is greater than he! He has said it. Christ was begotten of God. He was not born without the aid of Man, and that Man was God!'*[20]

Later we shall see that the Bible makes clear that within the *unified* one God of Israel, none is greater than the other.

## The Non-Biblical View of Jesus' Pre-existence

I have mentioned that as a small child I was taught as truth that all people first existed in a pre-mortal life, and that we were one huge spirit family. It was explained to me that during that existence a rebellion transpired which resulted in a heavenly battle. I was taught that at a time in pre-earth history, a huge family council meeting was held where Jesus, our spirit brother, was appointed as savior to all mankind. Our spirit brother, known now as Satan, contested that appointment - hence he became the devil. Two thirds of the spirit children (those who were to come to planet earth) voted for Jesus to be the Savior of this world. One third of the family of the Mormon God were cast out of heaven and became evil spirits.[21]

Mormons believe that Jesus became the Savior because He was intellectually and morally superior to His divine father and mother's children (us). The appointment of Jesus was contested by our spirit brother Lucifer.[22] The idea that we existed in a pre-earth and sided with Jesus to be Savior is wrong. No one ever voted for Jesus. The biblical Jesus never had a divine mother in a pre-earth life! This is definitely not the same pre-existing Jesus we read about in the Bible.

The Bible makes it clear that Jesus is the originator and first cause of all. Jesus cannot be a spirit brother to Satan; He created Satan! The Bible, unlike Mormon doctrine, reveals that Satan was created as an angel,[23] not a spirit brother of Jesus, and he is now a fallen angel.[24] Satan was created - not procreated! While Mormonism teaches that Jesus is a spirit brother to all of us including Satan,[25] the Bible, on the other hand, explains that Jesus is the Alpha and Omega.[26] Not only is Jehovah the first and last, He is the only God in all the heavens and their host.[27] He is Immanuel,[28] literally meaning God with us. He is the Everlasting Father.[29] He is absolute Deity in bodily fashion.[30] All the fulness of God dwells in Jesus.[31] As for his earthly existence, Jesus was supernaturally born of a virgin.[32] He was not procreated through a resurrected glorified God-man as Mormonism teaches! This is blasphemy! We all should rightfully exalt and honor Jesus. Jesus is God incarnate! He holds our destinies in His hands.

## Was Jesus a Product of a Virgin Birth?

According to Mormon theology, when the time came in the pre-mortal life for our oldest spirit brother Jesus to receive a body, God personally came to earth and had relations as husband to Mary in the same manner as mortal men are begotten by mortal fathers. The words of the early Mormon Apostle, Orson Pratt:

> *The fleshly body of Jesus required a Mother as well as a Father. Therefore, the Father and Mother of Jesus, according to the flesh, must have been associated together in the capacity of Husband and Wife; hence the Virgin Mary must have been, for the time being, the lawful wife*

*of God the Father: we use the term lawful Wife, because it would be blasphemous in the highest degree to say that He overshadowed her or begat the Savior unlawfully.*[33]

There are many Mormon references which demonstrate this Mormon heresy. Examine the following words by the Mormon Apostle Bruce R. McConkie which tells that God personally came to earth and copulated with Mary:

> *Only means* only; *Begotten means begotten; and Son means son. Christ was begotten by an immortal Father in the same way that mortal men are begotten by mortal fathers.*[34]

> *There is no need to spiritualize away the plain meaning of the scriptures. There is nothing figurative or hidden or beyond comprehension in our Lord's coming into mortality. He is the son of God in the same sense and way that we are the sons of mortal fathers. It is that simple.*[35]

Obviously then, Mormon theology sees nothing supernatural about Jesus' birth - it was simply an act of the flesh. My friend, in what sense were you begotten by your mortal father? The Mormon belief about the pre-earth life and the mortal birth of Jesus shows contempt for the true son of God. The belief that God physically fathered Jesus not only contradicts the biblical account of the virgin birth, but convicts the Mormon God of incest with Mary whom, according to Mormonism's doctrine of a pre-earth life, was a younger sister of Jesus.[36] Of this subject as with other Mormon doctrines, members are encouraged not to trust the Bible but to trust their prophets words instead. The Bible says of Jesus:

| |
|---|
| **Jesus was begotten by an immortal Father in the same way that mortal men are begotten by mortal fathers** |

> *And then he said, Listen now, O house of David! Is it too slight a thing for you to try the patience of men, that you will try the patience of my God as well . . . Therefore the Lord Himself will give you a sign: Behold, a virgin will be with child and bear a son, and she will call His name Immanuel.*[37]

In Hebrew *Immanuel* means *God with us*. The fact of the matter is that Jesus was supernaturally given a virgin birth, through the mediacy of the Holy Spirit.[38] He was not procreated through a resurrected glorified God-man as Mormonism teaches!

## Jesus Married? A Polygamist Too?

Although the Mormon belief that Jesus was married is not usually spoken of openly, a Mormon who understands church theology recognizes that it is intrinsic to the Mormon plan of self-Exaltation. The marriage of Jesus is not taught in the missionary lessons, but neither are the secrets of the Temple Ceremony, nor most laws necessary to the Mormon belief in achieving Exaltation to Godhood. As a young Mormon woman I learned about the necessity of Jesus' marriage. The posture the church takes regarding the subject of Jesus' marriage is illustrated in a letter by Joseph Fielding Smith. He replied to a letter of query from J. Ricks Smith, asking whether Jesus had been married, was married, and had children. In answer to the question Joseph Fielding Smith responded in his own handwriting:

> *\* Mosiah 15:10-12. Please Read Your Book of Mormon!*

> *\*\* Yes! But do not preach it! The Lord advised us not to cast pearls before swine!*

There is a photocopy of the letter in the Exhibit Section on page 207. Elsewhere, the Mormon Apostle, Orson Hyde, reiterates what used to be more openly taught:

| |
|---|
| **Jesus was married in Cana of Galilee** |

> *. . . There was a marriage in Cana of Galilee; and on a careful reading of that transaction, it will be discovered that no less a person than Jesus Christ was married on that occasion. If he was never married, his intimacy with Mary and Martha, and the other Mary also whom Jesus loved, must have been highly unbecoming and improper to say the best of it.*[39]

The Mormon Apostle, Jedediah Grant taught that Jesus' crucifixion was really related to polygamy:

> *The grand reason of the burst of public sentiment in anathemas upon Christ and his disciples, causing his crucifixion, was evidently based upon polygamy, according to the testimony of the philosophers who rose in that age. A belief in the doctrine of plurality of wives caused the persecution of Jesus and his followers.*[40]

The Mormon Apostle Orson Hyde said that Jesus saw his own seed before he was crucified.[41] In Mormonism, many references are cited showing that marriage was essential to the earthly ministry of Jesus Christ, and that without marriage he could not work out his salvation and exaltation. The Mormon Law of Eternal Exaltation necessitates that Jesus came to earth in order to work out his own salvation.[42] But the biblical Jesus never worked out His salvation. He is the giver of life and salvation![43]

As for the rest of the human family the same Mormon rule for working out one's salvation applies. The twelfth LDS Prophet Spencer W. Kimball said, "Only through Celestial marriage can one find the straight way, the narrow path. Eternal life cannot be had in any other way."[44] We see that Jesus told his listeners to enter the straight and narrow gate, the way that leads to life.[45] The Bible does not teach that a Celestial marriage is the straight and narrow path, or that eternal life with the Father comes through obedience to a temple marriage. The Bible does not teach that Jesus was married, nor that marriage of any sort is a requirement to live eternally with God. In fact, the Bible teaches that there is no marriage in heaven.[46]

As was noted earlier in the letter by Joseph Fielding Smith, Mormons are warned not to openly teach the Mormon doctrine of Jesus' marriage. The church uses the same subtle deception when it comes to the quest of the Mormon priesthood to take over our nation and world (more about this later). Mormons believe that one must graduate from milk to meat to learn Mormonism's key teachings that are necessary for Exaltation. None of these teachings are found in the *Book of Mormon,* although the church boasts that the *Book of Mormon* contains the *fulness of the gospel.*[47] These beliefs, like many others about God and man, are repulsive belonging in the catalog of peddling doctrines of devils and damnable heresies, denying the Lord that bought them, as warned against in the Bible.[48]

## The Blood of Jesus

During my youth, I heard rumors that the Mormon doctrine of Blood Atonement (the shedding of blood for personal Atonement for sin) was never practiced. I denied that the doctrine was actually practiced. I later learned that many members of the church, who did not live up to its principles, lost their lives by way of Blood Atonement. Brigham Young taught that the blood of Christ would never wipe out some sins and that only the transgressor's blood could pay the price. He also taught that among those condemned to death were Mormon apostates and covenant breakers.[49]

Like the Adam-God doctrine, there is overwhelming evidence that this doctrine was practiced, in spite of denials by Mormon leaders such as Bruce R. McConkie. While vehemently denying that this doctrine was practiced by the church, McConkie still admits that there are cases in which the blood of Jesus is not effective for one's own sin:

> *But under certain circumstances there are serious sins for which the cleansing of Christ does not operate, and the law of God is that men must then have their own blood shed to atone for their sins.*[50]

While doing research in the Garrett Library in Illinois, I checked out and read the book titled, *Mormonism Unveiled: The Life and Confessions of Mormon Bishop John D. Lee.* This account is one of many which convict the early LDS Church of being responsible for horrible deaths resulting from the Mormon doctrine of Blood Atonement. Even now, this nasty doctrine continues to surface among certain practicing Fundamentalist polygamist Mormons like Ervil LeBaron who was linked to more than a dozen deaths. This, and other examples, are described in Jon Krakauer's book *Under the Banner of Heaven.*[51] Of course LeBaron, like Brigham Young, believed Blood Atonement to be the only way to secure a covenant breaker's salvation. Although the doctrine is believed by many Mormons to this day, it is not practiced openly except by the Fundamentalist Mormons.

At one occasion while studying the Bible, it became crystal clear to me that throughout Mormon history the true significance of the *blood of Jesus* has never been properly taught. The high cost Jesus paid with His blood for redemption is misinterpreted and undermined in the LDS faith. Concerning the blood of Jesus the Bible states: "But if we walk in the light, as He is in the light, we have fellowship one with another, and the blood of Jesus Christ cleanseth us from all sin."[52]

In contrast, when attending the Mormon temple, water was used to wash me free from the blood and sins of this generation, and even that was according to my faithfulness. What a travesty, and an abomination. Only belief in Jesus' shed blood has power to wash away our sins! In addition the LDS Church believes that there are cases where neither water nor the blood of Jesus can remit sins. Apostasy is an example. When I recognized the true significance of the blood of Jesus, and saw through the false Mormon God, the church of my birth began to sour my stomach and made me think about becoming an apostate too. By doing so I certainly would break each of the covenants I had made in the temple. In the Mormon temple I vowed that I would rather have my life taken than be unfaithful to the temple vows. What if I had lived during Brigham Young's day? Let Brigham speak for himself:

> We have those that are amongst us that are full of all manner of abominations, those who need to have their blood shed, for water will not do, their sins are of too deep a dye . . . I would ask how many covenant breakers their are in this city and in this kingdom. I believe that there are a great many; and if they are covenant breakers we need a place designated, where we can shed their blood.[53]

Brigham Young explained the uselessness of the blood of Christ to cleanse the sins of an adulterer:

> Let me suppose a case. Suppose you found your brother in bed with your wife, and put a javelin through both of them, you would be justified, and they would atone for their sins, and be received into the kingdom of God. I would at once do so in such a case; and under such circumstances, I have no wife whom I love so well that I would not put a javelin through her heart, and I would do it with clean hands . . . There is not a man or woman, who violates the covenants made with their God, that will not be required to pay the debt. The blood of Christ will never wipe that out, your own blood must atone for it . . .[54]

In a small booklet published by the LDS Church and distributed at Mormon temples and provided to investigators, are these remarks:

> Christians speak often of the blood of Christ and its cleansing power. Much that is believed and taught on this subject, however, is such utter nonsense and so palpably false that to believe it is to lose one's salvation.[55]

In Mormonism, the blood of Jesus only provides universal resurrection, and does not pay for personal sin.[56] Believing that there are some sins that can only be paid for through the shedding of one's own blood makes human blood of equal and greater importance than the untainted shed blood of Jesus. The implications of such a belief is that man can do as much as Jesus did! What then is the point of a Savior? No wonder that some of the early Mormon apostles didn't believe there was any value in the death of Jesus for salvation.[57] How twisted and contorted the Mormon understanding of the blood of Jesus is.

Compare this quote from the prophet Isaiah:

> But he was wounded for our transgressions, he was bruised for our iniquities: the chastisement of our peace was upon him; and with his stripes we are healed.[58]

Sadly, the Mormon belief concerning the final Sacrifice and blood of Jesus was of no avail to King David because of the sins he committed. He lost his chance for Mormon Exaltation to Godhood. McConkie wrote, "When David was groaning under the crushing burden of those personal sins which caused him to lose his exaltation..."[59] Of murder the *Doctrine and Covenants* says, "Thou shalt not kill; and he that kills shall not have forgiveness in this world, nor in the world to come."[60]

> **caused him [David] to lose his exaltation**

David was responsible for murder and adultery[61] but he cried out to God in repentance. The truth is that David looked to the final Sacrifice for sins which would come through Messiah Jesus and His untainted shed blood. The true God of Israel is compassionate and full of loving-kindness (an old testament word for grace). He forgave David completely. In one of the beautiful Psalms, David wrote, "Create in me a new heart, O God; and renew a right spirit within me. Cast me not away from Thy presence; and take not thy holy spirit from me."[62] Anyone may call out to God for forgiveness as David did. The blood of Messiah Jesus will cleanse completely! Only His blood has power to remit sins. The blood of Jesus has already paid for our sins in full - but we must receive the gracious wonderful gift of redemption. God will never override our free will to choose or decline salvation through His amazing gift of grace. Worthiness is not achieved through Mormon Laws and Ordinances. Who is worthy to serve God? A list titled *Qualifications to Serve God* by pastor John MaCarthur is included in the Exhibit Section on page 227. The list evidences the truth about the matter of worthiness, and in contrast to Mormon rules and regulations, the reader will find this page so liberating! Such forgiveness, such wondrous grace!

## Who Forgives Sins?

> *a monumental presumption for unauthorized men elsewhere to claim to absolve people from sin*

The Mormon Prophet Spencer W. Kimball instructed the church:

*Since the power to remit sins is so carefully and strictly limited within the true Church of Jesus Christ, where so many men bear the true priesthood of God, it is a monumental presumption for unauthorized men elsewhere to claim to absolve people from sin.*[63]

*The Bishop will determine the case. He it is who will determine by the facts, and through the power of discernment which is his, whether the nature of the sin and the degree of repentance manifested warrant forgiveness . . . All this responsibility rests upon the bishop's shoulders.*[64]

Those words are very sad and untrue! The truth of the matter is that no one needs a Mormon bishop or the Mormon God's complicated perverted Gospel. Once again, we need only the legitimate Messiah Jesus. Jesus washed us from our sins in his own blood.[65] Believers overcome Satan by the blood of the Lamb, and by word of their testimony.[66] I am grateful that I am washed in Jesus' own precious blood, the only way sins are forgiven.[67]

## Atonement at Gethsemane?

In Mormonism, the importance of the Sacrifice of Jesus as He hung and shed His blood on the Cross at Calvary is conspicuously undermined. Mormons believe that it was in the Garden of Gethsemane that Jesus, sweating as if it were great drops of blood, atoned for most personal sins.[68] Within Mormonism the preaching of the Cross of Calvary and all it stands for dims into the background and Gethsemane takes the forefront. God's designated manner for the shedding of His dear Son's blood as the Atonement for our personal sin is diminished into sweating as if it were great drops of blood.

It is well established from Scripture that the blood of Jesus Christ cleanses from all sin,[69] and that it is the blood that makes Atonement for the soul.[70] I have no desire to rob the Cross of Calvary where Jesus shed His blood for us. Remember, "For the preaching of the cross is to them that perish foolishness; but unto us which are saved it is the power of God."[71] We ought never to undermine the Cross of Calvary and the cleansing power of the blood of Jesus, shed there in our behalf. Christ paid for all our sin, in His body on the cross.[72] Jesus didn't sweat for our sins in the Garden of Gethsemane. In the LDS Church salvation is obtained by people's works (e.g. obedience to Mormon Church leaders and dogma[73]). In contrast, the Bible teaches that salvation is obtained by God's grace; Christ's death on the Cross of Calvary as Atonement for our sins.[74] Good works are set apart and established as a natural loving response to God's grace. They have nothing to do with Mormonism's un-biblical works, like temple work.

The Mormon missionary lessons from which I taught during my mission say that the Atonement begins to be effective *after* repentance and baptism into the Mormon Church.[75] In contrast, the Holy Bible instructs that the Atonement goes into effect in our lives at the *instant* we believe in Jesus alone as Savior and advocate.[76]

## Honor and Exalt the Son, Even as the Father!

Recall the words of Jesus, "I and My Father are one,"[77] there Jesus not only speaks concerning the oneness of equality, but gives Himself first mention: not "The Father and I," but "I and the Father."

Jesus said:

> For the Father judgeth no man, but hath commited all judgment unto the Son: That all men should honour the Son, even as they honour the Father. He that honoureth not the Son honoureth not the Father which hath sent him. Verily, verily, I say unto you, He that heareth my word, and believeth on him that sent me, hath everlasting life, and shall not come into condemnation; but is passed from death unto life.[78]

Here, Messiah Jesus claims equal homage and worship with the Father. As for prayer, Jesus said, "If you ask Me anything in My name, I will do it."[79] The sinless humanity of Jesus is expressed in the Incarnation. When He was resurrected Thomas fell at Jesus' feet exclaiming, "My Lord and my God."[80] Such homage is blasphemy unless Jesus is Diety.[81]

It was while we lived in Illinois that Apostle Brockbank's speech (quoted earlier in this chapter) came out in the Ensign (an LDS Church magazine). Because I was seeking to know the truth about what my relationship with Jesus should be, the message was timely. I keep this magazine as a memento of a turning point in my life. At the time while I was examining the primary sources of Mormonism, and to this very day, I think to myself, "Yes, Apostle Brockbank and LDS President Hinckley are correct." The God of Mormonism is *very* different than the one of Christianity! Mormons answer to another Jesus, another spirit, and have a different way to be saved than is taught in the Bible. They are deceived

> *to believe Mormon doctrine is to believe the Bible teaches a lie*

in the same manner as was Eve. Thankfully, I now trust the Bible over the Mormon prophets who espouse doctrines contrary to God's Word. To believe Mormon doctrine is to believe the Bible teaches a lie! Embracing such un-biblical doctrines offends God! We ought take the following Scripture seriously:

> . . . *You are already following a different "way to heaven," which really doesn't go to heaven at all. For there is no other way than the one we showed you; you are being fooled by those who twist and change the truth concerning Christ. Let God's curses fall on anyone, including myself, who preaches any other way to be saved than the one we told you about; yes, if an angel comes from heaven and preaches any other message, let him be forever cursed. I will say it again: if anyone preaches any other Gospel than the one you welcomed, let God's curse fall upon him.*[82]

While the Mormon Church poses as Christian, the fact that Christians and Mormons pray to a different God is demonstrated by the fact that we carry irreconcilable differences concerning the God of the universe and His Gospel message. I felt cheated and betrayed by the Mormon Church when I discovered that I had not been taught the truth about what one's relationship with Christ should be - even though it was He that created us and saves our souls! Most of my life I sought only the Father (that is, the Mormon version of the Father). I was not taught about the true Father, nor the true Son, nor the true Holy Spirit. I only knew the teachings of men. In spite of it all I had an honest seeking heart, my motive was genuine, and I had a love for the truth. I believe that the true God honored that fact and accordingly brought me to Himself. To this day I think about how Mormon doctrine must grieve the very heart of God.

As true disciples, may we choose to follow the real prophesied Messiah Jesus, making the choice never to be guilty of redefining Him or His deeds in any way.

While chapter four introduced some of many unmanageable inconsistencies of the evolving God of the LDS Church, the information presented in this chapter concerning the Jesus of Mormonism is shocking and heartbreaking to those who embrace the ". . . simplicity that is in Christ."[83] From Strong's Exhaustive Concordance #572 we find the word *simplicity* in its Greek, means singleness without self-seeking. It is a bestowal of informed understanding.

When one embraces a false bridegroom one can expect a world view twisted and formed outside of biblical truth. In stern opposition to this Mormon system of belief, the Bible succinctly states in many places that accepting Jesus is the only way to the Father.[84]  Through accepting Jesus we enter the straight way, the narrow path to eternal life with the Father.  A Messiah outside of the whole of God's Word is no Messiah at all.

In contrast to the narrow path which Jesus taught leads to eternal life[85], we will now draw attention to the wide path of Mormonism in the next chapter.

1   Ensign, pp. 26-27, May, 1977.

2   2 Timothy 3:16.

3   Revelation 21:9.

4   John 3:29.

5   2 Corinthians 11:2.

6   2 Corinthians 11: 2-3, 4, 13-15.

7   Genesis 3:1-5.

8   Isaiah 14:12-15.

9   1 Timothy 4:1.

10  2 Timothy 4:3.

11  Ephesians 4:14.

12  2 Timothy 3:5, 7.

13  Proverbs 6:16-19.

14  Mark 11: 25-26.

15  The Provo Herald, January 12, 1984, p. 21.

16  BYU Devotional, March 2, 1982.

17  The Gospel Through the Ages, pp.114-115.

18  Book of Mormon, 2 Nephi 25:28-29.

19  Book of Mormon, 3 Nephi 19:30.

20  Doctrines of Salvation, vol.1, p.18.

21  Mormon Doctrine, p.828; Abraham 3:22-28; Doctrine and Covenants 29:36-38.

22  Gospel through the Ages, p.15; Pearl of Great Price, Abraham 3:19-28.

23  Ezekiel 28:13.

24  Isaiah 14:12-15.

25  Pearl of Great Price, Abraham 3:22-24.

26  Revelation 1:8, John 1:1-14; Colossians 1:15-17; Micah 5:2; John 1:1-3.

27  Isaiah 44:8, 45:6-12.

28  Isaiah 7:14.

29  Isaiah 9:6.

30  Colossians 2:9.

31  Colossians 1:19.

32  Isaiah 7:14.

33  The Seer, p. 158.

34  Mormon Doctrine, pp. 546-547.

35  The Promised Messiah, pp. 467-468.

36  Pearl of Great Price, Abraham 3:22-28.

37  Isaiah 7:13-14.

38  Luke 1:35; Matthew 1:18.

39  Journal of Discourses, vol. 4, pp. 259-260.

40  Journal of Discourses, vol. 1, p. 346.

41  Journal of Discourses, vol. 2, p. 82.

42  Journal of Discourses, vol. 6, p. 4 and The Promised Messiah, pp. 482,485.

43  Hebrews 12:2.

44  Deseret News, Church News section, November 12, 1977.

45  Matthew 7:13.

46  Mark 12:25.

47  Doctrine and Covenants 42:12.

48  2 Peter 2:1-3.

49  Journal of Discourses, vol. 3, p. 247.

50  Mormon Doctrine, p. 92.

51  Under The Banner of Heaven, Jon Krakauer, USA, Doubleday, 2003.

52  1 John 1:7.

53  Journal of Discourses, vol. 4, pp. 49-50

54  Journal of Discourses, vol. 3, p. 247.

55  What The Mormons Think Of Christ, p.20

56  Article of Faith #3.

57  Journal of Discourses, vol. 12, p. 66.

58  Isaiah 53:5.

59  Mormon Doctrine, p.153.

60  Doctrine and Covenants 42:18.

61  2 Samuel 12:9.

62  Psalms 51:10-11.

63  Miracle of Forgiveness, p. 334.

64  Miracle of Forgiveness, p. 327.

65  Revelation 1:5.

66  Revelation 12:11.

67  Hebrews 9:14; 1 John 1:7; Leviticus 17:11; Revelation 7:14; 1 Peter 1:18-19; Hebrews 10:19.

68  Deseret News, Church News Section, Oct. 9, 1982, p. 19; Doctrine and Covenants 19:16-19.

69  I John 1:7.

70  Leviticus 17:11.

71  1 Corinthians 1:18.

72  Colossians 1:20.

73  Article of Faith #3, also 2 Nephi 25:23.

74  1 Corinthians 15:1-4; Eph. 2:8, 9.

75  Missionary Lessons, concept 5:1-23; also Mormon Doctrine, p. 101.

76  John 1:12.

77  John 10:30.

78  John 5:22-23.

79  John 14:14.

80  John 20:28.

81  Exodus 20:3.

82  Galatians 1:6-9.

83  2 Corinthians 11:3.

84  John 10:9, John 14:6.

85  Matthew 7:13-14.

# 9. The Gods Concocted a Plan

*Now the serpent was more subtil . . . And he said unto the woman, Yea, hath God said . . .*

Genesis 3:1

It comes as a surprise for some members of the Mormon Church that the various mainstream Christian churches do not share more of their beliefs. Such was the case of my missionary companion in Illinois. She was a convert and was startled to learn that Christians do not believe that humans lived with a father and mother God in a pre-existent state. I wonder if, before her conversion to the Mormon faith, she was aware that non-members do not believe that God had to work out His own salvation. By Mormon standards doing so is a prerequisite to becoming a God. Obviously she didn't have a strong Christian upbringing, if she had one at all, or she would have known that a belief in a pre-earth life punctuates a glaring difference between the Christian and Mormon faiths. The belief in a pre-earth life is all tied up in the Mormon understanding of humans progression to Exaltation, that is, Godhood. A product of a strong Mormon heritage, I knew the differences between Christianity and Mormonism because I was taught them while growing up. Some Mormons know their doctrine fairly well. Others, I believe, are naive and only superficially know their religion.

It was Lorenzo Snow, the fifth Mormon Prophet, who coined the popular phrase "As man now is, God once was: As God now is, man may be."[1] This is the Mormon world view. This becomes more clear when one comprehends the Mormon Law of Eternal Progression and Exaltation. By definition, Mormon Exaltation comprises the belief in a plurality of Gods, and that humans may become Gods. This Mormon belief in polytheism (many Gods) diminishes God's centrality and heralds the age old appeal of humanism. By their own definitions of life and eternity, by their own values and needs, and as masters of their own destinies humans attempt to govern themselves without God's instruction manual of love safeguarded for us in the Bible. The exclusion or undermining of the Bible as God's Word, always brings unnecessary pain and sorrow. The Mormon Law of Eternal Progression and Exaltation, as defined in the Mormon Church, is the subject of this chapter.

> *as man now is,*
> *God once was:*
> *As God now is,*
> *man may be*

## A Mythical Pre-existence

Let's begin with the following quote from Joseph Smith:

*"Here, then, is eternal life –to know the only wise and true God; and you have got to learn*

*how to become Gods yourselves, and to be kings and priests to God, the same as all Gods have done before you, –namely, by going from one small degree to another, and from a small capacity to a great one, –from grace to grace, from exaltation to exaltation, until you attain to the resurrection of the dead, and are able to dwell in everlasting burnings and to sit in glory, as those who sit enthroned in everlasting power."[2]*

Present-day Mormonism sets forth the idea that the origins of life did not begin with creation. The Mormon *Pearl of Great Price*, gives the account that the heavens and the earth were organized and formed.[3] In contrast, the biblical account of the origins of life is one of creation. The Bible clearly states that through faith the worlds were formed by the Word of God, so that what is seen, was not made out of things which are visible.[4] Interestingly enough, and as is so often the case, the *Book of Mormon* does not teach present Mormon doctrine, but rather supports the Bible, that the world came about through creation.[5]

The Mormon Apostle Orson Pratt taught, "In the heaven where our spirits were born, there are many Gods, each of whom has his own wife or wives, which were given to him previous to his redemption while yet in his mortal state."[6] I was taught, and unquestioningly believed, that all persons born on planet earth first pre-existed as children of Celestial parentage. I used to sing about heavenly parents in the Mormon Hymn, *Oh My Father*.[7] Another church hymn that I sang, *If You Could Hie to Kolob*[8], concerned the planet Kolob, a planet, which according to Mormon theology is nearest to the Celestial residence of God, where Gods began to be.

Let's examine a couple of alleged proof-texts used to promote the LDS doctrine of a pre-existence. "Before I formed thee in the belly I knew thee; and before though camest forth out of the womb I sanctified thee, and I ordained thee to be a prophet to the nations."[9] As a missionary for the LDS Church, I was taught to use this verse to prove that we all, like Jeremiah, had a pre-earth life. This verse does not prove that Jeremiah or any human had a pre-existence. This passage is explained in the epistle of Paul to the Romans, ". . . God who quickeneth the dead, and calleth those things which be not as though they were."[10] The word "be" in the verse comes from a Greek verb denoting existence. So Paul is saying "those things which do not exist." You see, God, who is all-knowing knows all things before they happen. Jeremiah's life, as well as ours, were known to God before we came into existence.

*Job did not pre-exist. God's question to Job was one of rebuke*

Another proof text for a pre-earth life for humans is the conversation between God and Job: "Where wast thou when I laid the foundations of the earth . . . when the morning stars sang together, and all the sons of God shouted for joy?"[11] I was taught that Job had previously lived or God would never have asked him where he was before the foundations of the earth were laid. The point here is that Job did not pre-exist. God's question to Job was one of rebuke. In fact, rather than state that he was present, Job responds to God's question with the words, "Behold, I am vile; what have I to answer thee?"

It was not unusual among my Mormon friends to discuss the Mormon belief that in a pre-existence we chose our earthly parentage. Later, while studying the Bible, I discovered that Jacob and Esau never had a pre-earth parentage or existence. They, according to Romans,[12] did no good or evil before they were born. Why? Simply because they did not pre-exist. I'm certain that we, like Jacob and Esau, did no good or evil either, because nowhere does the Bible teach that humans pre-existed as spirit beings. First, comes the natural, not the spiritual.[13] The truth about the matter is that God forms our spirits within our mothers wombs.[14] Nowhere does the Bible teach that we chose our parents.

## The Place of the Fall

In Genesis, God instructs Adam and Eve that they must not eat of the tree in the middle of the Garden of Eden, lest they die. Satan, described in Scripture as the accuser, cast doubt on God's integrity by suggesting that God may be holding back something from them lest they find Him out. God said they would die, but would they? The temptation Satan tailored for Adam and Eve was to persuade them to be independent of their Creator, even exalting themselves to a place of power like God:

*Now the serpent was more subtil than any beast of the field which the LORD God had made. And he said unto the woman, Yea, hath God said, Ye shall not eat of every tree of the garden? And the woman said unto the serpent, We may eat of the fruit of the trees of the garden: But of the fruit of the tree which is in the midst of the garden, God hath said, Ye shall not eat of it, neither shall ye touch it, lest ye die. And the serpent said unto the woman, Ye shall not surely die: For God doth know that in the day ye eat thereof, then your eyes shall be opened, and ye shall be as gods, knowing good and evil.*[15]

Concerning God and His Word, Satan still accuses and instills doubt with the same words from Genesis: "Hath God said?" then quickly comes the follow up, "God doth know . . ." Notice the following version of Genesis chapter three-a segment of the Mormon Temple Ceremony as I experienced it:

*Lucifer:   Eve, here is some of the fruit of that tree. It will make you wise,*

*Eve:   But Father said that in the day we ate thereof, we should surely die.*

*Lucifer:   Ye shall not surely die but shall be as Gods; ye shall know good from evil, virtue from vice, light from darkness, health from sickness, pleasure from pain. And thus your eyes shall be opened and you will have knowledge.*

*Eve:   Is there no other way?*

*Lucifer:   There is no other way.*

*Eve:   Then I will partake.*

*Lucifer:   That is right. Now go and get Adam to partake . . .*

*Adam:   Eve, I see that it must be so . . . I will partake that man might be.*[16]

By appealing to human pride and imagination, Satan launched a plan against the integrity of God's Word. The fact that the suggestion was Satan's idea should have been reason enough for participants in the Mormon Temple Ceremony to seriously question the drama scene. Instead we put on our ceremonial green aprons –coverings like Adam and Eve made for themselves. God rejected those aprons; they represent man's own efforts. I pray that temple Mormons reject their green aprons and their inner Masonic-like undergarments (see exhibit on pages 229-231) and instead adorn themselves with God's salvation by grace through faith.

Why believe a word that Satan suggests? He is the father of lies and there is no truth in him.[17] Yet, we in the temple readily acquiesced to his ploy, and by doing so unwittingly placed ourselves and Satan above the centrality of God. The fall, to the Mormon mind was not a sin against God. Instead, the fall was a blessed event, a step toward personal Exaltation to Godhood. At this point in the Temple Ceremony, all of us should have quickly run out of the Mormon temple! Instead we were encouraged to follow the foolish idea of earning the positions of Gods and Goddesses for an eternal state.

While a Mormon, I held a pelagianistic view of man (the belief that there is no original sin or guilt). In agreement with the church I applauded Adam's rebellion as dramatized in the Temple Ceremony. I believed the account as recorded in the *Pearl of Great Price*.[18] Mormon Prophet Joseph Fielding Smith said:

*. . . I never speak of the part Eve took in this fall as a sin, nor do I accuse Adam of a sin. . . . this was a transgression of the law, but not a sin in the strict sense, for it was something that Adam and Eve had to do!*
*I am sure that neither Adam nor Eve looked upon it as a sin . . .*[19]

Do you believe that people can fall upward? One LDS General Authority, Sterling W. Sill, described the fall as a fall upward. "Adam fell, but he fell in the right direction. He fell toward his goal . . . . Adam fell, but he fell upward."[20]

> *Adam fell, but*
> *he fell upward*

Imagine how I felt when I learned that the goal of exalting himself to be like God caused Satan to fall (downward) from his heavenly station as the highest created angel (not Jesus' spirit brother or our spirit brother as LDS believe). How astonished I was to learn that the very goal Satan used to entice Adam and Eve[21] is the same goal which the Mormon Law of Eternal Exaltation extols.

By teaching that man is born spiritually dead the Bible strongly opposes Mormon doctrine concerning the fall of man, "Wherefore, as by one man sin entered into the world, and death by sin; and so death passed upon all men, for that all have sinned:"[22]

The Bible teaches that Jesus took all we inherited through Adam –eternal death, and replaced it with eternal life,[23] with Him.  The catastrophic effect of the fall is only remedied through the new birth.[24]

## Put Your Shoulder to the Wheel

From earliest childhood I was taught that temple marriage was a prerequisite to obtaining eternal life with the Father in the Mormon's highest kingdom (the Celestial kingdom).  Without a temple marriage one cannot become exalted to Godhood nor experience eternal child-bearing.  I explained earlier that the mirrors I viewed within the Mormon temple served as reminders that if faithful, in all things to the church, I would become a Goddess for all eternity, one among countless numbers of other Gods and Goddesses!  If my husband proved faithful he would be worshiped all through eternity.

I was taught that striving to become a Goddess was a noble goal —a goal which only an unselfish God would share with His children.  What loving Father, it was explained, would not want His children to become Gods, too?  The achievement of this goal was one which I understood required keeping all the Mormon Laws and Ordinances through lots of self effort.  McConkie explains this in his book *Mormon Doctrine*:

> *Baptism is the gate to the celestial kingdom; celestial marriage is the gate to an exaltation in the highest heaven within the celestial world (D.&C. 131:1-4).  To gain salvation after baptism it is necessary to keep the commandments of God and endure to the end (2 Ne. 31:17-21); to gain exaltation after celestial marriage the same continued devotion and righteousness is required.*[25]

The Mormon Prophet Joseph Smith said:

> *After this instruction, you will be responsible for your own sins; it is a desirable honor that you should so walk before our Heavenly Father as to save yourselves; we are responsible to God for the manner we improve the light and wisdom given by our Lord to enable us to save ourselves.*[26]

> **. . . so walk before our Heavenly Father as to save ourselves . . .**

The Mormon Apostle Milton R. Hunter states that those who keep all the commandments of Mormonism will actually be Gods.[27]  Hunter explains the concept further.  "Thus all men who ascend to the glorious status of Godhood can do so only by one method - by obedience to all the principles and ordinances of the Gospel of Jesus Christ."[28]  According to the Bible, the Mormon requirement and understanding of marriage does not exist in heaven.[29]

In Mormon doctrine, Jesus was the offspring of a mortal mother and an immortal, resurrected and glorified father.[30]  As part of working out his salvation, Jesus had to come to earth to receive a body and be married.  The same is required for the Exaltation of every LDS man and woman.  The achievement of eternal marriage enables Mormons to produce spirit children throughout all time.  The Mormon Apostle Orson Pratt says:

> *Each God, through his wife or wives, raises up a numerous family of sons and daughters; indeed, there will be no end to the increase of his own children: for each father and mother will be in a condition to multiply forever and ever.  As soon as each God has begotten many millions of male and female spirits, and his Heavenly inheritance becomes too small to comfortably accommodate his great family, he, in connection with his sons, organizes a new world, after a similar order to the one which we now inhabit, where he sends both the male and female spirits to inhabit tabernacles of flesh and bones . . . The inhabitants of each world are required to reverence, adore, and worship their own personal father who dwells in the Heaven which they formerly inhabited.*[31]

> **the inhabitants of each world worship their own personal father**

Busy men and busy women!

## Women's Place in Mormon Heaven

God's wives are not counted as part of the Mormon Godhead. Because they eternally bear children they (through necessity) must play an integral part in the the plan of self-Exaltation to Godhood. Every time her husband wants to begin a new world she observes her usual role as a perpetual spiritual baby bearer - that is how she is acclaimed! She is never equal to her husband but always yielding perfect obedience to her husband. The Mormon Apostle Orson Pratt explains the role of women in eternity this way:

> But if we have a heavenly Mother as well as a heavenly Father, is it not right that we should worship the Mother of our spirits as well as the Father? No; for the Father of our spirits is at the head of the household, and his wives and children are required to yield the most perfect obedience to their great Head. It is lawful for the children to worship the King of Heaven, but not the "Queen of heaven . . . we are nowhere taught that Jesus prayed to His heavenly Mother. . .[32]

Brigham Young taught that every earth has its redeemer and tempter.[33] If so, each Mormon Goddess will see one of her sons become a devil and one third of her spirit children cast out for rebellion. She and Mr. God will mourn at their loss of many grandchildren and great grandchildren, etc., as will most of their entire posterity, worlds infinitum. Poor women! Poor men!

Brigham Young, referring to the subject of polygamy, not just during mortality but through all eternity as well, said:

> "If you wish to be Eves and mothers of human families you ought to bear the burden . . . Woe to you Eves if you proclaim or entertain feelings against this doctrine!".[34]

The Mormon Apostle Heber C. Kimball taught:

> If you oppose what is called the 'spiritual wife doctrine,' the Patriarchal Order, which is of God, that course will corrode you with a spirit of apostasy, and you will go overboard; still a great many may do so, and strive to justify themselves in it, but they are not justified of God.[35]

Mormon women should reflect upon the present belief in Mormonism that polygamy must again be practiced, and will always be so throughout eternity. You see, when I went to the Mormon temple to be married for time and all eternity, I swore an *oath of obedience* to my husband and the *law of the priesthood*, which law, according to the *Doctrine and Covenants*, includes the practice of polygamy.[36] Instead of the New and Everlasting Covenant being the covenant God made with Israel as described in the Bible,[37] the LDS Church has reinvented this covenant to include the Celestial marriage bond of polygamy. While incidents of

> *I swore an oath of obedience to my husband*

polygamy in the Old Testament were an accepted cultural occurrence, God never approved of it; in fact, He disapproved of it.[38] Throughout history men and women have grieved their disobedience to God's plan of monogamy, which God originally gave to Adam and Eve. I wonder how many Mormon women are aware that they will actually be only the first wife of many her husband may acquire in the Celestial kingdom of glory. The eternal role of a women in Mormonism insults me - it's tyrannical! I think such women do not progress but are relegated to being mere machinery. I'm thankful that the Bible teaches that men and women are equal in heaven.

## Men's Place in Mormon Heaven

In the Mormon publication, *The Ensign*, the Mormon Prophet Spencer W. Kimball addressed the priesthood holders:

> Brethren, 225,000 of you are here tonight. I suppose 225,000 of you may become gods. There seems to be plenty of space out there in the universe. And the Lord has proved that he knows

*how to do it. I think he could make, or probably have us help make, worlds for all of us, for every one of us 225,000.*[39]

Men receive acclamation and power in the Mormon heaven according to the number of wives and children they have. The Mormon Apostle Orson Pratt said, "While the Patriarch with his hundred wives, would multiply worlds on worlds . . . the other who had only secured himself one wife, would in the same period, just barely have peopled one world."[40]

But what of the following words from the *Book of Mormon*, which oppose polygamy?

*Wherefore, my brethren, hear me, and hearken to the words of the Lord: For there shall not any man among you have save it be one wife, and concubines he shall have none; For I, the Lord God, delight in the chastity of women. And whoredoms are an abomination before me; thus saith the Lord of Hosts.*[41]

In addition, unless the Mormon Church erases an entire section from the *Doctrine of Covenants*, this doctrine will continue to justify its ungodly view upon church members. In direct contradiction to the *Book of Mormon* quote above, the *Doctrine and Covenants* says one will be damned if the law is not practiced:

*Verily, thus saith the Lord, unto you my servant Joseph, that inasmuch as you have inquired of my hand to know and understand wherein I, the Lord justified my servants Abraham, Isaac, and Jacob, as also Moses, David and Solomon, my servants, as touching the principle and doctrine of their having many wives and concubines– Behold, and lo, I am the Lord thy God, and will answer thee concerning this matter. Therefore, prepare your heart to receive and obey the instructions . . . For behold I reveal unto you a new and everlasting covenant; and if ye abide not that covenant, then ye are damned; for no one can reject this covenant and be permitted to enter into my glory . . . And let mine handmaid, Emma Smith [Joseph Smith's wife] receive all those that have been given unto my servant Joseph, and are virtuous and pure before me; and those who are not pure, and have said they were pure, shall be destroyed, saith the Lord . . . And again, as pertaining to the law of the priesthood– if any man espouse a virgin, and desires to espouse another . . . he is justified; he cannot commit adultery with that belongeth unto him and to no one else. And if he have ten virgins given unto him by this law, he cannot commit adultery, for they belong to him, and they are given to him; therefore is he justified.*[42]

> **the only men who become God . . . enter into polygamy**

It is also interesting to note that the Mormon Manifesto, which mandates the cessation of polygamy, does not claim to be a revelation from God.[43] Also, the 1835 edition of the *Doctrine and Covenants* stands in agreement with the *Book of Mormon*, clearly stating that a man must have only one wife. See the exhibit on page 212. To complicate the issue of monogamy further, Brigham Young said, "The only men who become God, even the Sons of God, are those who enter into polygamy."[44] To Mormon men who believe they shall achieve Godhood Brigham Young said, ". . . you will have all your children come and report to you of their sayings and acts; and you will hold every son and daughter of yours responsible when you get the privilege of being an Adam on earth . . ."[45]

## No Worry – All is Well in Zion and Hell?

Can one suffer to a point of cleanliness? The following words by the Mormon Prophet Joseph Fielding Smith contradict much of the Standard Works and other "Living Oracles" of the LDS Church:

*It is decreed that the unrighteous shall have to spend their time during this thousand years in the prison house prepared for them where they can repent and cleanse themselves through the things which they shall suffer.*[46]

The view that they may suffer themselves clean is an outright insult to Jesus who already suffered, purchased, and purged us from our sins on Calvary's Tree. It may be equated with the belief in Purgatory, which concept, I remember, Mormons mock.

The present God of Mormonism promotes a belief in universal salvation. The following words are those of the Mormon Apostle, John A. Widsoe, only one among many statements proclaiming the Mormon doctrine of universal salvation:

*The meanest sinner will find some place in the heavenly realm . . . . In the Church of Jesus Christ of Latter-day Saints, there is no hell. All will find a measure of salvation . . .The gospel of Jesus Christ has no hell.*[47]

In many places the *Book of Mormon* disagrees with present LDS doctrine of universal salvation:

*But remember that he that persists in his own carnal nature, and goes on in the ways of sin and rebellion against God, remaineth in his fallen state and the devil hath all power over him. Therefore, he is as though there was no redemption made, being an enemy to God; and also is the devil an enemy to God.*[48]

*And behold, others he flattereth away, and telleth them there is no hell; and he saith unto them: I am no devil, for there is none — and thus he whispereth in their ears, until he grasps them with his awful chains, from whence there is no deliverance. Yea, they are grasped with death, and hell; and death, and hell, and the devil, and all that have been seized therewith must stand before the throne of God, and be judged according to their works, from which they must go into the place prepared for them, even a lake of fire and brimstone, which is endless torment. Therefore, wo be unto him that is at ease in Zion.*[49]

I find that in Mormonism's Law of Eternal Progression, whatever subject is broached, a variety of definitions are used. The LDS Church has a way of escaping its contradictions - a comfortable zone to salve the conscience, and keep one from personal scrutiny of church doctrine. On the one side, the Mormon Apostle Milton R. Hunter, explained that one must keep all the Mormon Laws and Ordinances and commandments in order to be exalted to Godhood.[50] Yet, the lowest of the Mormon kingdoms in eternity offers a better life than this present existence. Dismissing the giant contradictions found in Mormonism jeopardizes one's intimacy with the author of salvation. The Bible warns against persons neglecting their opportunities to repent in this life, "It is appointed unto man once to die, but after that the judgment . . ."[51] The Bible teaches, "There is a way which seemeth right unto a man, and the end thereof are the ways of death."[52] The Mormon Church would rather interpret this verse as, "There is a way which seemeth right unto a man, and the end thereof are the ways of life."

> *a comfortable zone to salve the conscience and keep one from personal scrutiny of church doctrine*

## Redefining Creation, God and Humans

Joseph Smith said, "In the beginning, the head of the Gods called a council of the Gods; and they came together and concocted a plan to create the world and people it."[53] The Holy Bible knows nothing about a council of the Gods.

Although not an official Mormon General Authority, W. Cleon Skousen was a well known and highly respected Mormon and considered among Mormon ranks as an authority concerning scriptural themes. Mr. Scousen served for 16 years in the FBI, and also served on the Brigham Young University faculty. Following is a quote from his book *The First 2,000 Years.*

> *the Gods . . . came together and concocted a plan to create the world and the people*

*But who is it that occupies a position great enough in the universe to require of the exalted Elohim his Godhood in case He should violate any of the principles of truth and justice? That there is such a power to which the Father is subject would appear obvious from the above scriptures.*

*Through modern revelation we learn that the universe is filled with vast numbers of intelligences, and we further learn that Elohim is God simply because all of these intelligences honor and sustain Him as such . . . Therefore, the Father is actually dependent upon their sustaining influence or honor to accomplish His purposes . . . God's "power" is derived from*

> the power of God
> would disintegrate

*the honor and support of the intelligences over whom He rules . . . But since God "acquired" the honor and sustaining influence of "all things" it follows as a correlary [sic] that if He should ever do anything to violate the confidence or "sense of justice" of these intelligences, they would promptly withdraw their support, and the power of God would disintegrate . . .*[54]

Scousen's words show the limitations of the Mormon polytheistic God. They indicate that laws are greater than the Creator who made the laws. The words also indicate that persons of intelligence have power to dethrone the God who made them. Such a puny God!

One General Authority, Marion G. Romney, referred to the Father God this way: "God is a perfected, saved soul enjoying eternal life."[55] In chapter five I related a discussion between my father and mother where my dad insisted that the church teaches that there was a time when God was less powerful than He is today. Later, in agreement with my father, I came across these words by the Mormon Apostle Milton R. Hunter. Mentioned before, the following quote emphasizes how the Mormon God became God:

> *From day to day He exerted His will vigorously, and as a result became thoroughly acquainted with the forces lying about Him. As he gained more knowledge through persistent effort and continuous industry . . . He grew in experience and continued to grow until He attained the status of Godhood. He became God by absolute obedience to all the eternal laws of the Gospel - by conforming His actions to all truth, and thereby became the author of eternal truth. Therefore the road that the Eternal Father followed to Godhood was one of living at all times a dynamic, industrious and completely righteous life. There is no other way to exaltation.*[56]

## The Question of Polytheism

As a member of the LDS Church I applauded the idea that God is a glorified resurrected man with a physical body as taught in the Mormon Standard Works.[57] According to Mormonism humans are of the same species as God; little gods in embryo, and that people can exalt themselves to the station of Gods.[58] None of these beliefs are even hinted at in the Bible. The Bible sets the matter straight, showing we are not of the same species as God. Notice the italics as follows: "Which was *the son* of Enos, which was *the son* of Seth, which was *the son* of Adam, which was *the son* of God."[59] The reason "the son" is in italics is to point out their absence in the Greek manuscripts. The verse literally reads ". . . which was of God." This does not in any way suggest a co-existence of man and God. Adam was of God in the sense that God *formed man out of the dust.*

Later, I learned that the Bible contains many verses debunking the belief that God is a glorified man. "For I am God and not man . . ."[60] Another verse: "God is not a man, that he should lie; He doesn't change his mind like humans do".[61] God never had a human character. He created man! Instead of eternal progression to Exaltation, I view the Mormon doctrine concerning the fall of man and his journey to Godhood as an ungodly regression. I vote that Mormons fire the resurrected glorified imaginary God-man! We have already seen that the Bible does not teach that God is a saved soul. Instead, He is the author and giver of salvation. When I think of Mormonism's imaginary God-man, I always think of the entire first chapter of Romans. Making God in the image of corruptible man is a fulfillment of Bible warnings such as the one below:

> *. . . they did not honor Him as God, or give thanks; but they became futile in their speculations, and their foolish heart was darkened. Professing to be wise, they became fools, and exchanged the glory of the incorruptible God for an image in the form of corruptible man and of birds and fourfooted animals and crawling creatures.*[62]

I consider this verse a powerful warning against humans placing their ideas above God's standards for measuring truth. The Bible reveals that God is steady and reliably the same.[63] This means that God has never been in a state of graduation. Biblical prophets always reveal the same God. Yet, while professing to be wise Mormonism changed from one God to a plurality of Gods. In 1852, Brigham Young taught as doctrine that Adam is God, and that one must embrace the doctrine in order to receive salvation. Without faltering the Adam God doctrine was taught by the church for more than 50 years, and was included in the

Temple Ceremony. Yet, the time came that the LDS Church vehemently denied that the Adam God doctrine was ever taught. We have already noted that the Mormon Apostle Bruce R. McConkie admitted that Adam-God doctrine was in fact taught by Brigham Young (see the exhibit on pages 201-202). Additionaly, the exhibits on 198-199 demonstrate Brigham Young's doctrine about Adam-God. These are only a few of some 500 photo copies Melaine shared with me about Adam-God. The church no longer teaches that Adam is God. The fact that the church no longer holds to this doctrine should identify Brigham Young as a false prophet who received false revelation about who God is.

In its development, Mormonism switched from one God to Adam-God and then to the present view of a plurality of Gods. This trend certainly shows that Mormon prophets have led people astray on the most critical doctrines –God and salvation. What if a coming Mormon prophet gives another version of God? Will the present Mormon view of God be dismissed by stating again that the living prophet takes precedence over the dead prophets, carrying more weight than any of the Standard Works of the church? Such would be the Mormon pattern. Biblical prophets speak in accord about the nature of God. The true God of the Bible cannot and does not contradict Himself.

## Implications of Remaining Polytheists

From LDS history and its sacred writings, we see conclusively that the modern day Mormon Church embraces polytheism as part of the LDS Law of Eternal Progression. The polytheism of Mormonism puts Mormons in opposition to the Bible. Even so, Mormons attempt to persuade the world that they are Christian too. Although some members of the LDS Church may argue that they only worship one of the Gods, they remain polytheists because they believe that there are many Gods, and that they too may become Gods.

The Bible, in contrast to Mormon theology, teaches only one God. The Bible teaches, "For there is one God, and one mediator between God and men, the man Christ Jesus."[64] Yet, the LDS Church seems to interpret the same verse this way: "For there are many Gods, and two mediators between the God of this earth and men; Joseph Smith and The Church of Jesus Christ of Latter-day Saints." God explains that His desire for us is that we know, understand and believe that He alone is God:

*You are My witnesses declares the LORD, and My servant, in order that you my know and believe Me, And understand that I am He. Before me there was no God formed, and there will be none after me. I, even I, am the LORD; and there is no savior besides Me.*[65]

God declares that He *alone* stretched out the heavens, and all their host:

*Thus saith the LORD, your Redeemer, and the one who formed you from the womb, "I the LORD am the maker of all things, Stretching out the heavens by Myself, And spreading out the earth all alone . . ."*[66]

Here is one more reminder from God that a belief in polytheism is incorrect:

*See now that I, I am He, And there is no god besides Me; It is who put to death and give life . . .*[67]

While the Bible does not speak of many true Gods it does speak of *so-called* gods.[68] That some say there is more than one God does not make it so. In order to retain their theology about God, eternal progression and Exaltation, the church attempts to skirt biblical passages like the ones above. One such excuse to disregard the pure intent of the Bible is to insist that church members only worship one of the countless Gods; the one who is the God of this world. How pitiful; the Bible clearly teaches that Satan is the god of this world:

*But if our gospel be hid, it is hid to them that are lost: In whom the god of this world hath blinded the minds of those which believe not, lest the light of the glorious gospel of Christ, who is the image of God, should shine unto them.*[69]

The host of biblical evidence concerning the true God of Israel judges heavily against LDS doctrine. One such verse is: "Hear, O Israel! The Lord is our God, the Lord is one!"[70] This verse, called the SH'MA, in all its attending understanding, is the Jewish and Christian confession of faith. The central message is

> *the SH'MA is the Jewish and Christian confession of faith*

one of instruction –to listen, respect, honor and proclaim monotheism! The SH'MA totally refutes and nullifies the Mormon idea of many Gods, or that persons may graduate into Gods or Goddesses over their own worlds. When asked what is the greatest of all commandments, Jesus quoted the SH'MA. His words:

> . . . *Hear, O Israel; the LORD our God is one LORD; and you shall love the LORD your God with all your heart, and with all your soul, and with all your mind, and with all your strength.*[71]

In Hebrew the word for *one* is *echad* which denotes a plural oneness –a compound unity. Failing to recognize the truth of the SH'MA is to profane and make common the Name of God. Better to honor the true God of Israel! To honor Him, one must forsake the belief in polytheism. Humans receive salvation, not Godhood, and salvation comes only through God's gift of grace through faith.[72] Christ's death alone meets Atonement for our sins.[73]

It is a scriptural admonition that we pray for blinders to be removed from our eyes so that we may share in the light of the true glorious Gospel of grace. The very idea of polytheism goes against the entire grain of the Holy Bible. It is particularly offensive to God for persons to believe that more Gods than He exist. Look to the Bible! There is only One God! In fact, we have seen that the belief that any human can become like God- or a God - is Satan's big lie. This is the lie that Satan (the god of this world) used against Adam and Eve. One of the strongest teachings in the Bible is that man cannot become a God - period! But Satan knows our egos, and tempts man accordingly. Those who persist in the quest to become Gods will find themselves given over to a strong delusion to believe that lie.[74]

Joseph Smith taught that those who become Gods will be raised to dwell in everlasting burnings.[75] From the Scripture verses regarding the place called Hell, one can see that a definition of everlasting burnings involves and describes a place where Satan and his followers will spend eternity.[76] To remain a polytheist is to place oneself outside of God's care and protection.

The Mormon Law of Eternal Progression is a mere product of man trying to understand God through his own vain imaginings. God, with the strongest of terms counters the Mormon twisted perversion of the truth, with the true Gospel which the book of Jude explains was delivered once for all.[77] This verse denies any restoration in the manner the LDS Church proclaims. The true Gospel does not include the Mormon polytheistic doctrine of a self-Exaltation.

## Mormon Alleged Proof-texts

The LDS Church makes use of a few verses from the Bible to support the Law of Eternal Progression (also called Exaltation). Let us direct our attention to verses commonly used by the Mormon Church to support their view of God and man.

The first one I will mention concerns the word *image* in the verse, "Who (Jesus) being the brightness of His glory, and the express image of His person . . ."[78] I was taught to use this verse to show non-members that God has a body of flesh and bones like man has. But this Mormon explanation of the verse does not fit the Greek text used for the word *image*. The Greek word for *image* in this verse is *karakter*, from which we get our English word, *character*.[79] The character of Jesus was in the *image* of God, not his physical body.

Another verse Mormons use to promote their belief in polytheism is from the book of Psalms, "I have said, Ye are gods; and all of you are the children of the most High."[80] Because of the Mormon belief in polytheism, members of the LDS Church feel free to point to this verse as evidence that persons may be classified as Gods. But Jesus quoted this verse[81] against His accusers. Both Scriptures in the Old and New Testament refer to those who disobey God's laws. Both passages are an impeachment of unjust judges, who arrogantly ruled as gods. God renounces their behavior; pronouncing judgment upon them. God passes sentence upon them announcing that they, just like all men, will die. Moses was a prophet of God, and Pharaoh looked upon Moses as a God.[82] But Moses was not a God. Using these verses to uphold the Mormon belief in a plurality of Gods is to oppose the Word of God which countless times emphatically declares that there is only one God, and that there shall never be another God. Therefore man cannot become a God.

Another proof text is found in Matthew's Gospel and concerns the word *perfect*. "Be ye therefore perfect even as your Father which is in heaven is perfect."[83] As Mormons we used this passage to support our idea that man may become a God. This passage does not mean that man may become a God! The Greek word from which we derive our word *perfect* is *teleios*. In this verse *teleios* refers to *maturity within our roles*.[84] Paul uses this word in his letter to the Phillipians, "Let us therefore, as many as be perfect, be thus minded and if in anything ye be otherwise minded, God shall reveal even this unto you."[85] Again, the Greek word here is *teleios* which means *mature*. This passage does not support the Mormon belief that we are of the same species as God, or that God has a body like ours, or that people are entitled to do all the things that God

> *we are of the same species as God . . . and are entitled to do all the things that God has done*

has done. One may become a mature man but not a God! God creates from nothing that we see or comprehend. From the biblical text we read "By the word of the Lord were the heavens made; and all the host of them by the breath of his mouth."[86] Man creates from God's creation. God is the I AM - I am because He Is! Our perfection is in Jesus.

The LDS Church uses the same verse from Matthew's Gospel to show that through works one may achieve self-Exaltation. But in the context of the passage,[87] Jesus is speaking of those who display their good works without an inside change of the heart. We are called to take off the filthy rags of our good deeds[88] and put on the righteousness of Christ.[89] Through Christ we receive the new birth, our sins are paid for and we are able to mature into the full stature of what God's call is upon our lives. From the time of the new birth, which is the very moment the Holy Spirit makes His abode in us, we are better enabled to yield our lives to God. With good deeds following we begin the process of maturing in Godly *character*. Our responsibility is to heed the Holy Spirit, to meditate in God's Word, to pray, and to follow Godly examples. Believers are given the promise that as we co-operate with God, He will aid our maturity, "Being confident of this very thing, that he which hath begun a good work in you will perform it until the day of Jesus Christ."[90]

To embrace the idea that God is just a little above man instead of man being a little below angels is entirely wrong. God is always *other than* man. When we become born again we participate in the divine nature for the function of eternal fellowship. It is true that those who receive and believe truth become joint heirs with Christ, "And if children, then heirs; heirs of God, and joint-heirs with Christ; if it so be we suffer with him, that we may be glorified together."[91] But we participate in, not partake of, the divine nature, "Through these He has given us His very great and precious promises, so that through them you may participate in the divine nature and escape the corruption in the world caused by evil desires."[92]

## The Living Prophet and the First Presidency

As I see it, the only way to retain such a mythological system of belief as the Mormon Law of Eternal Exaltation is to indelibly print in the minds of church members the idea that their leaders supply all support for their earthly and heavenly needs. This necessitates an inordinate reliance on men rather than Scripture. A 1980 BYU Devotional address by Mormon Prophet Ezra Taft Benson (President of the Council of Twelve and once Secretary of Agriculture under President Eisenhower) outlined for the church what he termed the *Fourteen Fundamentals in Following the Prophet*.[93] Each of the fourteen take away one's personal accountability to God, and emphasize an unhealthy affection to men and church. Here are a few of the fourteen [taken directly from the official "Press Copy" version released by the LDS Church]:

SECOND: The living prophet is more vital to us than the standard works.

THIRD: The living prophet is more important to us than a dead prophet.

FOURTH: The prophet will never lead the Church astray.

SIXTH: The prophet does not have to say "Thus Saith the Lord" to give us scripture.

NINTH: The prophet can receive revelation on any matter, temporal or spiritual.

FOURTEENTH: The prophet and the presidency–the living prophet and the First Presidency–follow them and be blessed–reject them and suffer.

*God never told anyone to blindly honor men who lead churches*

Statements like these are prevalent among Mormon writings. God never told anyone to blindly honor men who lead churches. Instead, people ought to direct homage to God. In the end, it is He to whom we will answer.[94]

The Bible warns us that even demons recognize that there is only *one* God, a fact which makes them fear and tremble, "You believe that God is one. You do well; the demons also believe, and shudder."[95]

*Mormonism twists the true nature of God and exalts man*

Many Bible verses[96] give serious warnings to those who add anything to God's Word in an effort to present a different Gospel message. Without so much as a blush Mormonism adds to the Bible its doctrines concerning God, human salvation, and Exaltation through works. How ungodly the Mormon Laws and Ordinances are, and how futile and fatal it is to trust in them instead of God's Son alone as the means of salvation. A clear example of this twisting is how the Mormon Law of Eternal Exaltation exonerates the un-biblical belief in polytheism. Mormonism twists the true nature of God and exalts man. Mormon doctrine is man-centered, not God-centered. If the Mormon doctrine of God and man were correct, the first verse in the Bible would read: "In the beginning man . . ." rather than "In the beginning God . . ." The belief concerning both God and man as defined in the Mormon Law of Eternal Exaltation, separate Mormonism from biblical reality.

Trusting in the belief in polytheism, Mormons pursue their own personal enlightenment – Exaltation to Godhood. By Mormon requirements, few Mormons would reach the goal of Exaltation. As before mentioned, even if it were possible to become a God the position could be soured by the ever present possibility that if not careful one may in the future lose one's Godhood in a heaven where Gods can be dethroned. God dethroned? Such heaven! Such puny Gods! The Mormon God is only an imaginary God! In reality the Mormon Law of Eternal Progression is a mere mythical fantasy-an ungodly regression.

Rather than believing that the Gods came together and concocted a plan, one ought to exalt the one true God. I trust in the biblical message of redemption, not the prophets of Mormonism who profess another Gospel message. I rest my future into the hands of the gracious only true God, Who makes this promise to true believers, "But as it is written, Eye hath not seen, nor ear heard, neither hath it entered into the heart of man, the things which God hath prepared for them that love him."[97] Believers look foreword to eternal blessings inside the eternal city where there is no need of the sun or the moon to light it, for the glory of God and the Lamb illuminate it.[98]

An important question for a Mormon to come to grips with is "Do I worship God in spirit and in truth or do I worship the doctrine of men?" Jesus said, "God is a spirit; and they that worship Him must worship Him in spirit and in truth."[99] Members of the present Mormon Church are taught that God isn't a spirit, but that He has a spirit, and that He also has a resurrected body of flesh and bones just like ours. Far removed from the biblical measurement for truth, the Mormon Gospel does not worship God in spirit and in truth. Instead, it depicts only works of the flesh. By embracing the un-biblical doctrines of polytheism and the self-Exaltation of man the Mormon Church calls good evil and evil it calls good.[100]

This chapter provided several examples of how Mormonism was concocted by man. The next chapter delves deeper into the central Mormon claim to authority –the priesthood.

(Note that these LDS references use the capital letter G in the words Gods and Godhood.)

1    Student Manual Religion 345, Presidents of the Church, 1979, p. 140.
2    Journal of Discourses, vol. 6, p.4.
3    Pearl of Great Price, Book of Abraham 3 and 4.
4    Hebrews 11:3; Psalms 33:6.
5    Book of Mormon, 3 Nephi 9:15.
6    The Seer, p. 37.
7    Hymns, Church of Jesus Christ of Latter-Day Saints, p. 138.
8    Hymns, Church of Jesus Christ of Latter-Day Saints, p. 257.
9    Jeremiah 1:4-5.
10   Romans 4:17.
11   Job 38:7.
12   Romans 9:11.
13   1 Corinthians 15:46.
14   Zechariah 12:1; Isaiah 44:24.
15   Genesis 3:1-5.
16   What's Going On In Here?, pp.17-18.
17   John 8:44.
18   Pearl of Great Price, Moses 5:10-12.
19   Doctrines of Salvation, vol. 1, pp. 114-115.
20   Deseret News, Church News Section, July, 31, 1965, p. 7.
21   Isaiah 14:12-14; Genesis 3:5.
22   Romans 5:12.
23   John 3:16.
24   John  3:3.
25   Mormon Doctrine, p. 118.
26   Teachings of the Prophet Joseph Smith, compiled by Joseph Fielding Smith, p. 227.
27   Gospel Through the Ages, p. 117.
28   Gospel Through the Ages, p. 115.
29   Matthew 22:30.
30   Articles of Faith, p. 473.
31   The Seer, p. 37.
32   The Seer, p. 159.
33   Journal of Discourses, vol. 14, p. 71.
34   Journal of Discourses, vol. 12, p. 97.
35   Journal of Discourses, vol. 3, p. 125.
36   Doctrine and Covenants, section 132.
37   Isaiah 55:3; Jeremiah 33:20; Ezekiel 16:60, 37:26; Hebrews 13:20.
38   Deuteronomy 17:17.
39   The Ensign, November 1975, p. 80.
40   The Seer, p. 39.
41   Jacob 2:27-28.
42   Doctrine of Covenants 132:1, 4, 52, 61, 62.
43   The "Manifesto" is found at the very end of the Doctrine and Covenants.
44   Journal of Discourses, vol. 11, p. 269.
45   Journal of Discourses, vol. 4, p. 271.
46   Doctrines of Salvation, vol. 3, p. 60.
47   Joseph Smith —Seeker After Truth, pp. 177-178.
48   Book of Mormon, Mosiah 16:5.
49   Book of Mormon, 2 Nephi 28:22-24.
50   Gospel Through the Ages, p. 115.
51   Hebrews 9:27.
52   Proverbs 14:12.
53   Journal of Discourses, vol. 6, p. 5.
54   The First 2000 Years, pp. 354-355.
55   Salt Lake Tribune, April 3, 1977.
56   The Gospel Through the Ages, pp. 114-115.
57   Doctrine and Covenants 131:22.
58   Doctrine and Covenants 132:20; History of the Church, vol. 6, p. 306.
59   Luke 3:38.
60   Hosea 11:9.
61   Numbers 23:19.
62   Romans 1:21-23.
63   Malachi 3:6.
64   1 Timothy 2:5.
65   Isaiah 43:10-11.
66   Isaiah  44:24.
67   Deuteronomy 32:39.
68   1 Corinthians 8:5-6.
69   2 Corinthians 4:3-4.
70   Deuteronomy 6:4.
71   Mark 12:29-30,  see also Strong's Exhaustive Concordance of the Bible, Hebrew Dictionary, #259.
72   Ephesians 2:8-9.
73   1 Corinthians 15:1-4.
74   2 Thessalonians 2:9-11.
75   Teachings of the Prophet Joseph Smith, p. 347.
76   Revelation 20:10.
77   Jude 3.
78   Hebrews 1:3.
79   Strong's Exhaustive Concordance of the Bible, Greek Dictionary of the New Testament, #5481.
80   Psalms 82:6.
81   John 10:34.
82   Exodus 4:16, 7:1.
83   Matthew 5:48.
84   Strong's Exhaustive Concordance of the Bible, Greek Dictionary of the New Testament, #5046.
85   Phillipians 3:15.
86   Psalms 33:6.
87   Matthew 5:48.
88   Isaiah 64:6.
89   Colossians 3:9-10.
90   Philippians 1:6.
91   Romans 8:17.
92   2 Peter 1:4.
93   Provo Herald, Feb. 26,1980.
94   Hebrews 9:27.
95   James 2:19.
96   Deuteronomy 4:2,  Revelation 22:18,19, Galatians 1:6-7.
97   1 Corinthians 2:9.
98   Revelation 21:22-23.
99   John 4:24.
100  Isaiah 5:20.

# 10. Where Do You Get Your Authority?

*But as many as received him, to them gave he power to become the sons of God, even to them that believe on his name.*

John 1:3

## The First Vision

In the Mormon account of Joseph Smith's first vision, it is alleged that the Father and His Son Jesus Christ appeared on earth to instruct Joseph Smith that he was chosen to restore the lost truth and authority of the Gospel back to earth. Mormon Apostle McConkie admonishes members of the church to remember with reverence the visitation. The vision was a precursor to the restoration of the Mormon priesthood, where Mormons claim to get their authority and its attending ordinances and practices. In Bruce R. McConkie's own words:

> *That glorious theophany which took place in the spring of 1820 and which marked the opening of the dispensation of the fulness of times is called the first vision. It is rated as first from the standpoint of time and of pre-eminent importance. In it Joseph Smith saw and conversed with the Father and the Son, both of which exalted personages were personally present before him as he lay enwrapped in the Spirit and over-shadowed by the Holy Ghost . . . This transcendent vision was the beginning of latter-day revelation; it marked the opening of the heavens after the long night of apostate darkness . . . Through it the creeds of Christendom were shattered to smithereens . . . This vision was the most important event in all world history from the day of Christ's ministry to the glorious hour when it occurred.*[1]

> **the creeds of Christendom were shattered to smithereens**

Not many members of the LDS Church are aware that there are many contradicting versions of this vision. I have included a comparison on page 211 in the Exhibit Section. The quote below is the present standard version:

> *My object in going to inquire of the Lord was to know which of all the sects was right, that I might know which to join . . . I asked the personages who stood above me in the light, which of all the sects was right–and which I should join. I was answered that I must join none of them, for they were all wrong; and the Personage who addressed me said that all their creeds were an abomination in his sight; that those professors were all corrupt . . .*[2]

This vision and message is central to the Mormon belief that only they hold the authority of the priesthood. Mormons are taught that their priesthood will eventually prevail against all false abominable creeds and professors of religion and eventually cover the whole world.[3]

## Empty Claims to Priesthood Restoration

> **God restored power and authority through Joseph Smith**

The Mormon Church teaches that soon after the early apostles there came a great apostasy which lasted 1800 years until the *final dispensation of times* was ushered in by Joseph Smith, God's first latter-day prophet. For that long duration of time, Mormons are taught, there was no divine priesthood authority to officiate in the sacred ordinances of the Gospel. The Mormon Church proclaims that God restored power and authority, or in a word the *priesthood*, to usher in the the ordinances of the Gospel on earth through His latter-day servant Joseph Smith. The church preaches that all truth operates through the power of the Mormon Melchizedek priesthood. Members of the Mormon faith are taught that the Mormon priesthood holds the keys of the Kingdom of God. They hold strong the belief that outsiders claiming to hold the priesthood are impostors. Vested only within the Mormon faith, this priesthood is the channel for all of Mormon doctrine.

According to the LDS Church version of priesthood, it was on May 15th, 1829, that John the Baptist returned to the earth as a resurrected man and conferred the Aaronic priesthood upon Joseph Smith and Oliver Cowdery. The words of the ordination, so often repeated in Mormonism are as follows:

> *Upon you my fellow servants, in the name of the Messiah I confer the Priesthood of Aaron, which holds the keys of the ministering of angels, and of the gospel of repentance, and of baptism by immersion for the remission of sins; and this shall never be taken again from the earth, until the sons of Levi do offer again an offering unto the Lord in righteousness.*[4]

All of the present Section 13, (the words above) detailing the ordination are absent from the original *Book of Commandments*, later renamed the *Doctrine and Covenants*. How shocking it was for me to learn of its absence.

> **there is no difinitive account of the event conferring the Melchezedek Priesthood on Joseph Smith or Oliver Cowdery**

The resurrected apostles, Peter, James, and John, whom the Mormon Church believes held the keys to the Melchizedek priesthood, came back to earth to confer the Melchizedek priesthood to Joseph Smith and Oliver Cowdery. The account of this ordination is found in the *Doctrine and Covenants,*[5] and leads one to believe that the ordination from Peter, James, and John has always been common knowledge in the church. However, it is not common knowledge that this account concerning Peter, James, and John was added later to the Standard Works. Verses 8 and 12 of section 27 were not in the revelation as it first appeared in the *Book of Commandments*. All in all some 400 words were added to section 27 of the present *Doctrine and Covenants*. Shockingly, there is no definitive account of the event conferring of the Melchizedek priesthood on Joseph Smith or Oliver Cowdery in the *History of the Church*, or any of the early Mormon historical accounts. There is no support for the Mormon claim concerning Peter, James and John bestowing priesthood to anyone. How curious that these events are not mentioned in the early church history, unless they were added later.

Both accounts of the appearances and ordinations are crucial to the Mormon belief in a restoration of the Aaronic and Melchizedek priesthoods. They are common knowledge in Mormonism. Altogether, the history of the Mormon Church makes it difficult to believe the events ever happed at all. Even if they had happened they would have been demonic impostures because the account does not agree with God's Word concerning priesthood.

Mormons now receive their priesthood through a practice called the *laying on of the hands*. The practice of the laying on of the hands is a required procedure necessary for the transferal and reception of the Mormon priesthood to its members. The Mormon priesthood is presently given only to males and is always transferred by legal Mormon male administrators. It is expected that each worthy Mormon boy of twelve years of age receives the priesthood.

In bestowing the priesthood by the laying on of the hands, the LDS Church places the cart before the horse. Before receiving the true priesthood described in the Bible, persons must already be a child in the family of God. Note the future tense of the words to *become*, in the verse below:

> *But as many as received Him, to them gave He power to become the sons of God, even to them that believe on His name.*[6]

Also notice the word *power* in the same verse. From the original Greek language *Strongs Concordance* aids us to the proper understanding of the verse. The word *power* from the Greek language is *eksousia*, meaning "in the sense of ability); privilege, i.e. (subj.) force, capacity, competency, freedom, or (obj.) mastery of control), delegated influence:- authority, jurisdiction, liberty, power, right, strength."[7]

Therefore, *to become a child of God and to hold the authority* described in the above quote one must receive salvation just as the loving true God of the Bible instructed:

> *Verily, verily, I say unto thee, except a man be born again, he cannot see the kingdom of God . . . . That which is born of the flesh is flesh; and that which is born of the Spirit is spirit. Marvel not that I said unto thee, Ye must be born again.*[8]

It is at the time of the required new birth, (when one becomes a child by adoption into the family of God) that God bestows power and authority (priesthood) to the believer, not before. Believers in Christ become God's children –we have not always been children of God. Simply stated, true believers receive the priesthood through faith in the Son of God. It is then, regardless of age or sex, that God bestows authority and relationship. This event establishes humans as members of the God's Royal Priesthood, at which time there is a supernatural transferal out of darkness into God's marvelous light.[9]

While the Mormon priesthood is transmitted through the *laying on of the hands* by a Mormon priesthood holder, the biblical priesthood is non-transferrable:

> *But this man, because he continueth forever hath an unchangeable priesthood.*[10]

The word *unchangeable* comes from the Greek word *aparabatos*, which means, *"not passing away, i.e. untransferable, unchangeable."*[11] The margin in my King James Bible says: ". . . which passes not from one another." Therefore, the priesthood is not transferred through the laying on of hands, as Mormons practice. The truth is that God's Royal Priesthood was not restored to earth, since it never departed from the earth. Jesus is the only High Priest after the order of Melchizedek.

## Proper Lineage and Race?

In the Mormon faith, the Melchizedek priesthood is the authority behind the rituals that transpire within the walls of LDS temples. Without the Mormon priesthood there would be no temple ceremonies, ordinances, rites and sealings. In their temples ordinances of salvation and Exaltation are performed for themselves and on behalf of those who died before hearing the Mormon Gospel. McConkie explained that before ordinances for the dead can be performed within the temple, genealogical research is necessary for the identification of the dead.[12] Without the gathering of genealogy for names, the proxy work performed within the temples could not occur. That is the reason behind the vast genealogical resources of the Mormon Church. Patriarchal Blessings, which are channeled through the Mormon priesthood, allegedly reveal a church member's lineage.

When I was fourteen, I received from my Stake Patriarch a recommend of worthiness to receive my Patriarchal Blessing. Patriarchal Blessings, I was taught, are given only to Mormons because no one else holds the priesthood authority to bestow them. Here are excerpts from my Patriarchal Blessing:

> *. . . by the authority of the holy priesthood in me vested and my calling as a patriarch to the church of Jesus Christ of Latter-day saints, I give unto you a blessing which will be a comfort and a guide throughout life and declare you to be of the lineage of Ephraim . . . Dear sister, you are one of the chosen of God to come forth in the dispensation of the fulness of time . . . if you study the gospel you will be enlightened in its principles and be a savior in Zion to the*

*living as well as those who have gone beyond . . . You will find a mate who will accompany you to the house of the Lord and there receive the greatest blessings that can be given to you in this life and in the eternities — exaltation in the kingdom of God . . . Dear sister, I seal you up to come forth in the first resurrection of the just and ask you to bear in mind that all blessings are predicated upon your faithfulness and seal these blessings upon you by the authority vested in the name of Jesus Christ, Amen.*

This blessing guided me for many years and I was faithful to keep its admonitions, but the time came when I could see that the blessing given to me through the power of Mormon priesthood was not of God.

The blessing revealed other aspects concerning the direction I should direct my life, but I've not included them here. Then though, I was reassured that I descended from the tribe of Ephraim. As a female I could share in the blessings of the priesthood, but I could not hold the priesthood. Mormon sacred writings make known that their priesthood cannot be held by all races and is only given to male members. Tracing genealogy also determines whether one is of the proper designated lineage or race to hold the Mormon priesthood. I was shocked to discover that the lineage both as explained in Mormon extra-biblical Scripture, the writings of Mormon prophets, and Patriarchal Blessings show that their exclusive claim to the priesthood is flawed. Let me explain.

According to LDS doctrine anyone of Egyptian descent is forbidden to hold the priesthood.

Nearly all members of the Mormon Church are told in their Patriarchal Blessings (like mine quoted earlier) that they are of the lineage of Ephraim. There are a few from Manasseh. While it is possible that some Mormons may be of these tribes, we discover from the Old Testament that these two tribes do not qualify to hold the priesthood.

But a serious investigation of Mormon literature reveals most Mormons descend from either the tribes of Ephram or Manasseh which trace their roots to Egypt. The *Book of Abraham* (in the *Pearl of Great Price*), teaches that the Egyptians sprang from the Canaanites (Ham), who have no right (according to LDS doctrine) to hold the priesthood:

> *Now the King of Egypt was a descendant from the loins of Ham, and was a partaker of the blood of the Canaanites by birth. From this descent sprang all the Egyptians, and thus the blood of the Canaanites was preserved in the land. The land of Egypt being first discovered by a woman, who was the daughter of Ham, and the daughter of Egyptus, which in the Chaldean signifies that which is forbidden . . . and thus, from Ham, sprang that race which preserved the curse in the land . . . Now, Pharaoh being of that lineage by which he could not have the right of Priesthood, notwithstanding the Pharaohs would fain claim it . . .*[13]

We learn from the Bible, book of Genesis, that Ephraim and Manasseh are descended through Asenath, Joseph's Egyptian wife.[14] *The Book of Abraham* makes it very clear that anyone of Egyptian decent are of the wrong lineage to hold the priesthood. This makes the Mormon claim to priesthood through the lineage of Ephraim and Manasseh an impossibility!

The operation of the Mormon priesthood is further complicated as we look to the following words of Brigham Young concerning black people:

> *. . . the first presidency, the twelve, the high counsel, the Bishoprick, [sic] and all the elders of Israel, suppose we summon them to appear here, and here declare that it is right to mingle our seed, with the black race of Cain, that they shall come in with us and be partakers with us of all the blessings God has given to us. On that very day, and from the hour we should do so, the priesthood is taken from this Church and kingdom and God leaves us to our fate. The moment we consent to mingle with the seed of Cain, the Church must go to destruction, —we should receive the curse which has been placed upon the seed of Cain, and never more be numbered with the children of Adam who are heirs to the Priesthood until that curse be removed.*[15]

The church now shares its priesthood with the black race. So, if Brigham Young was correct, the LDS priesthood is lost.

Growing up in Mormonism, I was taught that one drop of Black blood disqualifies one from the priesthood, and that reason was always used as ammunition against intermarriage. Brigham Young taught that if the white man, who belongs to the chosen seed, mixes his blood with the seed of Cain, the penalty under the law of God is death on the spot.[16] However, it was on June 8, 1978 that the church, through the Mormon Prophet Spencer W. Kimball, caved into pressure from the outside and shared the priesthood with the African races. A 1978 *Deseret News*,[17] the church quoted the *Journal of Discourses*,[18] out of context, making it appear that it was now the Lord's will to give African races the priesthood. But, Brigham Young really said concerning the Blacks:

> *"How long is that race to endure the dreadful curse that is upon them? That curse will remain upon them and they never can hold the Priesthood or share in it until all the other descendants of Adam have received the promises and enjoyed the blessings of the Priesthood and the keys thereof."*[19]

The belief that the African race must not be given the priesthood was established by many prophets of the LDS Church, including Joseph Fielding Smith:

> *Not only was Cain called upon to suffer, but because of his wickedness he became the father of an inferior race. A curse was placed upon him and that curse has been continued through his lineage and must do so while time endures. Millions of souls have come into this world cursed with a black skin and have been denied the privilege of Priesthood and the fulness of the blessings of the gospel . . . . they have been made to feel their inferiority and have been separated from the rest of mankind from the beginning.*[20]

> *millions of souls have come into this world cursed with a black skin and have been denied the privilege of Priesthood*

Neither does the Bible agree with the LDS concept of genealogy. The Bible reveals the genealogical record necessary to identify the true Messiah. Jesus Himself completely fulfilled the genealogical Messianic prophecies. Biblical genealogy also aids in the comprehension of the end time prophecy as it relates to people and nations. There is no extra-biblical purpose for genealogy; not baptizing for the dead, not searching out individual lineage for the bestowal of Mormon priesthood, nor a requirement to live in the Mormon Celestial kingdom after mortality. Consider the Mormon usage of genealogy in the light of the following Bible verse: "Neither give heed to fables and endless genealogies, which minister questions rather than godly edifying which is in faith . . ."[21] The Bible makes no distinction between race and priesthood.

## Aaronic Priesthood

Let's take a moment to consider the biblical qualifications for the holding of the priesthood before and after Christ. While Mormons claim to have the Aaronic priesthood, the Bible teaches that the Aaronic priesthood was held only by descendants of Aaron, who were of the tribe of Levi, and only by the sons of Aaron, "And thou shalt appoint Aaron and his sons, and they shall wait on their priest's office: and the stranger that cometh nigh shall be put to death."[22]

Examine what the *Doctrine and Covenants* says about the Aaronic priesthood, "Why it is called the lesser priesthood is because it is an appendage to the greater or Melchizedek priesthood . . . No man has a legal right to this office, to hold the keys of this priesthood, except he be a literal descendant of Aaron."[23] Simply put, neither the *Doctrine and Covenants* nor the Bible support the Mormon idea of Aaronic priesthood, since very few Mormons claim to be of literal decent of Aaron. They are neither from Levi, nor the family of Aaron.

God was very serious about calling priests exclusively from the family of Aaron.[24] We read of God's displeasure that Jeroboam made priests from among all the people who were not of the sons of Levi. This was a great sin, and resulted in the destruction of Jeroboam's kingdom and the death of all his family. We also read of the case of Korah.[25] Korah was a cousin of Aaron. He was a Levite (correct tribe); but was not of Aaron's family, therefore he had no right to the priesthood. God was so displeased that Korah sought the priesthood that He caused the ground to open up and swallow Korah and his company.[26]

Since I was a small child I was taught to ask non-members the question, "Where do you get your authority?" Then I would quote the Mormon priesthood proof-text from the epistle to the Hebrews."And no man taketh this honour to himself, but he that is called of God as was Aaron."[27] But, within the church itself this method of reasoning is faulty. According to the *Doctrine and Covenants*, Aaron was called by the Lord's own voice.[28] According to the Bible, Aaron's ordination ceremony lasted a week and involved the sacrifice of a bull or a ram, and the using of oil, olives, and wine.[29] None of the above fits the Mormon priesthood calling.

The duties of the Priests are recorded in the Old Testament[30] and further expounded on in the New Testament.[31] These priests served in the sacrificial duties. Mormon priests do not fill these duties. The blood sacrificial duties of the Aaronic priesthood were replaced with the final blood sacrafice of the Messiah who gave his life for us.

This priesthood was replaced with the perfect lamb Sacrifice of Jesus.[32] Therefore, there was no more need for priests to mediate or for this type of blood sacrificial offering in the Old Testament. All was fulfilled in Jesus, the only mediator between God and man.[33]

## Melchizedek Priesthood

The biblical priests concerned themselves with the holiness of God and His remedy for sin. Mormon priesthood, on the other hand, deals with a human striving to become a God. According to the Bible, no one but the true Messiah holds the priesthood after the order of Melchizedek:

> . . . the new High Priest who came with the rank of Melchizedek, did not become a priest by meeting the old requirement of belonging to the tribe of Levi, but on the basis of power flowing from a life that cannot end.[34]

The Greek meaning of this verse expresses an indestructible or indissoluble life. Only Jesus meets the biblical standard: " . . . the blessed and only Potentate, the King of Kings, and Lord of Lords; Who only hath immortality, dwelling in the light which no man can approach unto . . ."[35]

The claims to which Mormons hold surrounding the origin of its priesthood are false. The Mormon priesthood is only an invented priesthood. The Bible in no way supports the Mormon version of priesthood.

The actual authority of the priesthood of all believers never left the earth because there was never a total apostasy from the Gospel. Even Elijah believed he was the only believer left in an evil world, but God revealed to him that there were seven thousand in Israel, who had not bowed unto the false god Baal.[36]

God has always kept His Kingdom and a remnant of believers on the earth. The following verse from the epistle of Paul to the Hebrews is one of many Scriptures which say so, "Wherefore receiving a kingdom which cannot be moved, let us have grace, whereby we may serve God acceptably with reverence and godly fear."[37]

The new birth (receiving God's means of redemption) gives me relationship, identification, and authority of the priesthood. This authority, or priesthood, comes to persons male and female, who become children of God through the new birth. The emphasis is on a personal relationship with God, not which church to join or locating a church which believes that it alone has the priesthood. A relationship with Christ is of primary importance. The Mormon claim to the priesthood is dispensed through man-made channels. On the other hand, the Bible explains that every person may come to Christ at which time God bestows authoritative power (the priesthood) to the believer,[38] based on His endless life.[39]

The priesthood of all believers is described below. It is the priesthood to which I hold.

> Ye also, as lively stones, are built upon a spiritual house, an holy priesthood, to offer up spiritual sacrifices, acceptable to God by Jesus Christ . . . But ye are a chosen generation, a royal priesthood, an holy nation, a peculiar people; that ye should shew forth the praises of him who hath called you out of darkness into his marvellous light, which in times past were not a people, but are now the people of God, which had not obtained mercy, but now have obtained mercy.[40]

The Mormon teaching about the priesthood is peculiar for certain, but not royal and peculiar in the same sense voiced in the quote above. The Mormon priesthood in no way resembles the priesthood of the Bible. All persons male and female are offered the true priesthood of God, and all may receive it through saving faith in Jesus, the Sacrificial Lamb, who shed His blood in our behalf. Praises to Him forever!

1   Mormon Doctrine, pp. 284-285.

2   Pearl of Great Price, Joseph Smith 2:16-20; History of the Church, vol. 1, pp. 5-6.

3   History of the Church, vol. 6. p. 365.

4   Doctrine and Covenants 13.

5   Doctrine and Covenants 27:8-13.

6   John 1:12.

7   Strong's Exhaustive Concordance of the Bible, Dictionary of the Greek New Testament, p. 30.

8   John 3:5-7.

9   1 Peter 2:9.

10  Hebrews 7:24.

11  Strong's Exhaustive Concordance of the Bible, Dictionary of the Greek New Testament, p. 13.

12  Mormon Doctrine, p. 308.

13  Pearl of Great Price, Book of Abraham 1:21-27.

14  Genesis 41:45, 50-52.

15  Brigham Young Addresses, Feb. 5, 1852, Ms d. 1234, box 48, Folder 3, LDS Archives.

16  Journal of Discourses, vol. 10, p. 110.

17  Deseret News, Salt Lake City, UT, June 17, 1978.

18  Journal of Discourses, vol. 10, p. 110.

19  Journal of Discourses, vol. 7, p. 291.

20  The Way to Perfection, p. 101.

21  1 Timothy 1:4.

22  Numbers 3:10.

23  Doctrine and Covenants 107:14-16.

24  1 Kings 12 and 13.

25  Numbers 16:1.

26  Numbers 16:32.

27  Hebrews 5:4.

28  Doctrine and Covenants 132:59.

29  Exodus 29:35-38.

30  Exodus 29:38-44.

31  Hebrews 5:1; 8:3.

32  Revelation 13:8.

33  1 Timothy 2:5; Hebrews 7:24-25; John 14: 6.

34  Hebrews 7:15-16.

35  1 Timothy 6:15-16.

36  1 Kings 19:18.

37  Hebrews 12:28.

38  John 1:12.

39  Hebrews 7:25.

40  1 Peter 2: 5, 9.

# 11. The Sixth Mormon Article of Faith

*We believe in the same organization that existed in the Primitive Church, viz., apostles, pastors, teachers, evangelists, etc.*

The Sixth Mormon Article of Faith

The Bible isn't specific about the organization of the true church. This is because the true church is not an organization –but an organism. Yet, in Mormonism we find that the physical organization is deemed to be of great importance. In fact, calling into question the structure of a potential convert's church organization has become an effective LDS missionary strategy. This chapter will show that the Mormon organization does not mirror the biblical church, and that the true church is expressed where there are two or three people gathered in the name of the true Messiah.

When I was a teenager, one of my brothers was temporarily sent home from a Mormon mission field until he recovered from yellow jaundice. I remember sitting in his room as he tutored with me on how to be a good missionary. I was impressed by the fact that he marked his Standard Works with a colored pencil. I believed he was knowledgeable about many important facts concerning Mormonism, which we both believed to be God's only true church. I was eager to learn from him all I could. While my brother was recovering I read some of his *Combination Reference* or *Missionary Pal,* as it is also called. This pocket sized ready reference compilation by Eldin Ricks is used by the church to promote Mormonism. I remember that my brother presented to my father and mother and myself a few of the missionary lessons in the manner the Mormon Church had prepared for proselyting purposes. One of the lessons taught ways to point out insufficiencies and inadequacies within the Christian Church. Pretending I was a non-Mormon, my brother asked, "Do you have apostles and prophets today in your church?" Then he helped me answer "no," as is hoped to be a non-member response. From these discussions I learned to present the Mormon view of insufficiencies and inadequacies within Christian denominations. Using this approach with non-member churches allows Mormons to claim there was indeed an apostasy and that God has restored the pristine form the New Testament church embodied.

In an earlier chapter I spoke of my childhood playmates who expressed to me that they didn't believe that the LDS Church was of God. Older now, and armed with the new ammunition and technique recently acquired from my brother's missionary discussions, I watched for an opportunity to pose questions to one of those friends hoping to point out to her an apparent fault within her church and the superiority of mine. A Mormon boy, who rode the same school bus beat me to her seat and the two of them had a conversation instead. She was one of the first to get off the bus and I never got another chance to share with her. She soon moved to Boise, Idaho, with her dad and stepmother and I never saw her again. To this day I would love to visit with her and her sister again and share with them that I am now a member of the true family of God. I often wonder what has happened in their lives.

At any rate the whole experience with my brother came in handy a few years down the road when as a new mother, I met the Jehovah's Witnesses. At that time, I owned my own little *Missionary Pal*, which I still have. It is all marked up as a reminder of experiences I had with my Jehovah Witness friends and others with whom I conversed concerning religious matters. The Jehovah's Witnesses had a small book which aided them the way my *Missionary Pal* did for me. We frequently used them as aids to point out the correctness of our personal yet opposing beliefs. One day in an effort to prove the Mormon Church true, I challenged them to find fault in the LDS sixth Article of Faith, "We believe in the same organization that existed in the Primitive Church, viz., apostles, pastors, teachers, evangelists, etc . . ." See the exhibit on page 224. To a Mormon mind this Article of Faith is a powerful proselytizing tool.

## What is the Church and Who Belongs to It?

I want to mention that the Bible does not say that the church is a building or an organization, or a denomination. *Strong's Exhaustive Concordance of the Bible* informs us that the word *church* comes from the Greek word *ekklesia* which means, *"a calling out, i.e. a popular meeting, espec. a religious congregation (Jewish synagogue, or Christian community of members on earth or saints in heaven or both);-assembly, church."*[1] The corresponding word for *ekklesia* in the Hebrew language is *qahal*.[2]

The Bible often refers to the term *the body of Christ*. This term is an expression used to describe the *called out ones*, or the *assembly of saints*. This is the true intent and meaning of the word *church*. It includes persons of the Old and New Covenant time periods who placed their faith in God's prophesied Messiah. This relationship with Christ has nothing to do with being baptized into the Mormon Church or having membership in any church organization or denomination. Christianity is not a religion, it is a relationship with the living God. That persons come to God's Messiah through faith alone is explained in many places in the Bible. One example to illustrate this truth is found in Hebrews chapter eleven, often described by Christians as the Bible's hall of faith chapter.

In chapter ten we noted from Scripture that persons do not qualify for the priesthood without first having a personal relationship with Christ. This relationship is received at the time of the required new birth. So it is with God's true church or assembly. No one is genuinely grouped with the called out ones, that is the church, without first receiving a true relationship with God's Son. One may occupy a seat, or be a part of an organized religion and still not have a genuine relationship with God. Salvation has nothing to do with the fact that one attends church or holds a church office. One does not become born again through membership or baptism into a church. Jesus did not die for an organization or denomination.

But, says McConkie:

> *There is no salvation outside this one true church, the Church of Jesus Christ. There is one Christ, one church, one gospel, one plan of salvation, one set of saving ordinances, one group of legal administrators.*[3]

**there is no salvation outside this one true church**

The LDS Church position is that when one passes the baptismal interview for worthiness of baptism into the Mormon Church and follows up with the baptism he or she becomes *born again*. In other words, Mormons are taught that in order to receive eternal life with God the Father, one must join and become baptized into the Mormon Church through its legal administrators:

> *The second birth begins when men are baptized in water by a legal administrator; it is completed when they actually receive the companionship of the Holy Ghost, becoming new creatures by the cleansing power of that member of the Godhead.*[4]

Note that McConkie explained that the second or *new birth* (being born again is the other term he uses in the same article) begins when persons are baptized in water by a legal (Mormon) administrator. This is but the beginning of saving ordinances in Mormonism. Ordinances, according to God's Word do not save. Obviously, the Mormon definition of the terms *born again* and *baptism* oppose the Christian view.

Regeneration, or the *new birth*, is the creation by the Holy Spirit of a new life in man, which the Bible calls the *new creation*, or the *new man*. The new birth comes by the acceptance of the good news of the true Gospel, which is that Jesus saves completely! It happens the instant one receives the true Jesus into one's heart by faith. At this time one *becomes* a child of God.[5] At this same juncture of faith, one receives the *priesthood of all believers*.[6] Everything begets after its kind –sinners beget sinners; a result of the Adam's fall. The new birth is the impartation of a different kind –God's Holy Spirit. This impartation sets in motion the process of regeneration. Baptism does not save, as the LDS believe. It is an outward symbol of a genuine conversion. Persons who receive the new birth are the true children of God.

## The Church Name: A Sign of the True Church?

The official title of the Mormon Church is *The Church of Jesus Christ of Latter-day Saints*. Mormons claim that the official name of their church is evidence of the truthfulness of their religion because it includes Christ's name. According to the *Book of Mormon* the true church should always contain Christ's name.[7] Actually, the name of the Mormon Church has been changed three times; *Church of Christ*,[8] *Church of the Latter-day Saints* (Christ's name is not used),[9] and presently, *The Church of Jesus Christ of Latter-day Saints*.[10] Why change the name? Did the Mormon authorities, as the Living Oracles, not believe the *Book of Mormon*?

## Church Organization

According to Joseph Smith's testimony, the Father and the Son appeared to him with the message that existing churches, their professors, and creeds are all corrupt and in God's sight are an abomination.[11] In chapter ten we noted that according to the *Doctrine and Covenants*, John the Baptist, Peter, James, and John, as resurrected men, returned to the earth and bestowed upon Joseph Smith the authority of the priesthood. This priesthood, according to Mormonism, had long before vanished from the earth. It was the power and authority of the restored priesthood bestowed upon Joseph Smith, that Mormons believe God directed him to restore the church to how it was in the days of the early apostles.

The Mormon Church emphasis on proper organization, expressed in the sixth Mormon Article of Faith, is a major selling point for the church. As a youth, I was taught that through the power of the Mormon priesthood the New Testament structure of the church was revealed to enable members of the church to spiritually grow and mature. I was encouraged to point out to non-members (the Gentiles) that the full official name of the Mormon Church and its organization are among the signs of the only true church. Believing that they alone are equipped with the proper understanding of the early church structure and organization, members of the LDS Church classify differences in Christian church structure and offices as deficiencies and errors, proof of an apostasy. Mormons believe that their organizational structure supports their claim of being the restored church. But we will now see why the LDS Church does not resemble the organization or function of the New Testament church.

> *the sixth Article of Faith is a major selling point for the church*

### Prophets

Mormons claim that they have a living prophet who stands unique and singular in the world. They also claim that there is never but *one* prophet on the earth at a time on whom this power and the keys of the priesthood are conferred.[12]

Jesus was the last of the prophets in the sense recorded and summed up in the Bible. "God who at sundry times and in divers manners spake in time past unto our fathers by the prophets, hath in these last days spoken unto us by his Son, by whom also He made the worlds . . ."[13]

The Old Testament prophets proclaim the coming Messiah. New Testament prophets expound upon the fact that Jesus is the Messiah. Furthermore, the Bible, unlike Mormonism, illustrates that a women may serve as a prophetess (while Mormons believe that only a man can be a prophet):

*"And there was a prophetess, Anna the daughter of Phanuel, of the tribe of Asher."*[14]

Unlike in Mormonism where there can be only one prophet at a time, the Bible teaches that there may be more than one prophet at at time: "Now at this time some prophets came down from Jerusalem to Antioch."[15] Among the spiritual gifts bestowed to Christians is the gift to prophesy, "Wherefore, brethren, covet to prophesy, and forbid not to speak in tongues."[16] "For the testimony of Jesus is the spirit of prophecy."[17] The role of prophet is not limited to a single, male, Mormon.

Finally, the prophet is of first importance to the organization of the Mormon Church. According to the Bible, however, the order is first, apostles, and second, prophets.[18] Apostles are first in order.

### Apostles

Mormons teach that in the true church there must always be twelve apostles. However, today the LDS Church has twelve apostles, plus three men in the First Presidency, who are also apostles. The Mormon Church didn't have twelve apostles until February 14, 1835, five years after the church was organized! The word *apostle* means *sent one* or *one sent forth*. Anyone who is a part of the true body of Christ is a *sent one*. Jesus did not direct this office to be limited in the sense it is in the Mormon Church. In fact, apostle is the only office without a strict and explicit list of qualifications in the Bible. Qualifications are listed for the offices of bishop and deacon, however.

The Bible states, "And he gave some, apostles; and some, prophets; and some evangelists; and some, pastors and teachers."[19] Consider the following:

### Evangelist

Mormons do not have an office titled evangelist, although some Mormons consider an evangelist the same as a patriarch. This is incorrect, for these two offices have different functions in the Bible. Evangelists preach good news, they do not bestow Patriarchal Blessings.

### Pastor

Mormons do not use an official title pastor, although some classify a bishop to be the same as a pastor. Why avoid the use of the biblical name if they have the same responsibilities, especially if they believe in preserving the original structure?

### Deacon

The Bible declares that a deacon must have only one wife[20] making it obvious that deacons were men, not boys. The question arises, why do Mormons have twelve year old boys serve as deacons?

### Bishop

A bishop must be a husband of one wife.[21] In the early history of Mormonism, bishops could have many wives!

### High Priest

No place in the New Testament is there record of a believer holding the office of High Priest. Jesus is both Sacrifice and High Priest. He is the *final* and *only* High Priest, and is now in heaven where He forever intercedes for us. To have such an office today is not only unscriptural, it is blasphemous! The early Mormon Church did not have High Priests, they came later.[22]

### Patriarch

The office of the patriarch is not found in the New Testament.

### First Counselors

Such an office is not found in the New Testament church.

### Seventy

The Mormon Church once had the Office of Seventy. Missionaries were once ordained as a Seventy before filling their missions. In the early 1980's the church had all of the seventies become either High Priests or return to being elders. Now there is the First Quorum of Seventy, although they do not go out two by two as Luke describes.[23] If this was a New Testament church office why did the Mormon Church omit it?

### First Presidency

The Bible never speaks of a First Presidency.

### Stake Presidency

The Mormon Office of Stake Presidency is composed of three men. There is no such office found in the New Testament church.

## Messiah Jesus

Messiah Jesus is our great High Priest,[24] apostle,[25] prophet,[26] evangelist,[27] shepherd,[28] teacher,[29] and so much more! Of Jesus we read, "For in him dwelleth all the fulness of the Godhead bodily."[30]

These are only a few of the problems showing that the sixth Mormon Article of Faith does not measure to its claim of New Testament church organization.

> *Messiah Jesus is our great High Priest, apostle, prophet, evangelist, shepherd, teacher, and so much more*

## The True Church Forever

I have already mentioned that Mormonism uses the term *fulness of times* to refer to the restoration of the Gospel of Christ (Mormonism) in the last days.[31] In contrast, rather than the expression the *fulness of times* referring to a restoration of the Mormon Gospel, the Bible shows the term to refer to the time beginning with the Incarnation of Jesus. It includes the time in history when Jesus was buried, conquered death, paid for our sins, and was resurrected. One's own privileged acceptance of salvation as an undeserved gift was produced and sustained by reason of this exultant and triumphal event in history. This is God's proclaimed message of the Gospel, and His true disciples are commissioned to carry it to all mankind.

Because the Mormon Church teaches that they alone have the truth restored and embodied, its members become more concerned about their church institution than about their relationship with true God of Israel. The Jehovah's Witnesses, Christian Scientists, as well as many Mormon splinter groups also claim to be the only true church. The Bible, interestingly, does not teach that one must join any kind of a church in order to get to heaven. The assembly, or church, as we have seen, is really comprised of all those who through faith put their trust in Jesus Christ who died for the assembly of believers, He did not die for an organization.

In closing this chapter, I conclude that the true church consists of all persons who have trusted in Christ alone for salvation; they make up the body of Christ.[32] The true church is located wherever two or three are gathered together in the name of the true Messiah.[33] There has never been a total apostasy from the Gospel. The LDS belief that the plain and precious things including the proper organization of the church of the New Testament were removed from the Bible and restored through Joseph Smith, does not hold true. God promised that His true church would never disappear from the earth, and it never did! Here is one of many

> *the true church is located wherever two or three are gathered together in the name of the true Messiah*

Scriptures which show so: "Wherefore receiving a kingdom which cannot be moved, let us have grace, whereby we may serve God acceptably with reverence and godly fear . . ."[34] There are many more biblical references to the faithfulness of God in securing and maintaining the Kingdom of God on earth.[35] Conclusively, the sixth Article of Faith does not concur with the early church organization.

1 Strong's Exhaustive Concordance of the Bible, Dictionary of the Greek New Testament, p. 26.

2 Strong's Exhaustive Concordance of the Bible, Hebrew and Chaldee Dictionary, p. 102.

3 Mormon Doctrine, p. 138.

4 Mormon Doctrine, p. 101.

5 John 1:12.

6 1 Peter 2:5, 9.

7 Book of Mormon, 3 Nephi 27:5-8.

8 Book of Commandments, 1833 edition, title page.

9 Doctrine and Covenants, 1835 edition, title page.

10 Doctrine and Covenants 115:3-4.

11 Pearl of Great Price, Joseph Smith 2:19.

12 Doctrine and Covenants 132:7.

13 Hebrews 1:1-3.

14 Luke 2:36.

15 Acts 11:27.

16 1 Corinthians 14:39.

17 Revelation 19:10.

18 1 Corinthians 12:28.

19 Ephesians 4:11-12.

20 1 Timothy 3:12.

21 1 Timothy 3:2.

22 An Address To All Believers In Christ p. 57.

23 Luke 10:1,17.

24 Hebrews 4:14.

25 Heberws 3:1.

26 Matthew 24.

27 Luke 4:18.

28 John 10:11.

29 John 3:2-3.

30 Colossians 1:9.

31 Mormon Doctrine, p. 200.

32 1 Corinthians 12:12-14; Romans 12:4-5.

33 Matthew 18:19-20.

34 Hebrews 12:28.

35 Psalms 100:5; Isaiah 55:11; Matthew 16:18, 24:35; 1 Corinthians 3:11; Ephesians 3:21; Hebews 12:28; John 14:16; Jude 3; 1 Peter 1:23-25.

# 12. Temples and Temple Work

*The spirits of the dead gathered around me wanting to know why I did not redeem them.*

Wilford Woodruff, Journal of Discourses, V.19, p. 229

Mormonism teaches that the dead may appear to members of the church, instructing them to do temple work in their behalf so that they may become members of the church. The fourth Mormon Prophet Wilford Woodruff quoted above, gave this account:

> *Every one of those men that signed the Declaration of Independence with General Washington called upon me as an apostle of the Lord Jesus Christ, in the Temple at St. George two consecutive nights, and demanded at my hands that I should go forth and attend to the ordinances of the house of God for them . . .I straightway went into the baptismal font and called upon Brother McAllister to baptize me for the signers of the Declaration of Independence, and fifty other eminent men, making one hundred in all, including John Wesley, Columbus, and others; I then baptized him for every president of the United States except three; and when their cause is just, somebody will do the work for them.*[1]

According to LDS theology people who die without hearing the Mormon Gospel go to a place called the *Spirit prison.* There they await to hear the Mormon version of the Gospel preached to them. Upon acceptance of the Mormon Gospel they await members of the church to perform proxy temple work: baptisms, ordinations, endowments, sealings etc., so that they too may receive eternal progression and Exaltation to Godhood. In their later years, my grandparents on my father's side worked in the Mormon temple at Logan, Utah. They completed 45,318 endowments and sealings, besides many baptisms for the dead. As a young woman I considered this a most impressive accomplishment. As referred to earlier, my Patriarchal Blessing promised me that if I were faithful to the leaders of my church, I too could be a savior in Zion and to many of the deceased. To fulfill such a calling required doing genealogy and temple proxy work.

The Mormon Prophet Joseph Fielding Smith explained it this way: " . . . the greatest commandment given us, and made obligatory, is the temple work in our own behalf and in behalf of the dead".[2] Nowhere in the Bible is there a command to baptize in a temple for the salvation of dead people. The opposite is true, "None of them can by any means redeem either himself or his brother, nor give a ransom for him; for the ransom of their life is too costly, and [the price they can pay] can never suffice."[3] There are, on the other hand, many Scriptures which teach that one must believe in the Lord Jesus Christ alone for salvation. The Bible does not teach a second chance after death. "It is appointed unto man once to die, but after that the judgment."[4]

Surprisingly, the following *Book of Mormon* quote is consistent with the Bible; that is, it contradicts today's LDS theology:

> *. . . do not procrastinate the day of your repentance . . . prepare for eternity . . . ye cannot say*

*when ye are brought to that awful crisis, that I will repent . . . For behold, if ye have procras-*
*tinated the day of your repentance even until death, behold, ye have become subjected to the*
*spirit of the devil, and he doth seal you his; therefore, the Spirit of the Lord hath withdrawn*
*from you, and hath all power over you; and this is the final state of the wicked.*[5]

After we die comes the judgment, not a preaching of the Mormon Gospel, nor a working of Mormon ordinances, nor becoming a God.  There are many biblical references to clarify this matter.[6]  The Mormon belief that one can assist salvation for themselves or for others by doing temple work parts company with the position taught in the Bible.

Likewise, the Bible parts company with the belief that Mormon temple ordinances assist one to prog-ress to the status of Godhood.  Instead, the Bible in many places emphatically informs us that no one will become a God: "That ye may know and believe me and understand that I am he: before me there was no God formed, neither shall there be after me.  I, even I, am the Lord; and beside Me there is no Savior . . . And beside Me there is no God."[7]

The Mormon belief that one may receive encounters with the dead for purposes of their salvation also is not biblical.  The Bible emphatically condemns communicating with the dead in any form:

*None of you . . . may practice black magic, or call on the evil spirits for aid, or be a fortune*
*teller, or be a serpent charmer, medium, or wizard, or call forth the spirits of the dead.  Anyone*
*doing these things is an object of horror and disgust to the Lord . . . The nations you replace*
*all do these evil things, but the Lord your God will not permit you to do such things.*[8]

*I will set my face against the person who turns to mediums and spiritists [familiar spirits] to*
*prostitute himself by following them, and I will cut him off from his people.*[9]

*If there is a prophet among you, or one who claims to foretell the future by dreams, and if his*
*predictions come true but he says, 'come, let us worship the gods of the other nations,' don't*
*listen to him.  For the Lord is testing you to find out whether or not you really love him with all*
*your heart and soul.*[10]

To participate in these practices is to encourage the activity of evil spirits who pose as the dead.  Com-munication with the dead are demonic counterfeits, "And no marvel; For Satan himself is transformed into an angel of light.  Therefore it is no great thing if his ministers also be transformed as ministers of righ-teousness; whose end shall be according to their works."[11]

Under the Old Testament law, people who communicated with familiar spirits were stoned to death.[12]  So were the false prophets who led them astray.[13]  God abhors such sin!  He says, "Thou shalt have no other gods before me."[14]  Communicating with demonic impostors breaks a commandment and invokes God's curse.[15]  Repentance breaks that curse.[16]  Jesus helps us understand that we do not communicate in this way with the dead: ". . . between us and you there is a great gulf fixed: so that they which would pass from hence to you cannot; neither can they pass to us, that would come from thence."[17]

Impostors from the unseen world make communion with the dead appear possible.  We are warned in the Book of Ephesians about the matter.

*For we are not fighting against people made of flesh and blood, but against persons without*
*bodies –the evil rulers of the unseen world, those mighty satanic beings and great and evil*
*princes of darkness who rule this world; and against huge numbers of wicked spirits in the*
*spirit world.*[18]

They pose as the dead but are demonic counterfeits who are highly organized, committed and disci-plined.  It is important to know how to equip ourselves against such powers, because Satan, the father of lies,[19] goes about as a roaring lion seeking whomever he may devour.[20]  How comforting it is that God has supplied deliverance to people who are trapped in the deceptions of Satan, the master deceiver, who comes to steal, kill and destroy.[21]  Jesus came to set such captives free:

*And I will bring the blind by a way that they knew not; I will lead them in paths they have not*
*known:  I will make darkness light before them, and crooked things straight.  These things will*
*I do unto them, and not forsake them.*[22]

Jesus has defeated Satan and gave the warning:

*And having disarmed the powers and authorities, he made a public spectacle of them, triumphing over them by the cross . . . . Do not let anyone who delights in false humility and the worship of angels disqualify you for the prize . . . . Such a person goes into great detail about what he has seen, and his unscriptural mind puffs him up with idle notions.*[23]

Jesus brings everlasting and inseparable love:

*I am persuaded, that neither death, nor life, nor angels, nor principalities, nor powers, nor things present, nor things to come . . . shall be able to separate us from the love of God, which is in Christ Jesus our Lord.*[24]

How comforting!

## Revealed Confusion

The Mormon Temple Ceremony is protectively secret and intense. As a temple patron I was bound with blood oaths, never to divulge what occurs inside. Most Mormons, because of the secret nature of the oaths they have participated in feel constrained and fearful about revealing or discussing the ceremony. I find it odd in that in several places the *Book of Mormon* teaches against secret societies (1 Nephi 20:16; 2 Nephi 9:9; Mormon 8:27; and Ether 8:14-16, 18, 22). LDS temple ceremonies and participants make up a secret society.

To members of the Mormon Church the temple is a secret sacred place. It is often repeated that the Temple Ceremony is sacred more than secret, its sacredness, not its secretness, they say, is the reason why the ceremonial details are never to be discussed. The fact remains that the ceremony is to be kept secret. While it is true that the temples of the Old Testament were sacred to the Hebrews, what transpired inside was not secret to anyone. The argument that the ceremony is too sacred to reveal what transpires within falls apart under any serious scrutiny of the Bible. Jesus said, "I spake openly to the world; I ever taught in the synagogue, and in the temple, whither the Jews always resort; and in secret have I said nothing."[25]

*ceremonial details of the temple are never to be discussed*

Mormon temples differ fundamentally from their old testament counterparts. Old Testament saints approached the temple acknowledging themselves as sinners in need of redemption. Moses gave the blueprint for the tabernacle. It served as a prototype of Salvation where the law expressed God's justice and the tabernacle expressed God's love, mercy, and pardon through Atonement. The purpose of the tabernacle and the temple that followed were the same: through the sacrifices, God conveyed the terrible price of sin which is death.[26] In contrast, Mormons approach their temple with recommends affirming their worthiness.

Since my own temple experience, many of the more bizarre aspects of the temple cermony have been removed or altered. In April, of 1990, the LDS Church made more changes to the Temple Ceremony. These changes include a number of blood oaths, the execution of the penalties, the five points of fellowship through the veil, the name of the second token of the Melchizedek priesthood and the patriarchal grip or sure sign of the nail. I'm grateful that the words, "Power in the Priesthood be upon me and upon all my posterity, throughout all generations of time and throughout all eternity," are gone as I believe this to be a demonic curse. The mocking of Christian clergy, the pay-lay-ale chant, and the woman's law of obedience to her husband, have all been deleted. The Temple Ceremony has been changed to omit some of the vows, but temple Mormons still retain the markings on their temple garments. My every day temple undergarments were to serve as reminders of all the the vows represented. For Mormons what do they represent now? The exact same things! Truthfully they are not a shield of protection as Mormons are taught. Messiah Jesus is the only true shield and protection! In 2005 the clothing worn in the washing and annointing rite was again modified.

Through the years the Mormon Church has made many other changes in the Temple Ceremony. Frankly, I believe the church has caved into pressure from the outside. Much of the recent pressure came to the church through William Schnoebelen and James Spencer, and Chuck Sackett's exposure of the Temple Ceremony. Other Christian ministries such as Dick Baer's, Ed Decker's, Jerald and Sandra Tanners, and others, are to be thanked for exposing Mormonism. Once again the temple changes were implemented without a sustaining vote of the church, which violates the Mormon law of common consent as defined the *Doctrine and Covenants*.[27] I believe this goes against the Mormon Church rules and abuses the trust of uninformed loyal members.

Endowments (see the glossary on page 195) are given only to those members who are deemed worthy to receive a Temple Recommend from their bishop and Stake President. This accounts for only about about 20 percent of all Mormons. All other Mormons are shielded and restricted from knowing the secrets of the Endowment Ceremony. The temple Endowment includes the ceremonies, ordinances and sealings which are administered for the living and for the dead. When I was a temple Mormon the endowment entailed sealings such as marriage, proxy baptisms for the dead, special instructions, secret oaths, special hand-shakes, and signs and covenants of the Mormon temple service. For examples see the exhibits on pages 228-231.

When Jesus died, the veil of God's Temple was torn in two, not by the hands of men but by the Holy Spirit. This supernatural event gives all persons freedom to go directly through the veil into the Holy of Holies.

> *And Jesus uttered a loud cry, and breathed His last. And the veil of the temple was torn in two from top to bottom.*[28] *Believers now have the Holy Spirit living in them.*[29]

Jesus is the last High Priest. He entered the Holy of Holies with His own blood, and sprinkled it on the mercy seat.[30] Jesus is our great High Priest of a superior priesthood, and His Sacrifice is effective and permanent. At the moment Jesus cried out his last words from the cross: "IT IS FINISHED!"[31] —temples and priests of this fashion ceased and the price of sin was then PAID IN FULL! Mormon temple rituals have never been in accord with the Bible, but even if they were, the crucifixion and resurrection made them obsolete.

## Offensive to God

The subject of Mormon temples and ceremonies cries out for an entire separate study. The *Book of Mormon* claims to contain the fulness of the everlasting Gospel, and the plain and precious things which were removed from the Bible. Yet the *Book of Mormon* contains no reference for today's temples, the unusual ceremonies they host, or other unique LDS doctrines. These ceremonies do not enjoy biblical sup-port. It was from Joseph Smith's association with the Masons that he derived the ceremonies and symbols known as the *endowment*. Consider the following:

> *today LDS deny Masonry, but continue to practice Masonic ceremonies*

**Masonic Connection** – Far from being revealed by God, Joseph Smith plagiarized from Masonic ceremonies in creating the Mormon Temple Ceremony.[32] The *History of the Church* records that he was a sublime 32nd degree Mason.[33] Brigham Young and many early members of the church were also proud Masons. Although today LDS deny ties to Masonry, they continue to practice Masonic ceremonies. Mormon's everyday temple garments sport several embroidered Masonic symbols. The exhibits on pages 203, 213 and 229-231 show Brigham Young's Masonic jewelry, Masonic architecture on the Mormon temple, and compare Mormon temple ceremonies to Masonic ceremonies, etc.

**The Veil** – The Bible explains that the veil separated the area of the temple where God's glory dwelt away from human access. Only once a year the High Priest could go therein. This veil separated sinful humans from the Holy and just God. The Bible does not teach anything about a human striving to go through the veil. Because of Christ's Sacrifice this veil has been permanently removed. This veil was not rent apart with human means but by the Holy Spirit from the top down. Now believers may go through the veil with boldness.[34] The Marks on the Mormon temple veil were not on the biblical temple veil, but are of Masonic origin.

**Oath of Vengeance** – With this *blood oath* members swore to defend the church against its enemies –which in the early days was the government. The oath said "to pray and never cease to importune high heaven to avenge the blood of the prophets on this nation, and to teach this to your children and your children's children to the third and fourth generation." This goes against the twelfth Mormon Article of Faith which says to recognize your secular leaders. The oath was removed from the Temple Ceremony sometime after 1930.[35]

**Principalities** – In the temple I prayed principalities and powers over my family. In the book of Ephesians the Bible has the following to say regarding principalities and powers: "For we wrestle not against flesh and blood, but against principalities, against powers, against the rulers of the darkness of this world, against spiritual wickedness in high places."[36] These powers are demonic.

**Mockery** – Christian pastors were said to be hirelings of Satan. During the Temple Ceremony, *Satan agrees to pay Christian pastors well* as they agree to teach a triune God, salvation by grace, and eternal Hell. What? *Why had I believed Satan?* No one should take Satan's counsel. Satan is the master of deceit! In the Bible we read that Satan ". . . was a murderer from the beginning, and abode not in the truth, because there is no truth in him. When he speaketh a lie, he speaketh of his own: for he is a liar, and the father of it."[37]

**Satan in God's Temple?** – Why does Satan play a role at all in the temple? In the Mormon temple Satan gets all the best roles. The Bible is explicit as to what transpired inside the Hebrew temples, and Satan never played a part. During the Temple Ceremony drama, Satan is portrayed by a temple worker. It is Satan – not God – who expounds LDS doctrine to the Mormons attending the Temple Ceremony. In the temple ceremonies I attended, *Satan shook his fingers at us and told us* that we would be under his power if we did not keep all the oaths we made in the temple. Mormons believe his words.

**Garments of the Priesthood** – I began to feel uncomfortable wearing my daily Mormon temple underwear sporting four Masonic symbols. In the Temple Ceremony, a priesthood holder plays the part of Satan. Dressed in his *own* apron, Satan explains that the apron is emblematic of his *power and priesthoods*. Lucifer instructs Adam and Eve to take some fig leaves and make themselves aprons. Then the worthy participants in the audience are told by the temple narrator, "Brethren and sisters, put on your aprons." We did this to simulate Adam and Eve's fig leaf aprons. The Mormon fig leaf like aprons carry the same *markings* which Lucifer claims in the temple ritual, represent his *power and priesthoods*. Very telling! Wearing the temple apron is an admission to the emblems of *Lucifer's power and priesthoods*. Furthermore, Mormons ignorantly cover themselves with aprons they believe *represent* the fig leaf aprons worn by Adam and Eve. But, as we read in the Bible, God took away their fig leaf aprons (because they were not acceptable), and gave Adam and Eve coats of skins. The skins represented the first sin covering. God Himself shed an animal's blood in order to cover Adam and Eve. This is a note of the blood redemption that is required to ransom sinners. We read, "For the life of the flesh is in the blood . . . for it is the blood that maketh an atonement for the soul"[38] Now through Christ, our Sacrificial Lamb, sin is covered *once for all*.[39] Jesus Himself is our righteousness and He justifies and accepts as righteous persons having true faith in Him.[40] I no longer saw any of my temple clothing as a *shield and protection* over me. I was certain they were an abomination to God, so I took them off! I renounced my Masonic involvement. Later, I came to see that God's own *garment of righteousness* and worthiness is my true *shield and protection*. The garment is Jesus Christ Himself!

**Temple Architecture** – Melaine, my friend, drew my attention to the decorative satanic symbols on Mormon temples and other Mormon architecture. One may see these symbols pictured in books like the LDS book, *The Salt Lake Temple -A Monument to a People*. In the Exhibit Section, page 213, I've included an example that shows the demonic symbols on the Salt Lake temple. I was ignorant of the origins of the symbols and I believe that most Mormons are. Most members of the LDS Church, no doubt, consider them merely ornate decorations. Nevertheless, the church claims divine revelation regarding their temples. Would the true God ever reveal satanic symbols for decorating His temple? Certainly not! I revere God and refuse to enter into a school of desperate and careless excuses, grasping to believe the Mormon Church to be the only true church, and such symbols to be simply ornate. God commands us to avoid even the appearance of evil.[41] The Temple Ceremony, as well as the symbols, go far beyond an appearance of evil. Consider the following two Scriptures: "Be ye not unequally yoked together with unbelievers: for what fellowship hath righteousness and what communion hath light with darkness?"[42] "And have no fellowship with the unfruitful works of darkness, but rather reprove them."[43]

**Temple Mormon Burial** – Temple Mormons are buried in green fig-leaf aprons emblematic of the aprons Adam and Eve in the Garden made for themselves. The aprons worn by Adam and Eve were an expression of their own righteousness, the merit of their own works, and the sweat of their own brow. God rejected Adam and Eve's aprons. All persons, whether LDS or not, need to understand that God offers to exchange the robes of our own righteousness with the robes of His righteousness. That exchange is freely offered, but is received only by our individual choice. I pray that my beloved family and friends within the Mormon faith will understand the prideful, futile character of the temple ceremonies and reject all temple garments. None of the Mormon clothing, or Laws and Ordinances (works) serve as a vehicle to salvation. God covers true believers with the garments of salvation, and the robe of righteousness.[44]

True believers are reminded to wear the full armor of God which is supplied in Jesus Christ as the shield and protection against the strategies and deceits of the devil. The armor is described and explained in Paul's epistle to the Ephesians[45]. Of course, the Mormon garments are not included in Paul's list. I pray the Mormons reflect on and understand that their temple garments are an offense to God. There are no references in the Bible, or in any of the Mormon Standard Works for that matter, for the Mormon temple garments. They carry secret talismanic symbols and are occultic good luck charms! I now believe that wearing any of the LDS temple attire as spiritual blindness. The exhibits on pages 229-231 show some examples.

**Plural Marriage** – The practice of plural marriage (polygamy) once made legal in Mormon temples, was at one time the standard prerequisite for achieving Godhood.[46] Current Mormonism, teaches that plural marriage is not essential to salvation or Exaltation.[47] The present *Doctrine and Covenants* 132 (the Law of Plural Marriage) replaced section 109 of the Book of Commandments, 1876 edition which states that one man should have but one wife. The present *Doctrine and Covenants* still refers to this doctrine and says that one will be *damned* if this law is not obeyed.[48] The Mormon Manifesto inserted at the end of the present *Doctrine and Covenants*, which effectively ended the practice of polygamy, does not claim to be a revelation from God. As long as section 132 remains in the *Doctrine and Covenants*, polygamy will continue to be practiced by Fundamentalist Latter-day Saints. If one believes the *Doctrine and Covenants* is for today – polygamy should be practiced or *one will be damned.*

> *damned if Polygamy isn't obeyed*

**Temple Marriage** – Temples of the Bible were never used for marriage of any kind. The Mormon concept of marriage goes against what Jesus proclaimed to the Pharisees when they questioned Him about marriage after the resurrection, "For when they shall rise from the dead, they neither marry, nor are given in marriage; but are as the angels which are in heaven."[49]

**Worship** – I am saddened as I recall a lack of worship in the Mormon temple. Mormon temples are devoid of worship, honor, or praise to the living Creator. Instead, it is a place of gnostic and demonic instruction to an imaginary false God. Jesus has only a minor role in the Mormon Temple Ceremony. In fact, as mentioned earlier, Satan plays a larger role in Mormon temples than Jesus. Would Jesus be the head of a church that, in its most sacred rites, pays Him little attention? Certainly not. There are no similarities between what occurs in the Mormon temples and that which occurred in the ancient biblical temples. In fact, a study of biblical temples and ceremonies completely destroys the Mormon concept of temples.

## Changes in the Mormon Temple Ceremony

**Adam-God, Oath of Vengeance, Law of Adoption** – Among the changes made through the years in the Temple Ceremony, each of the following has been removed: Brigham Young's lecture at the veil, which taught the Adam-God doctrine (addressed earlier), the oath of vengeance to our nation (more about this later), and the law of adoption which is the practice of sealing men to men.[50]

**Garments of the Priesthood** – According to the early Mormon Church, the designs of the undergarments worn by temple Mormons were revealed by God Himself, never to be changed in style; they were to be worn down to the wrist and ankles, and close around the neck. The promise that the garments would serve as a shield and protection was given only to the worthy Mormons who would not give way to the style of the Gentiles.[51] The garments have undergone dramatic style changes, which once was considered a violation of covenants.

Conclusively then, God does not dwell in temples made with hands, but within the believer's heart.[52] The God of Israel certainly did not author the Mormon Temple Ceremony. I pray for members of the LDS Church to discover that Mormonism is ". . . ever learning, and never able to come to the knowledge of the truth."[53] I pray also as did the Apostle Paul for his loved ones, that the eyes and hearts of Mormons everywhere will be flooded with truth, that they may be granted the spirit of wisdom and revelation from the Father of glory.[54]

Salvation does not include the Mormon endowment nor self-Exaltation to the station of Godhood. Salvation does not come to anyone by proxy. Instead salvation is like the Passover Lamb of the Israelites in Egypt.[55] Each of us must decide to post salvation to the doorpost of his own heart through faith. In the fulness of time Jesus became the last blood Sacrifice. True salvation does not require or include any part of the Mormon Temple Ceremony. Truly people die and are judged on the basis of their response to the true Messiah and His specific offer of salvation.[56]

One day many years ago, when I was still a Mormon, my neighbor came over for a visit. I mentioned to her something about wanting to go to the temple with some members of our ward. She did not realize that she planted a small seed in my heart as she tried to explain to me that Mormons do not need temples today. She reminded me of a verse in the Bible, "Know ye not that ye are the temple of God, and that the spirit of God dwelleth in you?"[57] In the Mormon Temple Ceremony I was instructed that God does not dwell in people's hearts. The very idea was mocked and made ludicrous. She hoped I would understand the sufficiency of the residence of God within persons who have relationship with Jesus. I hadn't heard the verse explained as she explained it to me before. I always kept her explanation in the back of my mind. Years later, when I invited the true Messiah Jesus into my heart, I came to understand experientially the workings of that verse. It is the Holy Spirit that leads us into all truth.[58] Christ is the Sacrificial Lamb.[59] Believers are now the temple of God.[60] The Spirit of God dwells in the hearts of true believers. As Jesus told the Samaritan woman at the well:

> . . . *Woman, believe me, the hour cometh, when ye shall neither in this mountain, nor yet at Jerusalem, worship the Father. Ye worship ye know not what: We know what we worship: for salvation is of the Jews. But the hour cometh, and now is, when the true worshippers shall worship the Father in spirit and in truth: for the Father seeketh such to worship Him. God is spirit: and they that worship Him must worship Him in spirit and in truth.*[61]

We too must worship God in truth; to worship Him in a lie is futile and fatal! Will we delight in reaping tomorrow what we are sowing today? I believe that Mormon temples and temple work are expressions of spiritual blindness.

In looking back on my life God certainly made use of the Mormon temple, but for a different reason than I expected. God used the temple to emphasize for me some horrid facts about Mormonism, and to draw me away from its evil. When I thought about the Temple Ceremony, I was grieved inside my soul! I thought about how it must grieve God too, as well as blinding Mormons from truth! I now believe that embracing the Mormon Temple Ceremony like other aspects of Mormonism is to ridicule and profane all that is exemplified and encompassed in the powerful Name of God. I believe that the church of my birth makes trivial the unique centrality of God. In the Mormon temple, God is not separate and other than all else —only a resurrected glorified man!

1   Temples of the Most High, pp. 87-88 from a report Woodruff made at General Conference, April 10,1898, pp. 89-90.
2   Doctrines of Salvation, vol. 2, p. 149.
3   Psalms 49:7-8.
4   Hebrews 9:27.
5   Book of Mormon, Alma 34:32-35; Moroni 8:22-23; Mosiah 15:24-27, 16:5.
6   Hebrew. 5:9, Romans 10:9-10.
7   Isaiah 43:10-11.
8   Deuteronomy 18:9-12.
9   Leviticus 20:6.
10  Deuteronomy 13:1-3.
11  2 Corinthians 11:14.
12  Deuteronomy 17:2-5.
13  Deuteronomy 13:5.
14  Exodus 20:3.
15  Exodus 20:5.
16  Exodus 20:6.
17  Luke 16: 26.
18  Ephesians 6:12.
19  John 8:44.
20  1 Peter 5:8.
21  John 10:10.
22  Isaiah 42:16.
23  Colossians 2:15,18.
24  Romans 8:38.
25  John 18:20.
26  Romans 6:23.
27  Doctrine and Covenants 26:2.
28  Mark 15:38.
29  1 Corinthians 3:16.
30  Hebews 9:11-24.
31  John 19:30.
32  Mormonism: Shadow or Reality, p. 484-492.
33  History of the Church, vol. 4, pp. 551-552.
34  Matthew 27:51.
35  Evolution of the Temple Ceremony, p. 22-26.
36  Ephesians 6:12.
37  John 8:44.
38  Leviticus 17:11.
39  Hebrews 9:12-26.
40  Romans 3:24-27.
41  1 Thessalonians 5:22.
42  2 Corinthians 6:14-17.
43  Ephesians 5:11.
44  Isaiah 61:10; Matthew 22:11-14; Revelation 19:8.
45  Ephesians 6:11-18.
46  Journal of Discourses, vol. 11, p. 269.
47  Mormon Doctrine, p. 578.
48  Doctrine and Covenants 132.
49  Mark 12:25.
50  Journal of Discourses, vol. 9, p. 269 and vol. 16, p. 186; Heber C. Kimball's Journal, Dec. 21, 1845; Journal of Abraham H. Cannon, Dec. 6, 1889; Brigham Young, cited in L. John Nuttall Manuscript, Feb. 7,1877.
51  The Improvement Era, vol. 9, p. 813, by President Joseph Fielding Smith; Temples of The Most High, p. 239; Messages of the First Presidency, J. R. Clark, 1971, vol. 5, p.110
52  Acts 7:48.
53  2 Timothy 3:7.
54  Ephesians 1:17-23.
55  Exodus 12:5-14.
56  John 3:16-18.
57  1 Corinthians 3:16.
58  John 14:26.
59  Revelation 13:8.
60  1 Corinthians 3:16
61  John 4:21-24.

# 13.  The Book of Mormon

*And it came to pass that after he had smitten off the head of Shiz, that Shiz raised upon his hands and fell; and after that he had struggled for breath, he died.*

Book of Mormon, Ether 15:31

Would you agree that believing the above *Book of Mormon* account of Shiz requires a huge leap of faith? Who in all history breathed after having his head cut off? When I was a little girl living on my father's farm I watched the lower bodies of chickens have muscle spasms after their heads were cut off, but not even in the *Guiness Book of World Records* have I heard of a man who could struggle for breath after his head was cut off! When one's head gets chopped off one doesn't have breath! I have to chuckle each time I think of this story, and then I chuckle more when I take into account that this story is from the *Book of Mormon* book "Ether."

The LDS Church claims that the *Book of Mormon* contains a history of God's dealings with the ancient inhabitants of the American continents from about 2247 B.C. to 421 A.D. No doubt you are familiar with the statue that is on top of Mormon temples. This statue represents the angel Moroni, an ancient prophet whose life is written about in the *Book of Mormon.*

In the *Doctine and Covenants,* Bruce McConkie explains that angels are resurrected personages with flesh and bones.[1] Moroni, according to the Mormonism, held the keys of the *Book of Mormon* record, a record the Mormons also refer to as the stick of Ephraim.[2] It is purported that long after his death, Moroni returned to the earth as a resurrected being, and according to Joseph Smith, it was this angel who led him to some gold plates on which were inscribed hieroglyphic language. The complete Gospel allegedly was written on gold plates and were deposited long ago and uncovered by Moroni from a hill presently known as the Hill Cumorah, near Manchester, New York. According to the *Pearl of Great Price,*[3] it was September 22, 1827, when the angel Moroni delivered the plates for Joseph Smith to translate. Joseph Smith supposedly translated from the Egyption language[4] into what now is known as the *Book of Mormon.* According to the *Doctrine and Covenants*[5] the *Book of Mormon* contains the *fulness* of the Gospel.

The *History of the Church*[6] describes each plate as six inches wide and eight inches long. The whole volume was something near six inches in thickness, and beautifully engraved. It is recorded by his mother[7] that Joseph Smith was attacked and saved from three assailants after he received the plates from the angel. Joseph's mother said that while in the process of getting away from his assailants Joseph Smith jumped over a log and ran at top speed more than a half mile. A little figuring shows that Joseph's run through the woods was quite a feat since the plates would have weighed around 200 pounds! A mental picture of such a run is amusing to the mind. After the plates were translated it is said that they were returned to the angel.[8]

The *Book of Mormon*[9] describes how difficult it was to engrave on the plates from which it is alleged to have been translated. In the *Book of Mormon* the phrase "and it came to pass" is used some 2,000 times, coupled with "behold" and "inasmuch". This is repetitive and unnecessary. As in all aspects of the Mormon faith, I find that placing one's trust in the *Book of Mormon* is to embrace a false sanctuary. There is no independent evidence to substantiate any of the story about the gold plates.

## An Empty Book

As a child, I was taken with the *Book of Mormon*. Just as I had been taught to do, I valued it more than the Bible. I often heard members of the church bear testimony at Fast and Testimony meeting to truthfulness of the *Book of Mormon* and of its being the most important book in the entire world. I was always proud to introduce it to my "Gentile" friends. I never knew that the *Book of Mormon* is packed with ludicrous and problematic verses. Even now, while thumbing through my old missionary *Book of Mormon*, I am astonished at what I overlooked whenever I read it. I can tell because after my departure from the church I underlined with a different color pencil than before. Now, in living color I can quickly reference verses through an LDS or bibical perspective. Now I see how badly my eyes were once blinded from the truth.

"I told the brethren that the *Book of Mormon* was the most correct of any book on earth, and the keystone to our religion, and a man would get nearer to God by abiding by its precepts, than by any other book,"[10] said Joseph Smith. The Standard Works of the church claims that the *Book of Mormon* contains a record of a fallen people, and the fulness of the Gospel of Jesus Christ to the Gentiles and to the Jews also.[11] The *Doctrine and Covenants* like the original Articles of Faith, define both the *Book of Mormon* and the Bible as carrying the fulness of the Gospel. Here is an example from the *Doctrine and Covenants*: "And again the elders, priests and teachers of this church shall teach the principles of my Gospel, which are in the Bible and the *Book of Mormon*, in the which is the fulness of the Gospel."[12]

> *the Book of Mormon is an effective, yet deceptive, missionary tool*

The claim that the *Book of Mormon* contains the fulness of the Gospel is misleading because the *Book of Mormom* contains very little Mormon doctrine. Mormon beliefs concerning Exaltation, pre-existence, and the Spirit prison are absent. No mention is made of temple work; Celestial marriage, endowments, baptisms for the dead, all are absent from the *Book of Mormon* text. A potential convert will never understand Mormonism using only the *Book of Mormon*. The *Book of Mormon* is an effective, yet deceptive, missionary tool. To understand Mormonism and its doctrines one must know the LDS Law of Eternal Progression (self-Exaltation). One must look elsewhere in the Mormon Standard Works, and within the Mormon Temple Ceremony for the most secret but essential aspects of Mormonism.

The *Book of Mormon* actually contradicts many current Mormon teachings. Still the *Book of Mormon* is trusted by the church over the Bible. Because Mormons view it as the most correct book on earth, the *Book of Mormon* also serves as an effective witnessing tool in exposing inconsistencies in Mormonism to Mormons. LDS Church members need to be asked questions such as "Do you believe God has a body?" "Do you believe that He had a father and mother?" "Does the *Book of Mormon* teach that Christ and God are really two separate Gods?" "Do you believe that as man is, God once was; and as God is, man may become?" Does man get a second chance? The *Book of Mormon* does not support any of these claims!

It is insightful to learn that today's foundational LDS doctrine of the Godhead cannot be supported in the *Book of Mormon*. However, there are many *Book of Mormon* passages that teach a closer biblical view of God. Consider the one below:

> *Now Zeezrom said: Is there more than one God? And he answered, No. . . . Now Zeezrom*
> *saith again unto him: Is the Son of God the very Eternal Father? And Amulek said unto him:*
> *Yea, he is the very Eternal Father of heaven and of earth, and all things which in them are; he*
> *is the beginning and the end, the first and the last; and he shall come to redeem his people . . .*
> *Christ the Son, and God the Father, and the Holy Spirit, which is one Eternal God . . .*[13]

This is only one example of many which refute the commonly held LDS view. There are many verses inside the *Book of Mormon* which do the same.[14]

The title page of *Book of Mormon* also expresses the belief in one God. The Testimony of Three Witnesses given just before the first chapter of the *Book of Mormon* also does. Such verses in the *Book of Mormon* are completely out of harmony with present-day Mormon doctrine concerning the nature of God. They contradict Mormonism's polytheistic doctrine altogether.

The *Book of Mormon* reflects the teaching of the early theologian Sabellius called modalism.[15] Modalism is the idea that there is only one God, Who becomes the other two of the Trinity. For example, He wears the hat, or title of the Father, then takes it off and places on the hat of the Son, wears that for a while, takes it off and places on the hat of the Holy Ghost. This view would indicate that God is ever-changing. This form of trinitarianism is not biblical, but does create opportunities to defend a more accurate understanding of God. The Bible teaches that, ". . .God was in Christ, reconciling the world unto Himself."[16] Still the Father remained the Father. Each one of the Godhead has existed from the beginning, fellowshipping together. None of the Godhead is superior or jealous of the other. God is a unified One.

## Other Problems

Since the first edition of the *Book of Mormon* there have been 3,913 word changes or 11,849 if punctuation errors are counted.[17] A comparison of your own can be made by reading Wilford C. Wood's 1830 First Edition, Volume 1, *Book of Mormon* reproduced from uncut sheets.[18] I was able to purchase Wood's volumes 1 and 2 from an LDS bookstore. Volume 2 contains other Standard Works.[19] Both volumes are available for purchase.[20] I refer to both of them in the writing of this book. I encourage you to examine for yourself the changes made from the early editions of the *Book of Mormon*. The following are significant changes concerning the *Book of Mormon*.

– In the *Book of Mormon* (Ether 4:1 and Mosiah 21:28) we read about King Mosiah. In the 1830 version (page 546) the name Mosiah was Benjamin. No doubt the change was made because King Benjamin had died a few chapters back (Mosiah 6:5).

– On page 303 of the 1830 first edition of the *Book of Mormon* the words *". . . yea, decreeth unto them decrees which are unalterable,"* have been removed. The present *Doctrine and Covenants 56:4* shows a contradiction to this verse and a reason for its deletion. Of the same verse the present *Doctrine and Covenants* reads, "Wherefore I, the Lord, command and revoke, as it seemeth me good; and all this to be answered upon the heads of the rebellious, saith the Lord." In Mormonism there are an embarrassing number of times this *Doctrine and Covenants* verse has come in handy in explaining Mormon doctrine.

– The 1830 first edition *Book of Mormon*, page 25, says of Mary, ". . . the virgin which thou seest, is the mother of God, after the manner of the flesh." The corresponding verse of 1 Nephi 11:18 was changed in 1837 to ". . . the virgin whom thou seest is the mother of the Son of God, after the manner of the flesh." Page 25 of the 1830 first edition reads ". . . behold the Lamb of God, yea, even the Eternal Father!" It has been changed in its corresponding verse, 1 Nephi 11:21, to "Behold the Lamb of God, yea, even the Son of the Eternal Father!" In like manner page 32 of the 1830 first edition says " . . . that the Lamb of God is the Eternal Father . . ." This verse has been changed in the present 1 Nephi 13:40 to read ". . . the Lamb of God is the Son of the Eternal Father,"- the words *the Son of* is added to each of the verses as they are rendered in the current edition. Adding the words *the Son of* makes a significant change in the meaning of these verses. Nothing that I am aware of has been more renovated than has the Mormon doctrine of God!

In the front of the *Book of Mormon* are two separate testimonies. One is a record of the Three Witnesses and the other of the Eight Witnesses. These men testify that they saw the gold plates from which the *Book of Mormon* was translated. Of these men, the Mormon Apostle John A. Widtsoe wrote:

*The Book of Mormon plates were seen and handled, at different times, by eleven competent men, of independent minds and spotless reputations, who published a formal statement of their experience. All these witnesses, of unchallenged honesty in the affairs of life remained true to their testimonies throughout their lives without deviation or variation.*[21]

As a Mormon, I believed the testimonies of the Three Witnesses and the Eight Witnesses to be power-ful proof of the truthfulness of the *Book of Mormon*. Great emphasis was placed on the honesty and clean reputations of these men. I was very much surprised, however, to discover that in the light of other LDS writings the characters of these men are not so spotless. For example, Hyrum Page, one of the Eight Wit-nesses, found a stone through which were received revelations contrary to those of Joseph Smith. Joseph Smith admitted that Hiram Page had a peep-stone, and that from it he received false revelations, which in-fluenced the other witnesses to the *Book of Mormon*.[22] By usual standards of definition, using a peep stone is an occultic practice.

Among the nine charges made against Oliver Cowdery, as recorded in the *History of the Church*, was that he was connected to a bogus money business.[23]

Joseph Smith characterized Martin Harris, another witness, as a wicked man.[24] During his lifetime, Harris changed his religion thirteen times.[25] The same reference points out that he joined the Shakers who believed Christ made his second return to earth in a chosen female known by the name of Ann Lee, acknowledged as our blessed Mother in the work of redemption.

Joseph Smith characterized another witness, David Whitmer, as a "dumb ass".[26]

He also stated that John Whitmer, David Whitmer, Oliver Cowdery, and Martin Harris were too mean to mention, and that he would like to have forgotten them.[27] These words from the first Mormon Prophet certainly are compelling and damaging against the witnesses to the *Book of Mormon*. Interestingly, all of the Three Witnesses to the *Book of Mormon* were excommunicated from the church.[28]

David Whitmer, one of the Three Witnesses to the *Book of Mormon*, who claimed that God told him to leave the church, wrote a fascinating booklet entitled, *An Address to all Believers in Christ*. In it he wrote the following concerning the witnesses to the *Book of Mormon*:

> *About the same time that I came out, the Spirit of God moved upon quite a number of the brethren who came out, with their families. All of the eight witnesses who were then living (except the three Smith's) came out; Peter and Christian Whitmer were dead. Oliver Cowdery came out also. Martin Harris was then in Ohio.*[29]

Mormon history records that six out of the eleven witnesses apostatized from the church.[30] In sum-mary, both Mormon and Non-Mormon sources depict the witnesses to the *Book of Mormon* as dishonest, incredulous, and gullible. There is no valid reason to believe their testimonies about the *Book of Mormon*.

In the face of all the damaging information concerning the character and gullibility of the witnesses, their testimonies to the *Book of Mormon* are revered by the LDS Church. The Mormon Apostle Orson Pratt emphatically declared:

> *. . . If investigation should prove the Book of Mormon is true . . . the American and English nations . . . should utterly reject both the Popish and Protestant ministry, together with all the churches which have been built up by them or that have sprung from them, as being entirely destitute of authority . . . the Book of Mormon claims to be a divinely inspired record . . . if false, it is one of the most cunning, wicked, bold, deep-layed impositions ever palmed upon the world, calculated to deceive and ruin millions . . .*[31]

I am certain that the *Book of Mormon* is false because it fails the test of reasonable scrutiny. Therefore, I agree with the last part of the words of Orson Pratt. I report that the *Book of Mormon* is indeed: ". . . one of the most cunning, wicked, bold, deep-layed impositions ever palmed upon the world, calculated to deceive and ruin millions . . ."[32]

There are many other startling issues surrounding the origins of the *Book of Mormon;* historical, cultural, linguistic, archaeological, biological, biblical, etc. There are too many to address in this chapter. As you read the sample list of *Book of Mormon* problems below keep in mind the quote by the Mormon Apostle Orson Pratt:

> *The nature of the message of the Book of Mormon is such that if true, no one can possibly be saved and reject it; if false, no one can possibly be saved and receive it.*[33]

## More Absurdities

### 1st NEPHI

- 1:2 Compare Nehemiah 13:3 Corrupt Language.

- Not inspired: vs.3, 16, 17, 19:4-6; 2 Nephi 11:1, 25:7-33:1; Mormon 1:2-6; Jacob 7:26-27.

- 2:5 Sam is a Yankee name, Samuel would have been the Jewish name.

- 2:8 No river, then or now, empties into the Red Sea.

- 5:14 A devout Jew did not know what tribe he was from until he saw the "plates?"

- 8:4 "me thought," an "old" English poetic word.

- 10:8 Exact quote from John 1:27.

- v.11 "Holy Ghost" a King Jamesism.

- v.17 "Faith" on the "Son of God": terms never used by an Old Testament writers.

- v.18 "same yesterday, today and forever" a quote from Hebrews 13:8.

- v.27 Baptism of Jesus - John 1:29-34. The one who wrote the *Book of Mormon* had read much of the New Testament.

- 12:23 People of unbelief became dark skinned, loathsome, idle, and full of abominations.

- 16:18 "bows of steel?"

- v.28, 29 Faith given to the "ball." Does God ask us to have faith in anything but Him?

- chapters 21-22 copied from Isaiah 49-50.

### 2nd NEPHI

- 1:3 "Land of Promise" for the Israelites was the land of Canaan, see Genesis 13:14-18.

- v.14 ". . . whence no traveler can return" from Shakespeare's Hamlet.

- chapter 4:17 "Oh wretched man that I am" is an exact quote from Romans 7:24.

- v.18 ". . . sins that do so easily beset me" from Hebrews 12:1.

- 5:21 Black skin is a curse?

- v.23 Don't marry a Laminite or you will be cursed. Mormons tell us that the Lamanites are the American Indians.

- chapters 6-8 copied from Isaiah 50-51.

- 10:7 A false prophecy. The Jews are back in their own land, only in unbelief.

- chapters 12-24 are Isaiah 2-14.

- chapter 13 is Isaiah 3.

- 25:19 "Christ" was not His last name. Christ means the Anointed One; the Messiah.

- 28:8, 9 Condemns Mormonism's doctrine of repentance after death.

- chapter 29 condemns the Bible.

- 29:1-13 Where are these many writings?

- 30:6 In 1981 the word *white* was changed to *pure*. Another skin color issue.

### JACOB

- 2:23 and 3:12 Condemns polygamy. *Doctrine and Covenants* 132 proclaims polygamy.

- 7:27 "Adieu," French in 544 B.C.?

### MOSIAH

- 2:3 the *Book of Mormon* 2 Nephi 5:10-11 states that no Manassite, (Alma 10:3) could give attendance at the alter according to the Law of Moses. Also firstlings of the flock never used as burnt offerings according to the Law of Moses (see Numbers 18:17-18; Exodus 13:2, 12).

- chapter 14 is copied from Isaiah 53.

- 15:10 his soul made offering for sin?  The Bible teaches it was Messiah's body and blood.

**ALMA**

- 7:10 Jesus born at Jerusalem?  See Matthew 2:1; Micah 5:2; Luke 2:4.

- 34:31-36  These versus disparage vicarious works for the dead.

- 46:15 "Christian" first called at Antioch (Acts 11:26).

- 44:12-16  Zerahemnah gets scalped and then gets angry and more powerful.

**ETHER**

- 1:34-37 Contradicts Genesis 11:9, God *did* confound the language of the *whole* earth.

- 2:16-25 Blunders all attributed to God.

- v.23 Glass thousands of years before Christ?

- 3:8, 13, 19 Saved from the fall because of seeing the "finger" of the Lord.

- 3:14 Jesus, the Father and the Son.  This is modalism.  This verse also refutes the doctrine of pre-exitence.

- 15:30, 31 Shiz struggles for breath after his head was cut off.

**HELAMAN**

- 9:6 Stab and murder with a *garb of secrecy?*


## Occultic Origins?

By the end of my studies, I no longer believed the *Book of Mormon* was from God.  Clearly, Joseph Smith had plagiarized entire chapters from the King James version of the Bible, even using the same italics.  I believe the *Book of Mormon* origins are clearly evil.  One way the Mormon Church explains the translation of the *Book of Mormon* is through the usage of the Urim and Thummim like in the Old Testament.  This is a wrong explanation because in the Old Testament the Urim and Thummim was never used for translating languages.  The Mormon claim that sentences would appear on the Urim and Thummim is reminiscent of ball gazing and not of the Urim and Thummim.  Consider the following account by David Whitmer, one of the Three Witnesses:

> *I will now give you a description of the manner in which the Book of Mormon was translated. Joseph would put the seer stone into a hat, and put his face in the hat, drawing it closely around his face to exclude the light; and in the darkness the spiritual light would shine.  A piece of something resembling parchment would appear, and on that appeared the writing.*[34]

This is only one of several accounts describing the occult origin of the *Book of Mormon*.  This account, like the account of the ball-like Liahona[35] of which the *Book of Mormon* refers is depictive of witchcraft.  The reference says the ball operated according to their faith in it - not according to their faith in God.  Practices like these are condemned in the Bible.[36]

My friend, Melaine, introduced me to Wesley P. Walters, who discovered the authentic Justice Albert Neely's bill recording Joseph Smith's conviction and fine for *glass looking*.  I have included a photo copy of this bill in the Exhibit Section on page 223.  Glass looking is the art of looking through stones to find buried treasure.  Such sorcery!  Joseph Smith had swindled people of their money in this way.  Wesley Walters introduced me to Joseph Smith's occultic practices by showing me the original *Doctrine and Covenants*.[37]  The words "gift of Aaron" in the present *Doctrine and Covenants*, first said, the "gift of working with the rod."  The divining rod, the *Doctrine and Covenants* explains, had told him many things.  Divining with the rod is and always has been associated with witchcraft.  Wesley Walters pointed out to me that the *Amboy Journal*,[38] shows that Joseph Smith took steps to join the Methodist Church.  Joseph Smith's name was removed from church records because he practiced necromancy, enchantments and

> *the words "gift of working with the rod" have changed to "the gift of Aaron"*

bleeding ghosts. Webster's dictionary defines necromancy as:1) conjuration of the spirits of the dead for purposes of magically revealing the future or influencing the course of events; 2) magic, sorcery.

Although Mormons believe it is an ancient document, Joseph Smith can be called the author of the *Book of Mormon*, after all the1830 Edition calls him "Author and Proprietor" on the title page.

## Biblical Support for the Book of Mormon?

In my research, I learned that the biblical proof-texts used by the Mormon Church to support the *Book of Mormon* are twisted and used out of context.

I pointed out at the beginning of this chapter that the angel Moroni, seen on the top of Mormon temples blowing a trumpet, is believed by members of the church to be an ancient war general written about in the *Book of Mormon*. The Mormon Church teaches that Moroni buried and fourteen centuries later delivered the *Book of Mormon* record to Joseph Smith. The Bible verse Isaiah 29:4 is used by the Mormon Church to support the existence of the angel Moroni, and the coming forth of the *Book of Mormon*. The Mormon Apostle LeGrand Richard states, "Isaiah saw the coming forth of this record [Book of Mormon] as the voice of one that hath a familiar spirit whispering out of the dust."[39] Richards then goes on to quote more from Isaiah: "And thou shalt be brought down, and shalt speak out of the ground, and thy speech shall be low out of the dust, thy voice shall be, as of one that hath a familiar spirit, of the ground, and thy speech shall whisper out of the dust."[40]

The term *familiar spirit* is used fifteen times in the Old Testament. In all instances it refers to witchcraft. For instance, Scripture clearly states, "Regard them not that hath familiar spirits, neither seek after wizards, to be defiled by them: I am the Lord your God."[41] Using the passage from the book of Isaiah in this manner is an example of Mormon twisting of God's Word. It illustrates the demonic roots of the *Book of Mormon*.

Another popular proof-text used by the Mormon Church as evidence for the coming forth of the *Book of Mormon* is found in the Old Testament book of Ezekiel:

> *Moreover, thou son of man, take thee one stick, and write upon it, For Judah, and for the children of Israel his companions: then take another stick, and write upon it, For Joseph, the stick of Ephraim, and for all the house of Israel and his companions: and join them one to another into one stick and they shall become one in thine hand. And when the children of thy people shall speak unto thee, saying, Wilt thou not shew us what thou meanest by these? Say unto them, Thus sayeth the Lord God; Behold, I will take the stick of Joseph, which is in the hand of Ephraim, and the tribes of Israel his fellows, and will put them with him, even with the stick of Judah, and make them one stick, and they shall be one in the hand.*[42]

Mormons claim this passage was fulfilled by the coming forth of the *Book of Mormon* in the last days. How so? Let me explain.

Mormons are taught that the word *sticks* refers to *scrolls*, the ancient form of a book. The stick of Judah is believed to be the Bible, since it is a record primarily of that tribe. Mormons view the stick of Joseph as the *Book of Mormon*, thought of by Mormons as a history of Jewish descendants in the Americas. For a Mormon, this passage is understood as a prophetic command to make two records and then at a later time in history combine them into a single record for a witness of Jesus Christ - the joining into one stick refers to this. However, the Mormon interpretation ignores what is stated clearly in this prophecy. It is important not to stop reading at verse 19. In fact, for proper context we must begin at chapter 34 and proceed through the end of the book. You see, starting at verse 20, God Himself explains the interpretation of the prophecy.

In its context, the chapter involves a specific point in history. At the time of the writing of Ezekiel, the Hebrews were divided into two kingdoms, Judah and Israel,[43] and each having their own king. Scripture plainly states that after their captivity Judah and Israel (Israel is called Ephraim here, as it is in Hosea and elsewhere) will no longer be separate kingdoms. Instead, they would become one kingdom with a single king (the Messiah) over them. These are the two sticks, Judah and Israel (not the *Bible* and the *Book of Mormon*). In order to fit the *Book of Mormon* into this Scripture one must ignore the context and disagree with God's own explanation of the passage.

Ezekiel 2:9 shows that Ezekiel knew the word for *scroll*. He did not use the word in Ezekiel 37:15-19. In fact, the word *stick* is never used in the Bible to symbolize a scroll as Mormons are taught. Instead, a *roll of the book* is the normal Bible expression to describe a *scroll*. Strong's Exhaustive Concordance[44] shows the Hebrew word for *roll of a book* or *scroll* is *cepher* (Strong's #5612). The Hebrew for the word *stick* in Ezekiel 37:15-19 is *ates* or a *tree, stick, or wood* (Strong's #6086). This word is found over 300 times in the Bible, and never refers to scrolls.

Besides conflicting with Ezekiel's own explanation, the Mormon interpretation is troubled further. The *Book of Mormon* never calls itself the *stick of Joseph*. According to Mormon history, the *Book of Mormon* was not written on a scroll, as Ezekiel describes, but on gold plates. Consequently, if a stick means a *scroll*, the *Book of Mormon* can have no relevance to Ezekiel 37.

Lastly, Joseph had two sons, Ephraim and Mannaseh.[45] According to the the *Book of Mormon* itself[46] the *Book of Mormon* is a history of Mannaseh's descendants, and not Ephraim's! Even the *Book of Mormon* does not support the Mormon interpretation of Ezekiel 37! It is obvious that Ezekiel did not prophesy the *Book of Mormon*.

## National Geographic and the Smithsonian

| |
|---|
| ***no archeological or scientific evidence*** |

Pages 218-220 of the Exhibit Section shows that the National Geographic Society and Smithsonian Institution report that there is virtually no archeological or scientific evidence to prove the claims of the Book of Mormon. On the other hand, there is massive archeological and historical evidence from numerous sources to prove the credibility of the Bible.

## DNA

*Book of Mormon*, 2 Nephi 33:8, teaches that forefathers of the American Indians were Jews by nationality. Through the scientific study of DNA it has been proven that the American Indians did not come through the Jewish line as the Mormons have always taught. You may want to watch an interesting video

| |
|---|
| ***American Indians were Jews*** |

about this subject. Information is available in Works Cited, page 233 under DNA vs. The Book of Mormon. The LDS Church is conceding again to pressure. Past editions of the *Book of Mormon* describe the Lamanites as the *principal* ancestors of the American Indians. Doubleday's second edition describes them as being *among* the ancestors of the American Indians. What a difference a word makes!

## Two Popular Book of Mormon Verses

Throughout my Mormon experience two frequently quoted verses in the *Book of Mormon* were used to undermine the Bible. The first verse is from the book of Alma:

> *And because my words shall hiss forth–many of the Gentiles shall say: A Bible! A Bible! We have got a Bible, and there cannot be any more Bible . . . Thou fool, that shall say: A Bible, we have got a Bible, and we need no more Bible. Have ye obtained a Bible save it were by the Jews?*[47]

This verse mirrors Satan's ploy with Eve in the third chapter of Genesis - to cast doubt on the integrity of God and His promise to protect it through the years. But God has kept His promise and the Word of God, the Bible, is still here and is perfectly reliable in every way to teach the purity of the Gospel of the Living God. God is a covenant keeping God, seeing to it that the Jews protect and provide His Word to the nations. They have faithfully done so. The other verse from Moroni:

*And when ye shall receive these things, I would exhort you that ye would ask God, the Eternal Father, in the name of Christ if these things are not true; and if ye shall ask with a sincere heart, with real intent, having faith in Christ, he will manifest the truth of it unto you, by the power of the Holy Ghost.*[48]

This verse makes it appear that disagreement with the *Book of Mormon* can only come through phony motives or unbelief. This is not true, and nowhere in the Bible are we told to pray for a testimony against what God has already revealed in the Bible. But God has in many places warned against adding to His Word and sadly, there are false Christs. The words of the biblical Messiah Jesus, ". . . Take heed that no man deceive you. For many shall come in my name, saying, I am the Christ; and shall deceive many."[49] God does not exclude believers from the responsibility to defend the truth. See the exhibit on page 226.

In recent editions, the title of the *Book of Mormon* reads "The Book of Mormon –Another Testament of Jesus Christ." I key in on the word *another*. The *Book of Mormon* is indeed a testament of *another* Jesus. Mormonism teaches about another Jesus, another Gospel, another spirit, and more even as we are warned against:

*For if he that cometh preacheth another Jesus, whom we have not preached, or if ye receive another spirit, which ye have not received, or another gospel, which ye have not accepted, ye might well bear with him . . .*[50]

*For such are false apostles, deceitful workers, transforming themselves into the apostles of Christ. And no marvel; for Satan himself is transformed into an angel of light. Therefore it is no great thing if his ministers also be transofromed as the ministers of righteousness; whose end shall be according to their works.*[51]

*But though we, or an angel from heaven, preach any other gospel unto you than which we have preached unto you, let him be accursed.*[52]

Better to repent from believing the *Book of Mormon* which equates to the warnings in Corinthians, Galations, and many others in the Bible, and embrace the true Gospel of Jesus Christ.

1   Mormon Doctrine, p. 36, also Doctrine and Covenants 129:1.
2   Mormon Doctrine, p. 514.
3   Pearl of Great Price, pp. 50-54.
4   Book of Mormon, 1 Nephi 1:2.
5   Doctrine and Covenants 20:9; 42:12; 135:3.
6   History of the Church, vol. 4, p. 537.
7   History of Joseph Smith by his Mother, p. 108.
8   Joseph Smith, 2. p. 54.
9   Book of Mormon, Jacob 4:1.
19  History of the Church, vol. 4, p. 461.
11  Doctrine and Covenants 20:9.
12  Doctrine and Covenants 42:12.
13  Book of Mormon, Alma 11:28, 29, 38-40, 44.
14  Book of Mormon, Alma 11:27-28; 3 Nephi 11:27, 36; 2 Nephi 11:7; 3 Nephi 11:27, 36; Mosiah 15:2-5; 2 Nephi 31:21; Mosiah 15:1-5.
15  Book of Mormon, Mosiah 15:3.
16  2 Corinthians 5:19.
17  Mormonism: Shadow or Reality, p. 89-93.
18  Book of Mormon, 1830 first edition, vol. 1, Wilford C. Wood's.
19  The Book of Commandments, The Doctrine and Covenants, The Lectures on Faith, and the Fourteen Articles of Faith, vol. 2, Wilford C. Wood's.
20  Sam Weller's bookstore Salt Lake City, or through Sandra and Jerald Tanner, Lighthouse Ministry, 1350 S. W. Temple, Salt Lake City.
21  Joseph Smith –Seeker After Truth, pp. 338-339.
22  History of the Church, vol. 1, pp. 109-110.
23  History of the Church, vol. 3, p. 16,17.
24  Doctrine and Covenants 3:12, 10:7.
25  The Millennial Star, vol. 8, pp. 124-128.
26  History of the Church, vol. 3, p. 228.
27  History of the Church, vol. 3, p. 232.
28  A Comprehensive History of the Church of Jesus Christ of Latter-day Saints, vol. 1, pp. 155.
29  An Address to all Believers in Christ, pp. 27-28.
30  A Comprehensive History of the Church of Jesus Christ of Latter-day Saints, vol. 1, pp. 155-156.
31  Divine Authenticity of the Book of Mormon, pp. 1-2.
32  Divine Authenticity of the Book of Mormon, pp. 1-2.
33  Divine Authenticity of the Book of Mormon, pp. 1-2.
34  An Address To All Believers In Christ, p. 12.
35  Book of Mormon, 1 Nephi 16:10, 28.
36  Leviticus chapters 19-20; Deuteronomy chapter 18.
37  Book of Commandments, chapter 7 (which is the present Doctrine and Covenants section 8).
38  The Amboy Journal, April 30, 1879, p. 1.
39  A Marvelous Work and a Wonder, p. 68.
40  A Marvelous Work and a Wonder, pp. 68-69.
41  Leviticus 19:31.
42  Ezekiel 37:15-19.
43  1 Kings 12:16-24.
44  Strong's Exhaustive Concordance of the Bible.
45  Genesis 41:50-52.
46  Book of Mormon, Alma 10:3.
47  Book of Mormon, 2 Nephi 29:3,6.
48  Book of Mormon, Moroni 10:4.
49  Matthew 24:5.
50  2 Corinthians 11:4.
51  2 Corinthians 11:13-15.
52  Galatians 1:6.

# 14.  Laughing and Crying

*Beloved, believe not every spirit, but try the spirits whether they are of God; because many false prophets are gone out into the world.*

1 John 4:1

## Question the Brethren?

Think seriously about the Bible verse, "For the leaders of this people cause them to err; and they that are led of them are destroyed."[1]  As to whether we are led astray from the Word of God, we should each examine the people and the teachings we hold dear.  What a cruel, sad delusion one experiences by trusting in false prophets!  I served in a false religion for thirty-seven years, during which I truly supported the leaders of my church.  Many beliefs of Mormonism are based on feelings more than on an honest investigation of the facts.  Feelings when not tested by God's Word leave an opening for great deception.  Here is how the Mormon General Authorities view the relationship between its human leaders and its written works:

*No man ever went astray by following the counsel of the authorities of the Church.  No man who ever followed the teachings or took advice or counsel from the one who stands as the representative of the Lord ever went astray.*[2]

*Brethren, keep your eye on the President of this Church.  If he tells you to do anything and it is wrong and you do it, the Lord will bless you for it.  But you don't need to worry; the Lord will never let his mouthpiece lead this people astray.*[3]

*. . . the living prophet and the First Presidency . . . follow them and be blessed, reject them and suffer . . . The living prophet is more vital to us than the Standard Works.*[4]

*When our leaders speak, the thinking has been done.  When they propose a plan - it is God's plan.*[5]

*. . . if you will follow the revelations and instructions which God gives you through me, I will take you to heaven on my back load.*[6]

> **when our leaders speak, the thinking has been done**

Should one simply bow to these human leaders, or should one sincerely seek God's truth for themselves?  Such blind obedience encouraged by the Mormon Church makes the blind to follow the blind, resulting in both falling into the ditch.  I had been injected with the above poisonous mind set which kept me from recognizing and responding to God's truth.  Never again!

Jesus expresses concern for people who put trust in men more than in the God who created them, "And fear not them [men] which kill the body, but are not able to kill the soul: but rather fear Him [God] which is able to destroy both the soul and the body in hell."[7]

The prophet Isaiah explains that we are to use Scripture as a means to test and determine truth: "To the law and to the testimony! If they speak not according to this word, it is because there is no dawn."[8] The meaning of the word *law* in the Bible is understood as God's guidance, teaching, and instruction. From Luke's Gospel we learn that Jesus validated and powerfully upheld the law and testimony as Scripture:

> *Then He said unto them, This is what I told you while I was still with you, that everything which is written concerning Me in the Law of Moses and the prophets and the Psalms must be fulfilled.*[9]

> *Then beginning with Moses and (throughout) all the prophets, He went on explaining and interpreting to them in all the Scriptures the things concerning and referring to Himself.*[10]

The words of Jesus, "Law of Moses and the prophets and the Psalms," are a description of our Old Testament. The New Testament was not yet written. All Scripture was written to reveal Jesus. Jesus said:

> *Search the scriptures; for in them ye think ye have eternal life: and they are they which testify of me.*[11]

The New Testament explains and expounds the Old Testament, and reveals God's Messiah. Jesus is revealed in each of the Old Testament feasts and throughout the entirety of the Bible. Revealing Messiah Jesus, the Bible contains all the truth necessary to receive salvation. Receiving Jesus as He is clearly revealed throughout the Bible results in liberating peace. No longer do I accept Joseph Smith's version of guidance, teaching and instruction.

## Joseph Smith the Ego Man

I shall never be other than shocked by the following pride-filled words of Joseph Smith. Here are words of Joseph Smith who structured my world view, until I fled Mormonism and accepted Jesus Christ alone for total salvation:

> **I meet the violence of mobs . . . I solve mathematical problems of universities . . . God is my right hand man . . . know more than all the world put together**

> *. . . I have more to boast of than ever any man had. I am the only man that has ever been able to keep a whole church together since the days of Adam. A large majority of the whole have stood by me. Neither Paul, John, Peter nor Jesus ever did it. I boast that no man ever did such a work as I.*[12]

> *God made Aaron to be the mouth piece for the children of Israel, and he will make me be God to you in his stead and the elders to be my mouth piece; and if you don't like it, you must lump it.*[13]

> *I am a lawyer; I am a big lawyer and comprehend heaven, earth and hell, to bring forth knowledge that shall cover up all lawyers, doctors or other big bodies.*[14]

> *Don't employ lawyers . . . or pay them money for their knowledge, for I have learned that they don't know anything. I know more than they all.*[15]

> *I combat the errors of the ages; I meet the violence of mobs . . . I cut the gordian knot of powers, and I solve mathematical problems of universities, with truth – diamond truth; and God is my right hand man.*[16]

> *I am learned, and know more than all the world put together.*[17]

From the Bible: "Pride goeth before destruction, and a haughty spirit before a fall."[18] and "For out of the abundance of the heart his mouth speaketh."[19] I decided that I would never again sing the Mormon hymns *Praise to the Man, Oh Give Me Back My Prophet, The Seer, Joseph, The Seer.* I would absolutely never sing *O My Father,* nor, *We Thank Thee, O God, for a Prophet.* God forbid! And I never have.

## Mormon Potpourri

Anyone who begins a study of Mormonism will find colorful speeches made by the Mormon General Authorities. The same goes for some LDS Scripture. After thoughtful consideration these parts of Mormonism make it difficult to determine whether one should laugh or cry. The comparatively small list below is not intended to hurt Mormons, but rather demonstrate some different aspects of Mormonism which are not in accord with God's Word:

**Dark Skin a Sign of Rebellion Among the Indians** – The idea that dark skin is a result of God's displeasure is taught in the *Book of Mormon*. The dark skinned people of the *Book of Mormon*, who are named Lamanites, were, according to the *Book of Mormon* story, first white in color. They became dark as they dwindled into unbelief.[20] When they repented, however, they became white again.[21] In the same way the *Book of Mormon* once taught that the Lamanites, in the last days, would repent and become a white and delightsome people once more.[22] In 1981, the church changed one *Book of Mormon* embarrassing phrase "white and delightsome"[23] to "pure and delightsome".

> *they became dark as they dwindled into unbelief*

In 1960, at the General Conference in Salt Lake City, the Mormon Prophet Spencer W. Kimball, stated:

> *... I saw a striking contrast in the progress of the Indian people today ... they are fast becoming a white and delightsome people. For years they have been growing delightsome, and they are now becoming white and delightsome, as they were promised .... The children in the home placement program in Utah are often lighter than their brothers and sisters in the hogans on the reservation. ... These young members of the Church are changing to whiteness and delightsomeness.*[24]

**Prejudice Toward Jews** – The Lamanites are the savage dark skinned people of the Book of Mormon. Making a comparison of them to the Jews, the Mormon Prophet Brigham Young said:

> *I would rather undertake to convert five thousand Lamanites, than to convert one of those poor miserable creatures whose fathers killed the Savior, and who say, "Amen to the deed," to this day. Yea, I would rather undertake to convert the Devil himself, if it were possible ... ELDERS, I WOULD SAY, LEAVE THEM, AND COME HOME, THE LORD DOES NOT REQUIRE YOU TO STAY THERE, FOR THEY MUST SUFFER AND BE DAMNED."*[25] [Upper case in original].

> *miserable creatures whose fathers killed the Savior*

Mormon history, however, does record a slim Jewish membership within their church. Brigham Young stated:

> *We have men among us who are Jews, and became converted from Judaism. For instance, here is brother Neibaur, do I believe there is one particle of the blood of Judah in his veins? No, not so much as could be seen in the point of a cambric needle, through a microscope with a magnifying power of two millions.*[26]

Such rhetoric about the Jews is odd considering that the people of the *Book of Mormon* are allegedly of that decent (see 1 Nephi 1:2). The preface of the *Book of Mormon* states that it is a witness to the Jew and Gentile alike. So it seems Brigham Young should have been more benevolent towards converting the Jews.

**Penalty for Inter-Marriage with the Blacks** – Brigham Young said:

> *Shall I tell you the law of God in regard to the African race? If the white man who belongs to the chosen seed mixes his blood with the seed of Cain, the penalty, under the law of God, is death on the spot. This will always be so.*[27]

**Negro Skin color and Priesthood** – Noah's son Ham married a descendant of Cain, preserving the negro lineage through the flood. Negros, according to the *Pearl of Great Price*,[28] are always denied the priesthood. I was taught that this inequality was not of man's making but was the Lord's doing. The LDS Standard Works teach that in a pre-earth life people earned their earthly status.[29] In the pre-existence all exhibited various degrees of devotion to the truth. Those who were less valiant were sent to the earth through the lineage of Cain. A mark of black skin was put upon Cain for his rebellion against God and his murder of Abel.[30] The negro "should not have the privilege of bearing the priesthood . . . until the far distant future . . . on some other world . . ."[31]

**Word of Wisdom** – (a revelation given as a code of health in 1833). "We then partook of some refreshments, and our hearts were made glad with the fruit of the vine."[32] ". . . . after the people had fasted all day, they sent out and got wine and bread . . . they ate and drank . . . some of the High Counsel of Missouri stepped into the stand, and, as righteous Noah did when he awoke from his wine, commenced to curse their enemies."[33]

> *when the Lord pours*
> *out the Holy Ghost upon*
> *that individual he will*
> *have spasms, and one*
> *would think he too was*
> *going into fits*

**Spasms and the Holy Ghost** – Brigham Young said, "Again, if a pure Gentile firmly believes the Gospel of Jesus Christ, and yields obedience to it, in such a case I will give you the words of Joseph — 'When the Lord pours out the Holy Ghost upon that individual he will have spasms, and one would think he too was going into fits.'"[34]

**Sun and Moon Inhabited** – Brigham Young said, "Who can tell us of the inhabitants of this little planet that shines of an evening, called the moon? . . . when you inquire about the inhabitants of that sphere you will find that the most learned are as ignorant in regard to them as the most ignorant of their fellows. So it is with regard to the inhabitants of the sun. Do you think it is inhabited? I rather think it is. Do you think there is any life there? No question about it; it was not made in vain."[35]

**Shaking Hands and Demonic Power** – "If it be the devil as an angel of light, when you ask him to shake hands with you he will offer you his hand, and you will not feel anything; you may therefore detect him."[36] Within the Bible, shaking hands is never mentioned as a means to determine whether a messenger is from God. The Bible states that one must test the spirits to see whether they are from God or the adversary, and warns against false prophets whose measurement for truth is outside of biblical counsel.

**Isaiah and the Doctrine and Covenants** – ". . . some of Moses, and some of Elias, and some of Esaias and some of Isaiah, and some of Enoch."[37] Esaias is the Greek form of the name Isaiah. Joseph Smith didn't know that Esaias and Isaiah are the same person.[38]

**The Marriage Supper of the Lamb** – "First, the rich and the learned, the wise and the noble; and after that . . . cometh the lame, and the blind, and the deaf . . ."[39] This is certainly is a doctrine of men. The Mormon Church is elitist!

**Polygamy** –The practice of plural marriage, or polygamy, was at one time preached as necessary toward achieving Godhood.[40] McConkie states that the practice will commence again after the second coming of Christ.[41] The present *Doctrine and Covenants* 132 (the Law of Plural Marriage) replaced section 109 of the *Book of Commandments*, 1876 edition, which states that one man should have but one wife. Still, the present *Doctrine and Covenants*, section 132, retains the doctrine of plural marriage and says one will be damned if this law is not obeyed. Polygamy is necessary to becomming a God, see the exhibit on page 206. Jon Krakauer's book, *Under the Banner of Heaven,* estimates that there are more than thirty thousand Fundamentalist LDS polygamists living in Canada, Mexico, and throughout the American West. Some experts estimate there may be as many as one hundred thousand. The Mormon Manifesto (at the end of the present *Doctrine and Covenants*), which gives the mandate to cease the practice of polygamy, does not claim to be a revelation from God. From biblical narratives we discover that polygamy underlined the beginning of the eventual downfall for many biblical characters. God pronounced a penalty to those who disobeyed His law of monogamy.[42]

> *a man who has only*
> *one wife . . .*
> *soon begins to*
> *wither and dry up*

**Live Polygamy or Dry Up** – Brigham Young said "I have noticed that a man who has only one wife and is inclined to that doctrine, soon begins to wither and dry up, while a man who goes into plurality looks fresh, young and sprightly . . . For a man to be confined to one woman is small business . . . I do not know what we should do if we had only one wife apiece."[43]

**Statue of a Lamb** – Until 1985, at the Visitors Center in Salt Lake City Temple Square, there was a bronze statue which graphically depicted the heretical teaching of the labor of one's hands and the absence of the cleansing blood of Jesus. The statue was of Adam and Eve kneeling at an altar. On the altar were fruits and vegetables, and a little lamb sitting at their side. The offering of fruits and vegetables is the same offering presented by Cain, which God rejected.[44] It was rejected because there was no blood in Cain's offering; his offering came from the earth, which was cursed, and it was the fruit of his own labor. Recent criticism by Christians precipitated the removal of the statue from the temple grounds. Still Mormonism emphasizes works to achieve salvation and in doing so dismisses the total efficacy of the blood of Jesus.

**Topics for the Elite** – Details shrouded within Mormonism and discussed usually by the doctrinally schooled are the following mysterious expressions: The Temple Oath of Vengeance, Political Kingdom of God, Welfare Plan, United Order, Grand Council of Fifty, Blood Atonement, Plural Marriage, Patriarchal Order, Polyandry, Church of the First Born, Calling and Election Made Sure, First Anointing, Second Endowment, the Second Comforter, Avenging Angels or Destroying Angels, Danites, the *Book of Mormon* account of Slippery Treasures and Gadianton Robbers. Naming only a few, these terms present for the reader a fascinating excursion through the veil of concealment and disguise of the Mormon cult.

**Mormon Kingdom of God** – The Mormon Apostle Orson Hyde said, "What the world calls Mormonism will rule every nation . . . This will make the heathen rage and the world imagine a vain thing."[45] Hyde actually is referring to Psalms 2, where God is speaking of His kingdom –not of Joseph Smith's Mormon Kingdom –such blasphemy! The Mormon Political Kingdom of God is promulgated by a secret Grand Council of Fifty that consists of 48 great LDS High Priests and two honorable non-Mormons of like power. It was organized for the purpose of counseling on the best way to respond to church enemies. This topic is cloaked in mystery. Following are additional references:

*Journal of Discourses,* vol.12, p. 204, vol.11, p. 53, vol. 2, p. 309, vol. 7, p. 15.
*General Conference Report,* April 1950.
*General Conference Report,* October 1987.
*Teachings of the Prophet Joseph Smith,* pp. 248-254, 322, 318.
*History of the Church,* vol.1, p. 196; vol.5, pp. 510-513, 1, 2, 139, 523; vol. 6, p. 365.
*Heber C. Kimball Journal,* 1845, Dec. 26, Church Archives.
*Mormon Doctrine,* p. 813.

**Hanging by a Thread** – In 1854, Brigham Young said, "Will the Constitution be destroyed? No: it will be held inviolate by this people," and, as Joseph Smith said, "The time will come when the destiny of the nation will hang upon a single thread. At that critical juncture, this people will step forth and save it from the threatened destruction. It will be so."[46]

**United Order** – The founders of Mormonism established what is known as the United Order, a legal organization to secure and distribute wealth. This order is expressed in the Mormon temple through a ritual called The Law of Consecration. Temple Mormons take a vow to prosper the Law of Consecration's intent and purpose. The implementation of the United Order as defined in various sections within the *Doctrine and Covenants*[47] failed. While the United Order failed, the Mormon Church plans its completed form and practice at a later date. Mormon Apostle Bruce McConkie explains:

*Early attempts to operate various United Orders failed, but the law of consecration must yet be put into full force, and so the United Order or its equivalent must again be brought into being. It appears that operation of the present Church Welfare Plan may be the beginning of this . . . It is not asserted that the Welfare Plan is the United Order, but perhaps there is a much greater nearness of approach that we have been accustomed to think. Safe it is to say that a complete living of the law governing this Plan, and the practice of the principles involved, would make transition to the organization of the United Order not too difficult.*[48]

> **I the Lord will that you should purchase lands . . . advantage over all the world . . .**

The following two quotes from the Standard Works concern the United Order:

*Wherefore, I the Lord will that you should purchase the lands, that you may have advantage over the world, that you may have claim on the world . . . wherefore the land of Zion shall not be obtained but by purchase or by blood, otherwise there is none inheritance for you.*[49]

*And now, verily I say unto you, and this is wisdom, make unto yourselves friends with the "mammon of unrighteousness," and they will not destroy you.*[50]

**Non-Profit** – Financially speaking, Mormonism is a covert power machine. The Mormon Church nets billions a year from tithing and spends millions a year for missionary endeavors. With it's power Mormonism is able to wield authority in any many settings. The Mormon Church owns cannaries, farms, ranches, land, insurance companies, radio and TV stations, lumber mills, newspapers, magazines, mines, railroads, and more. Members are taxed (tithed) at 10% –or over 4 billion dollars a year. *Mormon America,* by Richard Ostling and Joan Ostling in 2000, says that if the LDS Church were a U.S. Corporation, by revenues it would rank number 243 on the Fortune 500 list.

**Man versus God** – Joseph Smith said, "— the soul — the mind of man — the immortal spirit . . . men say God created it in the beginning. The very idea lessens man in my estimation; I do not believe the doctrine, I know better . . . I am going to tell of things more noble. The mind of man is as immortal as God Himself . . . God never did have power to create the spirit of man at all."[51]

**Poor Governor Ford** – Governor Ford did not support the Mormon cause. Of Ford Joseph Smith said: "I prophecy in the name of the Lord God that Governor Ford by granting the writ against me has damned himself politically and and his carcase will stink on the face of the earth food for the carrion Crow & Turkey Buzzard."[52] A copy of these words in Joseph's own handwriting may be seen in the Exhibit Section on page 222.

**President of the United States** – The Mormon Apostle Heber C. Kimball said, "The church and kingdom to which we belong will become the kingdom of our God and his Christ, and brother Brigham Young will become President of the United States . . . You may think I am joking; but I am perfectly willing that brother Long should write every word of it; for I can see it just as naturally as I see the earth and the productions thereof."[53]

> **brother Brigham Young will become President of the United States**

**Tithe or Burn** – The *Doctrine and Covenants* says that Mormon tithes are of necessity an important component to the building up of Mormon Zion. The LDS Church teaches its members that those who pay tithing will not be burned at the second coming of Christ.[54] Therefore, tithes play a role in a Mormon's safety during the end times. Incidentally, the payment of Mormon tithes are necessary for members to maintain a current Temple Recommend, an official document which serves as a ticket of entrance into a Mormon temple.

**Joseph Smith in a Gunfight** – The *Doctrine and Covenants* 135:4 states that Joseph Smith went like a lamb to the slaughter, but the *History of the Church*, in various places, says that he died in a gun fight. The following testimony given by the third Mormon Prophet, John Taylor, is one such example, "He, however, instantly arose, and with a firm, quick step, and a determined expression of countenance, approached the door, and pointing the six-shooter left by brother Whellock from his pocket, opened the door slightly, and snapped the pistol six successive times; only three of the barrels, however, were discharged. I afterwards understood that two or three were wounded by the discharges, two of whom, I am informed died."[55]

> **suppose you found your brother in bed with your wife, and put a javelin through both of them, you would be justified, and they would atone for their sins**

**Blood Atonement** – Brigham Young said, "Let me suppose a case. Suppose you found your brother in bed with your wife, and put a javelin through both of them, you would be justified, and they would atone for their sins, and be received into the kingdom of God. I would at once do so in such a case; and under such circumstances, I have no wife whom I love so well that I would not put a javelin through her heart, and I would do it with clean hands . . . There is not a man or woman, who violates the covenants made with their God, that will not be required to pay the debt. The blood of Christ will never wipe that out, your own blood must atone for it . . . ."[56]

**Blacks and their Curse** – Brigham Young described the Blacks in this manner ". . . black, uncouth, uncomely, disagreable and low in their habits, wild, and seemingly deprived of all the blessings of the intelligence that is generally bestowed upon man. How long is that race to endure the dreadful curse that is put upon them? The curse will remain and they can never hold the priesthood . . . until all of the other decendants of Adam have received the promises and enjoyed the blessings of the priesthood and keys thereof." See the exhibit on page 204.

**Reincarnation, Salvation, Diety, Spirits** – Of these subjects, Brigham Young states that "the Quorum of the Twelve disagree among themselves."[57]

**Blind Obendience –** Brigham Young said "if you will follow the revelations and instruction which God gives you through me, I will take you to heaven on my back load."[58]

**Brigham's Distillery** – Brigham Young had his own distillery and boasted that he could have made thousands of dollars.[59]

**Beat the World at any Game** – Brigham Young "dared the world to produce as mean devils as we can; we can beat them at anything. We have the greatest and smoothest liars in the world, the cunningest and most adroit thieves, and any other shade of character that you can mention. We can pick out Elders in Israel right here who can beat the world at gambling, who can handle the cards, cut and shuffle them with the smartest rogue on the face God's foot-stool."[60]

**Magic Charms** – Years ago at Wood's Museum in Salt Lake City, I was shown Jospeh Smith's Jupiter Talisman. The lady who showed me the display told me that Joseph Smith was wearing it when he was killed. The medallion relates to magic and astrology. You may read more about it in Tanner's book, *The Changing World of Mormonism.*[61]

There is an abundance of resources available that elaborate on Mormonism:

**Web sites:**
*Mormon Research Ministry,* www.mrm.org
*Recovery from Mormonism,* www.exmormon.org
*Living Hope Ministries,* www.lhvm.org
*The Bible vs. The Book of Mormon,* www.mormonchallenge.com
*The Story behind the Book of Abraham,* www.bookofabraham.info
*Watchman Fellowship,* www.watchman.org
*The Mormon Conspiracy,* www.mormonconspiracy.com, Charles L. Wood, Ph.D.
*Lighthouse Ministries,* www.utlm.org, Jerrald and Sandra Tanner
*Through the Maze,* www.mazeministry.com, Jim Spencer
*Saints Alive in Jesus,* www.saintsalive.com, Ed Decker
*Concerned Christians,* www.concernedchristians.org
*Out of Polygamy,* www.outofpolygamy.com

**Books:**
*The Mormon Conspiracy,* Charles L. Wood, Ph.D.
*The Changing World of Mormonism,* Jerald and Sandra Tanner.
*America's Saints, The Rise of Mormon Power,* Robert Gottlieb & Peter Wiley.
*The Mormon Corporate Empire,* John Heinerman and Anson Shupe.
*The Darker Side of Virtue,* Anson Shupe.
*The Mormon Hierarchy: Origins of Power,* D. Michael Quinn.
*Mormon America,* Richard N. Ostling and Joan K. Ostling.
*The Mormon Conspiracy,* Charles L. Wood.
*Early Mormonism and the Magic World View,* D. Michael Quinn.
*Evolution of the Mormon Temple Ceremony:1842-1990,* Jerald and Sandra Tanner.
*In Sacred Loneliness, The Plural Wives of Joseph Smith,* Todd Compton.
*No Man Knows My History –the life of Joseph Smith,* Fawn M. Brodie.
*Leaving the Saints,* Martha Beck.
*Wild Bill Hickman and the Mormon Frontier,* Hope A. Hilton.

1    Isaiah 9:16.
2    Doctrines of Salvation, vol. 1, p. 243.
3    Ensign, Alma P. Burton, October, 1972, p. 2.
4    14 Fundamentals in Following the Prophets, Provo Herald, Ezra Taft Benson, February 26, 1980.
5    The Improvement Era, Ward Teachers' Message, June, 1945 p. 354.
6    Brigham Young, Millennial Star, vol. 18, p. 743.
7    Matthew 10:28.
8    Isaiah 8:20.
9    Luke 24: 44-45.
10    Luke 24:27.
11    John 5:39.
12    History of the Church, vol. 6, pp. 408-409.
13    History of the Church, vol. 6, pp. 319-320.
14    History of the Church, vol. 5, p. 289.
15    History of the Church, vol. 5, p. 467.
16    History of the Church, vol. 6, p. 78.
17    History of the Church, vol. 6, p. 308.
18    Proverbs 16:18.
19    Luke 6:45.
20    Book of Mormon, 2 Nephi 5:21.
21    Book of Mormon, 3 Nephi 2:15.
22    Book of Mormon, 2 Nephi 30:6.
23    Book of Mormon, 2 Nephi 30:6.
24    Improvement Era, December 1960, pp. 922, 923.
25    Journal of Discourses, vol. 2, p. 143.
26    Journal of Discourses, vol. 2, p. 142.
27    Journal of Discourses, vol. 10, p. 110.
28    Pearl of Great Price, Abraham 1:20-27.
29    Pearl of Great Price, Abraham 3:22-24.
30    Pearl of Great Price, Moses 7:8, 22.
31    Answers to Gospel Questions, vol. 2, p. 188.
32    History of the Church, vol. 2, p. 369.
33    Journal of Discourses, vol. 2, p. 216.
34    Journal of Discourses, vol. 2, p. 269.
35    Journal of Discourses, vol. 13, p. 271.
36    Doctrine and Covenants 129:8.
37    Doctrine and Covenants 76:100.
38    Romams 9:27-29; Isaiah 10:22, 23.
39    Doctrine and Covenants 58:10,11.
40    Journal of Discourses, vol. 11, p. 269.
41    Mormon Doctrine, p. 578.
42    Deuteronomy 17:17.
43    Deseret News, April 22, 1857.
44    Genesis 4:3-5.
45    Journal of Discourses, vol. 7, p. 53.
46    Journal of Discourses, vol. 7, p. 15; vol. 12, p. 204.
47    Doctrine and Covenants, sections 82 and 51.
48    Mormon Doctrine, pp. 813-814.
49    Doctrine and Covenants 63:27, 29.
50    Doctrine and Covenants 82:22.
51    History of the Church, vol. 6, pp. 310-311.
52    Joseph Smith's Diary, June 30, 1843.
53    Journal of Discourses, vol. 5, p. 219.
54    Doctrine and Covenants 64:23.
55    History of the Church, vol. 7, pp. 102-103.
56    Journal of Discourses, vol. 3, p. 247.
57    Journal of Discourses, vol. 12, p. 66.
58    Millenial Star, vol 18, p. 743.
59    Journal of Discourses, vol. 10, p. 206.
60    Journal of Discourses, vol. 4, p. 77.
61    The Changing World of Mormonism, pp. 88-91.

# 15. Mormon Hymns

*Sing unto the Lord a new song; Sing to the Lord, all the earth. Sing to the Lord, bless His name; Proclaim good tidings of His salvation from day to day.*

Psalm 96:1-2

As a Mormon I took great pride in believing that Mormonism initiated their hymns.

When I left Mormonism I thought I would miss the Mormon hymns with which I had become so familiar. Then I discovered that my favorite words and melodies in Mormonism actually were taken from Christian hymns. Some hymns were modified to suit Mormon Church doctrine. Sometimes entire verses were eliminated, especially those that pertain to the cross, the blood of Jesus, or to grace.

This is important because it showed me that Mormonism is not unique in history, but is only a new twist on old traditions.

## Dora North Explains

My mother-in-law, Dora North, who had served as a Mormon organist for 40 years before coming to Christ, and then played at her Christian church, also made a list of such songs. We were astonished! We had assumed the hymns were mostly unique to Mormonism and were written by Mormon composers. How wrong we were. The Mormon Church had taken beautiful Christian hymns that proclaimed the true Gospel, yet with their doctrine had twisted that truth in order to proclaim their false Gospel. For the following contribution I thank my mother-in law.

> *As a Mormon organist, I was always instructed to avoid music that was secular or that pertained to the cross. I was led to believe that all Mormon hymns were written expressly for the Mormon Church.*
>
> *After I started playing from Christian hymn books, I discovered that many of the exclusive Mormon hymns were actually Christian hymns. Many times they had changed the words to conform to Mormonism, but the melodies were the same. This surprised me because many of the Christian hymns were much older than the Mormon Church! Since the Mormon Church claims that all other churches and creeds are an abomination to God, I feel that copying Christian hymns is unethical and hypocritical. Some examples:*
>
> > *A Mighty Fortress*
> > *Abide With Me*
> > *Christ the Lord is Risen*
> > *Come, Come, Ye Saints*
> > *Count Your Blessings*

*God Be With You*
*Guide Us, O Thou Great Jehovah*
*How Great Thou Art-(recently added to their hymn book)*
*How Firm a Foundation*
*I Stand All Amazed*
*In the Garden*
*I'll Go Were You Want Me to Go*
*I Need Thee Every Hour*
*If There's Sunshine in Your Heart*
*I Know that My Redeemer Lives*
*I'll be a Sunbeam*
*It May Not be on a  Mountain Top*
*Jesus, Savior, Pilot Me*
*Jesus Lover of My Soul*
*Jesus, the Very Thought of Thee*
*Praise God from Whom all Blessings Flow*
*Lead Kindly Light*
*Let the Lower Lights be Burning*
*Lord Dismiss Us with Thy Blessings*
*More Holiness Give Me*
*My Redeemer*
*Nearer My God to Thee*
*Now Thank We All Our God*
*Now the Day is Over*
*O My Father*
*Oh It is Wonderful*
*Onward Christian Soldiers*
*Rock of Ages*
*Softly Now the Light of Day*
*Sweet Hour of Prayer*
*There is Sunshine in My Soul*
*There is a Green Hill*

*The hymn, 'Praise God from Whom All Blessings Flow' is the Christian Church Doxology (Father, Son, and Holy Ghost - One God) - Ironically, LDS deny the orthodox view of TRIN-ITY!*

Thank you, Mom.

## Jeanette Tuxhorn Adds More

A friend of mine wrote an article about Mormon hymns, entitled, "*Mormonized Christian Hymns*". Here is an excerpt from her article.

*Joseph Smith purported that God told him not to join any of the churches because they were all wrong, their creeds were an abomination in his sight, their professors were all corrupt, and they taught for doctrines the commandments of men.*

*In view of God's conversation with Joseph, it is not immediately understandable why the LDS hymn book is padded with over 130 hymns written by Christian lyricists, some of the same corrupt professors of biblical Christianity that Joseph's God was talking about.*

*Offensive Christian lyrics had to be edited out before hymns were acceptable for the Mormon hymnal.  Mormon doctrine, or at least something harmless, was inserted in their place.*

*A prime example is the Christian hymn, All Creatures of Our God and King (1975 Edition Baptist Hymnal  p. 9).  Verses 3 and 4 of the Christian hymn read, "And all ye men of tender heart, Forgiving others, take your part, O sing ye!  Alleluia!  Ye who long pain and sorrow bear, Praise God and on him cast your care! Let all things their Creator bless, And worship him in humbleness, O praise him! Alleluia! Praise, praise the Father, praise the Son, And Praise the Spirit. Three in one!*

*And the Mormonized version of verses 3 and 4 read, "Thou flowing water, pure and clear, Make music for they Lord to hear, Alleluia! Alleuia! Thou fire so masterful and bright, That gives to man both warmth and light, Dear Mother Earth, who day by day, Unfoldest blessings on our way, Alleluia! Alleluia! That flow'rs and fruit that in thee grow, Let them his glory also show." If Mormonism were a Christian denomination, would the Trinity have to be replaced with Mother Earth, water and fire, flowers and fruit? Of course not!*

*Other hymns were changed simply to reflect Mormon hardships, reverence for the Prophet, outlook for the future, pride in Zion, Missionary zeal, and faith in the restoration and the church. It is understandable that songs in the Mormon Hymnal should reflect their doctrine and culture. However, it is unfortunate that some Christian Hymns have been Mormonized to reflect another Jesus, another gospel and another spirit, (2 Corinthians 11:4). Mormonism is NOT biblical Christianity!"*

Thank you, Jeanette.

These examples are but a few surprises most former Mormons discover when they embrace Christianity. They illustrate Mormon plagiarism and distortion of Christianity. Today's Mormons wish to be classified as Christian –yet avoid the basics of Christianity.

To close this chapter, I quote one more time from an old favorite Mormon hymn titled *Oh, Say, What Is Truth?*, by Jon Jaques:

> *Then say, what is truth? Tis the last and the first, For the limits of time it steps o'er.*
>
> *Though the heavens depart and the earth's fountains burst,*
>
> *Truth, the sum of existence, will weather the worst, Eternal, unchanged, evermore.*

The words to this song I keep in my heart. I rejoice that they are true! These words testify against the LDS faith.

> **today's Mormons**
> **wish to be**
> **classified as Christian**

# 16. Family Departure

*Therefore if any man is in Christ, he is a new creature; the old things passed away; behold, new things have come.*

2 Corinthians 5:17

## I Wanted Out and Counted the Cost

It is clear to me now that God worked the events of my life in such a way as to break down my resistance and to trust only in Him for salvation. This required repentance and turning my back on a false Gospel and leadership –even at the expense of family disapproval. I wanted to be obedient to God's Word. Jesus said:

*If anyone publicly acknowledges Me as his friend, I will openly acknowledge him as My friend before My Father in heaven. But if anyone publicly denies Me, I will openly deny him before My Father in heaven.*[1]

*Be ye not unequally yoked together with unbelievers: for what fellowship hath righteousness with unrighteousness? and what communion hath light with darkness? And what concord hath Christ with Belial? . . . wherefore come out from among them, and be ye separate, saith the Lord, and touch not that unclean thing; and I will receive you . . .*[2]

*And Jesus said unto him, No man, having put his hand to the plough, and looking back, is fit for the Kingdom of God.*[3]

*Don't imagine that I came to bring peace to the earth! No, rather, a sword. I have come to set a man against his father, and a daughter against her mother, and a daughter-in-law against her mother-in-law-a man's worst enemies will be in his own home.*[4]

I wasn't alarmed by these words. I considered them a loving warning from God to prepare for what may come. The message given by the true Messiah always separates and divides.

Jesus declared, "I am the light of the world he that followeth me shall not walk in darkness, but shall have the light of life."[5] He gave warning that some people would actually make a free will choice to embrace darkness more than light. Making that choice ends to their own condemnation.[6] He also said of some people, ". . . They hear, but don't understand; they look, but don't see! For their hearts are fat and heavy, and their ears are dull, and they have closed their eyes in sleep, so they won't see and hear and understand and turn to God again, and let me heal them."[7]

But the fact remains that a saving truth and proper relationship with the One who saves has been available all along. Our own ideas do not change the truth of God's Word. Not everyone who has ears listens with them. Jesus said that the Heavenly Father will give the Holy Spirit to those who ask Him.[8] We must ask!  The Holy Spirit opens our eyes and ears to the true salvation message.  If we do not listen and respond to the Holy Spirit as He speaks truth to our hearts, we may develop an unbelieving heart, "Beware, brethren, lest there be in any of you an evil heart of unbelief in departing from the living God; but exhort one another daily, while it is called "Today," lest any of you be hardened through the deceitfulness of sin."[9]

For me, discovering the Mormon Church to be false was like living through a great earthquake deep within me.  Increasingly, crystal clear evidence against the Mormon Gospel appeared, just as aftershocks follow an earthquake.  Deep in my heart I was certain that I must believe and rely only on Jesus and His shed blood to save me --- save me completely!  I was strongly urged by the words of Jesus concerning the new birth, "Verily, verily, I say unto thee, Except a man be born of water and of the Spirit, he cannot enter into the kingdom of God.  That which is born of the flesh is flesh; and that which is born of the Spirit is spirit.  Marvel not that I said unto thee, Ye must be born again."[10]

## A Saving Prayer

Finally in God's perfect timing, I arrived at a time in my life of great desire to surrender all to God!  The Holy Spirit led me to cry out in this type of prayer:

> *God of Abraham, Isaac, and Jacob, true God of all, I am willing to accept all that You choose to reveal to me.  Help me to do so without bias.  Please make Yourself known to me.  Teach me truth.  I know I'm a sinner.  Please continue showing me where my beliefs are wrong about You.  Please reveal Yourself to me in a way that I will know is genuine - I don't want to be deceived about religion ever again.  Dear Jesus, come into my heart, and forgive me of my sins.  Please make me Your servant.*

> **Mormon-colored glasses . . mis-translations and ommissions in the Bible**

After I gave my life to Jesus, rather than understanding God through the Mormon prophets, I received a fresh revelation from God.  When I first began to seriously doubt the church I felt empty inside, for I had always enjoyed reading Mormon Scripture and other church publications and apologetics.  I did not then have the trust, respect and regard for the Bible I now have.  God blessed me with the anointing of the Holy Spirit, quickening my soul with His refreshing comfort.  In the past I was accustomed to reading Bible passages in a Mormon context - through Mormon-colored glasses, and I was proud of the Mormon Scripture and prophets, each teaching about the mis-translations and ommissions in the Bible.

For the first time I began to read Bible verses with even more enthusiasm than ever before.  Bible reading, aside from being a tremendous joy for me, became a total surprise!  The surprise came not because I hadn't studied much of the Bible (I had), but because I began reading Bible verses from an altogether different vantage point.  The Holy Spirit was giving me supernatural assistance for understanding Scripture, just as was promised in the Bible:

> *But when He, the Spirit of Truth, is come, He will guide you into all truth . . .*[11]

> *And as for you, the anointing which you received from Him abides in you, and you have no need for anyone to teach you; but His anointing teaches you about all things, and is true and is not a lie, and just as it has taught you, you abide in Him.*[12]

God took away the fabrication of Mormonism and blessed me with true salvation; the Gift of His Son.  At the time I didn't understand all that had happened - but now I know that through my acceptance of the biblical Savior, I experienced the new birth, of which Jesus referred.[13]  According to the Bible, through the *new birth* I had passed from death to life.[14]  When Scripture speaks of death and life it always refers to relationship, not existence.  By receiving Christ as Savior I moved out from under Satan's government to live under God's government.  The Apostle Paul informs believers that through the Messiah Jesus, God "hath delivered us from the power of darkness, and hath translated us into the kingdom of His dear Son, in whom we have redemption, the forgiveness

> **Satan's government to God's government**

of sins."[15] Through the new birth my legal status with God is reconciled. My sins are pardoned and I have received the righteousness of Christ. The Bible refers to this pardoning as justification. Through the Messiah Jesus everyone who believes is justified.[16]

The Bible says that at the time of the new birth God begins a process in a believer's life which is termed *sanctification*. " . . . we are sanctified through the offering of the body of Jesus Christ once for all."[17] Through the process of sanctification one's character tunes and aligns itself to God's will for life. Drs. Gordon R. Lewis and Bruce A. Demarest, of Denver Seminary, explain the difference between justification and sanctification:

> *Justification is distinct from sanctification, although the former leads to the latter. Justification is a complete provision of Jesus Christ's atonement; sanctification is a progressive enabling by the spirit's ministries. That is, justification is once-for-all; sanctification is continuous.*[18]

Because of my new birth I was made a new creation.[19] As I co-operate with the enabling Holy Spirit sin no longer has power in my life. Sinning has become more obvious and repugnant and it is more difficult to continue in sin. While I may still fall in sin in many areas of my life, I sincerely desire to be obedient to His commandments and yield my life as a living sacrifice, holy, and acceptable unto God, which according to Scripture is my reasonable service.[20] I want to give Him preeminence by allowing Him to assist my growth and not let the world squeeze me into its mold. Part of the changes that occurred and are still taking place in my life are a cleansing and purging of old thought patterns, habits and problems which are not in accord with God's plan for my life. When I am faithful to let God rule in my life I am filled with His peace and joy. As I worship Him, I am bathed in His peace, light, life, grace, and truth.

Each day I am wonderfully amazed at all there is to glean and understand from God's Word! How very interesting this new me! One obvious new characteristic resulting from my new birth was an increased awareness of joy, love, laughter, hope and thanksgiving. I had compassion for my family and wanted to protect my loved ones and others from the snare of Mormonism. With great passion I recognized the presence of God. Within my heart I seemed to always rejoice and have a song of praise to God. In a deep intimate way I came to understand the meaning of the words of Jesus, "I am the way, and the truth, and the life; no man cometh unto the Father, but by Me."[21]

One day I was driving down the highway, thanking God for all the blessings He had given me. I was overwhelmed! I felt such love well up for Him and all He had led me through that I had to pull my car over and stop. Tears of gratitude and thanksgiving were flooding my eyes! I realized that I was experiencing the power of the Holy Spirit, as He testified again of the true person of Jesus. I prayed words like these:

> *Oh, Jesus - You are God! You truly are God Incarnate! I am so sorry that I never gave You full credit for who You actually are. I never understood all that I do now. Please forgive me. Thank You for answering my prayers and making Yourself known to me. I love You LORD, I praise Your Most Holy Name!*

There on the side of the road I magnified God. He alone is worthy of praise. Through the new birth I escaped Mormon cisterns filled with contaminated waters, exchanging them for cisterns of pure living water---washing with the pure Word of God.[22] Soon thereafter I experienced the waters of baptism into the true body of Christ.

Of Messiah Jesus, how true the Bible verse, "And there is salvation in no one else; for there is no other name under heaven that has been given among men, by which we must be saved."[23]

## A Remedial Twist

I now recognized the false doctrine of Mormonism as a cruel taskmaster imposing dire consequences.[24] How strange, knowing that even as I was once offended by accusations against the Mormon Church –my family still were offended. Even as I once believed that my friend Melaine was off-the-wall with her concern for my salvation, I was now burdened for my relatives' salvation, and all those that I recognized as being held hostage by the cult of Mormonism.

As I came to a clearer understanding of the beguilement and snare of Mormonism, the Holy Spirit

> *God's truth became a refreshing exchange for the endless maze of Mormonism*

prompted me to cry out to God for all of my family: my husband, his parents and family, our children, my parents, my brothers and sisters, each one by name. Prayer had always been important to me, but now it was unusually sweet and precious. I looked for time to be alone with God. I looked forward to reading the Bible. I was very hungry to learn what God was saying directly to me! God's truth became a refreshing exchange for the endless maze of Mormonism.

## My Husband Explains

My husband, Clyde, expresses his views of Mormonism and how his departure came about.

*Christine and I have quite different backgrounds. Though we were both raised as Mormons, she came from a strong Mormon family. My family were less involved in the Mormon Church. This difference caused some friction in our marriage during our early years together. I could never muster the religious intensity I needed to be a good Mormon. I made a few attempts to live the Mormon Gospel but just couldn't believe some of the teachings of Mormonism. They weren't logical or consistent. My going through the temple only reinforced my uneasy feelings.*

*During the 1970's in Illinois, Christine had accumulated a substantial library of both pro and anti-Mormon material. At Christine's urging I reluctantly began to read this material, which evolved into an in-depth study of LDS history. We examined Mormon history, its prophets, apostles, and revelations. Because I have a technical background, I expected some logical confirmation of the teachings of the church.*

*As our studies continued, I became more and more disenchanted with Mormonism. If Jesus is my Savior and atoned for my sins, as the Bible teaches, then the LDS Church must be a cultic social organization, not a Christian faith. After many months of deliberation and soul-searching, I wanted the Mormon officials to remove my name from their records. I asked Jesus to take control of my life. I am a child of God, and He will direct me, protect me and His will shall prevail. He is my way to Salvation.*

## Our Children

Clyde and I chose to tell our children the dreadful truth about Mormonism. Our eldest daughter was away attending Brigham Young University. We decided to tell the others first. I thought to myself, "This is going to be a difficult task!" The church was familiar and comfortable to them and I wondered what the outcome of telling them would be. One evening, we gathered our other children together and told them about our discovery. It seemed to me they were quiet for a long time. I wondered what they were thinking!

Gil, our then twelve year old son, finally looked up at us, and with big brown eyes and frank conviction said, "Well, if our Church isn't true, then I know God doesn't want us to be Mormons anymore!" All of us agreed. I thanked God! What seemed to be an unpleasant task, became a wonderful memory instead. Gil's words also spoke to what I knew must be done. We must request that our names be removed from the records of the Mormon Church!

As I said, our eldest daughter was attending Brigham Young University during this time, and had become engaged to marry a returned Mormon missionary. We did not want our daughter to be married in the Mormon temple. That was very difficult and sad for us, and the spiritual implication weighed heavy upon my mind. Becoming a Christian had given me Christian eyes with which to view the Mormon Temple Ceremony and the wearing of the temple garments. As I have previously mentioned, I had come to view the Temple Ceremony and all that is related to it as an abomination to God.

During this time I was very close to God and I noticed that as I surrendered my cares and broken dreams to Jesus, He began to fill me with His peace! I know now that Jesus had been drawing me my whole life long, and He had been with me through all my struggles. By grace I was saved through faith *unto* good works –biblical good works as opposed to Mormon extra-biblical works.

Now God was blessing me with freedom –not bondage; joy –not false guilt; rest –not false labor or competition; love –not false rules and regulations. In the meantime, our eldest daughter, Valerie, was traveling the Mormon road into false works –not grace; bondage –not freedom; guilt –not joy; competition and labor –not rest; false rules and regulations –not liberating love.

## Valerie Tells Her Story

Our oldest daughter, Valerie, describes the impact on her life.

*As a youth, I was very active in the church. I went to seminary every day before school (about 5:30 a.m.) and was involved in the church activities and meetings that were expected of a young person. My parents did an excellent job of raising a strong, upstanding young Mormon woman. We lived in Chicago at that time, and being a Mormon meant being different from the other kids in school. I was very proud of my faith and tried to set a good example for all of my non-Mormon friends. In fact, I felt a desire to make them curious about Mormonism in order to have an opportunity to convert them. I graduated from high school a year early and left for Brigham Young University when I was 17 years old. Shortly after I began school at BYU my parents left the Mormon Church.*

*While at BYU I met a wonderful, intelligent, returned Mormon missionary named Bob (not his real name) and we started dating. At my request, mom sent me some of the materials which had caused my parents to reject Mormonism. Bob and I examined them. I have to admit that my motivation was probably to learn enough to show my parents where they'd gone wrong. We met with and arranged for my mom to meet with our religion professors at BYU. We were astonished to discover that the professors did not agree amongst themselves about Mormon history and doctrines. Their differing opinions on subjects and answers to questions were perplexing to us, but we still had great faith in our Mormon leaders. I wanted desperately to save or fix my family. Months went by. Bob and I reached a point where we felt that the answers to our questions could only be resolved and explained by faith, prayer and learning through the front door. That is we agreed to quit studying the anti-Mormon material and focus on the Mormon Gospel. I put my best foot forward and continued teaching the Book of Mormon class for my college ward.*

*Bob asked me to marry him and we planned an August wedding in the Salt Lake City Temple. I had been taught that the temple was a sacred and special place. I was excited that I was finally going to personally experience the Temple Ceremony. I had performed baptisms for the dead on a few occasions, but the sacred secrets that would allow me into the Celestial kingdom were what I wanted to learn. I felt that the experience would surely resolve the questions I was still harboring.*

*I clearly remember my thoughts on the day I received my endowments and was married. The rooms in the temple were beautiful. All of the people were dressed in pure white and there was a sense of reverence and solemnity. But I recall feeling my mind switch channels. One minute I would be thinking how blessed I was to be there, enjoying the beauty and tranquility and feeling close to God. Then the channel would change and I would be thinking how goofy it was that the men were seated on one side, the women on the other, we were all wearing odd costumes, taking blood oaths, and learning secret handshakes. It was a lot to handle. I just wanted to learn and feel the truth in the temple.*

*Because my parents had resigned from the church, they were not permitted inside the temple to witness my marriage. Some of the worthy members of my mother's family did attend, including my grandmother. It was hard for me not to have my immediate family with me during the ceremony. They waited for us on the lawn outside the Salt Lake City Temple. Now I realize that it was much more difficult for my parents not to see their oldest daughter's wedding.*

*My husband and I began our lives together. We had a tacit agreement that the anti-Mormon issue would not be discussed. The temple ceremonies had not answered any of my questions -it had created more. I began to research again and plowed right into the history of the Temple Ceremony. I remember asking to see a certain document concerning the origins of the Mormon Temple Ceremony in the Special Collections rooms at the BYU library. The attendant hesitated and went to consult a supervisor. I finally pulled a corner of my temple garments out from under my blouse and showed it to the attendant. That convinced him that it was alright for me to see the documents, since I was a temple Mormon.*

*It was a long and tough personal struggle. I could accept a few discrepancies in Mormon doctrine, but I was beginning to realize that there were problems in just about every area of Mormonism, the Temple Ceremony being the last straw. Bob and I rarely discussed it. Months went by. I tried to ignore what I had been learning about Mormonism. I just couldn't forget about it. I made the decision to leave the church while walking down a residential street in Provo very early one morning. It was very quiet. I remember crying and asking God to guide me. I also remember looking out of our apartment window one Sunday morning with tears in my eyes watching all my friends going off to church. To date, I can honestly say that leaving Mormonism was the most difficult thing I've ever done. I lost most of my friends, and ultimately my marriage.*

*The next spring, Bob and I were traveling across the country to Provo, Utah. We stopped in Denver to visit my family. It had been a fun visit and we all spent the night in sleeping bags in the backyard. In the night my brother woke me saying, "Val, I think Bob is gone." He had packed up his car and left! There was a short letter explaining that he couldn't live with a pseudo-happiness and that he knew we wouldn't be together as husband and wife in heaven. The next time I saw him, he and a friend knocked on my apartment door in Provo and handed me divorce papers to sign. Apparently the divorce had been planned for months. The night Bob left, he met his mother at the Denver airport and they drove back together.*

*I did talk with him a few years later and he apologized for the way he had handled things. We agreed that we were both very young to have been dealing with such heavy issues and would definitely handle things differently now. It felt great to know that he had indeed loved me.*

*I still keep in touch with a couple of Mormon friends from my youth. They never ask why I left the church. It took years before I could say out loud that Mormonism is simply a man-made cult. I believe that as a whole, Mormons are people with good values and morals who are looking for the answers to life's questions –just like everyone else on the planet. Few of them have been exposed to or have opened their minds to the real facts and origins of Mormonism. I have traveled much of the world and learned that it is full of wonderful caring people with honorable values and morals.*

*I especially appreciate my mother for seeking the truth with such an honest heart. She has set an amazing example in the way she continues to study the Bible, genuinely appreciates different perspectives, and loves people.*

## Angela's Friend – No Friend

At an early age our daughter, Angela, lost her best LDS friend as a result of leaving the Mormon Church.

*When I was about 14, we moved from Illinois to Colorado, and I left behind my best friend Sue (not her real name). After about a year, I returned to Illinois to visit her. One evening, with reluctance, she raised the sensitive topic of the Mormon Church. I explained that I felt no alternative but to leave the church. Having appreciated the approach taken by my parents, I took a similar approach with Sue that night - I encouraged her to explore, offering to share information, if requested. She told me she would think about it, but seemed suspicious, since at a recent church meeting, members were warned against reading certain publications and listening to anyone who challenged the beliefs of the church.*

*The following morning, I overheard Sue talking to her father (a prominent church leader) regarding our discussion the night before. Sue was not aware that I overheard their discussion. When I arose, I sensed that I was no longer welcome, but nonetheless, I remained hopeful that our friendship was not in jeopardy.*

*Within a few days after my return to Colorado, I received a letter from Sue, confirming my suspicion that, for religious reasons, she had elected to end our friendship. I was very hurt, and it took many years to adjust to the reality of her actions. I never faulted Sue for her decision, having understood the great pressure she must have been facing. I relate this incident because it is one of my life events which I recall in vivid detail.  It had a significant impact in my life.  The following is an excerpt from her letter:*

*". . . I think our friendship needs to end.  I think you know why.  I wish you hadn't changed.  I'm sorry about Val and [Bob].  But [Bob] is correct because he needs an eternal companion.  Everybody does.  So this is the last letter you'll be receiving from me.  P.S.  This was my decision."*

Our departure from Mormonism didn't have as great an impact on our two younger children, although the discovery of the lie of Mormonism has left our entire family more critical in our thought, and more skeptical about accepting the doctrines people profess.

## A Curious and Disconcerting Observation

Not long after I asked Jesus into my heart, I requested my name be removed from the church records.  Doing so automatically labeled me an excommunicant and apostate.  The fact that Mormons excommunicate those who trust and believe in Jesus alone for salvation is an admission of the fact that the LDS Church considers itself in opposition to Christianity.  For a Mormon these terms are terrifying.  The Mormon Prophet Spencer Kimball explains:

> *the LDS Church considers itself in opposition to Christianity*

*The scriptures speak of the Church members being "cast out" or "cut off" or having their names "blotted out."  This means excommunication.  This dread action means total severance of the individual from the church.  The person who is excommunicated loses his membership in the church and all attendant blessings.  As an excommunicant he is in a worse situation than he was before he joined the church.  He has lost the Holy Ghost, his priesthood, his endowments, his sealings, his privileges and his claim upon eternal life.  This is about the saddest thing which could happen to an individual.  Better that he suffer poverty, persecution, sickness, and even death.  A true Latter-day Saint would far prefer to see a loved one in his bier than excommunicated from the Church.* [25]

The above quote paints the picture of how excommunicants are viewed by the Mormon Church.  Joseph Smith's first vision account,[26] the Temple Ceremony,[27] and the *Book of Mormon*,[28] all express that all Christian denominations, creeds and pastors are an abomination to God.  We who believe that God has preserved the salvation message in the Bible, are not "fools" as the *Book of Mormon* refers to us.[29]

It never bothered me to be called an apostate.  It became a pleasant reminder that I now belonged to the true Christ - I was now translated from death to life!  I did not apostatize from the truth because I hadn't had the truth.  I had not lost the Holy Ghost or the priesthood - I gained both.  My endowments and sealings and other Mormon claims upon eternal life are manufactured through the fallen heart of man, most certainly not authored by the Living God of Israel, so I never lost out there either.  I relinquished my life to the true and faithful God of Abraham, Isaac, and Jacob.  I wanted to be like the disciples of Jesus who left everything to follow Him –and not a church.  I asked God to take me as a new babe in Christ to a good Bible believing church where I could grow and fellowship with uncompromising Christians.  To this day I continually rejoice having made the choice to follow Christ.  Yet, it is God who calls us –we are the responders!

## A Christian Service

My husband and I went to a church service with Melaine and her husband.  The service presented a live re-enactment of the events leading up to the death, burial and resurrection of Jesus.  As the account unfolded, I found I could not keep the tears away, I simply let them flow.  The impact of the salvation message was penetrating my spirit.  Our dear Savior took away all our sins - past, present, and future.  They were nailed on the

> *a true Latter-day Saint would far prefer to see a loved one in his bier than excommunicated from the church*

cross with Jesus. The enactment at this church made me feel almost as though I were at Calvary observing all that was happening. I was hurting, I felt sorrow, but I was also rejoicing. My heart was flooded and spilling over with the joy of the Lord. I was so in love with Jesus! I wanted to live soley for Him! Jesus could have called out, "I'm not guilty!" Instead he gave Himself in our place. He did not have to take upon Himself our pain and guilt! But out of love He chose to do so. His crown of thorns was actually meant for us, but He wore it in our place.

In church that day as I pondered the events of the life of Jesus, it became crystal clear to me that I was experiencing the Holy Spirit moving in my life, testifying still more of the true Jesus of the Bible, contrasting Him for me with the false Jesus of Mormonism. I was radically amazed!

Alongside the wondrous peace I was then experiencing, I was struck by the extent to which Mormons completely redefine Jesus. In doing so they take great risk about their eternal destiny! Do you want to offend the Father? If you believe or teach incorrect things about His Son, or about the Holy Spirit or of salvation in order to place trust in a church, or a leader, you truly do offend the Father. The Bible informs us that who we say Jesus is and what we believe He personally did for us determines whether we spend eternity in heaven or in hell:

> And this is the record, that God hath given us eternal life; and this life is in his Son. He that hath the Son hath life; and he that hath not the Son of God hath not life. These things I have written unto you that believe on the name of the Son of God; that ye may know that ye have eternal life . . .[30]

> He who believeth on the Son hath everlasting life: and he that believeth not the Son shall not see life; but the wrath of God abideth on him.[31]

At this time, more than ever before in my life, I came to see that the only solid basis for truth and morality comes from the Bible, not through strict adherence to the Mormon code, which changes from time to time (consider the nature of God, polygamy, racial attitudes, temple rituals, revelation, etc.). I no longer embraced false revelation from Mormon prophets, whose revelations continually change and contradict previously held doctrine. Mormonism was ever more repugnant to my soul.

I continued to attend Christian churches, and embraced biblical truth with respect and enthusiasm. Several things about Christianity became a joy to me. I discovered the worship and knowledge of God in Christianity compared to that of the Mormon faith to be worlds apart. Many Christians praise and worship God openly. They do not hold back. They love to fellowship in homes for prayer and Bible study. Among Christians it is not uncommon to anoint with oil and pray for the sick. While a Mormon, I was led to believe that Mormons alone do so. Contrary to what I had been taught as a Mormon, I now understand that those who believe in Jesus as Savior do receive the true priesthood. God bestows it upon any person who trusts in Christ *alone* for salvation. In biblical Christianity the priesthood is referred to as the priesthood of *all* believers in Christ, male and female alike.

While still a new babe in Christ, God graciously surrounded me with people who desired to allow God to be the center of their lives. We had fire in our souls and an insatiable thirst to worship, grow in knowledge of God's Word, fellowship with other believers in Christ, and carry out the great commission.[32] I began to internalize the truth of God's Word in my heart. My love for God and His Word was like the closeness a mother feels inside her heart as she cradles a new-born child in her arms, making plans to shower her baby with all that is best in life. The difference was that I was the new-born babe and God Himself was cradling me in His arms, and supplying me with all that was tailor-made for my needs. He still does!

> **I was the new-born babe and God Himself was cradling me in His arms**

One contrast between a Christian and Mormon Church service that stood out boldly was that most Christians carried Bibles to church; and they used them! I was thrilled at the sound of Bible pages turning all at one time as we sought to learn from its pages. As a Mormon I had been taught that Christians do not understand the Bible, and often resort to writing down and reading formal prayers. Some Christians, especially those with liturgical worship, use prayers that are read, but this is not vain repetition in the way Mormons are led to believe. A closer fit to this criticism is the Mormon Temple Ceremony, which is rote, and always without deviation. So are Mormon sacramental and baptismal prayers, Celestial marriage, confirmation, etc.

I had been taught that people in the Christian world have a form of godliness but deny God's power; that they draw near to God with their lips but their hearts are far removed.[33] This statement, a quote lifted from the Bible[34] speaks of those who are hypocrites in their faith. To deny the power means to undermine and discredit all that is encompassed and embodied in the name of Jesus. I find the LDS Church guilty of doing so. Today I recognize that it is the LDS Church that has a form of godliness but denies the power thereof.

As I became acquainted with Christians I discovered that many of them understood and enjoyed God's Word to a degree that amazed me. The Mormon emphasis was geared to the church. The church *this* and the church *that*. But in Christianity the emphasis revolved around discussion of the majesty of God, worship, prayer, study and obeying His Word. My Christian experience has been with persons who fellowship and pray and worship with fervency! While I had been taught that only Mormons worship God properly and with real intent and genuineness, I must say that I never experienced such light and life in Mormonism as I find in Christianity.

## Remove Our Names From the Church Records, Please!

After moving back to Denver, my husband and our children agreed for me to send a letter requesting our excommunication from the Mormon Church. I addressed a letter to our local church presidency, requesting that our names be removed from the records of the church. I personally took the letter to the proper local Mormon authorities, requesting they take immediate action. Later on they came to our home, hoping to change our minds. Finally, they asked me personally to promise never to speak out against the church. I explained that with good conscience before God I could not make such a promise.

I was surprised by the fact that so few LDS Church members felt concern or curiosity as to our reasons for departure. Jesus said:

> *How think ye? If a man have an hundred sheep, and one of them be gone astray, doth he not leave the ninety and nine, and goeth into the mountains, and seeketh that which is gone astray.*[35]

Most people didn't express a caring heart, or perhaps they were indifferent toward seeking after us. The fact is that the Mormon Church is not the church of the true Shepherd! I lost friends. I thought I may lose relatives as well. Jesus also said:

> *Let Me assure you that no one has ever given up anything - home, brothers, sisters, mother, father, children, or property - for love of me and to tell others the Good News, who won't be given a hundred times over, homes, brothers, sisters, mothers, and fathers, and land - with persecutions.*[36]

The disciples of Jesus left all to follow Jesus! I wanted to join them.

A true child of God does not want religiosity, but does want an intimate relationship with the true Savior of mankind. Jesus said we should worship God in spirit and in truth. *In spirit,* refers exclusively to the new birth; the spiritual life-line which had been severed at Adam's fall is reconnected in Jesus, at the new birth, giving man immediate and continuous fellowship with God. To worship God in truth is to acknowledge and worship the true Jesus and cast away all false Christs, and false doctrines. The two commands are inseparable, and critically important. Any other form of worship is idolatrous, and therefore in vain.

May those whose hearts desire fellowship with the true God turn to the Bible for truth. "And that they may recover themselves out of the snare of the devil, who are taken captive by him at his will."[37] How blessed are those who, through faith, trust in Christ alone for their salvation! Can we agree together to bring our thoughts captive to Jesus Christ, and be truly liberated?

Continue reading to discover matters which the Holy Spirit clarified to my spirit after I gave my heart to Jesus –issues I needed to recognize and deal with in the continuing process of liberation from enemy territory. It is part-and-parcel of the santification process mentioned in this chapter.

1   Matthew 10:32.
2   2 Corinthians 6:14-17.
3   Luke 9:62.
4   Matthew 10:34-36.
5   John 8:12.
6   John 3:19.
7   Matthew 13:14-16.
8   Luke 11:13.
9   Hebrews 3:12-13.
10  John 3:5-7.
11  John 16:13.
12  1 John 2:27.
13  John 3:3-7.
14  John 5:24.
15  Colossians 1:13.
16  Acts 13:39.
17  Hebrews 10:10.
18  Integrative Theology, vol. 3, p. 152.
19  2 Corinthians 5:17.

20  Romans 12:1.
21  John 14:6.
22  Ephesians 5:26.
23  Acts 4:12.
24  Mark 7:7, 9, 13;  Jeremiah 14:14, 16:19.
25  Miracle of Forgiveness, p. 329.
26  Pearl of Great Price, Joseph Smith 2:19.
27  Sackett, Chuck, What's Going On In There?.
28  Book of Mormon, 2 Nephi 29:6.
29  Book of Mormon, 2 Nephi 29:6.
30  1 John 5:11-13.
31  John 3:36.
32  Matthew 28:19.
33  Pearl of Great Price, Joseph Smith 2:19.
34  2 Timothy 3:5.
35  Matthew 18:12.
36  Mark 10:30-31.
37  2 Timothy 2:26.

# 17. The Triunity of God: A Heresy?

*Go ye therefore, and teach all nations, baptizing them in the name of the Father, and of the Son, and of the Holy Ghost . . .*

Matthew 28:19

On one hand, the Mormon Church wants to portray itself as sharing mainstream Christian doctrines. But upon deeper analysis, Mormonism is at odds with, and even mocks, doctrines such as the triunity of God.

Unlike the biblical understanding of God which has remained constant to this day, Mormon doctrine has continually undergone revision. From the Mormon Living Oracles and the Standard Works, one confronts a very confusing, contradictory, changing God and Gospel message.

Through improper usage of Scripture and extra-biblical writings, Mormonism attempts to uphold its own version of the Gospel. In spite of insurmountable differences in doctrine, the LDS Church attempts to blend in as though they are another Christian denomination. Through persuasive advertising the LDS Church wants to be seen as the most pristine form of Christianity. The LDS view of the very nature of God, like other basics of the Mormon faith, stand out in bold contrast to Christianity and can only be upheld after the Bible is marginalized and stripped of its basic doctrinal tenets.

*like to blend in as though they are another Christian denomination*

## Two Great Heresies

In 1984, the popular Mormon doctrinal expert, Apostle Bruce R. McConkie, gave a lengthy sermon to the students at Brigham Young University in which he adamantly opposed the basic tenants of Christianity. In the speech he enlarged upon what he termed the two greatest heresies in the Christian world. McConkie declared that the first great heresy pertained to the nature of God, the doctrine of the Trinity, and the second greatest heresy was the doctrine of salvation by grace without works. (See the exhibit on page 221.)

Here we have, in a nutshell, the Mormon position on two foundational Bible tenets. In this chapter let us refer to the Bible which will provide a witness for the historically consistent view of the nature of God; the belief seen by the Mormon Church as the first great heresy. In the next chapter we shall consider the last part of McConkie's quote, the doctrine of salvation by grace without works, which is viewed by Mormonism as the second great heresy.

## Two Fundamental Themes

Two fundamental themes of the Bible are: 1) that in all the universe, the heavens above and the earth beneath, there is only one true God; and 2) there is a Triunity of God. That there is one God who eternally exists as a tri-personal God is the finale of God's progressive revelation of Himself in Scripture.

"Hear oh Israel, the Lord our God, the Lord is one." This verse, Deuteronomy 6:4, is compelling to anyone acquainted with God's relationship to the Hebrews. It is referred to in the Jewish faith as the SH'MA. This verse has always been the hallmark of Judaism, and to this day remains core to the faith of Jews and Christians alike. As we comprehend the SH'MA the Bible begins to unfold and blossom as the truth of God. The Hebrew word SH'MA means *to hear, obey, discern, attend to.*[1] Therefore, wisdom suggests that each of us pay strict attention to this Scripture verse. In reference to God, this verse is among the greatest theological statements made in the entire Bible. Interestingly, the SH'MA is, without a doubt, the most quoted verse in the entirety of Scripture. It has been and still is recited morning and evening by Jews throughout the world. The last testimony heard from the lips of many Jews through persecution and death has been the SH'MA.

> *as we comprehend the SH'MA the Bible begins to unfold and blossom as the truth of God*

> *the Hebrew word ECHAD denotes a plural oneness as in a cluster of grapes, never a solid unit*

Reflect on the word *one* as it appears within the SH'MA: "Hear oh Israel, the Lord our God, the Lord is one." The word *one* referring to God in the Old Testament is always translated from the Hebrew word ECHAD, which denotes a plural oneness, as in a cluster of grapes, never a solid unit. How we should tremble at the majesty of the ECHAD! It is the same word used in Genesis 2:24 which states, "Therefore a man shall leave his father and mother, and shall cleave unto his wife; and they shall be one [ECHAD]."[2] The SH'MA uncompromisingly holds to a monotheistic view of God, as opposed to Mormonism's polytheistic view of God. If the Mormon Church embraced the basic tenants of the SH'MA, it would have to give up the idea of polytheism. This would void the claim of Joseph Smith's vision where two gods appeared to him, a testimony primary to Mormon doctrine. Mormonism would cease to exist.

Even as polytheism has always been the most distinct characteristic of the pagans, monotheism has been the supreme characteristic of the Jewish and Christian people. God has always called His people out of polytheism into monotheism! In fact, the Hebrew Old Testament belief in monotheism sets its followers apart from all other peoples.

Because Christian roots are found in the Jewish faith, the belief in one God is characteristic of Christianity as well. Christianity does not believe in two Gods, or three Gods, or a countless number of Gods. The understanding of a plural oneness is disclosed in the first verse of Genesis and many other places throughout the Bible, as we shall see.

More than any other person, Jesus was an observant Jew. In the Bible, we see that Jesus cited and upheld the truth concerning the *one* God.[3] When asked which of all the commandments was the greatest, Jesus quoted from Deuteronomy 6:4. By doing so, He upheld and proclaimed the SH'MA as the greatest of all commandments:

> . . . *Hear, O Israel: the LORD our God, is one LORD; and you shall love the LORD your God with all your heart, with all your soul, and with all your mind, and with all your strength.*[4]

More than any other person, Messiah Jesus venerated the Ten Commandments. He certainly was conversant with the commandment which excludes worship of any other than God[5] and that one must never bow down before any other than God.[6] Yet, Jesus permitted people to worship and bow down before Him,[7] a blasphemous act if He were not God. By this act Jesus was declaring His Deity –He was declaring Himself to be God!

This is not all. Consider what Jesus did. We read that Jesus forgave sins.[8] Only God can forgive sins!

Furthermore, only God has power to raise the dead! Here are the words of Jesus:

> *Therefore doth the Father love me. because I lay down my life, that I might take it up again. No man taketh it from me, but I lay it down of myself. I have power to lay it down, and I have power to take it up again . . .*[9]

a blasphemous act
if he were not God

Jesus is expressing His Deity! Note how this is hinted at in the book of Matthew: "Go ye therefore, and teach all nations, baptizing them in the name of the Father, and of the Son, and of the Holy Ghost."[10] Notice the verse says in the name [singular] of the Father, and of the Son, and of the Holy Ghost. The word *name* is singular, even though it is ascribed as tri-personal. Yes, the one God of the Jewish and Christian faith is seen as Father, Son, and Holy Spirit.

The following examples are insightful: The Holy Spirit empowers, guides and directs us and is the giver of spiritual gifts to believers.[11] We are exhorted to pray to the Father[12] in the name of the Son[13] through the Holy Spirit.[14] Jesus invites prayer to Himself.[15] Believers are exhorted to call upon the name of Christ.[16] Believers will praise Messiah Jesus throughout eternity.[17]

Actually, the word *Trinity* is not found in the Bible and is a term attributed to a third century theologian named Tertullian. Arguing against the Trinity, the Mormon Church dates the origins of the doctrine of Trinity at the Council of Nicea in 325 A.D. and the Council of Constantinople in 381 A.D. Within the first few centuries after Christ, heretical teachings pertaining to the nature of God were creeping into the church. It was for the purpose of clarifying and defending the truth of Scripture that creeds and the expression Trinity came into existence. The fact is, the councils used the term to clarify biblical truth as it was understood among the first century saints. The term Trinity came into use to guard against the Gnostic view of Tritheism (three Gods), or of Modalism (the belief that God is one, but takes on different forms). The belief of Modalism would suggest that God changes, whereas, Scripture teaches that God never changes.[18] While some people misunderstand the term Trinity as a belief in three Gods, the early church creed clearly shows that this view was not the intent of the early church fathers. There are not three Gods; there is only one God.

Before the years of the councils, as early as 96 A.D., we find writings of the early church fathers explaining that God is one --- and yet the Father, Son, and Holy Spirit are God. Clement, a bishop of Rome, wrote to the church in Corinth in 96 A.D. affirming this doctrine. Ignatius, bishop of Antioch, wrote several letters, which still exist, to various churches before he was condemned to death for his faith in the year 117 A.D. These letters affirm the early espousal of the Trinity of God. Also, Justin and Irenaeus, bishops of Lyons in the late second century, held the view of Triunity of God.[19]

Furthermore, Jesus made statements that on the surface seem contradictory, although His Incarnation explains them. He spoke of a plurality; yet he spoke of each as the one God. How would you explain verses like Exodus 24:3; Ezekiel 37:19; Philippians 2:2; Exodus 26:11; Genesis 2:24; Acts 4:32; Judges 20:1,8,11; and Philippians 1:27? The examples below are biblical affirmations of the Triunity of God.

1. Giver of life
    a. Holy Spirit - 2 Corinthians 3:6, 8, 17, 18; Romans 8:11
    b. Jesus, The Word - John 1:3
    c. Lord God, (Jehovah Elohim) - Genesis 2:7

2. Leads, guides
    a. Lord (Jehovah) alone - Deuteronomy 32:12
    b. Holy Spirit - Isaiah 63:11-14
    c. Christ -1Corinthians 10:1-4

3. Convinces, convicts, draws
    a. Holy Spirit - 1 Corinthians 12:3
    b. Father - John 6:44

      c. Son - John 12:32

    4. Creator

      a. Father - Isaiah 64:8

      b. Holy Spirit - Job 33:4, 26:13

      c. Son - John 1:3; Col. 1:15-17; Hebrews 1:3

      d. Lord God Almighty - Revelation 4:8, 11

      e. God - Genesis 1:1

      g. Lord (Jehovah) Alone - Isaiah 44:24

    5. The resurrection

      a. Father - 1 Thessalonians 1:10

      b. Son - John 2:19, 10:17, 18

      c. Holy Spirit - Romans 8:11

      d. God - Acts 17:30, 31

    6. Indwells

      a. God - 2 Corinthians 6:16

      b. Christ - Colossians 1:27

      c. Holy Spirit - John 14:17

    7. The first and the last - the Alpha and Omega

      a. Lord (Jehovah) - Isaiah 43:10, 11, 44:6

      b. Lord, Almighty - Revelation 1:8

      c. Son of Man - Revelation 1:11-13

      d. Jesus - Revelation 1:17-18, 22:12, 13,16

The Bible describes God as a unified *One* having the same substance or essence.

One method Christians use to explain the Trinity is through analogy. Every actual thing or person is a multiplicity in unity. God, through all His creation, has shown us things that are tri-part; yet only one. Each of us, for example, is made up of body, soul, and spirit.[20] One family comprises a father, mother and child. One person thinks, loves and purposes. An atom is made up of electrons, protons, and neutrons. The sun can be seen and felt, felt and not seen, and neither felt nor seen. Similarly, a light bulb is made up of three components: the shell, the filament, and electricity, yet it is one unit - three parts contribute to the whole. The fact that I do not understand all there is to know about a light bulb does not mean that I cannot believe in or benefit from its usage. I know that it works and with simple faith I utilize it for my own benefit. Who are we to define God in our own terms? After all, He is the author of our limited three-dimensional perspective and creator of all dimensions.

> *analogies are man's attempts to convey complex information*

Keep in mind that analogies are man's attempts to convey complex information. The creeds of the early church fathers have both historical and present advantages and drawbacks. Our deeds, not just our creeds, need to be emphasized here. Balance is key. A true biblical emphasis will lead to right action. We must interpret Scripture as accurately as possible so that we may live out our lives in faithfulness.

## Thayer's Greek Lexicon and Strong's Concordance

Jesus claimed equality with God the Father. We see this in Philippians, John,[21] and elsewhere. In these verses the word *equal* according to *Thayer's Greek Lexicon*[22] means, "to claim for oneself the same substance or essence and be equal in quality as in quantity, and the nature, rank, authority, which belong to God." This is in agreement with *Strong's Exhaustive Concordance, of New Testament Greek words*.[23] Jesus said: "I and the Father are one."[24] Only Jesus could say that because He did not have a human Father, and was of the same essence or substance as the Father. Yet, because of His human mother, Jesus was also fully man. Jesus was both fully God and fully man.

## Humanity of Jesus – A Great Mystery

" . . . I go to the Father, for my Father is greater than I."[25] Jesus' humanity explains why He said that His Father was greater than He. Because of the fleshly body and the human nature He had taken on, He was subject to the Father. He became poor that through His poverty we might have eternal life. Confusion comes when we do not consider the humanity of Jesus. Remember that Jesus layed aside His glory, so that He prayed to His father just as you and I pray to the Father. Jesus ascribed all that is represented within the SH'MA to Himself. We see this in Bible verses such as are in the book of John,[26] where some among the number of Jews began to stone Him. They were angry because He was calling Himself God! This appears as a mystery. A mystery is something that cannot be comprehended by reason, and it is a blow to human opinions. The Incarnation is described as a great mystery, "And without controversy great is the mystery of Godliness: God was manifest in the flesh, justified in the spirit, seen of angels, preached unto the Gentiles, believed on in the world, received up into glory."[27] Praise be to God!

> *the Incarnation is described as a great mystery*

## Fulness of God's Revealed Person

The Incarnation is important to the understanding of the nature of God. The fulness of God's nature is expressed for us in the person of Jesus. Notice these verses from Colossians:

> *For it was the Father's good pleasure for all the fulness to dwell in Him.*[28] *[the margin of my New American Standard Bible reads, "i.e., fulness of diety"].*

> *Who is the image of the invisible God, the firstborn of every creature: For by Him were all things created, that are in heaven, and that are in the earth, visible and invisible, whether they be thrones, or dominions, or principalities, or powers: all things were created by Him, and for Him: And He is before all things, and by Him all things consist.*[29]

This is an awesome revelation, well worth our honor and respect.

## The Greek word *Protokos*

The word *first born* (Colossians 1:18), is *Protokos* which in the Greek language expresses His "priority to, and preeminence over, creation, not of being in the sense of being the first to be born . . ."[30] This is also expounded upon in *Word Pictures in the New Testament*.[31] This passage is consistent and parallel to the Logos passage in the first chapter of John:

> *In the beginning was the Word, and the Word was with God and the Word was God. The same was in the beginning with God. All things were made by Him; and without Him was not anything made that was made . . . . And the word was made flesh, and dwelt among us, (and we beheld His glory, the glory as of the only begotten of the Father,) full of grace and truth.*[32]

Yes, through the Incarnation, Jesus is the revealed person of the invisible God! If anyone is to be reconciled to God he must believe in Messiah Jesus. "He that believeth on the Son hath everlasting life: and he that believeth not the Son shall not see life, but the wrath of God abideth on him."[33]

## Foolish Plan?

The mystery of the nature of God is not whether God is revealed as Father, Son, and Holy Spirit, for that fact is clearly spoken of throughout the Bible. The mystery is how that fact is so. "The secret things belong to the Lord our God, but the things revealed belong to us and to our sons forever, that we may observe all the words of the law."[34] While no one can fully explain the nature of God, neither can anyone clearly explain the existence of God or the Atonement. As to how God reveals Himself to man, who are we to judge God? God Almighty may reveal and manifest Himself to man any way He chooses! We should not attempt to bring Infinity down to our own level of mind. In our finite minds it is impossible to comprehend Almighty God who created us. Metaphors only assist our understanding of God who is outside the realm of man's comprehension. Scripture reminds us:

> This so-called "foolish" plan of God is far wiser than the wisest plan of the wisest man, and God in His weakness – Christ dying on the cross – is far stronger than any man.[35]

> This plan of mine is not what you would work out, neither are my thoughts the same as yours! For just as the heavens are higher than the earth, so are my ways higher than yours, and my thoughts than yours.[36]

*without the Holy Spirit human wisdom can only come through the senses and intellect*

Presently we may not altogether understand but the Holy Spirit can bring man's wisdom up to a higher level. The so called foolishness of God can only be understood through faith. Without the Holy Spirit, human wisdom can only come through the senses and intellect. We are free to choose:

> For what if some did not believe? Shall their unbelief make the faith of God without effect? God forbid: Yea, let God be true, but every man a liar; as it is written, that thou mightest be justified in thy sayings, and mightest overcome when thou art judged.[37]

## Embrace the Name of the Lord

We read in Scripture that "whosoever" calls upon the name of the Lord shall be saved.[38] To call upon the name of the Lord is to acknowledge and embrace with faith, all that God reveals to humans concerning Himself through Jesus Christ. When we meet Jesus we have met with the Incarnation; the fullest revelation of God that our finite minds can comprehend. When we see in Scripture the term *name* it helps for us to think of the revealed representation or image of the invisible God. When we close prayer in the name of Jesus, we acknowledge and call upon all that God has revealed to man concerning Himself and the Incarnation.

*professing to be wise, they became fools, and exchanged the glory of the incorruptible God for an image in the form of corruptible man*

Personal accountability to biblical revelation is key to proper understanding of the nature of God. The true God, as described in the Bible, is unrelated to the polytheism of Mormonism. Embracing the Mormon view of God as a resurrected, glorified man, or that there is more than one God, is to mock the God of Israel, which makes one guilty in the manner explained and forewarned below:

> For since the creation of the world His invisible attributes, His eternal power and divine nature, have been clearly seen, being understood through what has been made, so that they are without excuse . . . professing to be wise, they became fools, and exchanged the glory of the incorruptible God for an image in the form of corruptible man . . . they exchanged the truth of God for a lie, and worshiped and served the creature rather than the Creator, who is blessed forever. Amen.[39]

This verse is directly expressive of the Mormon God who is only a corruptible man.  Our responsibility is to submit to God our lingering places of resistance.  God identifies with His followers, and commissions them to spread the true Gospel throughout the nations.

In conclusion, the Trinity is a theological term based on biblical doctrine.  We must be true to the authority of the Word of God that, in fact, does teach a triunity of the One God.  The purpose of the creeds of the early church was to expound upon the SH'MA and to battle against Gnosticism.  Disagreement on this issue clearly separates Christianity from other religions, such as Mormonism.

Remember that Jesus said, "All authority has been given to me in heaven and on earth.  Go therefore and make disciples of all nations, baptizing them in the name of Father and the Son and the Holy Spirit."[40]  Notice that Jesus said, "all authority is given to me."  This is a radical statement.  God does not confer His authority on anyone because it is part of who He is.  Truly this is expressive of the Incarnation.  Jesus is the Alpha and Omega, which is, and which was, and which is to come, the Almighty.[41]  Again, notice the structure of the verse.  It says the *name* –not the *names*.  True believers have been commissioned to preach His truth to the nations.  We who believe are not excused from preaching this message.  We must carry this message to the nations, in season and out –convenient or not.  We must do so lovingly and with true doctrinal purity.  It is to this end I have written this chapter.

1   Strong's Exhaustive Concordance of Hebrew Words, #8085.
2   Strong's Exhaustive Concordance of Hebrew Words, #259.
3   Mark 12:28-30.
4   Deuteronomy 6:4-5.
5   Exodus 20:3.
6   Exodus 20:5.
7   Matthew 28:9.
8   Mark 2:5, Matthew 9:2.
9   John 10:17-18.
10  Matthew 28:19.
11  Acts 20:28.
12  Matthew 6:6.
13  John 16:24.
14  Jude 20.
15  John 14:14-15, 16:23.
16  1 Corinthians 1:2.
17  Revelation 1:5-6.
18  Malachi 3:6; Hebrews 13:8.
19  Early Christian Fathers, Cyril Richardson, pp. 88, 90, 92, 103.
20  1 Thessalonians 5:23.
21  Philippians 2:5-11; John 5:17-18.
22  Thayer's Greek Lexicon, p. 307.
23  Strong's Exhaustive Concordance of New Testament Greek Words, p. 38
24  John 10:30.
25  John 14:28.
26  John 8:24, 58, 59.
27  1 Tim. 3:16.
28  Colossians 1:19.
29  Colossians 1:15-17.
30  An Expository Dictionary of the New Testament Words, p. 104-105.
31  Word Pictures in the New Testament, vol. 4, p. 477-479.
32  John 1:2, 14.
33  John 3:36.
34  Deuteronomy 29:29.
35  1 Corinthians 1:25.
36  Isaiah 55:8-9.
37  Romans 3:4.
38  Acts 2:21; Romans 10:9.
39  Romans 1:20, 22, 25.
40  Matthew 28:18-19.
41  Revelation 1:8.

# 18. Grace: A Heresy?

*For by grace you have been saved through faith; and that not of yourselves, it is the gift of God; not as a result of works, that no one should boast.*

Ephesians 2: 8-9

Grace is always underplayed by the Mormon Church, which portrays it as a false doctrine that excuses people from earning their salvation. Mormons believe that grace is earned. In this chapter I will show that grace is what sets Christianity apart from all other religions.

The *Book of Mormon* says:

*. . . for we know that it is by grace that we are saved, after all we can do."*[1]

Mormon Apostle Bruce McConkie said:

*The heresy of being saved by grace is burning like wildfire across the nation . . . The only "religious mania" to exceed it was the way the original heresy filled the early Christian church after Christ's death.*[2]

In the previous chapter we dealt with Mormon Apostle McConkie's speech to students at B.Y.U. in regards to what he terms the first great heresy of Christianity; the nature of God. Now we can examine what he terms the second great heresy of Christianity; the doctrine of salvation by grace apart from works.

Apostle James E. Talmage warned members of the LDS Church:

*The Sectarian Dogma of Justification by faith alone has exercised an influence for evil.*[3]

> the heresy of being saved by grace is burning like wildfire across the nation . . .

This understanding was prominent as I was growing up. These statements are strong words against Christian doctrine, but they are in total agreement with the founder of the Mormon faith, Joseph Smith. In a vision God cautioned Joseph Smith against joining any church within Christianity: "I was answered that I must join none of them, for they were all wrong; and the Personage who addressed me said that all their creeds were an abomination in his sight; that those professors were all corrupt . . ."[4] These and numerous other quotes basically establish that Mormonism is not only at odds with the Christian view of grace, but with the whole of Christianity. These statements are shocking to Bible believers who appreciate the total sufficiency of Christ's suffering for sins on the cross.

## My Nightmare

When I was in high school I had a strange and disconcerting dream which relates how at a young age the Mormon goal to strive for Eternal Exaltation was ingrained in me. The dream helps one understand the Mormon view of works and the need to endlessly reach for God's approval to abide in his domain. My dream:

> It was judgment time. God was busy judging people and assigning to them the kingdom they had earned during mortality. He assigned numerous people to assist Him in this monumental task. I was one of them. It seemed we took turns judging each other. How did God deal with the fact that His helpers would make mistakes of judgment? He gave us a way in which we could determine the correct kingdom people deserved. Each of us was given a dishtowel, of which the four corners were held by a frame. God also gave each of us a knife, a spoon, and a fork. Then He had rows and rows of people walk past us. As each person passed by us, they were to take the silverware and lay it on top of the dishtowel. If a person earned the highest, or Celestial Kingdom, the knife would mysteriously slip through the dishtowel. If he earned the second, or Terrestrial Kingdom, the fork would slip through the dishtowel. If the person only deserved the lowest, or Telestial Kingdom, the spoon would slip through in the same manner. Somewhere along the huge lines of people to which I was assigned to judge were my very own parents!

*the Temple Ceremony mocks God's merciful gift of salvation by grace*

The shock of seeing them in my line scared me. Well, I knew I must be obedient to God and do my part well. The silverware testing rewarded one of my parents a higher kingdom than the other. This frightened me more than ever because I found myself wondering if I could lie to God, in order to keep my parents together in the same kingdom. Fortunately I woke up before I made my choice to obey God or not. I hadn't been to the temple where I later learned about the necessary handclasps and other secrets a Mormon acquires there, to gain entrance through the Mormon veil and and eventually into God's presence. It was in the Mormon Temple Ceremony segment, The Lone and Dreary World, that I later experienced how blatantly Mormonism mocks God's merciful gift of salvation by grace. In live drama I witnessed a Christian preacher being mocked along with the doctrine of grace he was espousing.[5] The biblical message of grace is conspicuously absent in the Temple Ceremony. The coveted salvation for a Latter-day Saint is the achievement of Exaltation to Godhood. The LDS belief in Eternal Exaltation does not exist in the Bible.

Had I been taught the truth about salvation by grace through faith apart from works - I probably would not have had such a nightmare.

## Striving

True biblical salvation comes entirely from God's covenantal initiative - God's grace. God reaches downward to us and bestows us the gift of His presence throughout all eternity. The wondrous eternal gift of salvation comes apart from the efforts of man –if it were not so there would be no need for a Savior to die on our behalf. But Jesus did die for us; all our sins He bore. Appreciating the magnitude of this gift ought to result in our doing good deeds. So that we may understand the wondrous gift He has imparted to us, God has supplied us with teaching, guidance, and instruction. This is the true meaning of the law. The term *law* is misleading to some; it may hammer home the view of a mean or harsh disciplinarian. In actuality, the law defines sin and by doing so contrasts true sinlessness as is revealed to our human comprehension through the Incarnation of the Messiah, Who lovingly gave His life to free us from the ultimate penalty of sin.[6] This He did while we were yet sinners.[7]

Sometimes the Ten Commandments are treated more as ten suggestions. Truthfully speaking, the ten commandments should be classified as ten freedoms because they truly safeguard our lives. When we keep God's commandments we free ourselves from the misery which always comes when we break God's commands. The problem is that no one can keep all of the commandments - it is impossible to do so! And

Scripture teaches that if we break one we are guilty of breaking them all.[8] So ask yourselves if you have kept the command not to covet? All of us have broken that command. Accordingly then, all are guilty of breaking the commands. That is a reason the Bible informs us that all have sinned and come short of the glory of God.[9] The fact that we have all broken God's law points out our fallen nature and the need to be justified through faith in Christ.[10] The bright side to all of this is that although we all have sinned we may be made *right-standing*, (the biblical term is *justified*), through faith if we accept God's provision for us. It was through loving-kindness (an Old Testament term for grace), that Jesus kept the *law* in our behalf. The Bible does not teach the Mormon view of grace and salvation through human works.

Jesus, the Word of God, came in human form and dwelled among us.[11] He came to us full of grace and truth.[12] Do you want to understand the beauty of keeping the law, or the commands of God? Look into the Word made flesh - the face of Messiah Jesus! Jesus is the embodiment of the law. He bestows unmerited favor to us - such graciousness! Grace is free –but we must receive and accept it on the basis of its own true definition. If grace were earned it would not be a gift; it would be an award or wage earned. The Bible understands nothing of salvation by faith plus works, nor a mixture of grace plus works.[13] Biblical-based good deeds are a loving response to salvation.

> *if grace were earned it would not be a gift*

The Bible presents a credible and consistent message as to the relationship between grace and works. Works do not contribute to salvation. Many people in the world who do not claim Mormonism as their religion do good works. The fact that people do good deeds does not make them in any way approved or able to abide in the very presence of a Holy and righteous God. Jesus expounds upon the fact that one must be born again to inherit the Kingdom of God. The LDS Church may use the Christian term grace, but in relationship to the Atonement, for example, Mormon theology has a very different view of what the term means. To help Mormons comprehend the true meaning of grace and salvation, I ask questions such as: "Does my faith in Christ make me a Christian in the same way your faith in Christ does?" "If someone not in the Mormon Church accepted Christ alone for salvation could that one qualify to enter into the highest Mormon heaven?" An honest Mormon must answer "definitely not!" Please recall from an earlier chapter that Mormonism teaches that the Atonement begins to take place when one is baptized into the Mormon Church.[14] This is not salvation through God's gift of grace.

I find that members of the LDS Church confuse works and grace in the same breath. Such questions as those above help Mormons to realize they depend on Christ plus Joseph Smith and the Mormon Church for salvation. These questions remove a deadly and blurred concept of grace and salvation, and give a clear, distinct understanding of the Christian terms of salvation and grace. To understand the different language of words within Mormonism and those which are used by Christians I have included a terminology list, compiled by Sandra Tanner in the Exhibit Section on page 193. This list is of great value toward an honest dialogue with a Mormon.

Members of the Mormon faith are taught that one must satisfy several requirements in order to qualify for the coveted Celestial kingdom of glory. The third Article of Faith of the Mormon Church states, "We believe that through the Atonement of Christ, all mankind may be saved, by obedience to the Laws and Ordinances of the Gospel." The Laws and Ordinances intended in this Article of Faith are extra-biblical and have been dealt with throughout this book. Suffice it here to say, that a Mormon must rely on all of them to achieve their goal of Godhood.

When I was a young girl I was acquainted with a widely distributed booklet published by the LDS Church which illustrates the efforts of works and an absence of God's covenantal grace. The words on the final page of the booklet are by Spencer W. Kimball (who later became the twelfth Prophet) and are an adaptation of an address given to the students at BYU, May 4, 1954, "And when he has fasted enough, prayed enough, and when his heart is right, he may expect that forgiveness will come and with it the glorious peace that passeth understanding."[15]

This quote emphasizes the importance of works in the Mormon faith and shows the absence of a belief in the total sufficiency of Christ's Atonement for humanity. In no way am I undermining fasting and prayer, but how can praying and suffering of a sinner add anything to the suffering the Messiah Himself did for us?  Until the end of our days, how can we claim that we perfectly suffered enough or fasted and prayed enough?  No!  In my later years, I noticed in the LDS Church far more emphasis placed on works toward forgiveness and an undermining of grace and relationship with the giver of forgiveness.  There is no way to work for our salvation.

Jesus, the true giver of forgiveness, never suggested going to a church authority to receive forgiveness of one's sins.  It was Spencer W. Kimball (soon to be Mormon Prophet) who said:

> *Since the power to remit sins is so carefully and strictly limited within the true Church of Jesus Christ, where so many men bear the true priesthood of God, it is monumental presumption for unauthorized men elsewhere to claim to absolve people from sin.*[16]

> *The Bishop will determine the case.  He it is who will determine by the facts, and through the power of discernment which is his, whether the nature of the sin and the degree of repentance manifested warrant forgiveness . . . All this responsibility rests upon the bishop's shoulders.*[17]

How sad to have such devotion to a man and a church.  This is a way that church members come to identify more with their church and its leaders than with the true Messiah.  In all truthfulness, a Mormon bishop does not have the authority to make decisions about sin for a church member, and the power to remit sin is not limited to the Mormon Church - such blasphemy - if you please!  I believe that the LDS Church while using the name of Jesus in prayer and in the official title of their organization avoids the personal relationship that brings escape from bondage.  Using the Lord's name in the manner of which the LDS Church does, is to take the Lord's name in vain!  The power to absolve people from sin comes only through Messiah Jesus - He alone is our mediator.  The good news is that Jesus already suffered for us on the cross.  If we place our trust and faith in Him, we will have eternal life.  It is by God's initiative (His grace), through our faith, and by the power of the blood of the Lamb that we are reconciled to God.

Sin results in negative consequences and ultimately death.  While it is true that consequences come from sin, forgiveness, just like salvation, is a gift from God.  If we repent we will want to rectify our wrongs the best we are able and in behavior turn completely around.  The Holy Spirit enables us to do so.  As to the connection between grace and works, the Bible speaks blessings to those who believe in grace apart from works:

> *But to one who does not work, but believes in Him who justifies the ungodly, his faith is reckoned as righteousness, Just as David also speaks of the blessings upon the man to whom God reckons righteousness apart from works . . .*[18]

There are over one hundred verses in the Bible teaching that salvation is by grace through faith plus nothing!  This chapter contains only a few of many which clearly and simply affirm the truth of the Scripture.  Here are a few:

> *If we confess our sins, he is faithful and just to forgive us our sins, and to cleanse us from all unrighteousness.*[19]

> *For God so loved the world that He gave His only begotten Son, that whosoever believeth in Him should not perish but have everlasting life.*[20]

The record is further set straight:

> *For by grace are ye saved through faith; and that not of yourselves: it is the gift of God: not of works, lest any man should boast.  For we are his workmanship, created in Christ Jesus unto good works, which God hath before ordained that we should walk in them.*[21]

> *Not by works of righteousness which we have done, but according to his mercy, He hath saved us.*[22]

Through our own efforts of trying to keep the commands by our own initiative we will always fall short of the glory of God:

> *But that no man is justified by the law in the sight of God, it is evident: for, The just shall live by faith.*[23]

> *Therefore by the deeds of the law there shall no flesh be justified in his sight: for by the law is the knowledge of sin.*[24]

> *Well then, are God's laws and God's promises against each other?  Of course not!  If we could*

*be saved by his laws, then God would not have had to give us a different way to get out of the grip of sin - for the Scriptures insist that we are all its prisoners. The only way out is through faith in Jesus Christ; the way of escape is open to all who believe him.*[25]

Better to accept God's provision of grace to forgive our sin.

## The Greek word *Tetelestai*

Pause and reflect on the words Jesus cried out from the cross, "It is finished!"[26] He was referring to the giving of His life to end our separation and purchase our reconciliation to God. Our English words *It is finished* come from the Greek *tetelestai*. In the Greek, the perfect tense of this term is used, which means "the event is completed with continuing effects." *Strong's Exhaustive Concordance* of the Greek dictionary, defines *tetelestai* this way: "to end, i.e. complete, execute, conclude, discharge (a debt): - accomplish, make an end, expire, fill up, finish, go over, pay, perform."[27]

Adding works as a means to salvation totally contradicts the true meaning of the intent of the Greek word *tetelestai*. The actual meaning of *tetelestai* disavows the idea that Jesus showed us the way by His example, or that He was merely a way starter or that now we must add works as a means to salvation. If one believes that Jesus began the way of salvation and forgiveness for us - but that now we must work at it very hard to complete it - then we have not heard the true voice of Jesus Christ. Jesus is the final and only reconciliation of man to God! Jesus did not just die a martyr's death. He did not just give us a good example by which to abide. He was not simply a wonderful man and teacher. Through Jesus, the gift of reconciliation to God is final and complete. This is true grace. How we respond to the words of Jesus "It is finished!" is up to every individual, and is of eternal consequences. Eternal life will come to each of us, with or without God's loving companionship. Our eternal domain has to do with our response to the true meaning of those words of Jesus as He hung from the cross. Where do works fit in to all of this? Look below:

*. . . And now that I am away you must be even more careful to do the good things that result from being saved, obeying God with deep reverence, shrinking back from all that might displease Him. For God is at work within you, helping you want to obey Him, and then helping you do what He wants.*[28]

> **God is at work within you, helping you want to obey Him**

The King James version puts it this way:

*. . . Wherefore, my beloved, as ye have always obeyed, not as in my presence only, but now in my absence, work out your own salvation with fear and trembling. For it is God which worketh in you both to will and to do His good pleasure.*[29]

> **Saving faith produces good works**

While this verse seems to rationalize the LDS position, a closer look at the verse reveals that one cannot work out salvation until it is received. Some persons take lightly the wonderful gift of salvation. In the verse above, Paul speaks out against cold and dead orthodoxy that knows no struggle and growth. Saving faith produces good works and they flow as a result of salvation. As we yield to God, our deeds are in tune with the Holy Spirit, and not born of fleshly man-made motives or doctrines of unrighteousness.

## The Greek word *Dikaloo*

Those who place their faith in the finished work of Christ are saved by grace through faith.[30] This means they have been justified before God. In the Greek text, the word *justified* is *dikaloo* and conveys the meaning, "just as though I'd never sinned." This word in *Strong's Exhaustive Concordance* reads, "to render (i.e. show or regard as) just or innocent; to be free, justify, (-ier), be righteous."[31] How marvelous! God's provision for our sins, the most awesome supernatural event in history, entailed the shed blood and death of Jesus Christ on the cross at Calvary. Jesus has purchased true believers with His own blood.[32]

When we accept Jesus as Savior, God declares us NOT GUILTY –just as though we never sinned. When we obey God's command to be saved, or born again as it is referred to in the New Testament book of John,[33] we receive deliverance from eternal separation from God, and receive possession of eternal life with God. Eternal life is the gift from the Father - what an inexpressibly wonderful gift!

To say that Jesus didn't complete all that is necessary for our total salvation at Calvary is to cheapen and completely reject the clear message of Scripture. When we advocate human works as necessary to salvation, we reveal a lack of Bible understanding, and we deny the scriptural message of the cross and Sacrifice of the Lamb of God. Suppose I went to your bank and completely paid off your debt. Would there be any point of your going to the bank and insisting on paying an additional amount? No! When it's paid, it's paid for completely![34] Jesus said, "Truly, Truly, I say to you, he who hears My word, and believes in Him who sent Me, has eternal life, and does not come into judgment, but has passed out of death into life."[35]

What a promise! What resting knowledge! God has even assigned guardian angels to minister to those who receive the gift of salvation.[36] As the Father calls[37] have you felt the Holy Spirit[38] urging you to receive the true Christ as the only means of salvation?[39] Even as you've been sinning, God, in His lovingkindness, has been watching out for your future:

> *But God showed His great love for us by sending Christ to die for us while we were still sinners. And since by His blood He did all this for us as sinners, how much more will He do for us now that He has declared us not guilty? Now He will save us from all of God's wrath to come. And since we were His enemies, we were brought back to God by the death of His Son, what blessings he must have for us now that we are His friends, and He is living within us.*[40]

Conclusively, and clearly, the Bible teaches that grace is an unmerited gift to us from God. This awesome free gift is difficult to understand without an understanding of the meaning of sin and the nature of God. If we understood the extent of God's hatred for sin and how it has fractured our world and our lives, it would give us all chills, I am certain. Looking at sin through God's eyes would create within us a greater respect and wonderment for the grace God has extended to us through His Son. No doubt we would be fully persuaded to flee from sin, but without accepting God's genuine and gracious Atonement for our sins, running would be of no avail.

| |
|---|
| ***man is totally helpless to save himself*** |

How important it is to comprehend the seriousness and penalty of sin, for it is death. It is eternal separation from God. We all must repent and turn to God with the understanding that man is totally helpless to save himself. We must rely upon the grace of God. It will not do to have an intellectual knowledge of how to receive salvation. Truth without conviction from the heart does not please God.

Come to the Word of God for the honest truth about the Gospel of grace. The Holy Spirit helps us to understand that Jesus came to expound upon and explain the precepts, council, guidance and instruction of the the Bible to us.

May we each grasp firmly God's truth regarding salvation. Truly, humans must not approach God with a desire to exalt self to the status of a God. Although both here and in eternity God rewards believers for their good deeds, they are in no way aids to salvation. While a Mormon, I was taught that I could earn the Mormon Exaltation, but I now understand that I must trust Jesus Christ alone. Now I understand that good works are an expression of God's love through us. Anyone who thinks his own definition of truth will be accepted by God is deceived by a different Gospel and needs to be delivered from foolish thinking! God will not compromise, nor will anyone simply drift into heaven by his own good deeds or striving to keep man-made Laws and Ordinances. It is pure pride to say "I do not believe I can be saved by faith alone." God's gift of grace toward us comes from who He is, not because of who we are. Grace is God's goodness extending to our guilt. A gift is received, not earned! It was upon the Cross of Calvary that He took our sins upon Himself.[41] Jesus is our Passover Lamb.[41]

The extra-biblical laws for earning the Mormon highest kingdom of after-life is a way of adding to the Word of God. This is very serious, for the Word of God is pure and adding to it makes one a liar.[43] Such a lack of reverence for God's Word causes one to reap destruction.[44] Always, we should remember that the pure law is a picture of Messiah Jesus.  The law defines righteousness.  Grace bestows righteousness –we do not!  Thanks be to God!  How wondrous are the verses below:

> *This plan of mine is not what you would work out, neither are my thoughts the same as yours!*[45]

> *O the depth of the riches both of the wisdom and knowledge of God!  how unsearchable are his judgments, and his ways past finding out!  For who hath known the mind of the Lord?  Or who hath been His counseller?  Or who hath first given to him, and it shall be recompensed unto him again?  For of him, and through him, and unto Him, are all things: to whom be the glory forever Amen.*[46]

For a believer, God's grace grants a transference from death to life.

Amazing grace is the answer!  Such amazing Grace!

1   2 Nephi 25:23.
2   The Provo  Herald, January 12, 1984, p. 21.
3   Articles of Faith, p. 480.
4   Joseph Smith, 2:19.
5   What's Going On In There?,  p. 33-38.
6   Romans 3:20-25.
7   Romans 5:8.
8   James 2:10.
9   Romans 3:23.
10  Galatians 3:24.
11  John 1:4.
12  John 1:14.
13  Romans 11:6.
14  Mormon Doctrine, p. 101.
15  Repentance Brings Forgiveness, back page of booklet.
16  Miracle of Forgiveness, p. 334.
17  Miracle of Forgiveness, p. 327.
18  Romans 4:6.
19  1 John 1:9.
20  John 3:16.
21  Ephesians 2:8.
22  Titus 3:5.
23  Galatians 3:11.
24  Romans 3:20.
25  Galatians 3:21-22.
26  John 19:30.
27  Strong's Exhaustive Concordance of the Greek New Testament, #5055.
28  Philippians 2:12,13.
29  Philippians 2:12,13.
30  Hebews 10:38, and chapter 11.
31  Strong's Exhaustive Concordance of the Greek New Testament, #1344.
32  Acts 20:28.
33  John 3:7.
34  Galatians 2:16.
35  John 5:24.
36  Hebrews 1:14.
37  John 6:44.
38  1 Corinthians 12:3.
39  John 14:6.
40  Romans 5:8.
41  Revelation 13:8.
42  1 Corinthians 5:7.
43  Proverbs 30:5-6.
44  Proverbs 13:13; Revelation 21:8.
45  Isaiah 55:8.
46  Romans 11:33-36.

# 19. The Book Of Life

*. . . If any man shall add unto these things, God shall add unto him the plagues that are written in this book: and if any man shall take away from the words of the book of this prophecy, God shall take away his part out of the book of life, and out of the holy city, and from the things which are written in this book.*

Revelation 22:18-19

My friend, Melaine, encouraged me to ask the biblical Jesus into my heart. She explained that by doing so I would become God's child, a part of the true family of God. I sensed Melaine's sincerity, but thought "surely Christ is already in my heart!" Next, I thought, "Wait - I know the Mormon Jesus is different from the Jesus the Christians trust, and that the Mormon Gospel keeps changing doctrine about who God is. So perhaps there is a false Jesus in my heart, or even no Jesus at all." Of this subject I later learned that the Bible warns:

*Test yourselves to see if you are in the faith; examine yourselves! Or do you not recognize that Jesus Christ is in you unless indeed you fail the test?*[1]

The *Amplified Version* of this Bible verse uses the words: counterfeits, disapproved, on trial, and rejected.

Mormons believe all humans are children of God. While the Bible affirms that everyone is part of God's great creation, it also reveals that the fall severed our spiritual relationship with God, and so we must be reborn and adopted as children into the family of God.[2] According to the Word of God, until the new birth takes place we are spiritually dead. Spiritual and physical death, the seed of the serpent[3] is remedied through the new birth.[4] Notice the tense in the verse, "As many as received Him, to them gave He power to become the Sons of God. . ."[5] The verse does not say all people are His children, but that all may become so. We become children of God, at which time Jesus saves us from our sins, just as He came to do.

Even the Book of Mormon teaches that all must be adopted into the family of God.[6] Today Mormons believe that the new birth *begins* when one is baptized into the Mormon Church by a *legal* priesthood administrator.[7] Afterwards the Holy Ghost is conferred upon the new church member by the laying on of hands by a *legal* priesthood holder.

I continued to pursue truth as presented within the Bible. I contemplated puzzles within Mormonism such as "can God dwell in a man's heart?" We just noted that the Bible says yes. The Temple Ceremony which I experienced, and *Doctrine and Covenants*[8] both say no! Yet, the *Book of Mormon* says yes![9] Now I know that He lives within my heart.[10] I enjoy Him presently and will throughout all eternity. Joyfully, Scripture teaches that all persons may be saved and know that they too may live with God forever:

*And this is the record, that God hath given us eternal life; and this life is in his Son. He that hath the Son hath life; and he that hath not the Son of God hath not life. These things I have written unto you that believe on the name of the Son of God; that ye may know that ye have eternal life . . .*[11]

Sadly, Mormons do not have the sweet and absolute assurance that they will live with God forever. How obvious it is to me that Satan blinds eyes to the truth of the Gospel message.[12] I am thankful to the awesome God of the universe for His call to each of us to examine doctrine for its level of truth.[13] Examining Mormon doctrine removed the obstruction that kept me from seeing the true Gospel of Jesus Christ.[14] The truth set me free!

## What is Truth?

Through my years as a Mormon I was unable to separate the Mormon Church and its prophets from God. I couldn't see how one could exist without the other. One discussion I remember having as a child with a friend pertained to whether we would die for the Mormon Church. At an early age I learned that if I had to die someday for the Mormon Church I would please God in doing so. Strangely, years later in the temple I took a vow, –the Mormon oath to obey the the Law of Sacrifice which included the following words:

> *And as Jesus Christ has laid down his life for the redemption of mankind, so we should covenant to sacrifice all that we possess, even our own lives if necessary, in sustaining and defending the Kingdom of God.*[15]

> *I am the way, the truth, and the life: no man cometh unto the Father, but by me*

Within Mormonism, the Kingdom of God is the Mormon Gospel. In the Mormon temple I vowed to die if necessary for Mormonism!

"What is truth?" This is the famous question that Pilate asked of Jesus.[16] We have the answer to the question from Jesus Himself, "I am the way, the truth, and the life: no man cometh unto the Father, but by me."[17] The Bible also makes clear that in Jesus, dwells all the fulness of the Godhead bodily.[18] So Jesus is God!

If we choose not to believe Jesus' words, we will eternally sorrow. The words of Jesus, "I said therefore to you, that you shall die in your sins; for unless you believe that I am He, you shall die in your sins."[19] What is the penalty of sin? Death and separation from God for which there is no escape! "For the wages of sin is death, but the free gift of God is eternal life in Christ Jesus our Lord."[20] Jesus Christ alone is our eternal escape. He Himself gave warning:

> *Enter ye in at the strait gate: for wide is the gate, and broad is the way, that leadeth to destruction, and many there be which go in thereat: Because strait is the gate, and narrow is the way, which leadeth unto life, and few there be that find it.*[21]

From this verse we learn that in life there are two roads only, the broad road and the narrow road. Jesus claimed to be the only way to the Father. His words describe a narrow road. As I struggled for truth I thought to myself, "If Jesus is truly *Immanuel*, which means *God with us*,[22] then –His is the government! He is the Mighty God, the Prince of Peace![23]" Keeping this in mind, it is right that He is the gateway to life, and He renders all other ways as the broad way to destruction! I began to see that it was actually the blood of God; His blood Sacrifice which paid entirely for my sins.[24] There would have been no need for Jesus to die as defined in Scripture as the Lamb slaughtered from the foundation of the earth,[25] if we do not need redemption, nor if Jesus did not totally pay the ransom for us.

> *that Jesus spoke of the narrow road that leads to life does not make Him narrow-minded*

The fact that Jesus spoke of the narrow road that leads to life does not make Him narrow-minded. Jesus was being specific. He has been on earth and in heaven. He knows how to get back to heaven. To illustrate, if I told someone to go south from Denver to arrive at my house, but the person insisted going north because it seemed the reasonable way, that person would never arrive at my house. So it is with obedience to God's specific way to salvation, we must go the way God has ordained. I concur with the late Dr. Merrill Unger, of Dallas Theological Seminary. His words:

> *Heaven is for bad people. Hell is for good people. Heaven is for people so bad that they dare not approach God in their own right - they must have someone (Jesus) speak for them, and must be covered with the robes of the righteousness of Christ. Hell is for people good enough that they trusted in their own merits.*

## Heaven or Hell?

In my upbringing hell or damnation is not descriptive of a permanent abode. Indeed, hell was erased from its powerful biblical intent. Does the term *broad gate*[26] really mean eternal destruction? Destruction - a real hell, the way Christians describe it? In the past, I had dismissed this subject as a myth, or perhaps another bad translation. Just thinking such a thing was too horrid! I saw this and similar verses as a wrestling match between the Bible and Mormonism. I understand now that a literal hell is the truth of Holy Scripture. Without Jesus there is no way of escape! Choose life! The Incarnation of Jesus provides a way to escape from the clutches of Satan and separation from God.

> *the Incarnation of Jesus provides a way to escape from the clutches of Satan and separation from God*

But while LDS I held to church doctrine, which seemed to explain away biblical passages. Such included the view concerning people's final state in heaven or hell at the resurrection. I was troubled and perplexed by the concept of hell. I wondered, "What exactly is hell, anyway?" I wondered, "Is it true that all are resurrected to a measure of salvation? In heaven, are there really three kingdoms of glory as I was taught within Mormonism?" The Mormon Church believes in *universal salvation* which means that all will be saved in heaven. According to the LDS Church salvation is twofold. Joseph Fielding Smith explained:

> *In Mormonism salvation is twofold. General: –that which comes to all men irrespective of a belief (in this life) in Christ –and, Individual –that which man merits through his own acts through life and by obedience to the laws and ordinances of the gospel.*[27]

A strange contradiction about keeping all the commandments must be discussed here. In order to live with God, the LDS Church calls for perfection. As a missionary, I taught others from my church missionary lessons that true repentance must be a permanent one. "We also have to forsake the sin and never repeat it, not even in our minds . . . In order to remain forgiven, we must never commit that sin again."[28] In another place Joseph Fielding Smith said, "In other words, if there is one divine law that he does not keep he is barred from participating in the [Celestial] kingdom, and figuratively guilty of all, since he is denied all."[29] Being barred from God in a lower kingdom, I had been taught, is still separation from God the Father. A harrowing thought!

In Mormonism's three kingdoms, or heavens, the lowest is so wonderful that it surpasses our mortal understanding.[30] The second death, or outer darkness, as it is also referred to, is where the Sons of Perdition, and Satan and his followers are sent. This place of abode is not considered a kingdom in Mormonism. As the Mormon Apostles James E. Talmage and Joseph Fielding Smith explained, hell is the place termed Spirit prison, which eventually ends in progression to one of the three Mormon kingdoms.[31] Can you see then that Mormonism does not believe in a literal hell? This is explained in more detail in chapter nine. Oddly, the progression explained above contradicts the *Doctrine and Covenants* which makes the following reference to hell:

> *Nevertheless, is it not written that there shall be no end to this torment, but it is written endless torment . . . Again it is written eternal damnation . . . the punishment which is given from my hand is endless punishment, for Endless is my name . . .*[32]

The *Book of Mormon* agrees with the above quote and of the final state of the wicked:

> *For behold, if ye have procrastinated the day of your repentance even until death, behold, ye have become subjected to the spirit of the devil, and he doth seal you his; therefore, the spirit*

*of the Lord hath withdrawn from you, and hath no place in you, and the devil hath all power over you; and this is the final state of the wicked.*[33]

There are so many contradictory teachings in Mormonism like the ones above regarding hell. I asked myself, "What if the *three kingdoms* are really the *broad way* Jesus spoke of that leads to destruction? Supposing there really are not three compartments in heaven?" If that is so, Mormons may be among those using the Lord's name, but of whom the Lord would say, depart from Me, ye that work iniquity.[34] I didn't want to be among those who cross the line hardening themselves to the truth, and receiving a strong delusion. The Bible warns of this happening:

> *And with all deceivableness of unrighteousness in them that perish; because they received not the love of the truth, that they might be saved. And for this cause God shall send them a strong delusion, that they should believe a lie.*[35]

**they received not the love of the truth, that they might be saved**

I wanted to love truth and not sear my conscience or fall into self-deception. As I studied my Bible, I discovered that the Bible, unlike present Mormonism, doesn't equate resurrection as salvation. The Bible seriously instructs that people ought to receive salvation today and that it is possible to receive grace in vain:

> *As God's fellow workers we urge you not to receive God's grace in vain. For He says, "In the time of my favor I heard you, and in the day of salvation I helped you." I tell you, now is the time of God's favor, now is the day of salvation.*[36]

The Bible states that one doesn't get a second chance:

> *Just as man is destined to die once, and after that to face judgment, so Christ was sacrificed once to take away the sins of many people; and He will appear a second time, not to bear sin but to bear salvation to those who are waiting for Him.*[37]

## The Never-ending Culmination

In contrast to the Mormon doctrine of universal salvation let's briefly contrast the biblical understanding of hell. I learned that in the New Testament Jesus spoke of hell more than about any other subject. Hell is a place where God does not want people to go. The issue concerning a belief in hell is not so much whether or not there is a hell, as it is whether a person can handle the fact. One goes to hell by one's own neglect and default.

Hell is a place where the unregenerated person will forever be separated from God.[38] Those who disrespect and refuse the demands of God's justice and His *only* provision of mercy to cover man's sin are those who will take the broad way to hell. They refuse to receive into their hearts Jesus Himself, who shed His redeeming blood on their behalf. They have not chosen to be clothed in the gift of God's righteousness; God's only begotten Son. They prefer to clothe themselves with the garments of their own way.[39] Of their own choosing they have elected a course which keeps them unworthy and incapable of abiding in the presence of a Holy and righteous God. People who insist upon ruling their own life may do so - in hell. They, without the covering of God's righteousness will be defeated and tormented forever. After they have made the choice to cover themselves with their own righteousness for God's acceptance, it will be too late to cancel their decision. It will be too late to cry for mercy. They did not want God's provision for mercy, but mercy according to their own definition. This form of mercy is illusionary. It is not possible to slip into heaven:

**it is not possible to slip into heaven**

> *How shall we escape, [appropriate retribution] if we neglect and refuse to pay attention to such a great salvation [as is now offered to us, letting it drift past us forever]? For it was declared at first by the Lord [Himself], and it was confirmed to us and proved to be real and genuine by those who personally heard [Him speak]. [Besides these evidences] it was also established and plainly endorsed by God, Who showed His approval of it by signs and wonders. . .*[40]

*. . . they that go down into the pit cannot hope for thy truth.*[41]

*I said therefore unto you, that ye shall die in your sins: for if ye believe not that I am he, ye shall die in your sins.*[42]

*The wicked shall be turned into hell, and all the nations that forget God.*[43]

The Bible describes a wicked person as a sinner not washed in the cleansing blood of Jesus for the remission of sins, which accompanies God's salvation. On the other hand, a saved person is a sinner made positionally righteous through faith in the provision of God's Son, whose very Hebrew name, Yeshua, means *salvation*.

> **Jesus' Hebrew name means "salvation"**

Few object that heaven is eternal, why refuse to believe that hell is also eternal? The wrath of God rests on those who go to hell. The unbelieving will perish.[44] In the Bible, the word *perish* means eternal torment. Those who choose hell stand condemned.[45] The biblical word for hell is *Gehenna*. This word is found eleven times in the Gospels, and each time it is expressed by Jesus. In the New Testament alone there are 162 texts which speak of the doom which awaits the impenitent, and over 70 of these were uttered by Jesus Himself. Gehenna represents the Hebrew ge-hinnom or valley of Hinnom. This valley was used as a garbage pit where fires continually burned. Jesus used this foul valley as a graphic description of hell. There are so many Scriptures which define hell.[46]

Disregarding God's commands will bring certain consequences. The penalty of refusing the true Gospel will result in absolute devastation and everlasting punishment. As an immeasurable gift to us, Jesus literally gave up His life and went to hell in our place to end our separation from Him. Those who choose Christ will never be separated from God. Anyone, including the heathen, who truthfully want to know God may do so, for God reveals Himself to all persons.[47] The point in ones life when God reveals Himself is a critical time. One may choose a relationship with God, or elect to ignore Him. From the ends of the earth God will move a seeking person to understand the need to throw himself upon the merciful lovingkindness of God to receive reconciliation. The seeking person will recognize that he cannot, through his own efforts or merit, make himself acceptable to the Almighty Creator of all. For we humans, even one speck of sin separates us from the presence of the Almighty. That is why Jesus shed his life-saving blood on our behalf.

Rather than believing the true God, who has proclaimed in His Word that there is one literal heaven and one literal hell, Mormons are being deceived by their church to believe that all mankind will earn a place of habitation in one of *three kingdoms*. The revelations in the *Doctrine and Covenants* concerning three kingdoms[48] are fabrications of Satan who comes to steal, kill and destroy.[49] I concluded that the LDS doctrine about heaven and hell is false and only manufactured in the hearts of men led away by their own lusts,[50] thereby, giving license to Satan, the *god of this world*,[51] to sear their conscience from hearing the true Shepherd's voice. Thankfully, I came to see that what I thought was truth concerning this matter was not based on true evidence. I now have a clear understanding that the Mormon doctrine of salvation and the final state of humans is utterly debased and bogus; a substitute for truth. The true means of salvation and all of the loving warnings concerning the reality of hell, which are revealed through God's Word, are first dismissed, and then superseded by the pseudo-Gospel of Mormonism. We must not add or take away from God's Word.[52]

True salvation is available only to those who have placed their faith in the Atonement of Jesus apart from works.[53] At the time of the new birth, one passes from spiritual death to spiritual life, or from darkness to light. The saved will experience the joys of heaven –eternally!

Understanding the final state of humans, saved and lost, is a weighty matter. I recommend reading chapter eight in Volume three of *Integrative Theology*, by Drs. Gordon R. Lewis and Bruce A. Demarest. You will find it under the title *Life After Death, Resurrection, and the Final Judgment.*

1    2 Corinthians 13:5.

2    Galatians 4:5.

3    John 8:44.

4    John 3:7.

5    John 1:12.

6    Mosiah 5:7; 27:24-28, Alma 7:14.

7    Mormon Doctrine, p. 101.

8    Doctrine and Covenants 130:3.

9    Book of Mormon, Alma 34:36.

10   Galatians 2:20.

11   1 John 5:11-13.

12   2 Corinthians 4:3-4.

13   Acts 17:11.

14   2 Corinthians 11:3-4.

15   What's Going On In There?, p. 31.

16   John 18:38.

17   John 14:6.

18   Colossians 1:19.

19   John 8:24.

20   Romans 6:23.

21   Matthew 7:13.

22   Isaiah 7:14.

23   Isaiah 9:6.

24   1 John 1:7.

25   Revelation 13:8.

26   Matthew 7:13.

27   Doctrines of Salvation, vol. 1, p.134.

28   Uniform System for Teaching Families, Disscussion F, pp. 35-36.

29   Answers to Gospel Questions, vol. 3 p. 26.

30   Doctrine and Covenants, 76:89; Mormon Doctrine, p. 778.

31   Articles of Faith, p. 145, 147, 148; Doctrines of Salvation, vol. 2, p. 133.

32   Doctrine and Covenants 19:6-8, 10.

33   Book of Mormon, Alma 42:6.

34   Matthew 7:22.

35   2 Thessalonians 2:10-11.

36   2 Corinthians 6:1-2.

37   Hebrews 9:27-28.

38   2 Thessalonians 1:8, 9.

39   Judges 17:6; Isaiah 5:21; Proverbs 12:15; Proverbs 18:13; Jeremiah 7:24.

40   Hebews 2:3.

41   Isaiah 38:18.

42   John 8:24.

43   Psalms 9:17.

44   John 3:16.

45   John 3:18.

46   Luke16: 24-27; Revelation 2:11, 19:20, 20:6, 10, 14, 21:8; Matthew 13:42, 25:46; 2 Thessalonians 1:10; Philippians 3:19; Jude 13; 2 Peter 2:17.

47   Romans 1:18-32.

48   Doctrine and Covenants 76 and 88.

49   John 10:10.

50   James 1:14.

51   2 Corinthians 4:3-4.

52   Galatians 1:6-9.

53   Leviticus 17:11; Ephesians 2:8.

# 20. The Real Self

*A good tree cannot produce bad fruit, nor can a rotten tree produce good fruit. Every tree that does not bear good fruit is cut down and thrown into the fire. So then, you shall know them by their fruits. . . . And the rain descended, and the floods came, and the winds blew, and burst against that house; and it fell, and great was its fall.*

Matthew 7:18,19, 27

Someone said, "A man's character is like a fence; it cannot be strengthened by whitewash." Although God is pleased by good behavior, we cannot make ourselves approved by God for salvation on this basis. To believe so is to completely miss the point of salvation. By our own efforts we may change our behavior, but that does not justify us before God. God informs us that all have sinned and come short of the glory of God."[1] There still needs to be the inward heart acceptance of God's gift of grace.

Before I could escape the snare of Mormonism, I had to confront irreconcilable problems of doctrine. In other words, I had to see holes in the ship before I could look to the lifeboat. When I saw Mormonism crumble, I was not willing to continue justifying the church by skirting important issues. I saw Jesus, so to speak, as the lifeboat. I had served God in a lie through most of my life. Today I shudder as I think about the many Mormons who are entrusting their eternal existence into the hands of Mormonism and its false prophets! The true Messiah fades into the background. Now it gives me the chills when I think about the extreme differences between Mormonism and God's instructions and guidance.

> *I was not willing to continue justifying the church by skirting important issues*

I'm so grateful to God for loving and sustaining me even through all of my Mormon life. Through the providence of God, His timing and the Holy Spirit's nudging, my eyes were opened up to the full range of deception I had lived through as a Mormon. I now grasp with clearer understanding our fallen nature and estrangement from God and have learned the importance of recognizing Satan's devices.[2] The deceptions I recognized were serious. Now I believe that LDS Church members are in great need of rescue. I began asking God how people can be so wrong and still sincerely believe they are correct. The answer is revealed in the Bible.

## Nicodemus

Does God look upon our potential, our intelligence, or any earthly means, to qualify us for salvation? Nicodemus, the Pharisee, was no doubt shocked when Jesus informed him that in spite of all his good works, there was a problem in Nicodemus's life that needed to be dealt with. The problem Nicodemus had is universal among humans. You see, through Adam's fall all people inherit a sin nature. That is why Jesus explained to Nicodemus: "Truly, truly, I say to you, unless one is born again, he cannot see the kingdom of God."[3] You see, the whole human race has been spiritually poisoned through the fall. The fact that man has a sin nature explains the reason people are self-centered and rebellious. Sin is rebellion against God. Our ill-behavior, conduct, actions, and beliefs are indicators of what is already in our hearts. We need to be willing to reject false teachings, some of which we receive from our loved ones. The Bible teaches that the sins of the fathers fall upon the children to the fourth generation:

> *Thou shalt have none other gods before me . . . Thou shalt not bow down thyself unto them, nor serve them: For I the LORD thy God am a jealous God, visiting the iniquity of the fathers upon the children unto the third and fourth generation of them that hate me.*[4]

I believe that my Mormon family and friends fit the description of the verse above, for they have been serving a false God for generations. My whole family inherited a non-saving Gospel. We were taught that the Mormon Church was the only true church, but the facts prove differently. Generations of my family have come and gone since my ancestors embraced Mormonism and it is time to come out from the darkness of Mormonism to serve the true and Living God of the Bible. The bright side of the generational sin predicament is that through repentance the wrong sinful beliefs we have inherited and nurtured need not be passed on to future generations. We may choose life.[5] As for me, I didn't want generational problems passed on to my children and grandchildren. God's truth is liberating, coherent, and unwavering!

I confessed the sin of Mormonism to God. Seeking God for more direction, and with undivided attention I set my heart like flint to learn what should be my next step. I felt badly about my past and I certainly didn't want to take to heart Brigham Young's advice to church members:

> *Keep your follies that do not concern others to yourselves and keep your private wickedness as still as possible; hide it from the eyes of the public gaze as far as you can, and make it appear that you are filled with the wisdom of God.*[6]

It was also the Mormon Prophet Brigham Young who said:

> *We have the greatest and smoothest liars in the world, the cunningest and most adroit thieves, and any other shade of character that you can mention. . . . We can beat the world at any game.*[7]

How sad! More trustworthy are the words, "Confess your faults one to another, and pray for one another, that ye may be healed. The effectual fervent prayer of the righteous man availeth much."[8]

## The Old and New Creation

True Scripture teaches that many people are lost[9] and many are perishing.[10] But God, through His Son, has provided the solution.

To the Lost:

- spiritual things are not understood and cannot be until the new birth.[11]
- the Gospel is hidden.[12]
- the Gospel and the cross are foolishness.[13]
- the god of this world (Satan) has blinded their eyes.[14]
- a veil blinds them.[15]
- believers are a bad odor of death and doom.[16]
- to some, the Gospel is an offense.[17]

To the Saved:

- the Gospel is the power of God.[18]
- the Gospel gives spiritual discernment.[19]

The Gospel Provides Jesus as a Complete Covering of:

- righteousness.[20]
- healing.[21]
- worthiness.[22]

- fellowship.[23]
- peace.[24]
- sanctification.[25]
- protection.[26]
- forgiveness of rebellion against God –sin.[27]
- and even more –such treasures!

Jesus came to seek and save the lost.[28] When our hearts turn to the Lord He removes a veil from our eyes.[29] Then we are commanded to fulfill the great commission, which is to spread the Gospel throughout the world.[30]

## Anathema – God's Curses

Scripture is plain that there are false plans of salvation which cannot save, but do in fact, incur bondage in our lives. We should take heed that we are properly grounded in the truth of God's Word:

> . . .You are already following a different way to heaven, which really doesn't go to heaven at all. For there is no other way than the one we showed you; you are being fooled by those who twist and change the truth concerning Christ. Let God's curses fall on anyone, including myself, who preaches any other way to be saved than the one we told you about; yes, if an angel comes from heaven and preaches any other message, let him be forever cursed. I will say it again: if anyone preaches any other Gospel than the one you welcomed, let God's curse fall upon him.[31]

*Anyone* includes ourselves. Scripturally-speaking, curses are the natural consequences of shrinking away from God's teaching, instruction, and guidance.

The Greek word for *curse*, used in the verse above, is *anathema*. When used in conjunction with the word *maranatha*, which means *come Lord Jesus"*[32] it conveys the meaning *to be cut off without remedy at the coming of the Lord Jesus*. God warns about false prophets and apostles, of them is said:

> God never sent those men at all; they are "phonies" who have fooled you into thinking they are Christ's apostles. Yet I am not surprised! Satan can change himself into an angel of light, so it is no wonder his servants can do it too, and seem like godly ministers. In the end they will get every bit of punishment their wicked deeds deserve.[33]

*curses are the natural consequences of shrinking away from God's teaching, instruction, and guidance*

We ought not be fooled by men in sheep's clothing, nor by their words concerning salvation. How terrifying the ultimate result for not believing in and loving the true Gospel. To believe in a "god who is only a glorified, resurrected man" is to bend the knee to a false god and a false Gospel with no power to save. Remember the warning:

> I hope you will be patient with me as I keep on talking like a fool. Do bear with me and let me say what is on my heart. I am anxious for you with the deep concern of God himself---anxious that your love should be for Christ alone, just as a pure maiden saves her love for one man only, for the one who will be her husband. But I am frightened, fearing that in some way you will be led away from your pure and simple devotion to our Lord, just as Eve was deceived by Satan in the Garden of Eden. You seem so gullible: you believe whatever anyone tells you even if he is preaching about another Jesus than the one we preach, or a different spirit than the Holy Spirit you received, or shows you a different way to be saved. You swallow it all.[34]

Jesus explained:

> Heaven can be entered only through the narrow gate! The highway to hell is broad, and its gate is wide enough for all the multitudes who choose its easy way. But the Gateway to Life is small, and the road is narrow, and only a few ever find it.[35]

Notice that these verses absolutely deny a *broad way* (the Mormon term is universal salvation) to heaven and keeps in accord with Jesus' statement that He alone is the way to the Father. With this in mind heed and respect the biblical warning that there is indeed a literal place called Hell. Are you gambling with your eternity by assuming that the Bible and its message of salvation are wrong? Is that what you have been taught or have come to believe? False leaders and their teachings do influence our dogma and may consequently keep us from the eternal presence of God.

## Filters

I do not know who wrote the following paragraphs that drive home a powerful message:

> *Let's say I rob a bank. That makes me guilty of robbery. Let's say I don't feel guilty about it. If robbery can be established as wrong, then I am guilty of robbery, regardless of how I feel. The feeling - or lack of feeling - does not change the fact. Let's say I worship a false God. That makes me guilty of idolatry. Let's say I don't feel guilty about it. If idolatry can be established as wrong, then I am guilty of idolatry, regardless of how I feel. The feeling - or lack of feeling - does not change the fact.*

> *There once was a man who thought he was dead. As you can imagine this caused his wife considerable grief. The man was finally sent to a psychiatrist. In an effort to convince the man that he was not dead the doctor proposed that dead men do not bleed. He had the man read medical textbooks and watch a number of autopsies and after several weeks of efforts the man finally agreed that dead men don't bleed. At this point the doctor reached over and pricked the back of the man's hand with a needle and blood began to flow. The man looked down with a contorted ashen face and declared, "Good Lord, dead men bleed after all."*

The moral of the story is that if you hold unsound presuppositions with sufficient tenacity, facts will make no difference at all, and you will be able to create a world of your own, totally unrelated to reality, and totally incapable of being touched by reality. Such a condition which the philosophers called presuppositions, psychiatrists called autistically psychotic and lawyers call simply insane is tantamount to death, for connection with the living world is severed. The man thought he was dead and in a very real sense he was dead for facts no longer meant anything to him.

How are you filtering truth? No one likes to admit to being wrong. We love the bondage of our own ideas. Inside our hearts and minds we carry the badge of a church, a philosophy or any man-made substitute for truth, usually of our own determined preference. If someone questions us we take it personally; our pride, our self-esteem is threatened. If you are a Mormon, please consider the question: "If I accept you as a Christian, will you accept me as a Mormon?" To become a member of the Mormon Church requires the acceptance of Joseph Smith and the Mormon priesthood (only a couple among the attending Mormon requirements). The obvious Mormon response, "no!" to this question should drive home the fact that Christianity and Mormonism are not compatible.

While still a Mormon I could not separate the Mormon Church from God. This inability was not intentional, but somehow building up Mormonism for the glory of God took precedence over seeking God Himself. I believe this often happens to Mormons –unwittingly the church they are building obscures and eclipses the true God. I do not believe Mormons are necessarily hardened against truth. I believe many are Bible illiterate, naive and deceived. I also believe that many Mormons ignore the scriptural truth of who God is more than wanting to reject Him. Being deceived doesn't make a person dishonest or evil, it simply means being wrong. Sometimes we are afraid to examine the facts presented. This is natural. By not confronting our fears, we deny the grace of God to sustain us while seeking truth which sets us free.

As a little child trusts his parents to meet his needs we too ought accept all which God has revealed concerning Himself and the redemption of man. The things God has revealed to us are totally reliable and sufficient to make a proper choice about the Gospel of Christ. We ought not speculate or add to the already preserved truth of God.

Our purpose in life is to repent of our sins and receive relationship with Messiah Jesus, making Him our precious Lord and Savior. Jesus Christ is our redemption! Choosing the right by keeping our walk in accordance with the revealed truth of God's Word will keep us safe. Participation of both the heart and mind are necessary to a relationship with God. A personal relationship with the one true God is wonderful –and results in spontaneous praises to God. God inhabits our praises.[36] Worshiping the true God eradicates impurity of thought, filling us with the joy of the Lord. The joy of the Lord is our strength.[37] Intimacy with the Father is a righteous goal and comes to us when we receive Christ into our hearts permitting our relationship with Him to change our lives. It is the Holy spirit that draws us to that relationship. Intimacy with the Holy Spirit increases as we yield to His promptings.

On the other hand, there are unseen rulers of the darkness in this world. These principalities and powers are evil spirits who rule in Satan's unseen realm, where all of our spiritual battles take place. They are highly organized, disciplined and committed. Are we? These rulers of darkness impact our beliefs and consequently our behavior. This is a serious matter, for Satan comes to kill, steal and destroy.[38] We must be aware of his tactics. Satan wants us to remain ignorant, apathetic or neutralized. But as to what transpires behind the scenes we have been informed and forewarned. Take note of the following:

> *Satan wants us to remain ignorant, apathetic or neutralized*

**Principalities and Powers:**

> *. . . Lest Satan should get an advantage of us: we are not ignorant of his devices.*[39]

> *For we wrestle not against flesh and blood, but against principalities, against powers, against the rulers of the darkness of this world, against spiritual wickedness in high places.*[40]

**People are Destroyed for Lack of Knowledge:**

> *My people are destroyed for lack of knowledge: because thou hast rejected knowledge, I will also reject thee . . ..seeing thou hast forgotten the law of thy God . . .*[41]

**People Inherit Lies:**

> *Surely our fathers have inherited lies, vanity, and things wherein there is no profit.*[42]

It is wise to ask God to reveal to us the lies we have inherited or bought into. We are instructed to openly confess the lies and the iniquities of our fathers which we have inherited just as did the Israelites of Nehemiah's day.[43] We each may be assured of the promise, "Come now, and let us reason together, saith the Lord: though your sins be as scarlet, they shall be white as snow; though they be red like crimson, they shall be as wool."[44]

In the Garden of Eden mankind fell from his pristine state. Man's entire person and nature became fractured; his mind became subject to confusion and his understanding and relationship with God became distorted and blurred. It is our fallen nature that leads us to the making of standards of right and wrong which supersede the standards of God. God has spoken of man's unregenerated heart.

**Deceitful Heart**

> *There is a way which seemeth right unto a man, but the end thereof are the ways of death.*[45]

> *The heart is deceitful above all things, and desperately wicked: who can know it?*[46]

> *For from within, out of men's hearts, come evil thoughts of lust, theft, murder, adultery, wanting what belongs to others, wickedness, deceit, lewdness, envy, slander, pride, and all other folly. All these vile things come from within: they are that which pollute you and make you unfit for God.*[47]

> *Let no man say when he is tempted, I am tempted of God: for God cannot be tempted with evil, neither tempteth any man: But every man is tempted, when he is drawn away of his own lust, and enticed. Then when lust hath conceived, it bringeth forth sin: and sin, when it is finished, bringeth forth death.*[48]

The Bible speaks of a time when people went their own way and never sought to submit or have fellowship with our Creator. We read:

> *In those days there was no king in Israel, but every man did that which was right in his own eyes.*[49]

> **every man did
> that which was right
> in his own eyes**

Let's not do likewise. There is no point running from God:

*Can any hide himself in secret places so that I will not see him? says the Lord.  Do I not fill heaven and earth? says the Lord.*[50]

We are given warning:

*He who trusts himself is a fool, but he who walks in wisdom is kept safe.*[51]

People who distort the truth regarding God and his commandments are under a powerful delusion to believe a lie:

*Even him, whose coming is after the working of Satan with all power and signs and lying wonders, and with all deceivableness of unrighteousness in they that perish; because they received not the love of the truth, that they might be saved.  And for this cause God shall send them strong delusion, that they should believe a lie: that they all might be damned who believed not the truth, but had pleasure in unrighteousness.*[52]

### Therefore We Must Test the Spirits

*Beloved, believe not every spirit, but try the spirits whether they are of God: because many false prophets are gone out into the world.*[53]

To rearrange and delete truth to suit our own beliefs or notions, is termed "situational ethics."  Running from truth eventually catches up with us.  Sometimes we plug our ears so as not to hear God, but our spiritual senses are sharpened as we become obedient to the promptings of the true Holy Spirit.  I believe it is time to pull our fingers out of our ears and respond to God.  Let's be sure we are rooted and grounded in truth.  When we hear truth as God reveals it within the Bible, we become responsible for what we choose to do with it.  Truth can be our best friend or our worst enemy.  "Above all else, guard your affections, for they influence everything else in your life."[54]

It is so rewarding to agree with God's purpose in our lives, and acknowledge Him in all our ways.  Unlike the ever-changing Gospel of Mormonism, through which I and many have journeyed, God's truth never changes.  It has been with us all along.  If by now you see Mormonism as a counterfeit, I pray you also have more confidence in the truth of God's Word.  Do not be discouraged, God is still on the throne.  He has a wondrous plan for your life!  If you have not experienced salvation you may do so.  Look to Jesus Christ and His Word, the Bible, and discover the true plan of redemption, and our reconciliation back to the One God, the majestic King of the Universe.  Actually, the Bible is an autobiography given to mankind by God Himself.  How often does one get to read a book in the presence of its author?

God loves us passionately and with Godly jealously - even in the midst of our sin of neglect toward Him!  Regardless of past carelessness toward God, our awesome Creator is faithful to extend His loving kindness (grace) upon us.  He can put a new song in our hearts.  His promises are abundantly sufficient for our needs:

### His Abundant Promises

*As many as I love, I rebuke and chasten: be zealous therefore and repent.  Behold, I stand at the door and knock: if any one hears my voice and open the door, I will come in to him and eat with him, and will sup with him, and he with Me.*[55]

*. . . For whoever would come near to God must (necessarily) believe that God exists and that He is the Rewarder of those who earnestly and diligently seek Him (out).*[56]

*The fear of the Lord is the beginning of wisdom: and the knowledge of the holy is understanding.*[57]

*For God giveth to a man that is good in his sight wisdom, and knowledge and joy . . .*[58]

*When my anxious thoughts multiply within me, Thy consolations will delight my soul.*[59]

*The fear of the Lord leads to life: Then one rests content, untouched by trouble.*[60]

*Thou shalt guide me with thy counsel, and afterward receive me to glory.*[61]

Those promises are a bargain!  A true  bargain!

1   Romans 3:23.
2   2 Corinthians 2:11.
3   John 3:3.
4   Deuteronomy 5:7, 9.
5   Deuteronomy 30:19.
6   Journal of Discourses, vol. 8, p. 362.
7   Journal of Discourses, vol. 4, p. 77.
8   James 5:16.
9   2 Corinthians 4:3.
10  1 Corinthians 1:18.
11  1 Corinthians 2:14.
12  2 Corinthians 4:3-4.
13  1 Corinthians 1:18.
14  2 Corinthians 4:3-4.
15  2 Corinthians 3:14.
16  2 Corinthians 2:15-16.
17  1 Peter 2:7-8.
18  1 Corinthians 1:18.
19  1 Corinthians 2:14.
20  2 Corinthians 5:21.
21  Matthew 8:16-17.
22  Romans 6:16-18.
23  Ephesians 3:11-12.
24  Isaiah 55:3.
25  Hebrews 10:10.
26  Hebrews 13:5.
27  1 John 1:7.
28  Ezekiel 34:15-16; Matthew 18:11.
29  2 Corinthians 3:14-16.
30  Matthew 28:18-20; 2 Corinthians 2:15-16.
31  Galatians 1:6-9.
32  1 Corinthians 16:22.
33  2 Corinthians 11:13-15.
34  2 Corinthians 11:1-4.
35  Matthew 7:13.
36  Psalms 22:3.
37  Nehemiah 8:10.
38  John 10:10.
39  2 Corinthians 2:11.
40  Ephesians 6:12.
41  Hosea 4:6.
42  Jeremiah 16:19.
43  Nehemiah 9:2.
44  Isaiah 1:18.
45  Proverbs 14:12.
46  Jeremiah 17:9.
47  Mark 7:21-23.
48  James 1:13-15.
49  Judges 17:6.
50  Jeremiah 23:24.
51  Proverbs 28:26.
52  2 Thessalonians 2:9-12.
53  1 John 4:1.
54  Proverbs 4:23.
55  Revelation 3:19-20.
56  Hebrews 11:6.
57  Proverbs 9:10.
58  Ecclesesiastes 2:26.
59  Psalms 94:19.
60  Proverbs 19:23.
61  Psalms 73:24.

# 21. Surrendering

*No one can serve two masters; for either he will hate the one and love the other, or he will hold to one and despise the other.*

Matthew 6:24

As a Latter-day Saint, I believed the doctrines of Mormonism to be the restored and undefiled truth from God. One doctrine (man achieving Godhood) to my way of thinking was a lofty goal which God wanted his children to achieve. I once believed that the LDS priesthood and its ordinances authorized people to exalt themselves to Godhood. I strived to perfect myself, working for Exaltation to Godhood in Mormonism's Celestial kingdom, the eternal abode and reward for the Mormon faithful. My belief in Exaltation to Godhood and the belief in countless other Gods clearly identified me as a polytheist. A belief in polytheism separates one from biblical instruction. In order for one to embrace this doctrine, basic Bible verses must be discarded and replaced with man's own version of God's forever truth. Polytheism disregards the true nature of the self-existent God. God did not graduate to Godhood! Man shall never become a God, but the salvation offered to humans results in unspeakable joy which lasts eternally! This is made possible only through Jesus, Who carried away our sins as He hung from the Cross of Calvary. God's plan of redemption for humankind appears foolish to some. The Bible says:

*For Christ sent me not to baptize, but to preach the gospel: not with wisdom of words, lest the cross of Christ should be made of none effect. For the preaching of the cross is to them that perish foolishness; but unto us which are saved it is the power of God.*[1]

The Bible teaches the sound and fundamental doctrine that Christ's death on the cross brought total ransom for the human race - not so in Mormonism. I was taught to dismiss the cross and not to wear a cross as jewelry. We avoided music that pertained to the cross. It was explained to me that crosses must not decorate Mormon meeting houses or Mormon temples. I find this odd, especially since demonic symbols are seen decorating Mormon temples. See the Exhibit Section page 213.

While Mormonism downplays the work of the cross and promotes its complex and false Gospel, the biblical Gospel fades into the background. A strong reliance on the Mormon testimony derived from a burning bosom helps dismiss fundamental Bible teaching. The following *Doctrine and Covenants* quote describes the way Mormons are encouraged to acquire a testimony:

*But, behold, I say unto you, that you must study it out in your mind; then you must ask me if it be right, and if it is right I will cause that your bosom shall burn within you; therefore, you shall feel that it is right.*[2]

Whenever a testimony (by Mormon standards) is born, Joseph Smith and the present Mormon prophet must be attested to - as God's mouthpiece on earth. From the April, 1995, report of the 165th annual General Conference of the Mormon Church, David B. Haight of the Quorum of the Twelve Apostles, voiced the following concerning Gordon B. Hinckley the presiding Mormon Prophet in 1995:

> *With all the inspiration and love that I possess, I testify that Gordon B. Hinckley was foreordained to become the President of The Church of Jesus Christ of Latter-day Saints; to be the mouthpiece of God on the earth at this time; and to lead God's people as prophet, seer, and revelator . . . President Gordon B. Hinckley now wears the mantle given to the Prophet Joseph Smith. He was foreordained to this high and holy calling in premortal councils.[3]*

In the same speech, members of the church are instructed to heed the *Doctrine and Covenants* in respect to the Mormon prophet. So, in regards to Gordon B. Hinckley, this volume of alleged Scripture states:

> *Wherefore, meaning the church, thou shalt give heed unto all his words and commandments which he shall give unto you as he receiveth them, walking in holiness before me; for his word ye shall receive, as if from mine own mouth, in all patience and faith.[4]*

| |
|---|
| ***feelings . . .*** |
| ***are confused with faith*** |

I now view the reliance and emphases on the Mormon testimony (the burning bosom) and the need for a Mormon prophet as mere idol worship. Both carry major importance within Mormonism, even to the degree that for some members any other means of testing truth is dismissed. I believe that feelings and emotion, rather than reason, sets the tone in Mormonism. Feelings, for many LDS people, are confused with faith. The expression, *burning of the bosom*, used to describe the Mormon testimony, is a highly subjective way in which to determine truth.

We ought to conform to God's truth –rather than dress Him in our own style of religion. It's good, I think, to remind ourselves that God is the potter and we are the clay:

> *Woe to the one who quarrels with his Maker –An earthenware vessel among the vessels of earth! Will the clay say to the potter, 'What are you doing?'[5]*

> *But now, O Lord, Thou art our Father; We are the clay, and Thou our potter; And all of us are the work of Thy hand.[6]*

Why not agree to God's protective message recorded in the Bible?

Finally, I understand that God doesn't even deal with feelings like the Mormon's *burning bosom*. Feelings result from thoughts that may be void of truthful facts. The battle is in our minds –where all victory and defeat take place. The Holy Spirit aids us to bring captive our thoughts, and our feelings, to the obedience of Jesus Christ:

> *For though we walk in the flesh, we do not war after the flesh: (For the weapons of our warfare are not carnal, but mighty through God to the pulling down of strongholds;) Casting down imaginations, and every high thing that exalteth itself against the knowledge of God, and bringing into captivity every thought to the obedience of Christ . . .[7]*

Extra-biblical writings and imaginations ought to be surrendered to God in exchange for His own true words. That is what is meant by worshipping in spirit and in truth.[8]

## Doubts and Fears

While I was growing up my peers and myself were taught to believe that anyone's rejecting of Mormonism must be the consequence of grievous sin, rebelliousness, lack of good works or some other moral infraction. The possibility of the church being wrong or its members being deceived seemed inconceivable to my Mormon peers and myself. Or, if we doubted, it seemed we never dared admit to it or do anything about it. Part of the problem, as I see it now, is that Mormons are taught never to bring reproach upon their church and their leaders. And leaving the church for some may bring a loss of respect in a Mormon community, or a loss of job. The fear of doing injury to their church and their leaders may cause many Mormons to abandon a search for truth. Also, the experience of doubting some aspect about their church frightens many Mormons. As a Mormon, I often heard it expressed that doubting the church stems from Satan. Satan can indeed tempt us to fear examining the truth for ourselves. He may tempt us to depend on others whom we may assume are better qualified to make those kinds of choices, but Satan does so in order to keep us in darkness. I now believe it is dangerous to rely so much on others' opinions for the definition of right and wrong, "For the leaders of this people cause them to err; and they that are led of them are destroyed."[9]

When fear is present we experience weakness, self-centeredness and double-mindedness. God removes those kinds of problems from our lives, "For God hath not given us the spirit of fear; but of power, and of love, and of a sound mind."[10] My own experience has taught me that it is okay to doubt. I find it a stimulant to maturing faith! I've heard it said that there is more faith in honest doubt than in blind obedience. I agree! Lining the difficulties of our life alongside the Word of God shrinks them down to a workable size. If we meditate on the Word of God we protect ourselves. God implores us to love Him with all our hearts, minds and souls.[11] This verse doesn't in any way suggest that we hide away the mind. If we ask for the Holy Spirit to reveal truth, the result will be a sound mind.

> *it is dangerous to rely so much on others' opinions for the definition of right and wrong*

We are admonished to show ourselves approved unto God, and correctly handle the Word of God.[12] To study God's Word is a form of worship and shows respect to our creator. Satan wants to destroy our lives using deception and seduction. To repeat an important point- God's truth is always liberating, coherent, unwavering, harmonious, stable, constant, and consistent. When one takes personal responsibility and accountability to God, the Mormons "follow the leader" mentality must go. Adding to God's Word is a most serious matter ending in catastrophy.[13]

No one need fear the truth or be afraid to examine doctrine for its level of truth. Life is not over after discovering that Mormonism is false. If you have been saddened by the deceit and waste of Mormonism, be assured that God is sovereign; there is not one thing that happens in our lives which God has not permitted or somehow ordained. When we settle that issue in our hearts we come to peace with the adventures and trials of life. God's power is love, Satan's power is fear, and our power is choice, through the enabling Holy Spirit. God works all things together to those who love Him! I once heard the comforting words, "Hope is the ability to hear the music of the future. Faith is dancing to it in the present." May we each seek God! May we trust, obey, and follow Him the remainder of our days on earth.

## The Developing Room

As a young person I had a desire to serve God with all my heart, soul and mind. During my early married life God sent various people into my path who tested my understanding about God, the Mormon plan of Eternal Exaltation, grace, and other doctrines of Mormonism. They argued that crucial church doctrines upheld in the past were now changed or disbanded altogether. The matters they brought to my attention attacked the very foundation of the Mormon Church. Armed with unswerving confidence in the Mormon Church and its leaders, I set about to defend the purity of the church before the very eyes of its opposition and stop what I believed to be lies perpetrated by the *enemies of the church* (a common expression used by Mormons). As a response to the command of the *Doctrine and Covenants*, "Wherefore, confound your enemies; call upon them to meet you both in public and private; and inasmuch as you are faithful their shame shall be made manifest,"[14] I began a quest to study the defense of the Mormon Church. I sought to be faithful to all of the commandments the church espoused. How could I hope to teach the Mormon Gospel effectively if I could not live and defend it?

I honored the admonition of my Patriarchal Blessing, to study the Mormon Gospel, teach it, and seek the council of my leaders. In accordance to the admonition of my blessing, when I could not resolve problems by myself, I sought out the council of those who resided over me. The men who presided over me didn't have answers to the accusations and challenges which I had encountered, and sometimes were totally unfamiliar with critical issues which definitely deserved to be addressed and dealt with in a fair manner.

At the end of my research, and in accordance with the direction of my Patriarchal Blessing, I went to my bishop with the problems I had discovered during my study. Specifically, I mentioned the Tanners' book *Shadow or Reality*, which to me proved to be a shocking but faithful report of Mormon History. The bishop repeated for me the familiar response - all I had been reading was deceit and even outright distortions from the enemies of the church. The bishop remarked that he was acquainted with the Tanners' writing. According to him the Tanners, like other apostates, intentionally discredit "God's true church." Our bishop never bothered to demonstrate one reason to substantiate his words about the Tanners.

I learned from experience that in Palatine, just as in Aurora and in Vernal, that most Mormons seldom felt the need to give a defense for the faith as is commanded in the *Doctrine and Covenants*.[15] Few were the times anyone had been willing to discuss issues which were obviously of great significance to the authenticity of the Mormon Church. Often, when I brought questions to the attention of friends and family, and those who presided over me, the responses demonstrated a lack of basic reading of the Mormon Standard Works. To me, the usual response to the charges about which I had inquired carried no weight. They were reactionary emotions---certainly not answers. What happened to the command set forth by the Mormon Church to understand and defend the faith?

All through the years, LDS people with whom I had discussed problems about Mormonism, shared many of the same attitudes and responses, and although I've mentioned some of them before, I believe at this point in our journey they bear repeating:

1.  No interest - flee the issues.
2.  That's your interpretation.
3.  But, I have a testimony!
4.  I feel a spirit of contention here.
5.  Ask the missionaries - they will know!
6.  Can't you feel the truth?
7.  Don't cultivate a spirit of apostasy.
8.  You are too weak to keep the Mormon Gospel.
9.  We are always being persecuted!
10. You look only to ridicule the church!
11. Avoid the issue by attacking the character of the messenger.

I believe these restrictions are due to an inordinate embedded fear. Rather than study the evidence, it seemed a most frequent approach was to attack the character of anyone who may not agree with some aspect of the church. This is very sad. I am reminded of the words of Jesus, "But I say unto you, that every idle word that men shall speak, they shall give account thereof in the day of judgment."[16] Thankfully, God patiently waits for us to respond to His truth instead of our feelings. Now, I understand that when our feelings do not line up with the Word of God, we must not give place to them.[17]

## Counting the Cost

Persons receiving a Mormon *Temple Recommend* must answer "yes" to the qualifying questions from the General Handbook of Instruction of the Church. Among the questions I was asked was whether or not I had any connection, in sympathy or otherwise, with any of the apostate groups of individuals who are running counter to the accepted rules and doctrines of the church. The same questions were asked of my parents and brothers and sisters when they sought out their *Temple Recommend*. Therefore, what kind of connection would my parents and siblings carry on with me after I spoke to them of my departure from Mormonism? How would my aging parents hold up under this? What would my ten brothers and sisters think? If I left the church, I would offend my Mormon family and friends, and perhaps lose their friendship as well. And when I became aware of the ugly truth about the Mormon Church, naturally I also wondered how the results of my research would affect our children, all four of whom had been baptized into the church, the eldest then attending Brigham Young University.

I fully realized that there are obvious convicting evidences against the church which are inexcusable by any fashion and are matters not to be taken lightly. It is true that I diligently and sincerely studied Mormonism and the Bible, discovering the church I had been a member of for 37 years was a false Gospel. The Mormon Church had betrayed and deceived me! The more I searched for answers to my questions the more questions arose, and less and less answers came forth. In light of the research I embarked upon as well as diligence in prayer and fasting, Mormonism fell apart. It was an arduous journey, a battle outside the realm of flesh and blood,[18] not simply an intellectual or emotional battle. For me the obvious falsity of Mormonism resulted in a crisis of conscience. The leaders of the church preached doctrine which if had I continued to embrace would have utterly closed my ears to the truth of God's Word.

> *it was an arduous journey, a battle outside the realm of flesh and blood*

As I looked back through my life I became aware that through the years God had sent various messengers and means into my life enabling me to examine Mormonism in a fair and truthful fashion. In my upbringing I was taught that it is possible to put off repentance too long. I began to experience a need within my soul to *repent* for believing and practicing a false Gospel. I recalled an old adage repeated by my father, "A person convinced against his will is of the same opinion still." I didn't want people or any other form of deception to override truth and to keep me away from God. My world had been turned upside down, and I realized that my journey in life would now take a new direction. I had to make a choice and move on with life. In my heart and in my head I realized that my choices were either to forget about spiritual things altogether, which went against the grain of my nature, or pursue the truth of God with the same vigor I had served the LDS Church. My heart cried out for God's truth. I continued to think about the ramifications of leaving Mormonism. I weighed the cost. I knew I must be true to my convictions! I surrendered myself to God. I wanted to fellowship with true believers wherever they may be. I still had faith and hope that God would establish my feet on the proper path. I continued to pray and study. I never felt abandoned nor angry with God, but I was continually appalled about the discoveries unveiled before my eyes concerning the church I was raised in. As difficult as the task at hand appeared at times, I depended solely on God and was very confident that He was with me.

In my home, I have a poster of a rag doll being put through an old fashioned clothes wringer (shown in the Introduction on page iii). The caption on the picture depicts my personal journey to becoming a Christian. It reads, "The truth will make you free, but first it will make you miserable!" Actually, these words refer to a Scripture verse that reads "If ye continue in my Word, then ye are my disciples indeed; and ye shall know the truth and the truth will make you free."[19] In this verse Jesus is speaking to believers in Him. Jesus informs us that through obedience to the truth of God's Word our minds become renewed, enabling us to have clear understanding. Faith comes by hearing the Word of God.[20] These words of Jesus are comforting. He instructs us that we find liberating truth lodged in His Word. By embracing Bible truth we allow God to work in our lives.

## The Truth is at Stake Here

Defending the truth of God's Word and exposing error is an important command from God. I've compiled a partial list of biblical dictates titled *Biblical Defense of Truth* which is in the Exhibit Section on page 226. I felt a need to share the truth of my discoveries. For me to be silent about the false religion of Mormonism would be the equivalent of maintaining a lie.

Mormonism is a part of my family heritage and I believe that each family member has a right to know facts which I believe are hidden from view. The prospect of telling my family and friends may sometimes be unsettling, but I cannot think of a good reason that they should be kept in the dark. I have discovered there is only one fatal error in life. If we reject the sufficiency of Messiah Jesus for our *total* redemption we make a fatal and cataclysmic mistake –lasting for all eternity, "For the wages of sin is death but the free gift of God is eternal life in Christ Jesus our Lord."[21] There is no other way to come to God but through Jesus![22] It is crucial that my family discover that Mormonism is not the way to God! Families should have top priority in our earthly pilgrimage.

Mormonism opposes the pre-eminent doctrines of the Bible. All false religions are ever reaching and climbing up to please God. In comparison, the Bible reveals God reaching down to men with mercy and compassion through the awesome gift of eternal life through His Son. His forgiveness of sin is so necessary and costly that it required the life-blood of the true Messiah. How wonderful that Jesus should care enough for us to take humanity upon Himself, and die for our sins. Salvation is of such magnitude that it cannot be earned! It does not come through Joseph Smith and his alleged only true church - consisting of all the un-biblical works of the Mormon faith. Salvation comes through Jesus alone, not a church organization, or creed; neither brotherhood, nor principle, nor feeling, nor rules and regulations. God's truth is far more than a system of ethics. It is an intimate relationship with the Creator of the Universe. Embracing the Gospel message revealed in the Bible will cure false doctrinal diseases and keep one from spiritual cyanide. Our relationship with God must be on His terms! Otherwise we separate ourselves from the Holy One of Israel.

I have been set free from a massive and deadly deception. I see Mormonism as a new religion reinventing itself as it moves along its way. Convenience of the moment seems to dictate todays version of accepted church writings. I believe that the LDS Church rewrites history the way they wish it had been. The Mormon Church uses a rubber yardstick as their way of measuring, defining, and calculating truth. May its members reject that rubber yardstick and trust in Jesus Christ alone for complete salvation.

## Mormonism in a Nutshell

I wish I knew whom to credit the following quip which appropriately illustrates the Mormon warping of biblical Christianity:

> For God (the Father, who is a resurrected and glorified man with a body of flesh and bones) so loved the world that He gave (one of His pre-mortal spirit sons who became) His only begotten Son (in the flesh) that whosoever believeth in Him (and keepeth all his commandments and is baptized by immersion for the remission of sins by the authority of the (LDS) holy priesthood and is confirmed as a member of the one true (LDS) church and is married for all eternity in the House of the Lord which is an LDS temple) should not perish (which means to have ones' eternal progressions stopped in the telestial or terrestrial heavens so that one can cannot achieve godhood) but have everlasting life (in the highest or third level of the Celestial heaven where one shall be god over one's own world and beget spirit offspring eternally).

> – *16.6% written by God*

## Why I Oppose Mormonism

At the time of my departure out of Mormonism I concluded:

1. Joseph Smith was a false prophet and his followers fall prey to deceiving spirits.

2. The Mormon priesthood is an affront to God, and is authored by Satan, the father of lies.

3. The *Book of Mormon* is a contrived writing.

4. The *Doctrine and Covenants* has been rewritten, whole sections dropped making the very thought of divine authorization a preposterous claim.

5. The *Pearl of Great Price* is also a contrived writing, outside the realm of Christianity, and ought to be replaced with the genuine Pearl of Great Price –Messiah Jesus.

6. The Mormon Church has altered all of their *Standard Works* and most of their history making it impossible for it to be viewed as truth from the true God.

7. The Mormon belief in personal Exaltation to Godhood, and the belief in many Gods, is unbiblical and an absolute abomination to God.

8. Other Mormon doctrines concerning salvation, rituals, initiations, secret endowments, –not to mention Mormonism's understanding about the Bible, salvation, the nature of God, grace,

heaven and hell are all outside the biblical text. I believe they grieve God's heart. Such a blatant heretical departure from the true God of Israel! They are mere works of the flesh.

9.  The LDS Church is not the *restored* truth as it claims. The Bible establishes that there never was a total apostasy. God has always had a remnant of believers, just as in the days of Elijah. Elijah believed himself to be the only one who followed God. But the God of Israel informed him of 7,000 more who had not broken relationship with Him.[23] Mormonism is a natural result of undermining God's truth in order to make *God* into the *image of man*. Romans 1:23 says, "And changed the glory of the incorruptible God into an image made like to corruptible man..."

10. The LDS Church is guilty before God for concealing truth from its members and for hiding from critical examination. For the sake of their public image, the Mormon Church has elected to suppress or change doctrine that provokes bad publicity and criticism. Rather than admitting before others where it has been wrong, the Mormon Church calls forth another band-aid of new revelation. How many times the LDS Church has concealed facts to preserve itself! I agree with the old saying, "Fool me once, shame on you; fool me twice, shame on me." It is also said, "A thousand lies never make a truth."

11. Mormonism's chameleon-like revelations are the product of pressure from within or without. Examples of this are seen in in its conflicting doctrines of God, polygamy, Blacks receiving the priesthood, the change of the Temple Ceremony, and the literal gathering of the saints, to name a few. These changes support the argument that the current General Authorities themselves believe that the earlier prophets were false prophets, or why would they continually revise what has been handed down to them? It also points to the fact that the current General Authorities believe themselves superior in revelation to their predecessors. Primarily it shows that Mormonism's modern revelation is not authored by the true God, whose revelations never change.

12. I believe that many LDS Church members unwittingly surrender their faith and allegiance to their leaders and a burning bosom rather than to God. I see Mormonism as a highly organized religious heresy that has perverted the truth of the Bible into vain imaginations[24] centering around an allegiance to Joseph Smith and his spurious doctrines. The Mormon Church fails God's established test of truth. In the Mormon Church the true biblical Gospel message is not preached. In fact, Mormonism fits the standard definition of a cult. Webster's Dictionary defines *cult* as: "1. a system of religious beliefs and ritual; also, its body of adherents  2. a religion regarded as unorthodox or spurious  3. a great devotion to a person, idea, or thing."

> **Mormonism fits the standard definition of a cult**

Mormonism:

-   Demands unquestioning obedience
-   Denies grace; exalts man-made works
-   Downgrades Scripture
-   Humanizes God
-   Deifies man
-   Perverts sex
-   Downplays sin
-   Cannot withstand sound investigation
-   Centers around and magnifies one individual
-   Claims to speak for God
-   Has a persecution complex

People who know the biblical message of salvation often find it difficult to share the truth with Mormons because they have a prejudice against the Bible and an inordinate affection to the LDS faith.

## Taking Offense

I have not made up the evidence against Mormonism. Coupled with biblical evidence the LDS Church history is its worst enemy.

Jesus warned us about false prophets with verses such as this one: "Beware of false prophets, which come to you in sheep's clothing, but inwardly are ravening wolves. Ye shall know them by their fruits."[25] This warning necessarily includes doctrinal fruits. It has been seen that the doctrinal fruits of Mormonism change often, and the changes are serious and damaging to the church. In fact, I'm shocked to this very day of all the changes the Mormon Church continues to make to its already fabricated Gospel message. What a disagreement between the actual facts and these words written in the *Deseret News* editorial, which said of the Mormon God and His Gospel:

> But since He never changes, and since human nature is always the same, identical conditions are required to bring that human nature into harmony with the unchangeable God . . . For that reason, the gospel must always be the same in all its parts.[26]

What a blatant contradiction quotes such as this one are in the face of the facts I uncovered concerning the LDS Church! Because the Mormon Gospel was authored by man it is not surprising that man has changed it along the way. The Mormon Church is not only a blatant apostasy from Bible, but has become an apostasy from early Mormonism itself, which altogether negates its claim to restoration. God doesn't change![27] Nor is He the author of confusion.[28]

Conclusively, the truth which is in Jesus Christ does not in any way relate to the Mormon plan of salvation. Therefore, it is wise to escape the snare of Mormonism. The time we have on earth is too short and critical to waste living for a false salvation or to spend our lives in narrow self-interest rather than the way the Lord would have us live. The LDS Church grasps its false prophets and Gospel now, but ultimately it will answer to God. Falling into the hands of the living God while fighting against His true nature and means to salvation will be dreadful beyond measure.

Remaining inside of the organization while realizing its false origin would clearly be an act of open rebellion and idolatry before God. Most members in the Mormon faith, I hope, would not want to profane the name of God by clinging to a false Gospel.

*choosing not to decide they have already decided*

There are many reasons why people disregard God's command to test doctrine for its level of truth, but a strong dedication to truth will cause some to seek God with all their heart, soul and mind. Fearing a loss of the security based feeling of the *burning bosom* may keep some from examining the facts. For others, a fear of departure from the familiar may smother a need to pursue the facts. Some may choose not to decide at all. However, choosing not to decide they have already decided.

Regardless of how the news is finally handled, at such a juncture, a personal choice takes place resulting in the future and eternity of each member of the church to whom God supplies evidence for choice. I hope most members of the LDS Church would say with Joshua, ". . . Choose you this day whom ye will serve; . . . but as for me and my house, we will serve the Lord!"[29] Especially now in my life, I thank God for parents who taught me to trust in God. Honoring God and parents entails telling the truth. Truth, for me, holds eternal significance!

To those who are lost in false doctrine, I care enough for your souls that I must risk offending you. It is healthy to be warned, "A prudent man foreseeth the evil, and hideth himself: but the simple pass on and are punished."[30] I am also concerned that I don't offend God by ignoring His strong words:

> When I say to the wicked, O wicked man, you shall surely die, and you do not speak to warn the wicked from his way, that wicked man shall die in his perversity and iniquity, but his blood will I require at your hand.[31]

It is good to ask ourselves if we believe something because we were taught it, or because it is true. We should not be offended by having the truth magnified before our eyes. Consider the cluster of verses below:

*Am I therefore become your enemy, because I tell you the truth?*[32]

*Faithful are the wounds of a friend; but the kisses of an enemy are deceitful.*[33]

*Let the righteous smite me in kindness and reprove me; it is oil upon the head; do not let my head refuse it . . .*[34]

*For I am not ashamed of the gospel of Jesus Christ: for it is the power of God unto salvation to everyone that believeth . . .*[35]

## Be Encouraged!

I realize that when a person invests so much of themselves into the Mormon Church it becomes difficult to see the open truth. Although it may be difficult to forsake false traditions of family, friends, and loved ones, God's arm is not shortened. He supplies grace abundantly as we embrace the truth revealed in Scripture. One way God supplied me with peace was through the ministry of music. My friend, Melaine Layton, gave me a music tape by Bill and Gloria Gaither. One of the songs on the tape was called "Something Beautiful." This song is an expression of my journey out of Mormonism. The lyrics reveal my life before and after my departure. They are:

*Something beautiful, something good; All my confusion – He understood. All I had to offer Him was brokenness and strife, But He made something beautiful of my life.*

He can make anyone's life beautiful. I sang these words inside my heart. Now Jesus has become my righteousness. Jesus, the promised Messiah, gave Himself for me that I might have everlasting life with Him. What more could be added to His atoning Sacrifice? He saves completely, even from the maze and web of Mormonism!

How refreshing and straight on the mark is the true Gospel of Jesus Christ as it is preserved in the Bible, compared to the very complex system of Mormonism's false Gospel. True peace is found in a personal relationship with the real Messiah Jesus. When we meet with the true Jesus we hear the final Word of God! The desire to order our lives from our own will decrease as we surrender our own will to the true Shepherd's voice. God has spoken through Jesus Christ. Believers listen. Jesus describes a believer as one who knows, hears, listens and heeds His voice.[36] Do we accept the Incarnation, the shed blood of Jesus as God's only provision for our sins? Will we believe in what God instructs us, or will we decide on our own definition of truth? God offers each of us free pardon along with accompanying spiritual union with Him. But many refuse His pardon. They will themselves be at fault, for it is revealed through Scripture that God makes truth evident to all people.

I pray that loved ones and friends inside Mormonism will see that they have been led astray by their leaders, and realize the serious consequences of the Mormon false Gospel. I pray that they will be truthfully equipped to testify that they have worshipped an idol - only a god formed in the mind of man. It is my fervent prayer that before my LDS loved ones leave this world they will cease bearing the usual Mormon testimony (the burning bosom). This testimony, which is taught to children, I see as a mere expression of the Mormon creed. It must include the LDS prophet, priesthood, and LDS Church as God's only authority administered on earth.

I encourage Mormons to examine their faith in light of the truthful Holy Bible. See the comparison between the biblical Gospel and the LDS Gospel in the Exhibit Section on page 197. Come to know and testify of the true God of the Holy Bible, and reject the false God of Mormonism. Do not be discouraged. To members of the LDS faith who now may recognize how deceitful Mormon theology is, may I encourage you to faithfully keep pursuing God's holiness. Give Jesus your years and burdens of life. Drink in the love of God by becoming a true child of God.[37] Blessings beyond measure await those who recognize the true God and honor His means of salvation. Experience the reality of these beautiful words of Jesus:

*For this reason I say to you, do not be anxious for your life, as to what you shall eat, or what you shall drink; nor for your body, as to what you shall put on. Is not life more precious than clothing?  Look at the birds in the air, that they do not sow, neither do they reap, nor gather into barns, and yet your Heavenly Father feeds them.  Are ye not worth much more than they? . . . Observe how the lilies of the field grow; they do not toil nor do they spin, yet I say to you that even Solomon in all his glory did not clothe himself like one of these.  But if God so arrays the grass of the field, which is alive today and tomorrow is thrown into the furnace, will He not much more do so for you, O men of little faith? . . . Do not be anxious for tomorrow; for tomorrow will care for itself.  Each day has enough trouble of its own.*[38]

*And even to your old age, I shall be the same, And even to your graying years I shall bear you! I have done it, and I shall carry you; And I shall bear you, and I shall deliver you.*[39]

To conclude this chapter, I select the following magnificent, classic hymn, which captures and stirs the heart of man to grasp hold of the majesty of God and His reconciliation to mankind.

## Amazing Grace

John Newton

Amazing grace! How sweet the sound
that saved a wretch like me!
I once was lost, but now am found;
was blind, but now I see.

'Twas grace that taught my heart to fear,
and grace my fears relieved;
how precious did that grace appear,
the hour I first believed.

Through many dangers, toils, and snares,
I have already come;
'tis grace hath brought me safe thus far,
and grace will lead me home.

The Lord has promised good to me,
his word my hope secures;
he will my shield and portion be,
as long as life endures.

Yea, when this flesh and heart shall fail,
and mortal life shall cease,
I shall possess, within the veil,
a life of joy and peace.

When we've been there ten thousand years,
bright shining as the sun,
we've no less days to sing God's praise,
than when we first begun.

1    1 Corinthians 1:17-18.
2    Doctrine and Covenants 9:8-9.
3    Ensign, May, 1995, p. 36.
4    Doctrine and Covenants 21:4-5.
5    Isaiah 45:9.
6    Isaiah 64:8.
7    2 Corinthians 10:3-5.
8    John 4:24.
9    Isaiah 9:16.
10   2 Timothy 1:7.
11   Deuteronomy 6:5.
12   2 Timothy 2:15.
13   Galatians 1:8.
14   Doctrine and Covenants 71:7.
15   Doctrine and Covenants 71:7.
16   Matthew 12:36.
17   Proverbs 30:5-6, 13:13.
18   Ephesians 6:12.
19   John 8:31, 32.
20   Romans 10:17.

21   Romans 6:23.
22   John 14:6.
23   1 Kings 19:18.
24   Romans 1:21.
25   Matthew 7:15-20.
26   Deseret News, Church News Section, June 5, 1965.
27   Malachi 3:6.
28   1 Corinthians 14:33.
29   Joshua 24:15.
30   Proverbs 22:3.
31   Ezekiel 33:8-9.
32   Galatians 4:16.
33   Proverbs 27:6.
34   Psalms 141:5.
35   Romans 1:16.
36   John 10:4-5.
37   John 1:12.
38   Matthew 6:25-34.
39   Isaiah 46:4.

# 22. Reconciliation

*For since in the wisdom of God the world through its wisdom did not come to know God, God was well-pleased through the foolishness of the message preached to save those who believe.*

1 Corinthians 1: 21

The Bible discloses to us that those persons who wrote Scripture were directed to do so by the power of the Holy Spirit. Over a period of 1500 years, by 40 men, the Old Testament was written. The Old Testament contains several hundred references about the coming of Messiah. Those prophecies are fulfilled in Jesus. He is the giver of salvation. If His death on the cross was not necessary to our salvation, I'm certain it would not have happened. Let's examine what the Bible teaches.

In the first few chapters of Genesis we read about creation and how sin entered into our world. In prophetic form, the third chapter of Genesis contains the first preaching of the good news of salvation; the remedy for sin. Genesis, like the rest of the Bible is a revelation instead of an in-depth explanation of creation or of salvation. In Genesis we see that God decreed to permit sin. Sin came after the creation. It is not part of God's creation. It is not self-existent or necessary. It is not even a step of creativity to something higher or better. It is the result of chosing self over God.

We were created to be the object of God's love. God wanted humanity to return that love, since a true relationship is only possible through intellect, faith, will, emotions, and most importantly, by choice. God created man with these characteristics which sets them apart from all other creation. Although we are wonderfully made in the image of God, we are still created ones. We are reliant on God for our very breath.

The only thing God kept for Himself in the entire Garden of Eden was the tree of the Knowledge of Good and Evil,[1] of which God instructed Adam and Eve not to partake lest they die.

The serpent we read about in the account of the fall, is identified throughout Scripture in various ways i.e.: Serpent,[2] Satan,[3] Devil,[4] Lucifer,[5] Dragon.[6] The Bible does not reveal a great deal about Satan before his involvement with Adam and Eve, but in Scripture we are given some clues.[7] Satan was created as the most glorious of angels. In the Bible we learn that it was his prideful goal to become as God that launched Satan's downfall! Before the fall, Satan turned against his Creator! After God cast Satan from heaven, he still held fast to his goal to be as God.

In the Bible, the Serpent presents a life-like image of revolt against God.[8] It is seen that humans and the power of evil are at constant warfare. With accusation and lies Satan attempted to destroy God's integrity and purpose. It was he who cast doubt in Eve's mind as to the reasonableness of God's command concerning the eating of the tree of Knowledge of Good and Evil. Satan sold the lie to Eve that partaking of the tree of Knowledge of Good and Evil would not bring about death but would instead cause them to be as God. He seduced Eve to believe that breaking God's commands would profit her. Adam followed her and also partook of the tree. Now as then, Satan boldly casts doubt about God's integrity and the credibility of God's Word. Satan continually challenges God's boundaries and truth. Many people today are deceived into believing the same lie which Satan used to tempt Eve - that they may become as God. How reckless!

God's gift of volition to humans is always accompanied with responsibility on our part. It is here that the test of our character is manifested. Adam chose opposition and rebellion, severing his spiritual relationship with God. He did so in the light of the knowledge that breaking this command from God would carry the penalty of death.[9] The truth is that God is a loving Father and would have continued to bless Adam and Eve, thinking only of their utmost peace. Had their choice been to obey God, they still would have fulfilled God's command to multiply and replenish the earth.

> **Adam and Eve covered themselves, hid themselves, experienced fear and insecurity, and they criticized and blamed. So do we!**

As a result of rebellion against God, the fall brought sin and death to the entire human race. As a result of Adam's rebellion his descendants were not covered with God's righteousness. History illustrates that mankind has broken fellowship with God. We see this through wars and bloodshed rather than peace and harmony. The Bible explains that our sins have caused separation and a lack of intimacy with God.[10] In the instant of humanity's disobedience came separation, death, guilt and sorrow into Adam's and Eve's natures. The same followed for the entire human race. Adam and Eve covered themselves, hid themselves, experienced fear and insecurity, and they criticized and blamed. So do we!

In an attempt to cover their sense of shame they made themselves aprons of fig leaves. The Bible makes it clear that such an apron is symbolic of the works of human hands apart from God. God found the fig leaf aprons Adam and Eve made for themselves, unacceptable. To remedy Adam and Eve's broken human relationship with Him, He took away the fig leaf aprons and replaced them with the covering of skins from a sacrifice. Actually God killed a lamb and made coats of skins for Adam and Eve. God provided a blood sacrifice as a way to cover their sin. This was the first sacrifice, a gift offered to them showing them a way of forgiveness. This act was representative of the coming of the Messiah; the Sacrificial Covering of Jesus Christ. The Bible identifies Jesus as the Lamb Who takes away the sins of the world.[11] Jesus is the *garment of salvation* provided for us!

The killing of the sacrifice became Adam and Eve's first experience with physical death. They realized that God had sacrificed an innocent animal and that their own sin had made the offering necessary. From this act of God on their behalf, Adam and Eve were taught that they and their offspring were to offer animal sacrifice as a temporary covering for their sin until there came the Ultimate Sacrifice for sin provided by the Lamb of God Himself. In today's so-called civilized world many consider the idea of animal sacrifices as uncivilized, primitive, archaic and bloody. In biblical Old Testament times sacrifices illustrated the deadliness of sin. They demonstrated that breaking God's law resulted in death.

## Justice and The Fall

Paul explained in the book of Romans[12] that the result of the fall of Adam and Eve was fatal and widespread - because the whole of mankind was in Adam. We, therefore, are all sinners. Christ came to bridge the gap of our separation from God. If persons enter into the Glory of God's presence, they must do so through God's appointed means. This comes through accepting the final and Ultimate Sacrifice of Jesus, the Lamb of God who takes away the sins of the world. The message of the Sacrificial Offering must not be tainted by man.

Holiness is the intrinsic nature of God, and means that He is free from all defilement and imperfection. A Holy God, because His perfect nature is one of justice, cannot fellowship with anyone who is not righteous, nor can an unrighteous man withstand the very holiness of God's presence. In fact, we would not survive one second. His holiness would consume us! But, at the fall, when humanity broke fellowship with God, the justice of God demanded that a barrier be placed between Himself and His creation.

God did not want Adam and Eve to live eternally in their fallen state. Had Adam and Eve remained in the garden, they may have also partaken of the tree of life[13] and consequently lived forever in their fallen state. Whatever was to be done in order to rectify the dire consequences of the fall had to be compatible with God's nature, because it is not consistent with His nature to do anything outside of the scope of perfect holiness.

If the nature of God were exclusively one of justice, He would supply no mercy. God's justice and mercy are companions, and these two traits together are a revealing of His holiness. God's very nature cannot allow His love for us to take precedence over His justice. He cannot condone sin; that would be inconsistent with His holy attributes.[14] After the fall God still loved His creation, even though their relationship had been torn away by rebellion. Although God's nature is one of boundless love, God's Justice demands that our sin be paid for.[15]

Unlike the Mormons, the Israelites did not think of the fall as a blessing nor a prerequisite to exalt self to the station of a God. As pointed out before, one General Authority, Sterling W. Sill, defined the fall spoken of in Genesis an "upward fall."[16] For partaking of the tree of Knowledge of Good and Evil, Mormonism exonerates Adam and Eve. It teaches that breaking that command of God was necessary to one's achievement of Eternal Exaltation. While in reality it is impossible to fall upward, by teaching that the fall of Adam and Eve was not downward, the church sides with Satan! This is serious! Holy Scripture describes Satan as a murderer and a liar in whom there is no truth at all.[17] Clearly the Bible teaches that rather than upward the fall was downward. The sin of Adam and Eve was not an avenue to become Gods over planets as Mormonism teaches. Not to believe this basic fact of Scripture is to live outside of reality. The Bible does not include Adam in the hall of faith chapter of the Bible (Hebrews 11). The first man of saving faith is Abel, not Adam!

The fig leaf aprons of Adam and Eve should not be looked to with respect. In the Mormon Temple Ceremony I was taught to respect them. I wore a green fig leaf apron in the temple. It was a part of the temple attire. This fig-leaf like apron is also worn by deceased temple Mormons at burial services. I am reminded also of the Mormon garments, or the *regulation undergarments* as they are also called, which are worn daily by temple Mormons. In style and purpose neither the Mormon priesthood nor the temple garments, including the apron, resemble the biblical priesthood or temple attire. Instead, they are like the attempt of Adam and Eve to cover their shame with fig leaf-like aprons. The wearing of such a covering reminds me of the futility of the works of Mormons who aspire to become a God over their own planet. The garment which God offers to humans, the garment of salvation does not refer to LDS temple garments, but to the perfect covering of the righteousness of Christ.[18]

> *I wore a green fig leaf apron in the temple*

When we compromise God's Word we begin hearing another voice, not God's voice. Why question and rebel against God's commands and boundaries as they are revealed in the Bible? To accept the truth of Scripture makes for a better life. It is safe to believe the actual biblical account of the fall, and thankfully rid oneself of untrue traditions,[19] like those within the Mormon Church. True reconciliation to the God of the Bible does not come through Mormonism's Laws and Ordinances. Reconciliation is through faith in Jesus:

> *For by grace are ye saved through faith; and that not of yourselves; it is the gift of god: not of works, lest any man should boast. For we are his workmanship created in Christ Jesus. Unto good works, which God hath before ordained that we should walk in them.*[20]

## The Protevangelium

The term "Protevangelium" is a word used to describe the first preaching of the Good News of the Gospel –the remedy for the fall of man. The Israelites recognized sin, guilt, and death to be consequences of the fall. They understood sacrifice to be temporary. Ridding themselves of sin, guilt and death became a theme for the children of Israel. They understood that because of the fall of Adam and Eve, humans needed Atonement or restoration to God. In fact, the word *Atonement* comes from the Hebrew word *Kapar* as in

Yom Kippur, the Day of Atonement.  It means to cover, or to secure the sinner from guilt and punishment; to atone for an offense.[21]

Certainly by the time of Isaiah,[22] the Old Covenant Saints learned that the perfect, permanent, and final offering would come through the the Messiah.  Sacrifice continued in type and shadow until Jesus became the Ultimate and Final Sacrifice –the Sacrificial Lamb, transferal and Atonement for the sins of the whole world!

Soon after the fall of Adam and Eve, with lovingkindess the hand of God extended out to humans.  We see in the very genesis of Scripture God's beautiful provision to remedy the effects of the fall.  The key to salvation through Jesus (the Lamb of God) is found in Genesis chapter three, the account of Adam and Eve and the fall.  The Protevangelium is unveiled in verse fifteen of chapter three of Genesis.  It is a prophecy and is seen by believers as the pivot point of the entire Bible.  To the serpent God announced:

> And I will put enmity between thee and the woman, and between your seed and her seed; He [Jesus] shall bruise you on the head, and you [Satan] shall bruise him on the heel.[23]  [my emphasis]

The Protevangelium foretells the coming defeat of Satan through the seed of the woman.  There is a blending of literal and allegorical understanding within this verse of Scripture.  In this passage the seed of the woman, refers to Christ the Messiah, bringing salvation to fallen man.  It is in Jesus that the seed of the woman crushes the serpent's head, "And the God of peace will soon crush Satan under your feet,"[24] refers back to the Protevangelium.  The Bible says:

> And so it is written, The first man Adam was made a living soul; the last Adam was made a quickening spirit . . . The first man is of the earth, earthly: the second man is the Lord from heaven.[25]

The first man, Adam, gave in to Satan's temptation.  The second Adam, Jesus, defeated Satan.  Jesus restores the spiritually dead (unbelievers) to life.  Adam, the first man, was made in the image of God.  The last Adam is Jesus, Who *is* the image of God".[26]  Of Jesus the Bible says, "He made Him who knew no sin to be sin on our behalf, that we might become the righteousness of God in Him."[27]

The need for solving the magnitude of man's dilemma, resulting from the fall of separation, required God to do something very radical.  In order for mankind to be delivered from sin and its catastrophic effects, certain qualifications were necessary.

We discover by reading in Leviticus,[28] that life is in the blood and the blood makes Atonement for the soul.  The blood sacrifice for sin requires purity beyond man's measurement.  Because sin had been transferred to all men through one man, payment for the sin also had to come through one man.  Because sin had passed through the entire human race, this person would have to be born without sin, or else he could not pay for the sins of others.  This one, in order to qualify to pay the penalty for sin, had to be a human being.  To be the Savior for humankind, one would have to be true man but he could not have a human father, or else he would carry original sin, which would disqualify him for dying for the sins of others.  Besides, the God of Israel prohibits human sacrifice.  Only God could be that exchange.  Jesus was fully God and fully man.  Only holy can exchange holy, only man can exchange man.

*the God of Israel prohibits human sacrifice*

Because Jesus was born of a virgin there was no defilement in His blood.  By the Holy spirit, Jesus was miraculously kept from the taint of Mary's sinful nature, therefore Jesus had no original sin and He never sinned.  That is why the blood of Jesus perfectly paid the penalty for humanity's sin and bought back our spiritual relationship with God.  The virgin birth of Christ spoken of by the prophet Isaiah,[29] broke the cycle of original sin.  Regaining human relationship to God required that God Himself bear the demands of His own character (justice and mercy) on our behalf.  And that is exactly what happened through the Incarnation when He took upon Himself the nature of man.  Consider how wonderful this truth is.  Jesus, because His Father was not human, was not of the human race, and had no original sin.

The most awesome, ponderous, and inexplicable event in history came when God without ceasing to be God, entered into His creation and took upon Himself human nature, and poured out His redemptive blood to expiate our sins. Remarkably supernatural was the birth of Jesus through the virgin Mary. But Mary, because she had original sin, spoke of her need of redemption. In the Magnificat, the virgin Mary uttered: "My soul doth magnify the Lord, and my spirit hath rejoiced in God my Saviour."[30] We need Him too! God has satisfied the demands of His perfect justice and mercy on our behalf. In Jesus is the total expression of God's love without compromising His justice. Unmerited grace has been extended to humans. At the cross, when Jesus cried out, "It is finished!"[31] He was referring to Himself as the final and perfect Sacrificial Lamb.

Through Jesus, God has done all that is necessary to save the human race. The only barrier left is that of our own making. That barrier is our stubborn foolishness to refuse the free gift of pardon for our sins, by neglecting to receive salvation through faith in Jesus Christ and His shed blood. Adam was created in righteousness and holiness, but he fell from that likeness. This is why the Bible commands us to put righteousness back on! We put on righteousness when we make God's provision of salvation operative in our lives through the *new birth*. The Bible says, ". . . be renewed in the spirit of your mind, and put on the new self, which in the likeness of God has been created in righteousness and holiness of the truth."[32] When we receive Christ into our hearts we are born of the Holy Spirit, and partner with Jesus Christ. He completely reconciles us to the Father.[33] This is when we recieve the *priesthood of all believers* as spoken of by the Apostle Peter.[34]

It is so important that we ask God to strip off the foreskin of our hearts to make them soft, so that we recognize the need to repent of false doctrine and be saved by grace, through faith, and be willing to embrace His will for our lives. We need a humble heart most of all. How true the words which head this chapter:

> *For since in the wisdom of God the world through its wisdom did not come to know God, God was well-pleased through the foolishness of the message preached to save those who believe.*[35]

In denying truth how long can we resist? Today is the day of salvation. Do not neglect so great a salvation! There can be no compromise with a pseudo Gospel. At judgment we will be responsible for what we knew to do, but did not.

Do you recall that Rabbi Nicodemus was a very religious man, but not a saved man? He came to Jesus with important questions. Jesus shocked Nicodemus by speaking to the core of his personal problem and need. Jesus matter-of-factly declared, " . . . I tell you the truth, no one can see the kingdom of God unless he is born again!"[36] The new birth is necessary because at the fall there came a universal severing of our relationship with God. Each human being has the same need as did Nicodemus -- we too must be born again. The new birth gives us back that spiritual relationship.

Listen to the heart call of God:

> *His purpose in all this is that they should seek after God, and perhaps feel their way toward him and find him-though He is not far from any one of us. For in him we live and move and are.*[37]

> *This is good and acceptable in the sight of God our Savior, who desires all men to be saved and come to the knowledge of the truth.*[38]

> *For God so loved the world that he gave his only begotten son, that whosoever believeth in him should not perish, but have everlasting life.*[39]

> *. . . whosoever shall call upon the name of the Lord shall be saved.*[40]

> *That if thou shalt confess with thy mouth the Lord Jesus, and shalt believe in thine heart that God hath raised him from the dead, thou shalt be saved.*[41]

*whosever shall call upon the name of the Lord shall be saved*

It is true that only Messiah Jesus reconciles man to God. In keeping with Jesus' Hebrew name, *Yeshua*, which means *salvation*, we find Jesus in the New Testament forgiving sins. One less than Divine cannot save us from our sins! Will we accept His full payment for our sins? Such reconciliation!

Remember too, that the biblical term *Gospel* means *Good News*. There can only be one Gospel or

Good News concerning Jesus. The news is very simple: Jesus Christ suffered and died for our sins, was buried, and rose again for our personal salvation. God's will is that everyone believes in His Son, in order to have everlasting life.[42] The true Gospel does not include laws,[43] or ordinances,[44] or works,[45] as a means to salvation, but rather, works are a result of salvation. When asked of Jesus what must be done to work the works of God, the Savior replied that one must believe in Him whom the Father had sent.[46]

> *"He that believeth on the Son, hath everlasting life: and he that believeth not the Son shall not see life; but the wrath of God abideth on him."*[47]

True salvation is received only through faith in the finished work of Christ. It is a contradiction to claim salvation by grace, yet claim that eternal life must be earned. Good works do not serve as an aid to salvation. Good works verify and validate commitment and they must conform to the teachings of God's Word. Faithfulness and obedience to His guidance and instruction is the proper response.

If you are trying to be acceptable to God through your own work, you need no longer carry that heavy burden, because the blood of Christ redeems one from the guilt and penalty of sin.[48] The power of the Holy Spirit delivers one from the dominion of sin.[49] Do you want God to give you His garment of salvation and righteousness and praise in exchange for the garment of your own endeavor? Do you want to be numbered among the blessed "whosoever" group spoken of in the famous Bible passage John 3:16? Do you want to have eternal life in the presence of God? You may do so. Do you know where you would spend eternity if you were to die this hour? Be assured, and remember that unlike Mormon doctrine, the Bible teaches that you can know.[50] What a blessed assurance! I no longer try to be acceptable to God. I am acceptable, but not through any righteousness of my own. I am clothed in God's righteousness. By your own choice, you can be also. I urge you to be made acceptable before God through faith in Jesus Christ, by God's gift of grace! Then you choose liberty, not bondage. Remember that God gives us choice:

> *. . . I have set before you life and death, blessing and cursing: therefore choose life, that both thou and thy seed may live . . . cleave unto him: [the Lord thy God] for he is thy life.*[51]

The Son of God loves *you* and delivered Himself up for *you*.[52] If you have not received the true Savior for your redemption, I encourage you to do so *now*. There is not a neat little formula one must go through to receive Christ for salvation. Don't worry –God knows the intent of your heart. By the true Messiah's definition of truth, give Him preeminence in your life.

Here are a few simple guides often used to lead people to receive Christ.

## How to Receive Salvation

1. Recognize your need for salvation and that God sent His Son to die for you personally.[53]

2. Repent. You must do this so that you do not perish.[54] Repent means a change of direction. It is not enough to just be sorry.

3. Believe. Believing is not just acknowledging, but trusting Christ alone for salvation. This means you stop wearing your own fig leaf apron; an expression of your own endeavor.[55]

4. Receive Christ. You must do this to become a child of God.[56] Pray like this: "Jesus, I believe You are the Son of God, and that You died in my place as my sin Substitute on Calvary's Cross. I repent of my sins. I invite You into my heart *now* to be my Savior and Lord. Amen."

5. Be baptized. It is required.[57]

6. Jesus says to confess Him publicly so that He will confess you before the Father.[58] Telling someone brings you strength and courage.

If you did this you are now reconciled to God. You have the assurance of spending eternity with the true God Himself! Rest in His everlasting arms! He will keep on guiding you throughout your life with wisdom and counsel; and afterwards receive you into the glories of heaven.[59] May we each ask God to deal with us as bond servants according to His mercy, and teach us His statues.[60]

Please accept this book as my labor of love to you.  God bless you!

## "Maranatha!"
## Come Lord Jesus
*Revelation 22:20*

| | | | |
|---|---|---|---|
| 1 | Genesis 2:17. | 31 | John 19:30. |
| 2 | Revelation 12 :9. | 32 | Ephesians 4:23, 24. |
| 3 | Job 1:6. | 33 | 1 Corinthians 15:45. |
| 4 | Matthew 4:1. | 34 | 1 Peter 2:5, 9. |
| 5 | Isaiah 14:12. | 35 | 1 Corinthians 1: 21. |
| 6 | Revelation 12:17. | 36 | John 3:3. |
| 7 | Isaiah 14:12-15; Ezekiel 28:13-17. | 37 | Acts 17:27, 28. |
| 8 | Genesis 3:15. | 38 | 1 Timothy 2:3-4. |
| 9 | Genesis 2:17. | 39 | John 3:16. |
| 10 | Romans 6:23. | 40 | Acts 2:21. |
| 11 | Revelation 5:6, 21:23; John 1:29. | 41 | Romans 10:9. |
| 12 | Romans 5:16-18. | 42 | John 6:40. |
| 13 | Genesis 2:9. | 43 | Romans 3:19-20. |
| 14 | 1 John 1:5; Psalms 99:9. | 44 | Colossians 2:16-17. |
| 15 | Ezekiel 18:4; Genesis 2:17; Romans 6:23. | 45 | Titus 3:5-7. |
| 16 | Deseret News, Church News section, July 31, 1965, p. 7. | 46 | John 6:28. |
| 17 | John 8:44. | 47 | John 3:36. |
| 18 | 2 Corinthians 5:21. | 48 | 1 Peter 1:18-19. |
| 19 | Mark 7:8-9; Matthew 15:3. | 49 | Romans 8:2. |
| 20 | Ephesians 2:8-10. | 50 | 1 John 5:11-13. |
| 21 | Wilson's Old Testament Word Studies, p. 24. | 51 | Deuteronomy 30:19-20. |
| 22 | Isaiah 53. | 52 | Galatians 2:20. |
| 23 | Genesis 3:15. | 53 | John 3:16. |
| 24 | Romans 16:20. | 54 | Luke 13:3. |
| 25 | 1 Corinthians 15:45, 47. | 55 | Genesis 3:7. |
| 26 | Colossians 1:15, and Hebrews 1:3. | 56 | John 1:12. |
| 27 | 2 Corinthians 5:21. | 57 | Matthew 28:19. |
| 28 | Leviticus 17:11. | 58 | Matthew 10:32. |
| 29 | Isaiah 7:14;  Matthew 1:20-23. | 59 | Psalms 73:24. |
| 30 | Luke 1:46,47. | 60 | Psalms 119:10-12. |

# Exhibits

Terminology Differences . . . . . . . . . . . . . . . . . . . . . . . . . . . . . . . . . . . . . 193
Mormon Plan of Eternal Progression. . . . . . . . . . . . . . . . . . . . . . . . . . . . 194
Mormon Glossary . . . . . . . . . . . . . . . . . . . . . . . . . . . . . . . . . . . . . . 195-196
The Biblical Gospel / LDS Gospel. . . . . . . . . . . . . . . . . . . . . . . . . . . . . . 197
Adam-God - Journal of Discourses . . . . . . . . . . . . . . . . . . . . . . . . . . 198-199
Denouncing Adam-God, Kimball Article . . . . . . . . . . . . . . . . . . . . . . . . . . 200
Denouncing Adam-God- England letter . . . . . . . . . . . . . . . . . . . . . . . 201-202
Brigham Young's Tie Clasp. . . . . . . . . . . . . . . . . . . . . . . . . . . . . . . . . . . 203
Blacks and the Priesthood, Journal of Discourses . . . . . . . . . . . . . . . . . . . 204
How Many in the Godhead?, Lectures on Faith . . . . . . . . . . . . . . . . . . . . . 205
Polygamy -a necessity to Godhood, Journal of Discourses . . . . . . . . . . . . . 206
Marriage of Jesus, Joseph F. Smith's Letter. . . . . . . . . . . . . . . . . . . . . . . . 207
Blood Atonement, Journal of Discourses . . . . . . . . . . . . . . . . . . . . . . . . . 208
First Vision, Joseph Smith's Handwriting . . . . . . . . . . . . . . . . . . . . . . 209-210
First Vision Comparisons . . . . . . . . . . . . . . . . . . . . . . . . . . . . . . . . . . . . 211
Condemns Polygamy, Doctrine and Covenants . . . . . . . . . . . . . . . . . . . . . 212
Salt Lake Temple Decorated with Satanic Symbols . . . . . . . . . . . . . . . . . . 213
Flaws in the Pearl of Great Price . . . . . . . . . . . . . . . . . . . . . . . . . . . . . . . 214
Min is not God! . . . . . . . . . . . . . . . . . . . . . . . . . . . . . . . . . . . . . . . . . . . 215
Doctrine and Covenants Changes -sample . . . . . . . . . . . . . . . . . . . . 216-217
Archeology and the Book of Mormon, National Geographic. . . . . . . . . . . . . 218
Archeology and the Book of Mormon, Smithsonian Institute . . . . . . . . . 219-220
Grace and Trinity a Heresy - McConkie article . . . . . . . . . . . . . . . . . . . . . 221
Governor Ford Prophecy . . . . . . . . . . . . . . . . . . . . . . . . . . . . . . . . . . . . 222
Joseph Smith —the Glass Looker, Justice Albert Neely . . . . . . . . . . . . . . . 223
Articles of Faith: Original and Current. . . . . . . . . . . . . . . . . . . . . . . . . . . . 224
More Accurate Articles of Faith . . . . . . . . . . . . . . . . . . . . . . . . . . . . . . . . 225
Biblical Defense of Truth . . . . . . . . . . . . . . . . . . . . . . . . . . . . . . . . . . . . 226
Qualifications To Serve God . . . . . . . . . . . . . . . . . . . . . . . . . . . . . . . . . . 227
Mormon Priesthood Secrets Chart . . . . . . . . . . . . . . . . . . . . . . . . . . . . . 228
First Token of the Aaronic Priesthood . . . . . . . . . . . . . . . . . . . . . . . . . . . 229
Second Token of the Aaronic / First Token of the Melchizedek Priesthood. . . 230
Second Token of the Melchizedek Priesthood . . . . . . . . . . . . . . . . . . . . . 231

# Terminology Differences   <small>compiled by Sandra Tanner</small>

## Pre-existence:
LDS - teach that everyone pre-existed - that we all exist eternally.

Bible - Only Christ pre-existed, not man (John 8:58; Col. 1:17). We didn't have a spiritual existence prior to earth (I Col. 15:46).

## Fall
LDS - teach it brought mortality and physical death - not fallen nature - believe Adam was given two conflicting commandments and was supposed to fall.

Bible - God tempts no one (James 1:13-14). Man is basically sinful (Rom. 8:5-8; I Cor. 2:14).

## Sin
LDS - Specific acts - not man's basic nature.

Bible - We are in spiritual rebellion until conversion (Eph. 2:3; Rom. 5:6). We do not just commit sins - we are basically sinful (Matt 1:21)

## Repentance
LDS - Repent of individual acts - not sinful nature.

Bible - Must repent of basic rebellion (Jer 17:9; Luke 5:32).

## Atonement -Salvation by Grace
LDS - believe Christ's death brought release from grave and universal resurrection - Salvation by grace is universal resurrection - beyond this man must earn his place in heaven.

Bible - Salvation is not universal but based on belief of each individual (Rom. 1:16; Heb. 9:28; Eph. 2:8-9)

## Redeemed
LDS - from mortal death only - not sinful rebellion or spiritual death.

Bible - Christ redeems from more than mortal death - redeems us from spiritual death (Rom. 6:23; Eph. 2:1).

## Gospel
LDS - Mormon church system and doctrines.

Bible - Message of Christ's death and resurrection as atonement for our sins (I Cor. 15:14; Gal 1:8).

## Born Again
LDS - Baptism into LDS Church.

Bible - We are spiritually dead until our spiritual rebirth (I Peter 1:23; 2 Cor. 5:17).

## True Church
LDS - Only Mormon church - true church taken from earth until Joseph Smith restored it.

Bible - As a born-again Christian we are part of God's Church (I Cor. 12:12-14; Matt. 18:19-20; Matt. 16:18).

## Authority - Priesthood
LDS - believe only LDS have authority to baptize, ordain, etc. - Have two-part system of priesthood - Melchizedek and Aaronic.

Bible - Christ brought end to Aaronic priesthood and is ONLY high Priest after manner of Melchizedek (Heb. 5-9, II Tim. 2:2).

## Baptism
LDS - Must be performed by LDS priesthood.

Bible - Emphasis is on Believer - not priesthood authority (Mark 16:15-16).

## Sons of God
LDS - We are all literal spirit children of God.

Bible - We become a child of God at conversion (John 1:12).

## Eternal Life
LDS - Exaltation in Celestial Kingdom - ability to bear children in heaven - must have a Temple marriage.

Bible - Not limited to certain ones in heaven - no mention of parenthood or temple marriage but is given to All Christians (I John 5:12-13).

## Immortality
LDS - Universal gift - ability to live forever but not Eternal Life.

Bible - Makes no distinction between immortality and eternal life (2 Tim. 1:10).

## Heaven
LDS - Divided into three kingdoms - Celestial, Terrestrial and Telestial - place for almost everyone (misuse I Cor. 15:40-41).

Bible - Only mentions two conditions - everlasting punishment or life eternal (Matt. 25:31-46).

## Kingdom of God
LDS - Means Celestial Kingdom - only those in Celestial Kingdom are in God's presence. Those in Terrestrial or Telestial Kingdoms aren't in presence of Father.

Bible - All redeemed will be in God's presence (Rev. 21:1-3). All believers are part of Kingdom (Matt 13:41-43).

## Hell
LDS - Hell as an institution is eternal - inmates come and go as in jail - don't spend eternity there - stay until one has paid debt to God.

Bible - No mention of people getting out of Hell (Rev. 21:8, Matt. 13:24-43 and 47-50; Luke 16:26).

## Godhead
LDS - Father God is a resurrected man with physical body, Christ is a separate resurrected man with physical body. Holy Ghost is a separate man with a spiritual body - 3 totally separate Gods.

Bible - God not a man (Num 23:19). Only one God (Isa. 43:10-11; 44:6; 45:21-22). Father is Spirit and Invisible. (John 4:24; I Tim 1:17).

## Holy Ghost
LDS - Is a separate God from Father and Son - different from Holy Spirit - Holy Ghost is a person - Holy Spirit is influence from Father and not personal.

Bible - Same Greek word used for Holy Ghost and Holy Spirit (1 Cor. 3:16 and 6:19).

## Virgin Birth
LDS - believe God, as a resurrected, physical man, is literal Father of Jesus - same manner in which men are conceived on earth - believe Matt. 1:18 in error.

Bible - says Mary was "with child of the Holy Ghost" (Matt. 1:18).

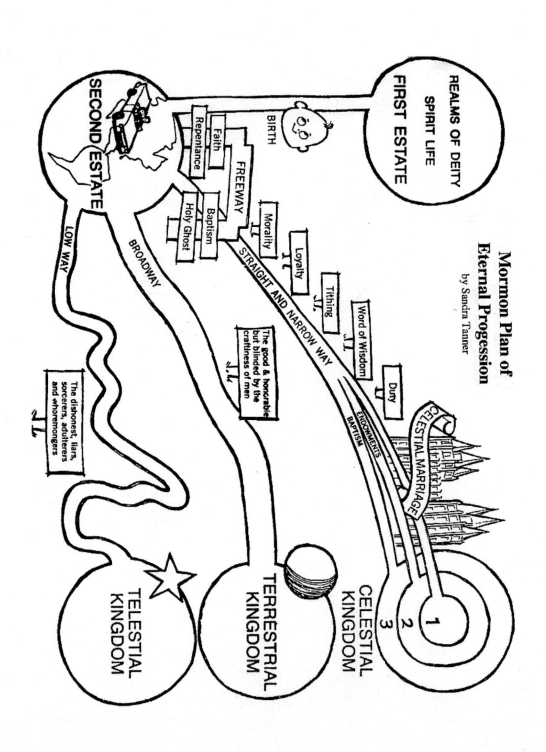

# Mormon Glossary —*some primary Mormon definitions*
compiled by Christine Carroll

**Baptism** - By immersion. Usually performed after age eight. Valid *only* when administered by the Mormon priesthood. Performed for the living and the dead, and makes one a member of the *only* true church (Mormon). It is the gate into the Mormon Celestial kingdom (Mormon Doctrine, pp. 69-74).

**Blood Atonement** - Refers to the shedding of a man's blood to remit various sins not covered by the blood of Jesus Christ (Mormon Doctrine p. 92).

**Born Under the Covenant** - Those whose parents achieved a temple marriage. In strict meaning the term refers to the New and Everlasting Covenant of marriage (see New and Everlasting Covenant).

**Celestial glory** - The highest level of Mormon heavens, which includes Godhood. It is earned by obedience to the Mormon Gospel (Mormon Doctrine p. 115-116; Doctrine and Covenants 76 and 132). See Endowments.

**Endowments** - The ceremony which includes sealing, special instructions, secret oaths, special handshakes, and signs and covenants of the Mormon temple service. These ordinances are administered for the living and for the dead (Doctrines of Salvation, v. 2, pp. 252-267). Endowments are reserved only for worthy Mormons. Approximately 20% of all Mormons have endowments. "All temple ordinances, except baptism for the dead, pertain to Exaltation in the Celestial kingdom and not merely to admission to that world." (Mormon Doctrine p. 227).

"Your endowment is, to receive all those ordinances in the house of the Lord, which are necessary for you, after you have departed this life, to enable you to walk back to the presence of the Father, passing the angels who stand as sentinels, being enabled to give them the key words, the signs and tokens, pertaining to the holy Priesthood, and gain your exaltation in spite of earth and hell." (Discourses of Brigham Young, p. 416).

**Exaltation** - The reward for strict obedience to the Mormon Gospel. The Law of Eternal Progression (Exaltation) is a term referring to those who earn the highest pinnacle of the Celestial kingdom. "They have eternal increase, a continuation of their seeds forever... they stand in the same position that God the Father stands to us. They inherit, in due course, the fulness of the glory of the Father, meaning that they have all power in heaven and on earth." (Mormon Doctrine p. 257; Doctrine and Covenants 76:50-119; 93:10-40). Exaltation is synonymous with Godhood.

**Fundamentalist Mormon** - One who still follows and practices the doctrines as taught by the early Mormon prophets, i.e. polygamy or plural marriage, blood atonement, "Adam-God" doctrine, etc. (see Doctrine and Covenants 132: 4-5).

**Garments / regulation garments** - Special underwear worn by temple Mormons, which have four Masonic-like marks sewn into them. The garments represent the coats of skin Adam received in the Garden of Eden (Gen. 2:21). Mormon garments serve as shield and protection and a continual reminder of the covenants the wearer made in a Mormon temple so long as the temple vows are kept. The garments have undergone much change through the years. The Mormon prophet Joseph F. Smith stated that they should be regarded as "...the most sacred of all things in the world... They should hold these things that God has given unto them sacred, unchanged and unaltered from the very pattern in which God gave them. Let us have the moral courage to stand against the opinions of fashion, and especially where fashion compels us to break a covenant and so commit grievous sin." (The Improvement Era, v. 9:813, as cited in Temples of the Most High, p. 239, N.B. Lundwall).

**Gods** - ...there is *"a God above the Father of our Lord Jesus Christ. ...* If Jesus Christ was the Son of God, and John discovered that *God the Father of Jesus Christ had a Father*, you may suppose that he had a Father also. Where was there ever a son without a father? ...Hence if Jesus had a Father, can we not believe that *he* had a Father also?" (*Teachings*, pp. 370, 373.) In this way both the Father and the Son, as also all exalted beings, are now or in due course will become Gods of Gods. (*Teachings*, pp. 342-376). (Mormon Doctrine, pp. 322-323).

**Kolob** - "And thus there shall be the reckoning of the time of one planet above another, until thou come nigh unto Kolob, which Kolob is after the reckoning of the Lord's time; which Kolob is set nigh unto the throne of God, to govern all those planets which belong to the same order as that upon which thou standest." (Pearl of Great Price, Abraham 3:9).

**Lamanites** - Dark skinned American Indians. The Lord placed a curse (skin of blackness) upon the Lamanites (Mormon Doctrine p. 528).

**Law of Eternal Progression** - See Exaltation.

**LDS** - The full title of the Mormon Church is The Church of Jesus Christ of Latter-day Saints. "LDS" is an acronym for Latter-day Saints and is used interchangeably with "Mormon."

**Living Oracles** - "Members of the First Presidency, Council of the Twelve, and the Patriarch to the Church–because they are appointed and sustained as prophets, seers, and revelators to the Church - are known as the living oracles." (Mormon Doctrine p. 547).

**Mormon** - "*Mormon* was the ancient Nephite prophet who abridged and compiled the sacred records of his people under the title *The Book of Mormon* . . . Accordingly, unoffically and by way of nickname, members of this restored church have become known as *Mormons*, a name which is in no sense offensive or objectionable to them." (Mormon Doctrine p. 513).

**Mormon Temple** - "Holy sanctuaries wherein sacred ordinances, rites, sealings and ceremonies are performed which pertain to salvation and Exaltation in the kingdom of God..." (Mormon Doctrine, p. 779).

**New and Everlasting Covenant, Plural Marriage, Polygamy, Celestial Marriage** - all synonymous. "For behold, I reveal unto you a new and an everlasting covenant; and if ye abide not that covenant, then are ye damned; for no one can reject this covenant and be permitted to enter into my glory." (Doctrine and Cov-

...continued

enants 132:4). Although a *revelation* and *commandment*, it was replaced with the *Official Declaration,* located at the end of the Doctrine and Covenants. The familiar name, the *Manifesto,* is not described as a revelation. Section 132 was deferrred until the Law of the Land gives way to this Mormon Covenant of Marriage. The Covenant will be practiced in the Mormon Celestial kingdom by those who earn the status of Godhood (see exhibit p. 206). Mormon Doctrine p. 578 says the revelation will be practiced during the millennium.

**Patriarchal Blessing** - A sacred blessing given by an ordained Mormon Patriarch to worthy Mormons. As the Patriarch lays his hands on the Mormon's head, the Holy Ghost manifests to the Patriarch the Mormon's lineage, and gives prophetic utterances regarding his life's mission (Mormon Doctrine, p. 558).

**Priesthood** - The authority to act in the name of God; exclusive to Mormonism. The two branches of Mormon priesthood are the Aaronic (preparatory or lesser) and Melchizedek priesthoods.

**Prophet** - God's mouthpiece. One living Mormon prophet at a time –the President of the Mormon Church (Mormon Doctrine, p. 608).

**Recommends** - "It is the practice of the church to issue certificates, commonly called *recommends,* in order to identify persons as members of the church or to certify to their worthiness to receive certain ordinances or blessings. ... when a worthy church member desires to obtain a patriarchal blessing or participates in the sacred ordinances of the temples, he is given a recommend certifying as to his worthiness to gain the desired blessings." (Mormon Doctrine, p. 620).

**Salvation** - Although *salvation* may be defined in many ways to mean many things, in its most pure and perfect definition it is a synonym for *Exaltation (Mormon Doctrine, p.* 257).

**Sons of Perdition** - One-third of the spirit hosts of heaven who followed Satan during the Mormon pre-existence. "Those in this life who gain a perfect knowledge of the divinity of the Gospel cause, a knowledge that comes by revelation from the Holy Ghost, and who then link themselves with Lucifer and come out in open rebellion, also become sons of perdition." (Mormon Doctrine, p. 746).

**Stake** - For administrative purposes the church is divided into *Stakes* and *Missions.* Each stake (composed of *wards* and *branches*) is so organized as to carry on the full program of the church... (Mormon Doctrine, p. 140).

**Standard Works** - "By the *standard works* of the church is meant the following four volumes of Scripture: The Bible, Book of Mormon, Doctrine and Covenants, and the Pearl of Great Price. The church uses the King James version of the Bible, but acceptance of the Bible is coupled with a reservation that it is true only insofar as translated correctly. The other three, having been revealed in modern times in English, are accepted without qualification." (Mormon Doctrine, p. 764). The Doctrine and Covenants and the Pearl of Great Price include direct revelations received by Joseph Smith while in Kirkland, Ohio, and Nauvoo, Illinois.

**Other set-apart works:** The words of Mormon prophets are viewed as Scripture (see Brigham Young's words in the Journal of Discourses, v. 9, p. 297; v. 13,

p. 95; Articles of Faith, Talmage, p. 7; Doctrine and Covenants 68:4).

The church views **Official Statements** made by LDS leaders as Scripture (Ensign Nov. 1976, p.63).

The **Journal of Discourses** was once ranked as valuable as the Standard Works of the church (i.e. Journal of Discourses prefaces 3, 4, 8, and 20).

The **1835 Doctrine and Covenants** is, by virtue of its Preface, viewed as Scripture.

The **1833 Book of Commandments** is, by virtue of its Preface, viewed as Scripture. Chapter headings declare the content to be revelations from God.

The Mormon **13 Articles of Faith**, which are published as part of The Pearl of Great Price, are also Scripture (Mormon Doctrine, p. 53). Also included as doctrine were the original 14 Articles of Faith. The eighth article declares the Bible to be the Word of God; this does not agree with the present day Articles of Faith.

The **Lectures of Faith** were voted as doctrine (Teachings of the Prophet Joseph Smith, p. 7-8). They were a part of the Doctrine and Covenants for 86 years, at which time (1921) they were removed without the vote of the church.

The **Inspired Version** is Joseph Smith's own version of the Bible. Some dismiss it saying that Joseph Smith never co*mpleted* the version (see Answers to Gospel Questions, v. 2 p. 207). The Doctrine and Covenants 124: 89, 94:10; 104:58 says that this version was to be completed, published, and sent out to the world. The Inspired Version is not honored nor promoted in the manner dictated in the revelation (a false revelation). Many Mormons are surprised to learn that Joseph Smith *did complete* both the Old and New Testaments (History of the Church, v. 1, pp. 324, 368).

**Temple Marriage** - also referred to as Celestial marriage, and the New and Everlasting Covenant, the gate to Exaltation in the highest Mormon heaven (Mormon Doctrine, p. 118).

**Temple Mormon** - A Mormon who has been through the Temple Endowment Ceremony, and thereby receive his/her own Endowments. One having special knowledge withheld from the world and disclosed only to the faithful Saints in a Mormon Temple (Mormon Doctrine, p. 227).

**Ward** - Members of a ward form a congregation. "...It is by faithfulness and service in ward organization (in the main) that the Lord's saints work out their salvation." (Mormon Doctrine, p. 827).

**Word of Wisdom** - A revealed law of health found in section 89 of the Doctrine and Covenants. It's keeping is a requirement for receiving recommends for temple entrance and for approving members for church positions or ordinances (Mormon Doctrine, p. 845).

**Zion - Mt. Zion** - The pure in heart. The Church of Jesus Christ of Latter-day Saints *is* Zion. Members are citizens of Zion (Doctrine and Covenants 97:21). The Mount Zion spoken of by latter-day revelation as the New Jerusalem, was to be built in Jackson County, Missouri, and built in the generation the prophecy was delivered: 1832 (a failed prophecy). (Doctrine and Covenants 84:4-5).

# The Biblical Gospel

# The LDS Gospel

**"If any man preach any other gospel unto you than that ye have received, let him be accursed."**
**Galatians 1:9**

"Moreover, brethren, I declare unto you the gospel which I preached unto you...how that Christ died for our sins according to the scriptures; And that He was buried and that He rose again the third day according to the scriptures." I Corinthians 15:1-4

"Christ sent me not to baptize, but to preach the gospel." I Corinthians 1:17

"We believe that the first principles and ordinances of the Gospel are: first, Faith in the Lord Jesus Christ; second, Repentance; third, Baptism by immersion for the remission of sins; fourth, Laying on of hands for the gift of the Holy Ghost." 4th Article of Faith

"And this is my gospel - repentance and baptism by water..." Doctrine and Covenants 39:6

## Do you see how the true gospel is opposed by the Mormon gospel?

The LDS Church teaches that Christ died for Adam's transgression, not for ours. They teach that our sins as individuals must be washed away in obedience by baptism (Articles of Faith, pp. 87, 122-123, 128). The true biblical gospel tells us that Christ died for "our sins." I John 1:7 says, "the blood of Jesus Christ His Son cleanseth us from all sin." If all my sins are cleansed by His precious blood, if they were borne "in His own body on the tree" (I Peter 2:24), then how many are left to be cleansed by baptism?

### What about baptism "for the remission of sins" in Acts 2:38?

Reading this, we see the meaning of baptism for the purpose of the remission of our sins. However, the word translated "for" is the Greek preposition eis, which in this verse means "because of." We are baptized "because of" the remission of our sins. Eis is used the same way in Matthew 12:41: "They repented at (eis) the preaching of Jonas." Here, they repented "because of" the preaching of Jonas, not "for the purpose of" his preaching.
The same applies in Acts 2:38; we are baptized "because of" the remission of our sins.

## How is this another gospel?

These principles are all taught in the Bible as instructions for believers in Christ. But they are not the gospel. Mormonism does teach that Christ died, was buried, and rose again, but it doesn't teach that as the gospel. Instead, the LDS Church teaches that Christ's death and resurrection are events leading to the gospel of Mormonism - which is repentance and Baptism.

The Mormon gospel requires man's laws to achieve salvation, which is "by obedience to the laws and ordinances of the gospel" (3rd Article of Faith). The true gospel states what Jesus Christ has done for our salvation.

# Why we need the gospel according to the Bible

**We have sin, and are therefore separated from God.**
"But your iniquities have separated between you and your God, and your sins have hid His face from you, that He will not hear" (Isa. 59:2).
*What is sin?* Not only is sin lawlessness (I Jn. 3:4), there is a vast array of sins mentioned throughout the Bible. To name a few: coveting, envy, boasting, disobedience to parents (Rom. 1:29-32), favoritism (Jam. 2:9), immoral thoughts as well as actions (Matt. 5:27-28), and not doing what you know you should do (Jam. 4:17).
*All of us have sin.* "For all have sinned and come short of the glory of God" (Rom. 3:23). "There is not a just man upon earth, that doeth good, and sinneth not" (Eccl. 7:20). "If we say that we have no sin, we deceive ourselves, and the truth is not in us" (I John 1:8).

**Because of our sin, we have no way to enter God's kingdom on our own.**
Jesus said, in comparing us with the scribes and Pharisees (religious leaders who diligently kept the law): "Except your righteousness shall exceed the righteousness of the scribes and Pharisees, ye shall in no case enter into the kingdom of heaven" (Matt. 5:20). You see, to God, "we are all as an unclean thing, and all our righteousnesses are as filthy rags" (Isa. 64:6).

**Because God is loving and merciful, He sent Jesus Christ to pay the penalty for our sins.**
"But God commendeth His love toward us, in that, while we were yet sinners, Christ died for us" (Rom. 5:8). "God was in Christ, reconciling the world unto Himself..For He hath made Him to be sin for us" (2 Cor. 5:19-21).
The whole Bible is about one great transaction that Christ performed on our behalf, which is centered in the "gospel." By His death and resurrection, He paid for our sins and provided the way for us to come to God, "For Christ also hath once suffered for sins, the just for the unjust, that He might bring us to God" (I Peter 3:18).

**Christ's payment for sin is available only to those who personally trust Him as Savior and Lord.**
"For God so loved the world, that He gave His only begotten Son, that whosoever believeth (literally "places trust") in Him should not perish, but have everlasting life...He that believeth on the Son hath everlasting life: and he that believeth not the Son shall not see life; but the wrath of God abideth on him" (John 3:16,36).
"But as many as received Him, to them gave He power (literal Greek: "authority") to become the sons of God, even to them that believe on His name" (John 1:12). The phrase "believe on His name" has much stronger meaning in the original Greek. "Name" here signifies both character and power: We must completely place our trust and confidence in who He is and what He has done!

**Our trust in Jesus Christ begins a wonderful lifelong relationship!**
*God completely forgives our sins.* "For I will be merciful to their unrighteousness, and their sins and their iniquities will I remember no more" (Heb. 8:12).
*We have assurance of eternal life.* "These things have I written unto you that believe on the name of the Son of God; that ye may know that ye have eternal life..." (I John 5:13).

## Does the LDS gospel lead to salvation?

The Book of Mormon says "it is by grace that we are saved, after all we can do" (2 Nephi 25:23). Are you honestly doing all you can do?
The Bible says "For whosoever shall keep the whole law, and yet offend in one point, he is guilty of all" (James 2:10).
The Mormon prophet Joseph F. Smith agreed: "Therefore the words of James are true. Unless a man can abide strictly in complete accord, he cannot enter there, and in the words of James, he is guilty of all. In other words if there is one divine law that he does not keep he is barred from participating in the kingdom" (Answers to Gospel Questions, vol. 3, p. 26).
Do you always keep the law and never sin, or does the LDS gospel present you with a "Mission Impossible" salvation?
Paul's warning to the Galatians about preaching any other gospel was given because some were teaching that works must be added to God's grace for salvation. This is transgressing against God (Gal. 2:16, 18, 21), and Mormonism presents this same teaching ("it is by grace that we are saved, after all we can do").
Works in the Bible are for believers to gain rewards in heaven, not to achieve salvation.

For a free booklet write to *Truth in Love Ministries*, P.O. Box 7373, Orange, CA 92613

**Adam God**
The Journal of Discourses
photocopy of original, volume 1 page 50
Brigham Young

lead me." I was trying to think of the place where God is not, but it is impossible, unless you can find *empty* space; and *there* I believe He is not. If you can find such a place, it will become useful for a hiding place to those who wish to hide themselves from the presence of the Lord, in the great day of accounts. I will close this sermon, as I intend to preach another before I present the subject I more particularly wish to speak upon. My next sermon will be to both Saint and sinner. One thing has remained a mystery in this kingdom up to this day. It is in regard to the character of the well-beloved Son of God, upon which subject the Elders of Israel have conflicting views. Our God and Father in heaven, is a being of tabernacle, or, in other words, He has a body, with parts the same as you and I have; and is capable of showing forth His works to organized beings, as, for instance, in the world in which we live, it is the result of the knowledge and infinite wisdom that dwell in His organized body. His son Jesus Christ has become a personage of tabernacle, and has a body like his father. The Holy Ghost is the Spirit of the Lord, and issues forth from Himself, and may properly be called God's minister to execute His will in immensity; being called to govern by His influence and power; but *He* is not a person of tabernacle as we are, and as our Father in Heaven and Jesus Christ are. The question has been, and is often, asked, who it was that begat the Son of the Virgin Mary. The infidel world have concluded that if what the Apostles wrote about his father and mother be true, and the present marriage discipline acknowledged by Christendom be correct, then Christians must believe that God is the father of an illegitimate son, in the person of Jesus Christ! The infidel fraternity teach *that* to their disciples. I will tell you how it is. Our Father in Heaven begat all the spirits that ever were, or ever will be, upon this earth; and they were born spirits in the eternal world. Then the Lord by His power and wisdom organized the mortal tabernacle of man. We were made first spiritual, and afterwards temporal.

Now hear it, O inhabitants of the earth, Jew and Gentile, Saint and sinner! When our father Adam came into the garden of Eden, he came into it with a *celestial body*, and brought Eve, *one of his wives*, with him. He helped to make and organize this world. He is MICHAEL, *the Archangel*, the ANCIENT OF DAYS! about whom holy men have written and spoken — HE *is our* FATHER *and our* GOD, *and the only God with whom* WE *have to do.* Every man upon the earth, professing Christians or non-professing, must hear it, and *will know it sooner or later.* They came here, organized the raw material, and arranged in their order the herbs of the field, the trees, the apple, the peach, the plum, the pear, and every other fruit that is desirable and good for man; the seed was brought from another sphere, and planted in this earth. The thistle, the thorn, the brier, and the obnoxious weed did *not* appear until after the earth was cursed. When Adam and Eve had eaten of the forbidden fruit, their bodies became mortal from *its effects*, and therefore their offspring were mortal. When the Virgin Mary conceived the child Jesus, the Father had begotten him in his own likeness. He was *not* begotten by the Holy Ghost. And who is the Father? He is the first of the human family; and when he took a tabernacle, it was begotten by *his Father* in heaven, after the same manner as the tabernacles of Cain, Abel, and the rest of the sons and daughters of Adam and Eve; from the fruits of the earth, the first earthly tabernacles were originated by the Father, and so

**Adam God**
The Journal of Discourses
photocopy of original, volume 1 page 51
Joseph Smith

SELF-GOVERNMENT—MYSTERIES—ETC.                 **51**

on in succession. I could tell you much more about this; but were I to tell you the whole truth, blasphemy would be nothing to it, in the estimation of the superstitious and over-righteous of mankind. However, I have told you the truth as far as I have gone. I have heard men preach upon the divinity of Christ, and exhaust all the wisdom they possessed. All Scripturalists, and approved theologians who were considered exemplary for piety and education, have undertaken to expound on this subject, in every age of the Christian era; and after they have done all, they are obliged to conclude by exclaiming "great is the mystery of godliness." and tell nothing.

It is true that the earth was organized by three distinct characters, namely, Eloheim, Yahovah, and Michael, these three forming a quorum, as in all heavenly bodies, and in organizing element, perfectly represented in the Deity, as Father, Son, and Holy Ghost.

Again, they will try to tell how the divinity of Jesus is joined to his humanity, and exhaust all their mental faculties, and wind up with this profound language, as describing the soul of man, "it is an immaterial substance!" What a learned idea! Jesus, our elder brother, was begotten in the flesh by the same character that was in the garden of Eden, and who is our Father in Heaven. Now, let all who may hear these doctrines, pause before they make light of them, or treat them with indifference, for they will prove their salvation or damnation.

I have given you a few leading items upon this subject, but a great deal more remains to be told. Now, remember from this time forth, and for ever, that Jesus Christ was not begotten by the Holy Ghost. I will repeat a little anecdote. I was in conversation with a certain learned professor upon this subject, when I replied, to this idea—" if the Son was begotten by the Holy Ghost, it would be very dangerous to baptize and confirm females, and give the Holy Ghost to them, lest he should beget children, to be palmed upon the Elders by the people, bringing the Elders into great difficulties."

Treasure up these things in your hearts. In the Bible, you have read the things I have told you to-night: but you have not known what you did read. I have told you no more than you are conversant with: but what do the people in Christendom, with the Bible in their hands, know about this subject? Comparatively nothing.

I will now again take up the subject of tithing. The brethren have done well. They have been willing and obedient, no people could have been more so: for this I thank my Father in Heaven. I could not wish a people to work more kindly in the yoke of Jesus than this people do: the yoke grows more and more easy to them. It seems that every man will not only pay his tithing, but give all he has, if the Lord requires it: still I see wherein they may do better. I asked the people to day to assist to pay our Church liabilities. The offer of three or four yoke of oxen only, we do not want: but I will lay before you what we wish you to do. By the manifesto which has been read, you have learned the precise situation of the property of the Church. What has incurred this debt? Why does it exist in the shape in which it now appears? And wherein could we have obviated the difficulty, and done better? A fourth part of the money already paid out, did not come in upon tithing. This money we have had to borrow in order to keep the public works in progress. You may say, wherein could we have done better, for we have paid our tithing punctually? But has that brother, who sent $100 back to the

## Denouncing Adam-God Doctrine
Kimball Article

# Our Own Liahona

### President Spencer W. Kimball

**We each have a personal Liahona, our conscience, to unfailingly guide us through the wilderness and storms of life**

Beloved brethren, I should like to say a few words to you if I may. What an opportunity it is to meet together under these auspices, 230,000 of us, possibly more. We welcome you again this night and ask the Lord to bless us while we are thus convened.

There are two or three matters I would like to bring to your attention. We have written a letter to all the stake presidencies in the western United States saying that in the past the Primary Children's Medical Center received substantial financial support through the annual Penny Parade. These funds enabled the hospital to admit children in need of assistance without regard to race, creed, religion, or ability to pay. Since this source of support is no longer available, the hospital has organized a children's fund and will be conducting a penny-by-the-inch fund drive in the month of February 1977. All funds received will be used to continue charity services. We think the program is worthy of your support.

I wish also to call your attention to another matter deserving your attention and support. The general presidency of the Relief Society more than a year ago proposed to the First Presidency and the Twelve the erection of a monument to the women of the Church. In view of the fact that the Prophet Joseph Smith organized the Relief Society in Nauvoo on March 17, 1842, it was felt that this monument should stand in Nauvoo. The First Presidency and the Quorum of the Twelve, after consideration, felt to endorse this proposal with the understanding that the project would be funded primarily through the voluntary contributions of the women of the Church. Work on the monument has been going forward, and contributions are being received.

We earnestly ask that stake presidents and bishops give their endorsement to this undertaking and encourage their respective Relief Society presidents in their efforts to secure the needed contributions. We are confident that, with support from you brethren, these funds can be gathered without doing any injury to anyone. If many contribute, the individual amount need not be large. We would also hope that some of the brethren might feel inclined to make a contribution to this worthy project. The general Relief Society presidency are anxious to conclude the fund drive before March 17 of next year, their anniversary date. Your efforts in this direction will be greatly appreciated. Each sister could make a small contribution to the Relief Society.

and she would then feel a part of it.

Another matter. We hope that you who teach in the various organizations, whether on the campuses or in our chapels, will always teach the orthodox truth. We warn you against the dissemination of doctrines which are not according to the scriptures and which are alleged to have been taught by some of the General Authorities of past generations. Such, for instance, is the Adam-God theory. We denounce that theory and hope that everyone will be cautioned against this and other kinds of false doctrine.

Now, just a few words to you young men. Have you ever imagined yourself to be the Prophet Joseph Smith when he was fourteen and received his glorious vision? Or David when he was playing his harp for King Saul? Or Joseph who had dreams and visions and saw in a dream how his father and mother and all his brothers and their families would bow down to him? Have you ever thought of yourself as being Nephi, who, under very difficult circumstances, defied his rebellious brothers and went into the city of Jerusalem and singlehandedly obtained the plates which were vital to the posterity of Lehi and his family? Have you ever thought of yourself as being the young Nephi who gave leadership in large measure to his older brothers and to his father's family?

Can you think of yourself as being Nephi who heard his father excitedly call attention to something he had found just outside the door of his tent? It was a round ball that made it possible for father Lehi to fulfill the commandment he had received during the night when visited by the Lord who told him to resume his journey into the wilderness on the morrow. There must have been great excitement in the family when the ball was shown to them. They found it to be "a round ball of curious workmanship," made "of fine brass," and none had ever seen anything like it before. (1 Ne. 16:10.) It had two spindles or pointers which were designed to indicate the direction of movement of the party as they went forward. For no reason that could be figured out, one of the spindles pointed a specific direction which was identified by Lehi as the direction that should be followed into the wilderness.

If you were greatly interested and observed very carefully the workings of this unusual ball, you would note that it worked "according to the faith and diligence and heed" which were given unto it concerning the way you should

THE CHURCH OF JESUS CHRIST OF LATTER-DAY SAINTS

The Council of the Twelve
47 East South Temple Street, Salt Lake City, Utah 84150

February 19, 1981

Mr. Eugene England
C/O Honors Program
4012 Harold B. Lee Library
Provo, Utah 84602

Dear Brother England:

This may well be the most important letter you have or will receive. It is written in reply to an undated letter from you which came in an envelope postmarked, September 4, 19__ Your letter enclosed a 19-page document which you had __ under the title, "The Perfection and Progre___ Spheres of Existence and Two Modes of ___

In your ___
set forth th___
pert___

**Denouncing Adam-God**
Bruce R. McConkie responsed to Eugene England in an eleven page letter in 2-19-81. To save space half of the first page and half of the last page are seen here. All of page 6, which addresses Adam-God, is shown on the next page.

___ message.
___ heart. I pray
___ y office is
___ he very astute
___orities said to me when I chanced to
___ the subject of your letter to me. He said:
___ haven't we rescued him enough times already."

Now I hope you will ponder and pray and come to a basic understanding of fundamental things and that unless and until you can on all points, you will remain silent on those where differences exist between you and the Brethren. This is the course of safety. I advise you to pursue it. If you do not, perils lie ahead. It is not too often in this day that any of us are told plainly and bluntly what ought to be. I am taking the liberty of so speaking to you at this time, and become thus a witness against you if you do not take the counsel.

I repeat: I have every good wish for you, pray that the Lord will bless you and hope that things will work out properly and well in your life.

Sincerely,

Bruce R. McConkie

Bruce R. McConkie

BRM:vh

February 19, 1981
Page 6

He was guided by the Holy Spirit in his teachings in general.
He was a mighty prophet. He led Israel the way the Lord wanted
his people led. He built on the foundation laid by the Prophet
Joseph. He completed his work and has gone on to eternal
exaltation.

Nonetheless, as Joseph Smith so pointedly taught, a prophet
is not always a prophet, only when he is acting as such. Prophets
are men and they make mistakes. Sometimes they err in doctrine.
This is one of the reasons the Lord has given us the Standard
Works. They become the standards and rules that govern where
doctrine and philosophy are concerned. If this were not so, we
would believe one thing when one man was president of the Church
and another thing in the days of his successors. Truth is eternal
and does not vary. Sometimes even wise and good men fall short
in the accurate presentation of what is truth. Sometimes a
prophet gives personal views which are not endorsed and approved
by the Lord.

Yes, President Young did teach that Adam was the father of
our spirits, and all the related things that the cultists ascribe
to him. This, however, is not true. He expressed views that are
out of harmony with the gospel. But, be it known, Brigham Young
also taught accurately and correctly, the status and position
of Adam in the eternal scheme of things. What I am saying is
that Brigham Young, contradicted Brigham Young, and the issue
becomes one of which Brigham Young we will believe. The answer
is we will believe the expressions that accord with the teachings
in the Standard Works.

Yes, Brigham Young did say some things about God progressing
in knowledge and understanding, but again, be it known, that
Brigham Young taught emphatically and plainly, that God knows all
things and has all power meaning in the infinite, eternal and
ultimate and absolute sense of the word. Again, the issue is
which Brigham Young shall we believe and the answer is: We will
take the one whose statements accord with what God has revealed
in the Standard Works.

I think you can give me credit for having a knowledge of
the quotations from Brigham Young relative to Adam, and of knowing
what he taught under the subject that has become known as the
Adam God Theory. President Joseph Fielding Smith said that
Brigham Young will have to make his own explanations on the points
there involved. I think you can also give me credit for knowing
what Brigham Young said about God progressing. And again, that
is something he will have to account for. As for me and my house,
we will have the good sense to choose between the divergent
teachings of the same man and come up with those that accord with

**Brigham Young's Masonic Tie Clasp**
*copy of a 1988 calendar page*
*published by Collier's Publishing Company*
*Box 1886, Salt Lake City, Utah  84110*

## Blacks and the Priesthood
Journal of Discourses, volume 7, p. 290-291
Brigham Young

birth of that man. He was fore-ordained in eternity to preside over this last dispensation, as much so as Pharaoh was fore-ordained to be a wicked man, or as was Jesus to be the Saviour of the world because he was the oldest son in the family.

Abraham was ordained to be the father of the faithful,—that is, he was ordained to come forth at a certain period; and when he had proved him-self faithful to his God, and would re-sist the worship of idols, and would trample them under his feet in the presence of their king, and set up the worship of the true God, he obtained the appellation of "father of the faithful." "For whom he did foreknow he also did predestinate to be conformed to the image of his Son." He knew, millions of years before this world was framed, that Pharaoh would be a wicked man. He saw—he under-stood; his work was before him, and he could see it from the beginning to the end. And so scrutinizing, pene-trating, and expanded are his visions and knowledge, that not even a hair of our head can fall to the ground un-noticed by him. He foreknew what Joseph, who was sold into Egypt, would do. Joseph was foreordained to be the temporal saviour of his father's house, and the seed of Joseph are ordained to be the spiritual and tem-poral saviours of all the house of Israel in the latter days. Joseph's seed has mixed itself with all the seed of man upon the face of the whole earth. The great majority of those who are now before me are the descen-dants of that Joseph who was sold. Joseph Smith, junior, was foreordained to come through the loins of Abraham, Isaac, Jacob, Joseph, and so on down through the Prophets and Apostles; and thus he came forth in the last days to be a minister of salvation, and to hold the keys of the last dispensa-tion of the fulness of times. The whole object of the creation of

this world is to exalt the intelligencies that are placed upon it, that they may live, endure, and increase for ever and ever. We are not here to quarrel and contend about the things of this world, but we are here to subdue and beautify it. Let every man and woman worship their God with all their heart. Let them pay their devotions and sacrifices to him, the Supreme, and the Author of their existence. Do all the good you can to your fellow-creatures. You are flesh of my flesh and bone of my bone. God has created of one blood all the nations and kingdoms of men that dwell upon all the face of the earth: black, white, copper-coloured, or whatever their colour, customs, or religion, they have all sprung from the same origin; the blood of all is from the same element. Adam and Eve are the parents of all pertaining to the flesh, and I would not say that they are not also the parents of our spirits.

You see some classes of the human family that are black, uncouth, un-comely, disagreeable and low in their habits, wild, and seemingly deprived of nearly all the blessings of the in-telligence that is generally bestowed upon mankind. The first man that committed the odious crime of killing one of his brethren will be cursed the longest of any one of the children of Adam. Cain slew his brother. Cain might have been killed, and that would have put a termination to that line of human beings. This was not to be, and the Lord put a mark upon him, which is the flat nose and black skin. Trace mankind down to after the flood, and then another curse is pro-nounced upon the same race—that they should be the "servant of servants;" and they will be, until that curse is re-moved; and the Abolitionists cannot help it, nor in the least alter that de-cree. How long is that race to endure the dreadful curse that is upon them? That curse will remain upon them,

and they never can hold the Priest-hood or share in it until all the other descendants of Adam have received the promises and enjoyed the bless-ings of the Priesthood and the keys thereof. Until the last ones of the residue of Adam's children are brought up to that favourable position, the children of Cain cannot receive the first ordinances of the Priesthood. They were the first that were cursed, and they will be the last from whom the curse will be removed. When the residue of the family of Adam come up and receive their blessings, then will the curse be removed from the seed of Cain, and they will receive the blessings in like proportion.

I have but just commenced my remarks, and have presented you a few texts; and it is now time to ad-journ. The exertion required to speak to you somewhat at length seems to injure me. I will therefore stop. I bless you all, inasmuch as you have desired and striven to do right, and to revere the character of his Son, and to exalt the name of Deity, and to revere the character of his Son on the earth. I bless you in the name of Jesus Christ! Amen.

---

### DEVOTEDNESS TO "MORMONISM"—RESPONSIBILITY.

*Remarks by President D. H. Wells, made in the Tabernacle, Great Salt Lake City, October 16, 1859.*

REPORTED BY G. D. WATT.

Brethren and Sisters,—I arise before you this afternoon without having any particular subject on my mind upon which to speak, hoping and believing that the Lord will help me, that I may say what I shall say to your edification and comfort.

"Mormonism" presents themes sufficient for our consideration at all times and upon all occasions. We never need be at a loss for a subject, for there is no part of it that we can contemplate that is not fitting and suitable to almost any occasion that may arise.

I feel that the principles of the holy Gospel are all-absorbing. In them are concentrated all my hopes of happi-ness—my life, my business, all my

interests, both temporal and spiritual, in time and eternity, and I trust will ever be. There is nothing else that I esteem worthy to engage my attention in comparison, and I have no hopes outside my interest in this kingdom, neither do I wish to have.

When I embraced "Mormonism," I let go everything else; and since then I have had no wish or desire but to attend to those things required at my hands. I take peculiar pleasure and delight in doing anything that is for the advancement of this kingdom.

I feel an ardent anxiety to see Israel rise triumphant over every op-posing object that may lie in their onward course. With me it is. 'Hosanna!' and "Glory to God!" when

# How many in the Godhead?
## The Lectures on Faith

(part of the *Doctrine and Covenants*
from 1835-1921)

---

**52**

Q. Where are the revelations to be found which give this relation of the attributes of God?

A. In the Old and New Testaments, and they are quoted in the fourth lecture, fifth, sixth, seventh, eighth, ninth, and tenth paragraphs.*

Q. Is the idea of the existence of those attributes, in the Deity, necessary in order to enable any rational being to exercise faith in him unto life and salvation?

A. It is.

Q. How do you prove it?

A. By the eleventh, twelfth, thirteenth fourteenth, fifteenth and sixteenth paragraphs in this lecture.*

Q. Does the idea of the existence of these attributes in the Deity, as far as his attributes are concerned, enable a rational being to exercise faith in him unto life and salvation?

A. It does.

Q. How do you prove it?

A. By the seventeenth and eighteenth paragraphs.*

Q. Have the Latter Day Saints as much authority given them, through the revelation of the attributes of God, to exercise faith in him as the Former Day Saints had?

A. They have.

Q. How do you prove it?

A. By the nineteenth paragraph of this lecture.*

*Note.* Let the student turn and commit those paragraphs to memory.

---

### LECTURE FIFTH.

### Of Faith.

#### SECTION V.

1 In our former lectures we treated of the being, character, perfections and attributes of God. What we mean by perfections, is, the perfections which belong to all the attributes of his nature. We shall, in this lecture speak of the Godhead: we mean the Father, Son and Holy Spirit.

2 There are two personages who constitute the great, matchless, governing and supreme power over

---

**53**

all things—by whom all things were created and made, that are created and made, whether visible or invisible: whether in heaven, on earth, or in the earth, under the earth, or throughout the immensity of space—They are the Father and the Son: The Father being a personage of spirit, glory and power: possessing all perfection and fulness: The Son, who was in the bosom of the Father, a personage of tabernacle, made, or fashioned like unto man, or being in the form and likeness of man, or, rather, man was formed after his likeness, and in his image;—he is also the express image and likeness of the personage of the Father: possessing all the fulness of the Father, or, the same fulness with the Father; being begotten of him, and was ordained from before the foundation of the world to be a propitiation for the sins of all those who should believe on his name, and is called the Son because of the flesh—and descended in suffering below that which man can suffer, or, in other words, suffered greater sufferings, and was exposed to more powerful contradictions than any man can be. But notwithstanding all this, he kept the law of God, and remained without sin: Showing thereby that it is in the power of man to keep the law and remain also without sin. And also, that by him a righteous judgment might come upon all flesh, and that all who walk not in the law of God, may justly be condemned by the law, and have no excuse for their sins. And he being the only begotten of the Father, full of grace and truth, and having overcome, received a fulness of the glory of the Father—possessing the same mind with the Father, which mind is the Holy Spirit, that bears record of the Father and the Son, and these three are one, or in other words, these three constitute the great, matchless, governing and supreme power over all things: by whom all things were created and made, that were created and made: and these three

---

**55**

*Question.* Of what do the foregoing lectures treat?

*Answer.* Of the being, perfections and attributes of the Deity. [§5. ¶1.]

Q. What are we to understand by the perfections of the Deity?

A. The perfections which belong to his attributes.

Q. How many personages are there in the Godhead?

A. Two: the Father and the Son. [§5. ¶1.]

Q. How do you prove that there are two personages in the Godhead?

A. By the Scriptures. Gen. 1:26. Also §2. ¶6. And the Lord God said unto the Only Begotten, who was with him from the beginning, Let us make man in our image, after our likeness:—and it was done. Gen. 3: 22. And the Lord God said unto the Only Begotten, Behold, the man is become as one of us: to know good and evil. John, 17: 5. And now, O Father, glorify thou me with thine own self with the glory which I had with thee before the world was [§5. ¶2.]

Q. What is the Father?

A. He is a personage of glory and of power. [§5. ¶2.

Q. How do you prove that the Father is a personage of glory and of power?

A. Isaiah 60: 19. The Sun shall be no more thy light by day, neither for brightness shall the moon give light unto thee: but the Lord shall be unto thee an everlasting light, and thy God thy glory. 1 Chron. 29: 11. Thine, O Lord, is the greatness, and the power, and the glory. Ps. 29: 3. The voice of the Lord is upon the waters: the God of glory thunders. Ps. 79: 9. Help us, O God of our salvation, for the glory of thy name. Romans 1: 23. And changed the glory of the incorruptible God into an image made like to corruptible men.

Secondly, of power. 1 Chron. 29: 4. Thine, O Lord, is the greatness and the power, and the glory. Jer. 32: 17. Ah! Lord God, behold thou hast made the earth and the heavens by thy great power, and stretched-out arm; and there is nothing too hard for thee. Deut 4: 37. And because he loved thy fathers therefore he chose their seed after them, and bro't them out in his sight with his mighty power. 2. Samuel 22: 33. God is my strength and power. Job 26. commencing with the 7 verse, to the end of the chapter. He stretches out the north over the empty place, and hangs the earth upon nothing. He binds up the waters in his thick clouds; and the cloud is not rent under them. He holds back the face of his throne, and spreads his cloud upon it. He has compassed the waters with bounds, until the day and night come to an

---

**57**

visible and invisible; whether they be thrones or dominions, principalities or powers; all things were created by him and for him; and he is before all things, and by him all things consist. Gen. 1: 1. In the beginning God created the heavens and the earth. Heb. 1: 2. [God] Has in these last days spoken unto us by his Son, whom he has appointed heir of all things, by whom also he made the worlds.

Q. Does he possess the fulness of the Father?

A. He does. Col. 1: 19. 2: 9. For it pleased the Father that in him should all fulness dwell. For in him dwells all the fulness of the Godhead bodily. Eph. 1: 23. Which is his [Christ's] body, the fulness of him that fills all in all.

Q. Why was he called the Son?

A. Because of the flesh. Luke 1: 33. That holy thing which shall be born of thee, shall be called the Son of God.—Math. 3: 16, 17. And Jesus, when he was baptized, went up straitway out of the water; and lo, the heavens were opened unto him, and he [John] saw the Spirit of God descending like a dove and lighting upon him: and lo, a voice from heaven, saying, This is my beloved Son, in whom I am well pleased.

Q. Was he ordained of the Father, from before the foundation of the world, to be a propitiation for the sins of all those who should believe on his name?

A. He was. 1 Peter, 1: 18, 19, 20. For as much as you know that you were not redeemed with corruptible things, as silver and gold, from your vain conversation, received by tradition from your fathers; but with the precious blood of Christ, as of a lamb without blemish and without spot: who verily was foreordained before the foundation of the world, but was manifested in these last times for you. Rev. 13: 8. And all that dwell upon the earth shall worship him, [the beast] whose names are not written in the book of life of the Lamb slain from the foundation of the world. 1 Corin. 2: 7. But we speak the wisdom of God in a mystery, even the hidden mystery, which God ordained before the world unto our glory.

Q. Do the Father and the Son possess the same mind?

A. They do. John 5: 30. I [Christ] can of my own self do nothing: as I hear, I judge, and my judgment is just: because I seek not my own will, but the will of the Father who sent me. John 6: 38. For I [Christ] came down from heaven, not to do my own will, but the will of him that sent me. John 10: 30. I [Christ] and my Father are one.

Q. What is this mind?

A. The Holy Spirit. John 15: 26. But when the Comforter is come, whom I will send unto you from the Father, even the Spirit of truth, which proceeds from the Father, he

---

**58**

shall testify of me. [Christ.] Gal. 4: 6. And because you are sons, God has sent forth the Spirit of his Son into your hearts.

Q. Do the Father, Son and Holy Spirit constitute the Godhead?

A. They do. [§5. ¶2.]

Let the student commit this paragraph to memory.

Q. Does the believer in Christ Jesus, through the gift of the Spirit, become one with the Father and the Son, as the Father and the Son are one?

A. They do. John 17: 20, 21. Neither pray I for these (the apostles) alone, but for them also who shall believe on me through their word; that they all may be one; as thou, Father, art in me, and I in thee, that they also may be one in us, that the world may believe that thou hast sent me.

Q. Does the foregoing account of the Godhead lay a sure foundation for the exercise of faith in him unto life and salvation?

A. It does.

Q. How do you prove it?

A. By the third paragraph of this lecture.

Let the student commit this also.

---

### LECTURE SIXTH.

### Of Faith.

#### SECTION VI.

1 Having treated, in the preceding lectures, of the ideas of the character, perfections and attributes of God, we next proceed to treat of the knowledge which persons must have, that the course of life which they pursue is according to the will of God, in order that they may be enabled to exercise faith in him unto life and salvation.

2 This knowledge supplies an important place in revealed religion; for it was by reason of it that the ancients were enabled to endure as seeing him who is invisible. An actual knowledge to any person that

---

**JOSEPH SMITH BEGINS HIS WORK**

Volume II

✦ ✦

The Book of Commandments

✦ ✦

The Doctrine and Covenants

✦ ✦ ✦

The Lectures on Faith

✦ ✦ ✦ ✦

Fourteen Articles of Faith

✦ ✦ ✦ ✦ ✦

**WILFORD C. WOOD**

## Polygamy –a necessity to Godhood
The Journal of Discourses
photocopy of original, volume 11 page 269

blessings which Abraham obtained, you will be polygamists at least in your faith, or you will come short of enjoying the salvation and the glory which Abraham has obtained. This is as true as that God lives. You who wish that there were no such thing in existence, if you have in your hearts to say : " We will pass along in the Church without obeying or submitting to it in our faith or believing this order, because, for aught that we know, this community may be broken up yet, and we may have lucrative offices offered to us; we will not, therefore, be polygamists lest we should fail in obtaining some earthly honor, character and office, etc,"— the man that has that in his heart, and will continue to persist in pursuing that policy, will come short of dwelling in the presence of the Father and the Son, in celestial glory. The only men who become Gods, even the Sons of God, are those who enter into polygamy. Others attain unto a glory and may even be permitted to come into the presence of the Father and the Son; but they cannot reign as kings in glory, because they had blessings offered unto them, and they refused to accept them.

The Lord gave a revelation through Joseph Smith, His servant; and we have believed and practiced it. Now, then, it is said that this must be done away before we are permitted to receive our place as a State in the Union It may be, or it may not be One of the twin relics—' they say, is aboli' however, " but if sk iron-hande by the bla I am glad of .eart is pained for that unfortunate race of men. One twin relic having been strangled, the other, they say, must next be destroyed. It is they and God for it,

and you will all find that out. It is not Brigham Young, Heber C. Kimball and Daniel H. Wells and the Elders of Israel they are fighting against; but it is the Lord Almighty. What is the Lord going to do? He is going to do just as he pleases, and the world cannot help themselves.

I heard the revelation on polygamy, and I believed it with all my heart, and I know it is from God— I know that he revealed it from heaven; I know that it is true, and understand the bearings of it and why it is. " Do you think that we shall ever be admitted as a State into the Union without denying the principle of polygamy?" If we are not admitted until then, we shall never be admitted. These things will be just as the Lord will. Let us live to take just what he sends to us, and when our enemies rise up against us, we will meet them as we can, and exercise faith and pray for wisdom and power more than they have, and contend continually for the right. Go along, my children, saith the Lord, do all you can, and remember that your blessings come through your faith. Be faithful and cut the corners of your enemies where you can—get the advantage of them by faith and good works, take care of yourselves, and they will destroy themselves. Be what you should be, live as you should, and all will be well.

Who ' 'l come ide in 'y the any .. Washington: .. in New York? or in ., State of the Union? are they more unvirtuous, are they more disloyal to the Government? But then there is polygamy." That has nothing in the least to do with our being loyal or disloyal, one way or the other. But is not the practice of

Burbank, California
March 17, 1963


President Joseph Fielding Smith
47 East South Temple Street
Salt Lake City 11, Utah

Dear President Smith:

In a discussion recently the question arose, "Was Christ married?" The quote of Isaiah 53:10 was given, which reads,

> Yet it pleased the ord to bruise him; he hath put Him to grief: when thou shalt make his soul an offering for sin, he shall see His seed❌he shall prolong His days, and the pleasure of the Lord shall prosper in his hand.

What is meant by "he shall see his seed"? Does this mean that Christ had children?

In the Temple ceremony we are told that only through Temple marriage can we receive the highest degree of exaltation and dwell in the presence of our Heavenly Father and Jesus Christ. Christ came here to set us the example and, therefore, we believe that he must have been married❌❌Are we right?

Sincerely,

*J. Ricks Smith*

J. Ricks Smith


1736 N. Ontario Street
Burbank, California

❌ *Mosiah 15:10-12 Please Read Your Book of Mormon!*

❌❌ *Yes! But do not preach it! The Lord advised us Not to cast pearls before swine!*

*Joseph Fielding Smith*

## Blood Atonement

The Journal of Discourses, 1856 edition
photocopy of original, volume 3 page 247
Brigham Young

A few of the men and women who go into the house of the Lord, and receive their endowments, and in the most sacred manner make covenants before the Almighty, go and violate those covenants. Do I have compassion on them? Yes, I do have mercy on them, for there is something in their organization which they do not understand; and there are but few in this congregation who do understand it.

You say, "That man ought to die for transgressing the law of God." Let me suppose a case. Suppose you found your brother in bed with your wife, and put a javelin through both of them, you would be justified, and they would atone for their sins, and be received into the kingdom of God. I would at once do so in such a case; and under such circumstances, I have no wife whom I love so well that I would not put a javelin through her heart, and I would do it with clean hands. But you who trifle with your covenants, be careful lest in judging you will be judged.

Every man and women has got to have clean hands and a pure heart, to execute judgment, else they had better let the matter alone.

Again, suppose the parties are not caught in their iniquity, and it passes along unnoticed, shall I have compassion on them? Yes, I will have compassion on them, for transgressions of the nature already named, or for those of any other description. If the Lord so order it that they are not caught in the act of their iniquity, it is pretty good proof that He is willing for them to live; and I say let them live and suffer in the flesh for their sins, for they will have it to do.

There is not a man or woman, who violates the covenants made with their God, that will not be required to pay the debt. The blood of Christ will never wipe that out, your own blood must atone for it; and the judgments of the Almighty will come, sooner or later, and every man and woman will have to atone for breaking their covenants. To what degree? Will they have to go to hell? They are in hell enough now. I do not wish them in a greater hell, when their consciences condemn them all the time. Let compassion reign in our bosoms. Try to comprehend how weak we are, how we are organized, how the spirit and the flesh are continually at war.

I told you here, some time ago, that the devil who tempted Eve, got possession of the earth, and reigns triumphant, has nothing to do with influencing our spirits, only through the flesh; that is a true doctrine. Inasmuch as our spirits are inseparably connected with the flesh, and, inasmuch as the whole tabernacle is filled with the spirit which God gave, if the body is afflicted, the spirit also suffers, for there is a warfare between the flesh and the spirit, and if the flesh overcomes, the spirit is brought into bondage, and if the spirit overcomes, the body is made free, and then we are free indeed, for we are made free by the Son of God. Watch yourselves, and think. As I heard observed, on the evening of the 14th, at the Social Hall, "think, brethren, think," but do not think so far that you cannot think back again. I then wanted to tell a little anecdote, but I will tell it now.

In the eastern country there was a man who used to go crazy, at times, and then come to his senses again. One of his neighbors asked him what made him go crazy; he replied, "I get to thinking, and thinking, until finally I think so far that I am not always able to think back again." Can you think too much for the spirit which is put in the tabernacle? You can, and this is a subject which I wish the brethren instructed upon, and the people to understand. The spirit is the intelligent part of man;

**The First Vision**
in Joseph Smith's handwriting
*The Changing World of Mormonism*, page 153

marvilous even in the likeness of him who created them
and when I considered upon these things my heart exclai
-med well hath the wise man said the fool saith in
his heart there is no God my heart exclaimed all all
these bear testimony and bespeak an omnipotant
and omnipreasant power a being who maketh Laws and
decreeeth and bindeth all things in their bounds who
filleth Eternity who was and is and will be from all
Eternity to Eternity and when I considered all these thin[gs]
and that that being seeketh such to worship him as wor
-ship him in spirit and in truth therefore I cried unto
the Lord for mercy for there was none else to whom I could go an[d]
to obtain mercy and the Lord heard my cry in the wilderne[ss]
and while in the attitude of calling upon the Lord in the 16th year of my age
a pillar of
fire light above the brightness of the sun at noon day
come down from above and rested upon me and I was filled
with the spirit of god and the Lord opened the heavens upon
me and I saw the Lord and he spake unto me saying
Joseph my son thy sins are forgiven thee go thy way walk in my
statutes and keep my commandments Behold I am the
Lord of glory I was crucifyed for the world that all those
who believe on my name may have Eternal life the world
lieth in sin and at this time and none doeth good no
not one they have turned asside from the gospel and
keep not my commandments they draw near to me with their
lips while their hearts are far from me and mine anger
is kindling against the inhabitants of the earth to visit
them according to their ungodliness and to bring to pass
that which hath been spoken by the mouth of the prophe[ts]
and Apostles behold and lo I come quickly as it wa[s]
written of me in the cloud clothed in the glory of my Father
and my soul was filled with love and for many days I
could rejoice with great joy and the Lord was with me
but could find none that would believe the hevnly
vision nevertheless I pondered these things in my heart
about that time my mother and but after many da[ys]

## The First Vision
in Joseph Smith's handwriting
...continued

with regard to the all important concern for the wel-
fore of my immortal soul which led me to searching the scriptures believing as I was taught, that
they contained the word of God thus applying
myself to them and my intimate acquaintance
with those of different denominations led me to
marvel exceedingly for I discovered that they did not
adorning their profession by a holy walk and Godly conversation agreeable to what I found contained in that sacred depository this was a grief to
my soul thus from the age of twelve years
to fifteen I pondered many things in my heart
concerning the situation of the world of mankind
the contentions and divions the wickeness and
abominations and the darkness which pervaded
the minds of mankind my mind become
exceedingly distressed for I became convicted of my
sins and by searching the scriptures I found
that mankind did not come unto the Lord but that
they had apostatised from the true and living
faith and there was no society or denomination
that built upon the Gospel of Jesus Christ as
recorded in the new testament and I felt to mourn
for my own sins and for the sins of the world
for I learned in the scriptures that God was
the same yesterday to day and forever that he was
no respecter to persons for he was God for I
looked upon the sun the glorious luminary of
the earth and also the moon rolling in their
majesty through the heavens and also the stars
shining in their courses and the earth also upon whic-
h I stood and the beast of the field and the fawls of
heaven and the fish of the waters and also man walking
forth upon the face of the earth in majesty and in
the strength of beauty whose power and intiligence
in governing the things which are so exceeding great and

**First Vision Comparisons**
compiled by Sandra Tanner

# Comparison of Various Accounts of the First Vision

| 1832 - SMITH | 1835 - COWDERY | 1835 - SMITH | 1838 - SMITH | PRESENT - SMITH |
|---|---|---|---|---|
| A vision of only the Lord as the heavens were opened to him. | An Angel came to him | First visitation of Angels. | The Father and Son appeared to him in the woods. | The Father and Son appeared to him in the woods. |
| Was praying to the Lord for mercy; a forgiveness of his sins. | He was seeking to know if God existed and wanted the forgiveness of his sins. | | He was seeking to know which denomination was right. | He was seeking to know which denomination was right. |
| Study of the bible showed him all denominations were wrong, before the vision came. | | | God told him, in the vision, that all denominations were wrong, and to join none of them. | God told him, in the vision, that all denominations were wrong, and to join none of them. |
| Knew all denominations were wrong by Bible study before the vision. | Was wondering about who was right. | | Never, before the vision, had it entered his heart that all were not right. | Deleted from the present version. |
| 16th year, 1821-22 | 17th year, 1823 | 14 years old, 1820 | 14 years old, 1820 | 14 years old, 1820 |

**Condemns Polygamy**
Doctrine of Covenants 1835 edition
photocopy of original, page 251

251

## SECTION CI.

## MARRIAGE.

1 According to the custom of all civilized nations, marriage is regulated by laws and ceremonies: therefore we believe, that all marriages in this church of Christ of Latter Day Saints, should be solemnized in a public meeting, or feast, prepared for that purpose: and that the solemnization should be performed by a presiding high priest, high priest, bishop, elder, or priest, not even prohibiting those persons who are desirous to get married, of being married by other authority. We believe that it is not right to prohibit members of this church from marrying out of the church, if it be their determination so to do, but such persons will be considered weak in the faith of our Lord and Savior Jesus Christ.

2 Marriage should be celebrated with prayer and thanksgiving; and at the solemnization, the persons to be married, standing together, the man on the right, and the woman on the left, shall be addressed, by the person officiating, as he shall be directed by the holy Spirit; and if there be no legal objections, he shall say, calling each by their names: "You both mutually agree to be each other's companion, husband and wife, observing the legal rights belonging to this condition; that is, keeping yourselves wholly for each other, and from all others, during your lives." And when they have answered "Yes," he shall pronounce them "husband and wife" in the name of the Lord Jesus Christ, and by virtue of the laws of the country and authority vested in him: "may God add his blessings and keep you to fulfill your covenants from henceforth and forever. Amen."

3 The clerk of every church should keep a record of all marriages, solemnized in his branch.

4 All legal contracts of marriage made before a person is baptized into this church, should be held sacred and fulfilled. Inasmuch as this church of Christ has been reproached with the crime of fornication, and polygamy: we declare that we believe, that one man should have one wife; and one woman, but one husband, except in case of death, when either is at liberty to marry again. It is not right to persuade a woman to be baptized contrary to the will of her husband, neither is it lawful to influence her to leave her husband. All children are bound by law to obey their parents; and to influence them to embrace any religious faith, or be baptized, or leave their parents without their consent, is unlawful and unjust. We believe that all persons who exercise control over their fellow

# Why is the Salt Lake Temple Decorated with Satanic Symbols?

Ever since ancient times and throughout the Medieval Ages, these symbols have been used in Satanic worship. What influence caused these symbols to be used to decorate Mormonism's most prominent temple and LDS architecture?

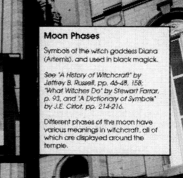

### Moon Phases

Symbols of the witch goddess Diana (Artemis), and used in black magick.

*See "A History of Witchcraft" by Jeffrey B. Russell, pp. 46-48, 158; "What Witches Do" by Stewart Farrar, p. 93, and "A Dictionary of Symbols" by J.E. Cirlot, pp. 214-216.*

Different phases of the moon have various meanings in witchcraft, all of which are displayed around the temple.

### Inverted Pentagram

This is the universal sign of Satan, and symbol of opposition to Christ.

*See "Aleister Crowley and the Hidden God" by Kenneth Grant, p. 12; "A Dictionary of Symbols" by J.E. Cirlot, p. 310, and "Magic - White and Black" by Franz Hartmann, M.D., pp. 290-291. Also displayed on the cover of "The Satanic Bible."*

This pentagram is all over the Salt Lake Temple above the doors and most of the side windows. It is also found very prominent in its more evil form (bottom point elongated) on the Eagle Gate at Temple Square and on the Logan Temple. Eleven large inverted pentagrams decorated the Nauvoo Temple.

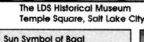

**The LDS Historical Museum**
**Temple Square, Salt Lake City**

### Sun Symbol of Baal

Throughout the Old Testament God punished the Israelites for the worship of the idol, "Baal", portrayed by this image of the sun.

*See "The Two Babylons" by Alexander Hislop, pp. 162-163; also I Kings 22:53; II Kings 23:4,5,11; II Cron. 34:4 and Jer. 11:13,17.*

This symbol also lined the walls of the Nauvoo Temple. Sun symbols in a different form are displayed around the Salt Lake Temple.

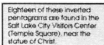

Eighteen of these inverted pentagrams are found in the Salt Lake City Visitors Center (Temple Square), near the statue of Christ.

## What Every Latter-day Saint Should Know

Satan's first lie recorded in the Bible is in Genisis 3:5, "ye shall be as gods." The doctrines of "exalta-tion" and "celestial glory" (that people can evolve into gods and goddesses) are rooted in ancient witchcraft (see "A History of Witchcraft" by Jeffrey B. Russell, pp. 158-159; "Drawing Down the Moon" by Margot Adler, p. 25, and "Gnosis" by Kurt Rudolph, pp. 92-93). Yet, these doctrines, complete with the same terminology, are being perpetuated through the Mormon Church today. Satan is deceiving innocent, God-loving people into unknowingly following his oldest and most predomi-nate lie, and he has left his mark all over Mormon temples.

Don't you wonder why the cross is nowhere to be found on Mormon temples and LDS Church buildings? The cross is where our victory over death took place, and yet the LDS Church won't have anything to do with it. The apostle Paul tells us that "the preaching of the cross is to them that perish, foolishness; but unto us which are saved it is the power of God" (I Cor. 1:18). Satan opposes the cross.

This evidence is being exposed to you, my friend, because of our deep love for the LDS people, and because you have the right to know. Our hope for Mormons throughout the world who deeply love God and who honestly want to worship God in truth, is that they will realize they've become victims of Satan's deception. Since the early 1800's, Satan has been blinding the minds of Mormons around the world from the true gospel; "But if our gospel be hid, it is hid to them that are lost: In whom the god of this world (Satan) hath blinded the minds of them which believe not " (ii Cor. 4:3-4). See reverse side.

from Truth in Love Ministries, P.O. Box 7373, Orange, CA 92613

## Flaws in the Pearl of Great Price
by Jerald & Sandra Tanner
photocopy, page 114

PAGE 16 - CONTINUED

CAIN - W.A.

THAT WHICH T.C.

FALLETH - T.C.

AND - T.C.

THY - T.C.

THOU - T.C.

THOU SHALT - T.C.

THY - T.C.

SHALT THOU - T.C.

W.D.

WROTH ALSO - T.C.

W.D.

THE LORD - T.C.

FINDETH - T.C.

THAT HE - T.C.

SLAYETH THEE T.C.

I - W.A.

W.D.

W.D.

ABEL, HIS BROTHER - T.C.

IT CAME TO PASS THAT - W.A.

ABEL, HIS BROTHER - T.C.

THY - T.C.

HAST - T.C.

HATH - T.C.

THOU TILLEST T.C.

IT - T.C.

THY - T.C.

TREE - T.C.

THOU DIDST ACCEPT - T.C.

NOT MINE - T.C.

THOU HAST - T.C.

W.D.

THY - T.C.

MINE INIQUITIES - T.C.

WHOSOEVER - T.C.

W.D. (MOSES 5:1)

I - W.A.

(MOSES 8:13)

THOSE - T.C.

AND - W.A.

THE - T.C.

And Cain went into the field and talked with his brother Abel. And while they were in the field, Cain rose up against his brother Abel and slew him. And Cain gloried in what he had done, saying, I am free; surely the flocks of my brother will fall into my hands.

But the Lord said unto Cain, Where is Abel, your brother? And he said, I know not. Am I my brother's keeper? And the Lord said, What have you done? the voice of your brother's blood cries unto me from the ground. And now you shall be cursed from the earth which has opened her mouth to receive your brother's blood from your hand. When you till the ground she shall not henceforth yield unto you her strength. A fugitive, and a vagabond also you shall be in the earth.

And Cain said unto the Lord, Satan tempted me because of my brother's flocks. And I was also angry; for his offering was accepted, and mine was not; my punishment is greater than I can bear. Behold, you have driven me out this day from the face of men and from your face shall I be hid also; and I shall be a fugitive and a vagabond in the earth; And it shall come to pass, every one that finds me will slay me because of my oath, for these things are not hid from the Lord. And the Lord said unto him, Therefore whoever slays Cain, vengeance shall be taken on him sevenfold. And the Lord set a mark upon Cain, lest any finding him should kill him."

\*     \*     \*     \*     \*     \*

"And it came to pass, that Noah and his sons hearkened unto the Lord, and gave heed, and they were called the sons of God. And when these men began to multiply on the face of the earth, and daughters were born unto them, that the sons of men saw that their daughters were fair, they took them wives even as they chose. And the Lord said unto Noah, the daughters of thy sons have sold themselves; for behold mine anger is kindled against the sons of men, for they will not hearken to my voice. And it came to pass, that Noah prophesied, and taught the things of God, even as it was in the beginning. And the Lord said unto Noah, my Spirit shall not always strive with man, for he shall know that all flesh shall die; yet his days shall be an hundred and twenty years; and if men do not repent, I will send in my floods upon them.

And in those days there were giants on the earth, and they sought Noah to take away his life; but the Lord was with Noah, and the power of the Lord was upon him.

# Min is not God!

**An Examination of Joseph Smith's "Explanation" of Facsimile #2 in the Book of Abraham**

In 1835 Michael H. Chandler arrived in Kirtland, Ohio. In his horse-drawn wagon he carried four Egyptian mummies...Along with the mummies were included displays of the papyri rolls found on the mummies themselves. Joseph Smith, the Mormon Prophet, was fascinated by Chandler's exhibit, so much so that his fledgling Church purchased the entire display from Chandler for a large sum of money: $2400.00. Joseph Smith said:

> Soon after this, some of the Saints at Kirtland purchased the mummies and papyrus...and with W. W. Phelps and Oliver Cowdery as scribes, I commenced the translation of some of the characters or hieroglyphics, and much to our joy found that one of the rolls contained the writings of Abraham, another the writings of Joseph of Egypt, etc...(Documentary History of the Church, 2:236, emphasis added).

It should be remembered that at this time the study of Egyptian was, on a scholarly level, in its infancy. Smith was claiming to be able to translate what was, for all practical purposes, an unknown language. Of course, he had claimed this same ability in translating the Book of Mormon, which was said to have been written in "Reformed Egyptian." That Smith was indeed claiming to translate in the normal sense of the term can be seen from his own words:

> The remainder of this month, I was continually engaged in translating an alphabet to the Book of Abraham, and arranging a grammar of the Egyptian language as practiced by the ancients (DHC 2:238).

Over the next nine years Smith continued to work on his translation of the Book of Abraham. The work was included in the Pearl of Great Price when it was accepted as Scripture in 1880.

The Book of Abraham is unique amongst the books of LDS Scripture; it is the only book that contains illustrations in the form of three "Facsimiles," each with an "Explanation" provided by Joseph Smith. Since the actual papyri were thought lost (some of the original papyri were found in 1967 and turned over to the LDS Church), the "Facsimiles" provided the only means of testing Joseph Smith's translation, and his understanding of the documents that were before him.

In this small tract we cannot discuss all the evidence that now exists regarding the Book of Abraham, the papyri that have been found, and the various explanations put forward by defenders of Joseph Smith. Instead, we wish to look at just one aspect of the Book of Abraham, Facsimile 2 (found on the front of this tract), and even more specifically, one section of this drawing and what it really means.

Here we reproduce one section of Facsimile 2 from the Pearl of Great Price, marked and explained by Joseph Smith as figure 7:

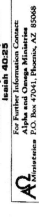

Represents God sitting upon his throne, revealing through the heavens the grand Keywords of the Priesthood; as, also, the sign of the Holy Ghost unto Abraham, in the form of a dove.

Is this indeed a representation of the one true God sitting upon His throne, revealing the grand Keywords of the priesthood? Was Joseph Smith a man of his time, able to decipher Egyptian writings in a time when scholarship was just starting to get a clue on the topic?

The object that Joseph Smith included in the Book of Abraham is, in reality, a "hypocephalus," a common item of Egyptian funeral literature (all of the facsimiles in the Book of Abraham are drawn from common Egyptian funerary documents). It was placed under the person's head, and was to aid them in making the journey through the netherworld by bathing their bodies in light. Many examples of this kind of hypocephalus are to be found. One of the many pagan gods pictured in this hypocephalus is shown above as it appears in the current edition of the LDS Scriptures. Egyptologists tell us that this is the god "Min." Min is an "ithyphallic god," that is, a sexually aroused male deity, as the picture clearly indicates. Min is the god of the procreative forces of nature. Joseph Smith told us that the Egyptian god Min was in point of fact the one true God.

And what is Min doing? Joseph tells us that he is revealing the grand Keywords of the priesthood, with the sign of the Holy Ghost in the form of a dove before him. In reality, he is holding up the "divine flail" in one hand, and is being approached by the figure Joseph Smith identified as the Holy Ghost in the form of a dove. In point of fact, Joseph's hypocephalus was damaged at the border so that only the head of the "dove" was visible. So, Joseph had to restore the picture. Did he do so correctly? No, he did not. The figure to the right provides us with the proper scene from another hypocephalus (Leyden AMS 62). The being that is approaching Min is not the Holy Ghost in the form of a dove; it is yet another ithyphallic figure, specifically, a serpent, probably the Egyptian God Nehebka, presenting to Min the uedjat eye, the symbol of good gifts.

The single LDS scholar who has written the most on the Book of Abraham, Dr. Hugh Nibley, has written of Min:

> As the supreme sex symbol of gods and men, Min behaves with shocking promiscuity, which is hardly relieved by its ritual nature...His sacred plants were aphrodisiacal...and he is everywhere represented as indulging in incestuous relationships with those of his immediate family; he had the most numerous and varied religious entourage of all the gods, consisting mostly of his huge harem...The hymns, or rather chanting, of his worshippers were accompanied with lewd dancing and carousing...to the exciting stimulus of a band of sistrum-shaking damsels (Abraham in Egypt, p. 210).

It must be remembered that Joseph Smith said that this figure represented God sitting on His throne! Incredible as it may seem, intelligent, well-read LDS are fully aware of the true nature of the hypocephalus, including the presence of Min and Nehebka (the vast majority of LDS, however, are not). How do they explain this? Mormon Egyptologist Michael Dennis Rhoades said,

> Joseph Smith mentions here the Holy Ghost in the form of a dove and God "revealing through the heavens the grand keywords of the priesthood." The procreative forces, receiving unusual accentuation throughout the representation, may stand for many divine generative powers, not least of which might be conjoined with the blessings of the Priesthood in one's posterity eternally (BYU Studies, Spring 1977, p. 273).

In other words, since the God of Mormonism is sexually active, begetting children in the spirit-world (indeed, God's power is often described by Mormons as being made up of the power of the priesthood and the power of procreation), and Min is obviously sexually active as well, this, then is the "connection."

We believe that Joseph Smith was utterly ignorant of what was represented in the Egyptian papyri that lay before him. Incapable of translating the figures, he made things up as he went along, claiming God's direction and inspiration as his guide. In the process he demonstrated his own inability as a "prophet, seer and revelator," for he grossly misidentified each of the items not only in this Facsimile, but in the other two as well.

Joseph Smith's defenders today seek to find any connection whatsoever between LDS belief and Egyptian religion, even to the point of seeing in the sexually aroused Min a picture of God upon His throne. But to grasp at this straw is to ignore the Biblical testimony to the one true God. Isaiah saw God upon His throne in Isaiah 6:1-10, but instead of an incestuous god, surrounded by lewd dancing girls, the angels surrounded His throne and cried, "Holy, holy, holy." God describes the gods of Egypt as "idols" that tremble before him (Isaiah 19:1); these false gods will literally be captured by God in His wrath (Jeremiah 43:12). God reveals the worship of these gods to be an abomination that brings His wrath (Jeremiah 44:8), and mentions one Egyptian god by name in speaking of the punishment he will bring against Egypt (Jeremiah 46:25). Those who worship such gods are "defiled" in God's sight (Ezekiel 20:7-8). The Bible has nothing but contempt for the gods of Egypt, which would include the abominable figure of Min, identified by Joseph Smith as his God.

We will gladly admit that there is a similarity between the pagan god Min and the Mormon doctrine of God developed in the later years of Joseph Smith's life. What is equally clear is that the God of the Bible is not similar to either Min, nor the LDS God. As God Himself said:

**"To whom will you compare me?"**
**Isaiah 40:25**

AΩ Ministries

For Further Information Contact:
Alpha and Omega Ministries
P.O. Box 47041, Phoenix, AZ 85068   (602)266-2537

# Journey from Mormonism

## Doctrine and Covenants Changes -sample

photocopy from *Mormonism: Shadow or Reality?* p. 18, by Jerald & Sandra Tanner
also in *The Changing World of Mormonism*, p. 44, 46, by Jerald & Sandra Tanner

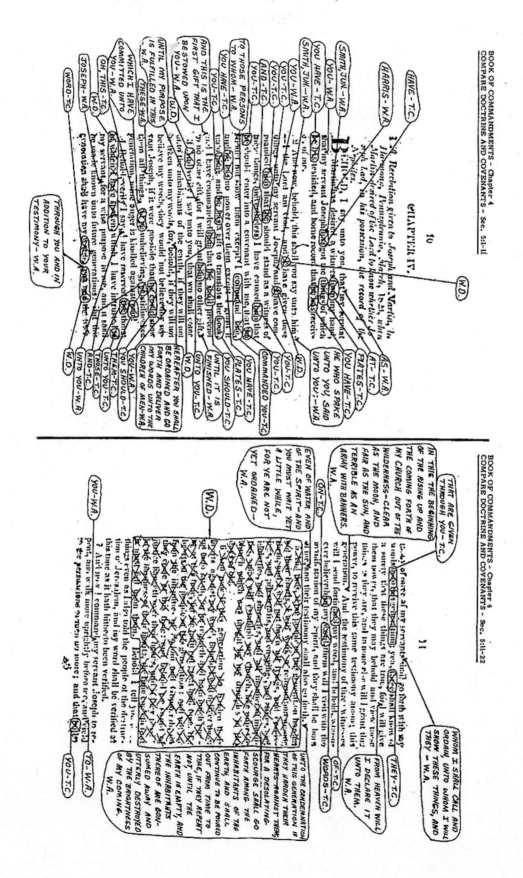

## Doctrine and Covenants Changes -sample
photocopy from *Mormonism: Shadow or Reality?* by Jerald & Sandra Tanner
also in *The Changing World of Mormonism*, p. 48, 50, by Jerald & Sandra Tanner

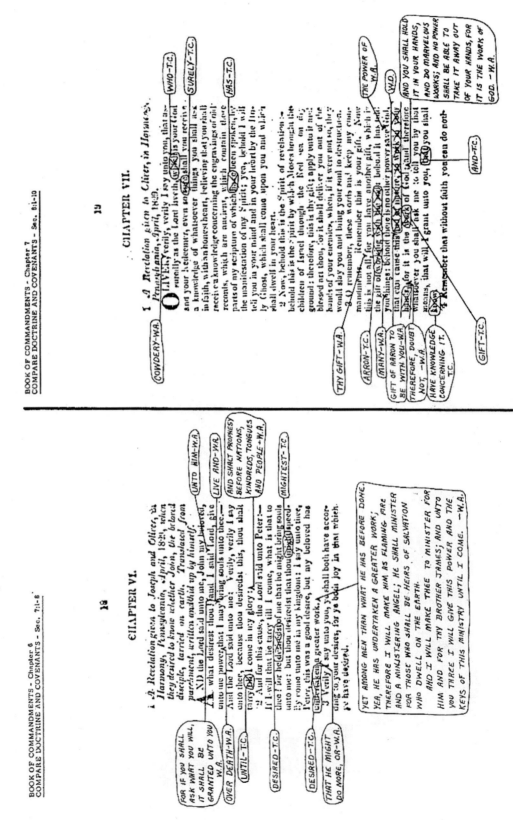

## Archeology and the Book of Mormon
Letter from the National Geographic Society
1979

# National Geographic Society
### WASHINGTON. D.C. 20036

August 7, 1979

Mr. Maurice Barnett
3928 W. Colter Street
Phoenix, AZ  85019

Dear Mr. Barnett:

We appreciate the interest that prompted you to write to the National Geographic Society.

The Society has been asked several times whether the Book of Mormon has been substantiated by archaeological findings. We referred this question to the late Dr. Neal M. Judd, noted archaeologist of the Smithsonian Institution, and his reply was as follows:

> Neither representatives of the National Geographic Society nor, to my knowledge, archaeologists connected with any other institution of equal prestige have ever used the Book of Mormon in locating historic ruins in Middle America or elsewhere.

I hope this information will prove helpful. It was a pleasure to be of assistance.

Sincerely yours,

Janet L. Shaw
Research Correspondence

JLS:rd

**Archeology and the Book of Mormon**
Letter from the Smithsonian Institution
1979

 *Information From the*
# SMITHSONIAN INSTITUTION
WASHINGTON, D. C.  20560

STATEMENT REGARDING THE BOOK OF MORMON

   1.  The Smithsonian Institution has never used the Book of Mormon in any way as a scientific guide.  Smithsonian archeologists see no direct connection between the archeology of the New World and the subject matter of the book.

   2.  The physical type of the American Indian is basically Mongoloid, being most closely related to that of the peoples of eastern, central, and northeastern Asia.  Archeological evidence indicates that the ancestors of the present Indians came into the New World--probably over a land bridge known to have existed in the Bering Strait region during the last Ice Age--in a continuing series of small migrations beginning from about 25,000 to 30,000 years ago.

   3.  Present evidence indicates that the first people to reach this continent from the East were the Norsemen who arrived in the northeastern part of North America around A.D. 1000.  There is nothing to show that they reached Mexico or Central America.

   4.  One of the main lines of evidence supporting the scientific finding that contacts with Old World civilizations, if indeed they occurred at all, were of very little significance for the development of American Indian civilizations, is the fact that none of the principal Old World domesticated food plants or animals (except the dog) occurred in the New World in pre-Columbian times.  American Indians had no wheat, barley, oats, millet, rice, cattle, pigs, chickens, horses, donkeys, camels, etc., before 1492.  The domesticated dogs of the Indians accompanied their ancestors from northwestern Asia.  Domesticated sweet potatoes occurred in both hemispheres, but probably originated in the New World and spread from there into the Pacific.

SIL-76
Summer 1979

- 2 -

5.  Iron, steel, glass, and silk were not used in the New
World before 1492 (except for occasional use of unsmelted meteoric
iron).  Nuggets of native copper were used in various locations in
pre-Columbian times, but true metallurgy was limited to southern
Mexico and the Andean region, where its occurrence in late pre-
historic times involved gold, silver, copper, and their alloys, but
not iron.

6.  There is a possibility that the spread of cultural traits
across the Pacific to Mesoamerica and the northwestern coast of
South America began several hundred years before the Christian era.
However, any such inter-hemispheric contacts appear to have been
the results of accidental voyages originating in eastern and
southern Asia.  It is by no means certain that even such contacts
occurred; certainly there were no contacts with the ancient
Egyptians, Hebrews, or other peoples of Western Asia and the Near
East.

7.  No reputable Egyptologist or other specialist on Old World
archeology, and no expert on New World prehistory, has discovered
or confirmed any relationship between archeological remains in
Mexico and archeological remains in Egypt.

8.  Reports of findings of ancient Egyptian, Hebrew, and other
Old World writings in the New World in pre-Columbian contexts have
frequently appeared in newspapers, magazines, and sensational books.
None of these claims has stood up to examination by reputable
scholars.  No inscriptions using Old World forms of writing have
been shown to have occurred in any part of the Americas before 1492.

9.  There are copies of the Book of Mormon in the library of
the National Museum of Natural History, Smithsonian Institution.

# McConkie Tells 'Y' Students Heresies

### By LAURA M. JANNEY
### Herald Staff Writer

Elder Bruce R. McConkie, an apostle of The Church of Jesus Christ of Latter-day Saints, called the doctrine of salvation by grace without works "the second greatest heresy" of Christianity during Brigham Young University's opening devotional Tuesday.

The first great heresy, he said, pertains to the nature of God, the doctrine of the trinity.

McConkie discussed the "great religious phenomenon of the 80's" which he says is sweeping the nation now.

The heresy of being saved by grace is burning like wildfire across the nation, he said. The only "religious mania" to exceed it was the way the original heresy filled the early Christian church after Christ's death.

McConkie said the doctrine of a "three-in-one" God filled the universe after Christ died, and the adoption of the false image "destroyed the true worship of God."

Because of the doctrine, organized religion became so powerful that only the Church could administer salvation, he said.

Present day religion has become even more distorted, he said. The doctrine of salvation by confessing one's faith has been a leading

contributor. McConkie said he heard a preacher on the radio admonish listeners in their cars to touch their radios in order to make contact with the preacher, while saying "Lord Jesus, I believe."

McConkie traced the doctrine to Martin Luther, and read a portion of Luther's biography. "We have to acknowledge that Luther's break with Catholicism was part of a divine plan," McConkie said, but contended that it doesn't justify Luther's belief in being saved by grace regardless of good works.

McConkie said the difference between the gospel of Christ as taught by the LDS Church and the doctrine of so-called Born-Again Christians is the difference between the straight and narrow path and the broad way available to all the world.

He said the doctrine of "saved by grace without works" is devised to allow people to live as part of the wicked world and at the same time satisfy their innate need to worship God.

"There is a true doctrine of grace," he said. That true doctrine is the plan of salvation — which consists of a creation, a fall, and an atonement.

"The grace of God is his mercy, his love, and his condescension." He said God's grace is seen in everything He does "for the benefit of His children which brings to pass the immortality and eternal life of man."

McConkie said the plan of salvation is provided through God's grace, and no works on our part were required.

He said that salvation is not in good works alone, either, but is in Christ and faith in Him.

"We are not saved by works alone, no matter how good. We are saved by the blood of Christ."

Thursday, January 12, 1984  THE HERALD, Provo, Utah, — Page 21

## Governor Ford Prophecy
diary of Joseph Smith

PERSONAL DIARY OF JOSEPH SMITH
ENTRY OF JUNE 30, 1843

"I prophesy in the name of the Lord
God that Governor Ford by granting
the writ against me has damned himself politically and and his carcase
will stink on the face of the earth
food for the carrion Crow & Turkey
Buzzard."

### Joseph Smith the Glass Looker
Justice A. Neely
1826

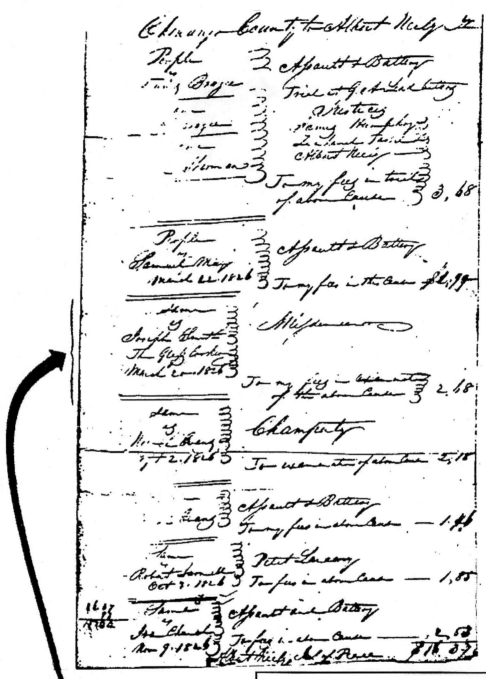

same
vs.
Joseph Smith
The Glass Looker
March 20, 1826

Misdemeanor

To my fees in examination
of the above cause    2.68

Above is a photograph of Justice Albert Neely's
Bill showing the costs involved in several trials in
1826. The fifth item from the top mentions the trial
of "Joseph Smith the Glass Looker." When the letter "P" was repeated in documents of Joseph
Smith's time, as in the word "glass" the two letters
appeared as a "P". We have typed out the portion
of this bill which mentions Joseph Smith. This bill
proves that the published court record is authentic.

## Articles of Faith: Original and Current

### Original 14 Articles of Faith

copies of uncut originals, circa 1830's

**Joseph Smith Begins His Work, vol. II, Wilford C. Wood, 1962**

THE ARTICLES OF FAITH OF
THE CHURCH OF JESUS CHRIST
OF LATTER-DAY SAINTS

1. We believe in God the eternal Father, and his son Jesus Christ, and in the Holy Ghost.

2. We believe that men will be punished for their own sins, and not for Adam's transgressions.

3. We believe that through the atonement of Christ all mankind may be saved, by obedience to the laws and ordinances of the Gospel.

4. We believe that these ordinances are: 1st, Faith in the Lord Jesus Christ; 2nd, Repentance; 3rd, Baptism by immersion for the remission of sins; 4th, Laying on of hands for the gift of the Holy Spirit; 5th, The Lord's Supper.

5. We believe that men must be called of God by inspiration, and by laying on of hands by those who are duly commissioned to preach the Gospel, and administer in the ordinances thereof.

6. We believe in the same organization that existed in the primitive church, viz., apostles, prophets, pastors, teachers, evangelists, etc.

7. We believe in the powers and gifts of the everlasting Gospel, viz., the gift of faith, discerning of spirits, prophecy, revelation, visions, healing, tongues, and the interpretation of tongues, wisdom, charity, brotherly love, etc.

8. We believe in the Word of God recorded in the Bible; we also believe the Word of God recorded in the Book of Mormon, and in all other good books.

9. We believe all that God has revealed; all that he does now reveal; and we believe that he will yet reveal many more great and important things pertaining to the Kingdom of God, and Messiah's second coming.

10. We believe in the literal gathering of Israel, and in the restoration of the ten tribes; that Zion will be established upon the western continent; that Christ will reign personally upon the earth a thousand years; and that the earth will be renewed, and receive its paradisaical glory.

11. We believe in the literal resurrection of the body, and that the dead in Christ will rise first, and that the rest of the dead live not again until the thousand years are expired.

12. We claim the privilege of worshipping Almighty God according to the dictates of our conscience unmolested, and allow all men the same privilege, let them worship how or where they may.

13. We believe in being subject to kings, queens, presidents, rulers, and magistrates, in obeying, honoring, and sustaining the law.

14. We believe in being honest, true, chaste, temperate, benevolent, virtuous, and upright, and in doing good to all men; indeed, we may say that we follow the admonition of Paul, we 'believe all things,' we 'hope all things,' 'we have endured very many things,' and hope to be able to 'endure all things.' Everything virtuous, lovely, praiseworthy, and of good report, we seek after, looking forward to the 'recompense of reward.'

JOSEPH SMITH

## Current 13 Articles of Faith

1. We believe in God, the Eternal Father, and in His Son, Jesus Christ, and in the Holy Ghost.

2. We believe that men will be punished for their own sins, and not for Adam's transgression.

3. We believe that through the Atonement of Christ, all mankind may be saved, by obedience to the laws and ordinances of the Gospel.

4. We believe that the first principles and ordinances of the Gospel are: first, Faith in the Lord Jesus Christ; second, Repentance; third, Baptism by immersion for the remission of sins; fourth, Laying on of hands for the gift of the Holy Ghost.

5. We believe that a man must be called of God, by prophecy, and by the laying on of hands, by those who are in authority to preach the Gospel and administer in the ordinances thereof.

6. We believe in the same organization that existed in the Primitive Church, viz., apostles, prophets, pastors, teachers, evangelists, etc.

7. We believe in the gift of tongues, prophecy, revelation, visions, healing, interpretation of tongues, etc.

8. We believe the Bible to be the word of God as far as it is translated correctly; we also believe The Book of Mormon to be the word of God.

9. We believe all that God has revealed, all that He does now reveal, and we believe that He will yet reveal many great and important things pertaining to the Kingdom of God.

10. We believe in the literal gathering of Israel and in the restoration of the Ten Tribes; that Zion will be built upon this [the American] Continent; that Christ will reign personally upon the earth; and, that the earth will be renewed and receive its paradisiacal glory.

11. We claim the privilege of worshipping Almighty God according to the dictates of our own conscience, and allow all men the same privilege, let them worship how, where, or what they may.

12. We believe in being subject to kings, presidents, rulers, and magistrates, in obeying, honoring, and sustaining the law.

13. We believe in being honest, true, chaste, benevolent, virtuous, and in doing good to all men; indeed, we may say that we follow the admonition of Paul - We believe all things, we hope all things, we have endured many things, and hope to be able to endure all things. If there is anything virtuous, lovely, or of good report or praiseworthy, we seek after these things.

# More Accurate Articles
Interpreted by a Bible believing Christian, Robert McKay

1.  *We believe that God the Father was once a man, became God, has a tangible body of flesh and bones, and could conceivably cease to be God; we believe that the Son is the spirit-brother of Lucifer, also became a god , and was conceived as Jesus Christ through a physical relationship between the Father and Mary; we believe that the Holy Ghost is a spirit in the form of a man who became a god without ever obtaining a body, even though a body is necessary for godhood; we believe that the members of the Godhead are three separate and distinct gods, who are united only in plan, purpose, and attributes. We also believe that there are many other gods.*

2.  *We believe that men are not naturally sinful, but become sinners when they commit sin. Therefore Adam's sin has no effect on us and all we have to worry about are our own specific sinful acts.*

3.  *We believe that Christ atoned for Adam's sin only, in the Garden of Gethsemane, and that by obeying the laws of Mormonism we can make amends for our sins and progress to godhood.*

4.  *We believe that a man must be called to a church position by the proper church authority, and it never hurts to be a successful businessman or a relative of a General Authority.*

5.  *We believe that the church must have a First Presidency, a total of 15 living apostles, a First Quorum of the Seventy with between 40 and 60 members, stake presidents, regional representatives, thousands of high priests, a Relief Society, and other features unheard of before 1830.*

6.  *We believe in the gifts of prophecy, revelation, and visions, but do not find it necessary to prophesy, see visions, or publish revelations.*

7.  *We believe the Bible to be the Word of God except where it contradicts Mormonism; we also believe the Book of Mormon to be the Word of God even though it contradicts LDS doctrine.*

8.  *We believe those revelations that agree with our doctrine; we believe that God is revealing many things to the leaders of the church even though those revelations are never made public; and we believe that God will yet reveal things such as the "lost books" of the Bible, a good portion of the golden plates that Joseph Smith did not translate, the location of all the Book of Mormon cities, and the answers to the questions asked by "anti-Mormons."*

9.  *We claim the right to worship who, where, when, and how we please, and for the time being grant the privilege to others. Of course it would be better if church and state were identical, as in the days of Brigham Young.*

10. *We believe in blindly following the General Authorities of the church, and in obeying the civil laws with the same dedication as non-Mormons.*

11. *We believe that the LDS church is the only true church; that non-Mormons cannot enter the kingdom of God; that we are superior to all other people; and that everyone is persecuting us by quoting our literature.*

# Biblical Defense of Truth

King James Version
compiled by Christine Carroll

Beloved, when I gave all diligence to write unto you of the common salvation, it was needful for me to write unto you, and exhort you that ye should earnestly contend for the faith which was once delivered unto the saints. (Jude verse 3)

Preach the word; be instant in season, out of season; reprove, rebuke, exhort with all longsuffering and doctrine. For the time will come when they will not endure sound doctrine; but after their own lusts shall they heap to themselves teachers, having itching ears... (2 Timothy 4:2-3)

And with all deceivableness of unrighteousness in them that perish; because they received not the love of the truth, that they might be saved. And for this cause God shall send them strong delusion, that they should believe a lie... (2 Thessalonians 2:10-11)

But sanctify the Lord God in your hearts: and be ready always to give an answer to every man that asketh you a reason for the hope that is in you with meekness and fear: (1 Peter 3:15)

And have no fellowship with the unfruitful works of darkness, but rather reprove them. (Ephesians 5:11)

He that answereth a matter before he heareth it, it is folly and shame unto him. (Proverbs 18:13)

But if thine heart turn away, so that thou wilt not hear, but shalt be drawn away, and worship other gods, and serve them; I denounce unto you this day, that ye shall surely perish, and that ye shall not prolong your days upon the land, whither thou passest over Jordan to go to possess it. (Deuteronomy 30:17-18)

I know thy works, and thy labour, and thy patience, and how though canst not bear them which are evil: and thou hast tried them which say they are apostles, and are not, and hast found them liars: (Revelation 2:2)

Beware of false prophets, which come to you in sheep's clothing, but inwardly they are ravening wolves. Ye shall know them by their fruits... (Matthew 7:15-16)

In meekness instructing those that oppose themselves; if God peradventure will give them repentance to the acknowledging of the truth... (2 Timothy 2:25-26)

For there shall arise false Christs, and false prophets, and shall shew great signs and wonders; insomuch that, if it were possible, they shall deceive the very elect. (Matthew 24:24-25)

But though we, or an angel from heaven, preach any other gospel unto you, than that which we have preached unto you, let him be accursed. As we said before, so say I now again, If any man preach any other gospel unto you than that ye have received, let him be accursed. (Galatians 1:8-9)

For I testify unto every man that heareth the words of the prophecy of this book, If any man shall add unto these things, God shall add unto him the plagues that are written in this book: And if any man shall take away from the words of the book of this prophecy, God shall take away his part out of the book of life, and out of the holy city, and from the things which are written in this book. (Revelation 22:18-19)

Ye shall not add unto the word which I command you, neither shall ye diminish ought from it, that ye may keep the commandments of the Lord your God which I command you. (Deuteronomy 4:2)

Every word of God is pure: he is a shield unto them that put their trust in him. Add thou not unto his words, lest he reprove thee, and thou be found a liar. (Proverbs 30:5-6)

To the law and to the testimony: if they do not speak according to this word, it is because there is no light in them. (Isaiah 8:20)

Now I beseech you, brethren, mark them which cause divisions and offences contrary to the doctrine which ye have learned; and avoid them. For they that are such serve not our Lord Jesus Christ, but their own belly; and by good words and fair speeches deceive the hearts of the simple. (Romans 16:17-18)

But sanctify the Lord God in your hearts: and be ready always to give an answer to every man that asketh you a reason of the hope that is in you with meekness and fear: Having a good conscience; that, whereas they speak evil of you, as of evildoers, they may be ashamed that falsely accuse your good conversation in Christ. (Peter 3:15-16)

Whosoever transgresseth, and abideth not in the doctrine of Christ, hath not God. He that abideth in the doctrine of Christ, he hath both the Father and the Son. (2 John verse 9)

But the fearful, and unbelieving, and the abominable, and murderers, and whoremongers, and sorcerers, and idolaters, and all liars, shall have their part in the lake which burneth with fire and brimstone: which is the second death. (Revelation 21:8)

# Qualifications to Serve God

from John MaCarthur's Bible studies - The Master's Men, Matthew 10:51-54, p. 56-57.

*What kind of people does god use for His purpose? What kind of men did Jesus choose? Well, when most people think of the twelve apostles, they are prone to think of stained-glass saints, men without faults, men who manifested none of the failures that beset the rest of humanity. But if you look at the apostles that way, you're wrong! They were people just like all of us. Even though they were specially called, specially transformed, specially sent by Christ -they were people just like us.*

*We live in a very qualification conscious society. There are qualifications for just about everything. For example, we have to qualify to buy a house, to buy a car, to get a credit card, to apply for a job, to pursue a career, to enroll in school, to train for a particular skill, to join a team - or whatever else we want to do. It seems everything we do requires that we qualify. Somebody establishes standards that we have to meet because society has determined that it's only going to use qualified people.*

*Now what qualifications does God have? What does God require of those who serve Him? What kind of people does Jesus use in His ministry to advance His eternal kingdom? Well, since nobody is qualified, God has only one alternative -to use the unqualified to do the impossible. That is essentially how God works. God uses unqualified people, moves into their lives and with saving, sanctifying grace, transforms them into useful instruments to perform His purposes. Look at some biblical examples of unqualified people that God has used.*

*If you'll just follow the flow of the people God used, you'll see a march of the unqualified. God uses unqualified people! And when you look at the twelve, you'll meet a group of unqualified men, just like all the rest.*

1. Noah got drunk and conducted himself in a lewd way.
2. Abraham doubted God, lied about his wife, and committed adultery.
3. Isaac sinned as his father had taught him, lying about his wife Rebekah to Abimelech.
4. Jacob extorted the birthright from Esau, deceived his father, and raised a family of immoral children.
5. Joseph was an outcast and was hated by his brothers.
6. Moses was a murderer and, acting in pride, tried to steal God's glory by striking a rock to get water from it, instead of obediently speaking to it as God has told him to do.
7. Aaron, the high priest, led Israel in the worship of the golden calf and the accompanying orgy.
8. Joshua was so deceived by the Gibeonites that he made a treaty with them instead of destroying them as God had told him to do, and because of this disobedience, Israel was troubled endlessly by them.
9. Gideon had no confidence in himself and even less confidence in God's plan and power.
10. Samson was marked as a man with a lustful love for a wretched woman.
11. Ruth was in the messianic line, yet she was an accursed Moabitess.
12. Samuel was only a little child when he began to serve God.
13. David was a ladies' man, an adulterer, a murderer, a poor father, and a man with such bloody hands that God wouldn't even let him build the Temple.
14. Solomon was the world's leading polygamist.
15. Isaiah put his trust in a human king.
16. Ezekiel was a brash, tough, strong-minded, crusty, say-what-you-think priest.
17. Daniel was educated in a pagan county and taught the wisdom of the bitter and hasty Chaldeans.
18. Hosea married a prostitute.
19. Jonah defied God in direct disobedience and got terribly upset when the Gentile city of Nineveh was converted.
20. Habakkuk questioned the divine plan.
21. Elijah was able to handle 850 false priests and prophets, but ran like a maniac from one woman -Jezebel.
22. Paul was a former Christian killer.
23. Timothy was ashamed of Christ and had to be rebuked by Paul.
24. Peter was a liar.

## The Mormon Priesthood Secrets Chart
*What's Going On In There?,* 1982, by Chuck Sackett
photocopy of page 57

# The Mormon Priesthood Secrets Chart
### AS ADMINISTERED IN THE TEMPLE ENDOWMENT RITUAL

| SECRET ELEMENT | AARONIC PRIESTHOOD | | MELCHIZEDEK PRIESTHOOD | |
|---|---|---|---|---|
| | FIRST TOKEN | SECOND TOKEN | FIRST TOKEN | SECOND TOKEN |
| LAW & COVENANT | OBEDIENCE: wives agree to obey their husband in righteousness, and husbands agree to obey the Law of Elohim and to keep his commandments. SACRIFICE: all agree to sacrifice all they possess, even their lives, if necessary, in sustaining and defending the Kingdom of God (the Mormon church) | GOSPEL: all agree to "obey the Law of the Gospel and to avoid all light-mindedness, loud laughter, evil speaking of the Lord's anointed,* the taking of the name of God in vain, and every other unholy and impure practice." * Refers to Mormon leaders, not Jesus. | CHASTITY: all agree that "no one of you will have sexual intercourse except with your husband or wife (wives) to whom you are legally and lawfully wedded." (changed ca. 1973 to include the prohibition of most popular forms of sex perversion, which were previously excluded) | CONSECRATION: all agree "you do consecrate yourselves, your time, talents, and everything with which the Lord has blessed you, or may bless you to the Church of Jesus Christ of Latter-Day Saints for the building up of the Kingdom of God on the earth and the establishment of Zion. (the Mormon Church) |
| TOKEN (handclasp) NOTICE → #9 Masonic equivalents are marked on reverse | Clasp right hands and and place joint of the thumb over the first knuckle of the other person's hand. 1 | Clasp right hands and place the joint of the thumb between the first and second knuckle of the other person's hand. 2 | Right hand in vertical position, fingers together, thumb extended. Giver places tip of forefinger in the center of the palm, and thumb opposite on back of the hand. | Clasp right hands, interlocking little fingers, and place the index finger tip in the center of the other persons wrist. (Similar to an age old Witchcraft handclasp.) |
| NAME (key word) | The "NEW NAME" which everyone recieves for this day in all LDS Temples worldwide. | The first given name of the person for whom the work is being performed | The SUN (Amon-Ra), later changed to "The SON-meaning the Son of God," but his name is not mentioned. | The "INCANTATION"1 while embracing in the Five Points of Fellowship2 through the Veil 3 |
| SIGN (gesture) | Standing with right arm raised to the square, palm forward, fingers together, thumb extended. | Standing with the right hand in front of you, hand in cupping shape, right arm forming a square, left arm raised to the square. 4 | Standing with the left hand, in cupping shape, in front of you, left arm forming a square, right hand palm down fingers together, thumb over the left hip. 5 | Standing with both hands, palm forward, fingers together, raised high above the head. Lower hands to waist while saying "Pay Lay Ale" three times in unison. 5 |
| PENALTY FOR REVEALING SECRETS SIGNIFYING | Place right hand, palm down, fingers together thumb under left ear, draw thumb quickly across your throat to your right ear, then drop hand to your side. 6  Having your throat slit from ear to ear, and your tongue torn out by its roots.* 9 | Place cup shaped right hand over left breast and draw it quickly across your body, then drop hands to your sides. 7  Having your chest cut open and your heart and vitals torn out and fed to the beasts of the field and the fowls of the air. *10 | In the Sign position above, draw the right thumb quickly across the waist to the right hip, then drop both hands to the sides. 8  Having your body cut assunder and your vitals and bowels gush out upon the ground. *11 | NO PENALTY IS REQUIRED  THE GARMENT MARKS The SQUARE "over the RIGHT BREAST signifying exactness and honor in living up to all of the covenants of the Temple" The COMPASS "over the LEFT BREAST signifying that desires, appetites and passions must be kept within certain bounds which the Lord has established, and that all truth may be circumscribed into one great whole." 12 |

* The wording of the penalties was subdued approximately 50 years ago due to complaints from younger participants. It now states that these morbid gestures "represent different ways in which life may be taken." The patron swears a blood oath that "rather than reveal them (these secrets), I would suffer my life to be taken" as everyone executes the morbid gestures.

The LEVEL mark over the NAVEL is "a reminder of the constant need of nourishment to body and spirit." The KNEE mark indicates "that every knee shall bow and every tongue confess that Jesus is the Christ."

FOOTNOTES: 1. The name of the Token is an incantation: "Health in the navel, marrow in the bones, strength in the loins and in the sinews. POWER IN THE PRIESTHOOD BE UPON ME AND UPON MY POSTERITY THROUGH ALL GENERATIONS OF TIME, AND THROUGHOUT ALL ETERNITY." (Whose PRIESTCRAFT POWER?)
2. "The Five Points of Fellowship are: inside of right foot by the side of right foot, knee to knee, breast to breast, hand to back, and mouth to ear." Right hands are also joined in the TOKEN described above, called "The PATRIARCHAL GRIP, or Sure Sign of the Nail." 3
3. Partons are told that "Pay Lay Ale" means "Oh God, hear the words of my mouth" in the "Adamic language." This expression has varied over the past 125 years in several published exposés; the original words are unknown. Joseph Smith was unlearned but pretentiously used his own version of "horrible Hebrew" to impress his clan. In Strong's Exhaustive Concordance of the Bible, Hebrew Dictionary--words #6382 and #1966 combine in an expression phonetically similar to this; "peh-leh hay-lale." Peh-leh (פֶּלֶא) meaning marvelous thing or wonderful, and hay-lale (הֵילֵל) meaning Lucifer or the morning star. Is this the god whom Mormons unknowingly PRAISE in the Endowment? When Adam prays using these words it is LUCIFER who answers him-- NOT GOD!! ADAM is CONVINCED BY LUCIFER THAT HE IS THE GOD OF THIS WORLD.

**First Token of the Aaronic Priesthood**
*Mormonism's Temple of Doom,* 1987
by W.J. Schnoebelen and J.R. Spencer
photocopy of page 37

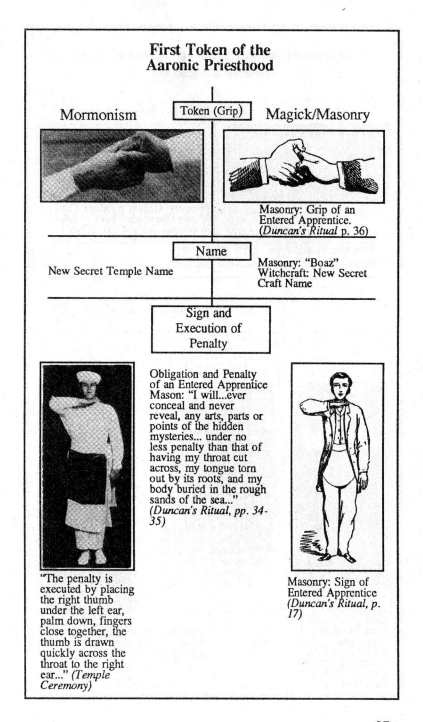

## The Second Token of the Aaronic Priesthood
## First Token of the Melchizedek Priesthood
*Mormonism's Temple of Doom,* 1987
by W.J. Schnoebelen and J.R. Spencer
photocopy of pages 38-39

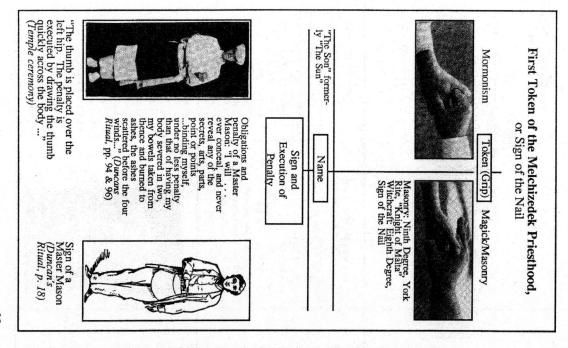

38

### Second Token of the Aaronic Priesthood

Mormonism | Token (Grip) | Magick/Masonry

Masonry: Grip of a Fellow Craft Mason (*Duncan's Ritual, p. 66*) Witchcraft 3rd°, "Sign of Pan"

Your own First (Given) Name.

Name

Sign and Execution of Penalty

Obligation and penalty of a Fellow Craft Mason: "I will ...ever conceal, and never reveal any of the secret arts, parts, or points of the Fellow Craft Degree... binding myself under no less than of having my breast torn open, my heart plucked out and placed on the highest pinnacle of the temple." (*Duncan's Ritual, pp. 64 & 65*).

Sign of a Fellow Craft Mason (*Duncan's Ritual, p.17*)

"The penalty is executed by placing the right hand on the left breast, and drawing the hand quickly across the chest..." (*Temple Ceremony*)

### First Token of the Melchizedek Priesthood, or Sign of the Nail

Mormonism | Token (Grip) | Magick/Masonry

Masonry: Ninth Degree, York Rite, "Knight of Malta" Witchcraft Eighth Degree, Sign of the Nail

"The Son" former-ly "The Sun"

Name

Sign and Execution of Penalty

Obligations and penalty of a Master Mason: "I will ... ever conceal, and never reveal any of the secrets, arts, parts, point or points ...binding myself, under no less penalty than that of having my body severed in two, my bowels taken from thence and burned to ashes, the ashes scattered before the four winds...." (*Duncans Ritual, pp. 94 & 96*).

Sign of a Master Mason (*Duncan's Ritual, p. 18*)

"The thumb is placed over the left hip. The penalty is executed by drawing the thumb quickly across the body ...." (*Temple ceremony*)

39

### The Second Token of the Melchizedek Priesthood
*Mormonism's Temple of Doom,* 1987
by W.J. Schnoebelen and J.R. Spencer
photocopy of pages 40-41

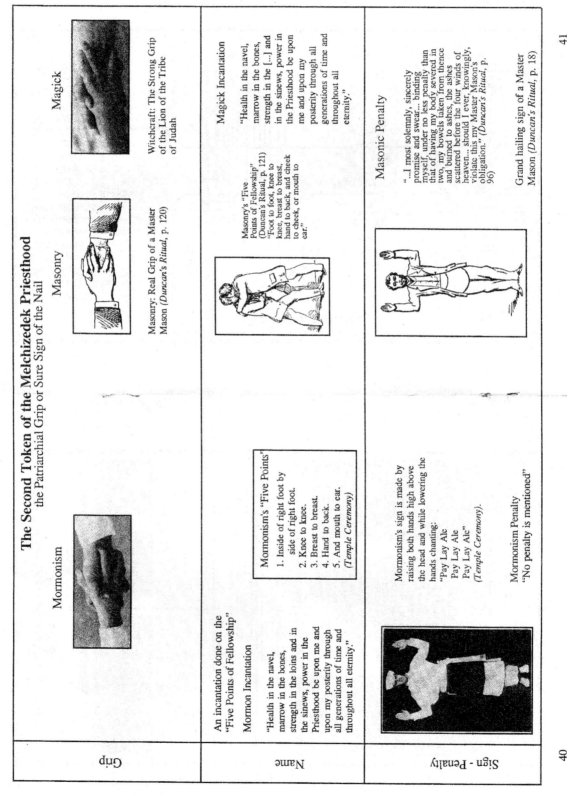

## The Second Token of the Melchizedek Priesthood
the Patriarchial Grip or Sure Sign of the Nail

|  | Mormonism | Masonry | Magick |
|---|---|---|---|
| **Grip** | | Masonry: Real Grip of a Master Mason (*Duncan's Ritual*, p. 120) | Witchcraft: The Strong Grip of the Lion of the Tribe of Judah |
| **Name** | An incantation done on the "Five Points of Fellowship" — Mormon Incantation — "Health in the navel, marrow in the bones, strength in the loins and in the sinews, power in the Priesthood be upon me and upon my posterity through all generations of time and throughout all eternity." | Masonry's "Five Points of Fellowship" (*Duncan's Ritual*, p. 121) "Foot to foot, knee to knee, breast to breast, hand to back, and cheek to cheek, or mouth to ear." | Magick Incantation — "Health in the navel, marrow in the bones, strength in the [...] and in the sinews, power in the Priesthood be upon me and upon my posterity through all generations of time and throughout all eternity." |
| **Sign - Penalty** | Mormonism's "Five Points" 1. Inside of right foot by side of right foot. 2. Knee to knee. 3. Breast to breast. 4. Hand to back. 5. And mouth to ear. (*Temple Ceremony*) — Mormonism's sign is made by raising both hands high above the head and while lowering the hands chanting: "Pay Lay Ale / Pay Lay Ale / Pay Lay Ale" (*Temple Ceremony*). Mormonism Penalty "No penalty is mentioned" | | Masonic Penalty "...I most solemnly, sincerely promise and swear... binding myself, under no less penalty than that of having my body severed in two, my bowels taken from thence and burned to ashes, the ashes scattered before the four winds of heaven... should I ever, knowingly, violate this my Master Mason's obligation." (*Duncan's Ritual*, p. 96) — Grand hailing sign of a Master Mason (*Duncan's Ritual*, p. 18) |

# Works Cited

*Books, pamphlets, newspapers, magazines, reference books, and journals listed alphabetically by:*
*author, "Article Title", Book or Periodical Name, City, State: publisher, date, and any other information.*

Benson, Ezra Taft. BYU Devotional. "Fourteen Fundamentals in Following the Prophets" *Provo Herald.* Provo, UT. February 26, 1980.

Benson, Ezra Taft. General Conference Report, Salt Lake City, UT, April 1950, October 1987.

Brockbank, Bernard P. "The Living Christ" *Ensign.* Salt Lake City, UT, May 1977, p.26.

Burton, Alma P. "Follow the Brethren" *Ensign*, Salt Lake City, UT, October 1972.

Cannon, Abraham. *Journal of Abraham C. Cannon.* Salt Lake City, UT, Collection in the Church Archives LDS Historical Department, December 6, 1889.

Clark, J. Reuben. *Messages of the first Presidency*, Salt Lake City, UT, 1971. v.5 p.110.

_____. *Deseret News,* Church News. Editorial. Salt Lake City, UT, June 5, 1965 p.16.

_____. *Deseret News,* Church News. Salt Lake City, UT, October 9, 1976 p.11

_____. *Deseret News,* Salt Lake City, UT, June 17, 1978

Compton, Todd. *In Sacred Loneliness, The Plural Wives of Joseph Smith.* Salt Lake City, UT, Signature books, 1999.

_____. *DNA vs. The Book of Mormon.* Order from: Living Hope Ministries, 48 N. Main St., Brigham City, UT, 84302. Free video offer to LDS members. www.lhvm.org

Douglas, Alban. *God's Answers to Man's Questions,* written and copyrighted by North American Copyright granted in 1976 to W.D. Kennedy. For extra copies write to W.D. Kennedy, Route 8, Box 260, Greenville, SC, 29611.

Geisler, Norman L. & William E. Nix. *From God To Us.* Chicago, IL, Moody Press, 1976.

_____. *Ensign.* General Conference Report. Salt Lake City, UT, October 1987.

_____. *Ensign.* General Conference Report. Salt Lake City, UT, April 10, 1898.

_____. *Ensign.* General Conference Report. Salt Lake City, UT, May 1995.

Gottlieb, Rober & Wiley, Peter. *America's Saints -The Rise of Mormon Power.* NY, G.P. Putnam's Sons, 1984.

Haight, David, B. "Sustaining A New Prophet" *Ensign.* Salt Lake City, UT, May 1995, p.36-37.

Heinerman, John & Shupe, Anson. *The Mormon Corporate Empire.* Boston, MA, Beacon Press 1985.

_____. *History of Joseph Smith by his Mother*, Salt Lake City, UT, Bookcraft, 1956.

_____. *History of the Church,* Salt Lake City, UT, The Deseret Book Company, 1978.

Howell, Eber D. *Mormonism Unveiled or a Faithful Account of That Singular Imposition and Discussion from It's Rise to the Present Time*, NY, AMS Printing Inc. (reproduction of the 1834 edition).

Hunter, Milton R. *The Gospel through the Ages.* Salt Lake City, UT, Steven and Wallis, 1945.

_____. *Hymns, The Church of Jesus Christ of Latter-Day Saints.* Salt Lake City, UT, The Deseret News Press, 1961.

_____. *Improvement Era.* "Sustaining the General Authorities of the Church" Ward Teachers Message. Salt Lake City, UT, June 1945, p.354.

_____. *Improvement Era.* Kimball, Spencer W., Salt Lake City, UT, December 1960, p.922-923.

_____. *Improvement Era.* General Conference Report. Salt Lake City, UT, April 1950.

_____. *Journal of Discourses.* Liverpool, England, Lithographed in USA, 1966 (26 volumes).

Kimball, Heber C. *Journal of Heber C. Kimball.* Collection in the Church Archives LDS Historical Department. Salt Lake City, UT, December 26, 1845.

Kimball, Spencer W. *The Miracle of Forgiveness*, Salt Lake City, UT, Bookcraft, 1971.

Kimball, Spencer W. *The New Era.* Salt Lake City, UT, 1975, p.9.

Kimball, Spencer W. *Improvement Era*, Salt Lake City, UT, December 1960, p.922-923.

Krakauer, Jon. *Under The Banner of Heaven.* USA. Doubleday, 2003.

Kraut, Ogden. *Michael-Adam.* Salt Lake City: Kraut's Pioneer Press. Book may be purchased through Sam Weller's Bookstore in Salt Lake City, UT.

Larson, Charles M. *...By His Own Hand Upon Papyrus, a new look at the Joseph Smith Papyri.* Grand Rapids, MI, Institute for Religious Research. 1985.

Layton, Melaine. *And this is Life Eternal that they might know Thee, the only True God? Adam?* Acquire from: 4383 Ruskin Rd., Rockford, IL, 61101.

Lewis, Gordon R. & Bruce A. Demarest. *Integrative Theology.* Grand Rapids, MI, 3 volumes, Zondervan Publishing House 1994.

Lundwall, N.B. *Temples of the Most High.* Salt Lake City, UT, Press of Zion's Printing & Publishing Company, 1945.

McConkie, Bruce R. *Letter to Eugene England.* February 19, 1981, photo of original letter.

McConkie, Bruce R. "McConkie Tells 'Y' Students Heresies" *The Provo Herald*, UT, January 12, 1984, p.21.

McConkie, Bruce R. *Mormon Doctrine.* Salt Lake City, UT, Bookcraft, 1979 and 1966 Edition.

McConkie, Bruce R. *The Promised Messiah.* Salt Lake City, UT, Deseret Books. 1978.

McConkie, Bruce R. *Deseret News.* "What Is Our Relationship to the Godhead?" BYU Devotional. Church News Section. Salt Lake City, UT, March 20, 1982, p.5.

McDowell, Josh. *Evidence That Demands A Verdict.* San Bernadino, CA, Here's Life Publishers 1975 (2 volumes).

McGavin, Cecil, E. *Cumorah's Gold Bible*, Salt Lake City, UT, Bookcraft, 1948.

_____. *Melchizedek Priesthood Study Guide.* Salt Lake City, UT, Corporation of the Church of Jesus Christ of Latter-Day Saints, 1984. p.129.

_____. *Millennial Star.* England 1840-1970 (official church voice in England) v.3 p.53, 71, v.8 p.124-128, v.25 p.797.

_____. *Missionary Lessons.* Salt Lake City, UT, Deseret Press. Corporation of the President of the Church of Jesus Christ of Latter-Day Saints, Concept 5, 1-23.

Nibley, Hugh. *No Ma'am, That's Not History.* Salt Lake City, UT, Bookcraft, 1946.

Nibley, Hugh. *Sounding Brass.* Salt Lake City, UT, Bookcraft, 1963.

Nibley, Hugh. *The Myth Makers.* Salt Lake City, UT, Bookcraft, 1961.

Nuttall, John L. *Journal of John L. Nuttall.* Collection in the Church Archives LDS Historical Department. Salt Lake City, UT, February 7. 1877.

Ostling, Richard and Joan. *Mormon America.* Harper Collins, 2000.

Peterson, Mark E. *Adam, Who Is He?* Salt Lake City, UT. Deseret Book company, 1976.

Peterson, Mark E. *As Translated Correctly.* Salt Lake City, UT. Deseret Book Company. 1966.

Pierce, Norman C. *The 3-1/2 Years.* Salt Lake City, UT, October 6, 1963.

Pratt, Orson. *Divine Authenticity of The Book of Mormon.* Liverpool, England, 1850.

Pratt, Orson. *The Seer.* Washington City D.C, 1852. Purchase reprint at Sam Weller's Bookstore, Salt Lake City, UT.

Pratt, Parley. *Key to the Science of Theology.* Revised Edition Salt Lake City, UT, Deseret Book Company, 1965. Originally Liverpool, F.D. Richards 1855 edition.

Quinn, D. Michael. *Early Mormonism and the Magic World View.* Salt Lake City, UT, Signature Books, 1987.

Quinn, D. Michael. *The Mormon Hierarchy: Origins of Power,* Salt Lake City, UT, Signature Books, 1994.

_____. *Repentance Brings Forgiveness.* The Church of Jesus Christ of Latter-Day Saint, Salt Lake City, UT, 1975.

Richardson, Cyril. *Early Christian Fathers,* NY, The MacMillian Company, 1970.

Richards, LeGrand. *A Marvelous Work and a Wonder.* Salt Lake City, UT, Deseret Book Company, 1973.

_____. *Salt Lake Temple -A Monument to a People.* Salt Lake City, UT, University Services Incorporated, 1983.

Ricks, Eldin. *Combination Reference.* Salt Lake City, UT, Deseret Book company, 1960.

Roberts, B.H. *A Comprehensive History of the Church of Jesus Christ of Latter-Day Saints,* Salt Lake City, UT, Brigham Young University Press, 1965.

Robertson, Archibald Thomas. *Word Pictures in the New Testament,* Baker Book House, Grand Rapids, MI, 49506, 1931.

Romney, Marion G. *Salt Lake Tribune,* Salt Lake City, UT, April 3, 1977.

Sackett, Chuck. *What's Going On In There?* copyright 1982 by Chuck Sackett. Write to: Sword of the Shepherd Ministries, P.O. Box 4707, Thousand Oaks, CA, 91359.

Shupe, Anson. *The Darker side of Virtue.* Buffalo, NY, Prometheus Books, 1991.

Shupe, Anson. *Wealth and Power in American Zion.* NY, E. Meller Printing. 1992.

Sill, Sterling. *Deseret News.* Church News Section. Salt Lake City, UT, July 31, 1965, p.7.

Skousen, W. Cleon. *The First 2000 Years.* Salt Lake City, UT, Bookcraft, 1953.

Smith, Hyrum & Sjodahl, Janne M. *Doctrine & Covenants Commentary.* Salt Lake City, UT, Deseret Book Company, 1968.

Smith, Joseph. *Book of Mormon.* Salt Lake City, UT, Deseret Book Company. 1976.

Smith, Joseph. *Doctrine and Covenants.* Salt Lake City, UT, Deseret Book Company, 1976.

Smith, Joseph. *History of the Church.* Salt Lake City, UT, Deseret Book Company, 1978, 7 volumes.

Smith, Joseph. *Inspired Version,* Independence, MI, Reorganized Church of Jesus Christ of Latter-Day Saints, 1959.

Smith, Joseph. *Joseph Smith's Diary,* June 20, 1843, photo-copy, Lighthouse Ministry, 1350 S.W. Temple, Salt Lake City, UT, 84115.

Smith, Joseph. *Private Journal.* Collection in the Church Archives LDS Historical Department. Salt Lake City, UT, January 17, 1844.

Smith, Joseph. *The Pearl of Great Price.* Salt Lake City, UT, Deseret Book Company, 1976.

Smith, Joseph Fielding. *Teachings of the Prophet Joseph Smith.* Salt Lake City, UT, Deseret Book Company, 1977.

Smith, Joseph Fielding. *The Way to Perfection.* Salt Lake City, UT, Deseret Book Company, 1978.

Smith, Joseph Fielding. *Answers to Gospel Questions.* Salt Lake City, UT, Deseret Book Company, 1957, 4 volumes.

Smith, Joseph Fielding. *Doctrines of Salvation.* Sermons of Joseph Fielding Smith compiled by McConkie. Salt Lake city, UT, Bookcraft, 1967, 3 volumes.

_____. *Strong's Exhaustive Concordance of the Bible.* Madison: Abingdon, Nashville, TN, 1976. 34th printing.

Tanner, Jerald & Sandra. *Evolution of the Mormon Temple Ceremony: 1842-1990.* Salt Lake City, UT, Utah Lighthouse Ministry, 1350 S.W. Temple, Salt Lake City, UT, 84115.

Tanner, Jerald & Sandra. *Flaws in the Pearl of Great Price.* Salt Lake City, UT, Lighthouse Ministry, 1350 S.W. Temple, Salt Lake City, UT, 84115.

Tanner, Jerald & Sandra. *Mormonism: Shadow or Reality?* Salt Lake City, UT, Modern Microfilm, 1972.

Tanner, Jerald & Sandra. *The Changing World of Mormonism,* Moody Bible Institue of Chicago, 1980.

Talmage, James E. *Articles of Faith.* Salt Lake City, UT, The Church of Jesus Christ of Latter-Day Saints, 1960.

Talmage, James E. *Jesus the Christ.* Salt Lake City, UT, The Church of Jesus Christ of Latter-Day Saints, 1961

Talmage, James E. *The Great Apostasy.* Salt Lake City, UT, The The Deseret News Press, 1909.

Taylor, Henry D. *The Ensign.* Salt Lake City, UT, The Church of Jesus Christ of Latter-Day Saints. p.63, November 1976.

Taylor, Henry D. *Gospel Principles.* Salt Lake City, UT, The Church of Jesus Christ of Latter-Day Saints. 1979.

_____. *Thayer's Greek Lexicon of the English New Testament.* Grand Rapids, MI, Baker Book House, 1978, 4th edition.

_____. *The Salt Lake Temple. –A Monument to a People.* Second Edition, University Services, Inc., SLC, UT 1983.

_____. *Times and Seasons.* Nauvoo, IL, an official organ of the Church 1839-1846, v.3, p.579, 6 volumes.

Tryk, Loftes. *The Best Kept Secrets in the Book of Mormon.* Redondo Beach, CA, Jacob's Well Foundation, 1988.

Tuxhorn, Janette. *Mormonized Christian Hymns,* 1904 Chama Ave., Loveland, CO, 80538, phone 970-667-6049.

Vine, W. E. *An Expository Dictionary of the New Testament Words,* 1966, Fleming Revell Company, Old Tappan, NJ.

Walters, Wesley P. *Justice Albert Neely's Bill -The Glass Looker.* March 20, 1826 (copy of Judge Neely's records) Amboy Journal, Amboy, Illinois, April 30, 1879 and June 11, 1879. Obtain from Utah Christian Tract, LaMesa, CA.

Walters, Wesley P. *New Light on Mormon Origins from the Palmyra (N.Y.) Revival.* Obtain from Utah Christian Tract, LaMesa, CA.

_____. *Webster's New Collegiate Dictionary.* Springfield, MO, G&C Merriam Co., 1980.

_____. *What the Mormons think of Christ.* Salt Lake City, UT, The Church of Jesus Christ of Latter-Day Saints, 1982.

Whitmer, David. *An Address To All Believers in Christ.* Richmond, MO 1877. Order from Pacific Publishing Company, Martinez, CA.

Widtsoe, John A. *Discourses of Brigham Young.* Salt Lake City, UT, Deseret Book Company, 1977.

Widtsoe, John A. *Joseph Smith - Seeker After Truth.* Salt Lake City, UT, Deseret Book Company, 1951.

_____. *Wilson's Old Testament Word Studies.* MacDonald Publishing Co, McLean, VA, 22102, date void.

Witte, Bob & Fraser, Gordon. *What's Going On In Here?* Gordon Fraser Publishing, P.O. Box 7251, Eugene, OR, 97401.

Wood, Wilford C. *Joseph Smith Begins His Work.* "The Book of Commandments, Doctrine and Covenants, The Lectures on Faith, Fourteen Articles of Faith"; v.2, Salt Lake City, UT, copyright by Wilford C. Wood 1962.

Wood, Wilford C. *Book of Mormon 1830 edition,* v.1, Salt Lake City, UT; copyright by Wilford C. Wood 1962.

Young, Brigham. *Joint Session of the Legislature.* "Views on Slavery" Salt Lake City, UT, February 5, 1852, Ms d. 1234, Box 48, Folder 3, LDS Archives.

Young, Dillworth, S. *BYU Stake Fireside Message,* Provo, UT, May 1974, n.p.

Other resources that elaborate on Mormonism:

**Web sites:**

Mormon Research Ministry, www.mrm.org

Recovery from Mormonism, www.exmormon.org

Living Hope Ministries, www.lhvm.org

The Bible vs. The Book of Mormon, www.mormonchallenge.com

The Story behind the Book of Abraham, www.bookofabraham.info

Watchman Fellowship, www.watchman.org

The Mormon Conspiracy, www.mormonconspiracy.com, Charles L. Wood, Ph.D.

Lighthouse Ministries, www.utlm.org, Jerrald and Sandra Tanner

Through the Maze, www.mazeministry.com, Jim Spencer

Saints Alive in Jesus, www.saintsalive.com, Ed Decker

Concerned Christians, www.concernedchristians.org

**Books:**

The Mormon Conspiracy, Charles L. Wood, Ph.D.

The Changing World of Mormonism, Jerald and Sandra Tanner.

America's Saints, The Rise of Mormon Power, Robert Gottlieb & Peter Wiley.

The Mormon Corporate Empire, John Heinerman and Anson Shupe.

The Darker Side of Virtue, Anson Shupe.

The Mormon Hierarchy: Origins of Power, D. Michael Quinn.

Mormon America, Richard N. Ostling and Joan K. Ostling.

The Mormon Conspiracy, Charles L. Wood.

Early Mormonism and the Magic World View, D. Michael Quinn.

Evolution of the Mormon Temple Ceremony:1842-1990, Jerald and Sandra Tanner.

In Sacred Loneliness, The Plural Wives of Joseph Smith, Todd Compton.

No Man Knows My History –the life of Joseph Smith, Fawn M. Brodie.

Leaving the Saints, Martha Beck.

Wild Bill Hickman and the Mormon Frontier, Hope A. Hilton.